European Yearbook of International Economic Law

EYIEL Monographs - Studies in European and International Economic Law

Volume 46

EYIEL Monographs is a subseries of the European Yearbook of International Economic Law (EYIEL). It contains scholarly works in the fields of European and international economic law, in particular WTO law, international investment law, international monetary law, law of regional economic integration, external trade law of the EU and EU internal market law. The series does not include edited volumes. EYIEL Monographs are peer-reviewed by the series editors and external reviewers.

Elisabeth Anna Lümkea Andersen

Regulation of Biotechnological Risks in a Multi-Level System

An Analysis of the EU Regulation of Genome Edited Plants in light of WTO Law and CETA

Springer

Elisabeth Anna Lümkea Andersen
Hamburg, Germany

ISSN 2524-6658 ISSN 2524-6666 (electronic)
EYIEL Monographs - Studies in European and International Economic Law
ISSN 2364-8392 ISSN 2364-8406 (electronic)
European Yearbook of International Economic Law
ISBN 978-3-032-02408-4 ISBN 978-3-032-02409-1 (eBook)
https://doi.org/10.1007/978-3-032-02409-1

Dekan/Dekanin (zum Zeitpunkt der Erscheinung): Prof. Dr. Jan Felix Hoffmann
Erstgutachter/Erstgutachterin: Prof. Dr. Silja Vöneky
Zweitgutachter/Zweitgutachterin: Prof. Dr. Paulina Starski
Tag/Tage der mündlichen Prüfung: 04./05.11.2024
Dissertationsort: Freiburg im Breisgau
Erscheinungsjahr: 2025

This Springer imprint is published by the registered company Springer Nature Switzerland AG
The registered company address is: Gewerbestrasse 11, 6330 Cham, Switzerland

To my daughter

Acknowledgments

The present volume is based on my doctoral thesis, which was accepted by the Faculty of Law of the University of Freiburg in November 2024. It was written under the framework of the Centre for Integrative Biological Signalling Studies, Cluster of Excellence at the University of Freiburg (EXC-2189 – 390939984) from 2020 to 2022. The thesis was finalised and submitted in December 2023.

Completing this dissertation was possible only with the support and guidance of many people, only some of which are mentioned here.

First and foremost, I wish to thank my family for their encouragement and understanding. Heartfelt gratitude goes to my husband for his unconditional support throughout the ups and downs of this time and the possibility to start again on this project only four months after I gave birth to my daughter. I am beyond grateful to have a husband with whom I can share a fulfilling family life and at the same time pursue my personal goals. Furthermore, I wish to thank my parents who always made me believe that I can achieve all the goals I have and equipped me with the capabilities to do so. Also, I wish to thank my mother for her unwavering support during my studies and through the first years of my daughter's childhood.

Beside my family, I wish to thank my doctoral supervisor, Prof Dr Silja Vöneky, and the whole Institute for Public International Law at the University of Freiburg for providing me with an environment in which I could pursue my research and build on the exchange with dear colleagues. Also, I thank Prof Dr Paulina Starski who very quickly reviewed my thesis as a second reader.

This book is dedicated to my daughter Charlotte. My dearest wish for her is to grow up in a world where she can pursue her dreams without obstacles.

Elisabeth Anna Lümkea Andersen

Competing Interests The author has no competing interests to declare that are relevant to the content of this manuscript.

Contents

Abbreviations

AB	Appellate Body of the World Trade Organization
ALOP	Appropriate level of protection
ASEAN	Association of Southeast Asian Nations
CA	Competent authority
CAC	Codex Alimentarius Commission
CBD	Convention on Biological Diversity
CCP	Common Commercial Policy
CETA	Comprehensive Economic and Trade Agreement
CJEU	Court of Justice of the European Union
CRISPR	Clustered Regularly Interspaced Short Palindromic Repeats
CSFP	Common Security and Foreign Policy
DNA	Deoxyribonucleic acid
DSB	Dispute Settlement Body of the World Trade Organisation
DSU	Understanding on Rules and Procedures Governing the Settlement of Disputes
EC	European Communities
ECJ	European Court of Justice
EFSA	European Food Safety Authority
ENGL	European Network of GMO Laboratories
ERA	Environmental risk assessment
EU	European Union
EURL GMFF	European Union Reference Laboratory for Genetically Modified Food and Feed
GATT	General Agreement on Tariffs and Trade
GM	Genetically modified
GMO	Genetically modified organism
HDR	Homology-directed repair
HGT	Horizontal gene transfer
IOE	International Office of Epizootics
IPPC	International Plant Protection Convention
ISPM	International Standard for Phytosanitary Measures

ITO	International Trade Organization
JRC	Joint Research Centre
LMO	Living modified organism
MPIA	Multi-Party Interim Appeal Arbitration Arrangement pursuant to Article 25 of the Understanding on Rules and Procedures Governing the Settlement of Disputes
NAFTA	North American Free Trade Agreement
NBTs	New breeding techniques
NGO	Non-governmental organisation
NGTs	New genomic techniques
NHEJ	Nonhomologous end-joining
NPBTs	New plant breeding techniques
ODM	Oligonucleotide-directed mutagenesis
OECD	Organisation for Economic Cooperation and Development
OJ EC	Official Journal of the European Communities
OJ EU	Official Journal of the European Union
PPMs	Processes and production methods
RCF	Regulatory Cooperation Forum
RNA	Ribonucleic acid
SCoPAFF	Standing Committee on Plants, Animals, Food and Feed
SDGs	Sustainable Development Goals
SDN	Site-directed nuclease
SPS Agreement	Agreement on the Application of Sanitary and Phytosanitary Measures
SPS Committee	Committee on Sanitary and Phytosanitary Measures
SPS measure	Sanitary and phytosanitary measure
STC	Specific trade concern
TALEN	Transcription activator-like effector nuclease
TBT Agreement	Agreement on Technical Barriers to Trade
TBT Committee	Committee on Technical Barriers to Trade
TEU	Treaty on European Union
TFEU	Treaty on the Functioning of the European Union
TPRM	Trade Policy Review Mechanism
UN	United Nations
UNCIO	United Nations Conference on International Organization
UNTS	United Nations Treaty Series
US	United States of America
VCLT	Vienna Convention on the Law of Treaties
WHO	World Health Organization
WOAH	World Organisation for Animal Health
WTO	World Trade Organisation
ZFN	Zinc finger nuclease

Chapter 1
Introduction

In July 2023, the Commission of the European Union ('EU') published its proposal for a regulation on plants obtained by certain new genomic techniques ('NGT plants') and their food and feed. According to the EU Commission the proposal is prompted by a significant demand in the Union and globally for NGT plants. It ascribes great potential to these plants in building up a more sustainable agriculture and food system which are resilient to the challenges coming along with climate change and biodiversity loss. Also, by supporting the use and application of new genomic techniques, the EU Commission hopes to decrease the EU's external dependencies on imports of plant proteins which have been revealed by the Covid-19 pandemic and the Russian war against Ukraine. The EU Commission does not consider the current EU regulation on genetically modified organisms ('GMOs') adequate to regulate NGT plants, but needs to be adapted to scientific and technological progress.

Due to the global demand for NGT plants and the international dimension of trade in genetically modified plants, the prospect of a new regulation of NGT plants in the EU brings up the question on how to best regulate NGT plants in a way that also meets the EU's obligations under international trade law. This also offers the opportunity to address problems that arise at the interface of the current EU GMO law and the EU's obligations under international trade law. The current framework is constantly criticised with regard to its negative implications on international trade in GMOs.

The present academic work therefore in a first step takes the EU Commission's proposal as an opportunity to examine the compliance of the current EU GMO law and its applicability on NGT plants with the EU's obligations under the law of the World Trade Organisation ('WTO'). In a second step, it analyses whether the proposal addresses these problems and to what extent.

The first question is not totally new but has already been discussed in the beginnings of the 2000s with regard to the first generation of GMOs, so-called

E. A. L. Andersen, *Regulation of Biotechnological Risks in a Multi-Level System*, European Yearbook of International Economic Law 46,
https://doi.org/10.1007/978-3-032-02409-1_1

conventional or transgenic GMOs. Back then, the EU revised their regulatory framework applicable to GMOs and meanwhile had enacted a *de facto* moratorium on the authorisation of GMOs. Also, several Member States had prohibited the cultivation of GMOs on their territory although these GMOs had already obtained EU-wide approval. This had prompted the US, Canada and Argentina to initiate panel proceedings before the WTO dispute settlement mechanism asserting a violation of WTO law by the EU's *de facto* moratorium and the Member States' safeguard measures. This judgment which is also discussed in the present work already showed the difficulties that arise for the adequate regulation of areas that are characterised by constant technological and scientific progress.

Additionally, the *Cartagena Protocol on Biosafety to the Convention on Biological Diversity*[1] ('Cartagena Protocol') had been adopted in 2000 and entered into force in 2003. The Cartagena Protocol is concerned with the transboundary movement of GMOs and its focus lays on regulations that ensure biodiversity and environment protection. With the Cartagena Protocol a substantially different approach in comparison to the WTO's one was adopted at the same time that the WTO dispute settlement mechanism dealt with the EU's regulation of GMOs under its regulatory framework. Accordingly, the question of the relationship between the Cartagena Protocol with its objectives on environmental protection and WTO law with its focus on free trade arose. It has not yet been finally decided.

This multidimensional issue on how to adequately regulate scientific progress in our multi-level system of international, EU and national regulation is also present in the current discussion on the regulation of genome edited plants. It has been brought up again by a judgment of the Court of Justice of the European Union ('CJEU') in 2018 where the CJEU had to decide whether targeted mutagenesis techniques[2] and plants derived thereof fall within the scope of the currently applicable EU GMO law.

These modification techniques have been developed over the past 20 years after the adoption of the currently applicable EU GMO legislation. They differ substantially in comparison to the modification techniques used to obtain transgenic GMOs for which the current EU GMO law was designed. While transgenesis techniques insert foreign deoxyribonucleic acid ('DNA'), targeted mutagenesis techniques only induce small mutations and do not insert foreign DNA. And what is important for the currently applicable GMO law: techniques to generate transgenic GMOs can be clearly distinguished from conventional breeding techniques which are not regulated by the EU GMO law. But such a clear differentiation does not exist between plants modified by targeted mutagenesis techniques and plants modified by conventional breeding techniques. It is said that plants modified by targeted mutagenesis techniques could also be obtained by conventional breeding techniques or even natural mutation methods. Out of these differences, the question arose whether plants obtained by targeted mutagenesis techniques should be regulated in the same

[1] *Cartagena Protocol on Biosafety to the Convention on Biological Diversity* ('Cartagena Protocol') (adopted 29 January 2000, entered into force 11 September 2003) 2226 UNTS 208.

[2] Targeted mutagenesis techniques are a subcategory of genome editing techniques, see Chap. 2, p. 8 for more details.

way as transgenic GMOs or whether they should rather be treated as plants obtained by conventional breeding methods.

The CJEU judged that organisms modified by these targeted mutagenesis techniques fall within the EU law governing the deliberate release and placing on the market of genetically modified organisms. Accordingly, authorisation procedures and labelling requirements, as part of the EU GMO law regulations, apply to plants modified by these techniques. This judgment provoked an outcry from the scientific community and biotech plant industry. According to them, the high burden that comes along with the EU's authorisation procedure and labelling requirements for GMOs is simply not justifiable for plants modified by targeted mutagenesis from a scientific point of view. The Court's findings would prevent the use of plants obtained by these techniques which are however necessary for a sustainable agriculture that can withstand climatic changes and ensure food security. Also, the judgment has been constantly criticised for its negative implications on international trade.

Furthermore, the EU Commission has taken the CJEU's judgment and the reactions to it as a reason to propose a new EU regulation on plants obtained by new genomic techniques[3] and their food and feed. The proposal aims to reduce regulatory burdens for plants obtained by new genomic techniques. Thereby, the EU Commission wants to facilitate the development and application of plants obtained by new genomic techniques because it considers these types of plants crucial to make the EU's agriculture more sustainable and resilient to climatic changes. Accordingly, the proposal is also part of the EU's Green Deal and its farm to fork strategy.

By embedding the proposal in the EU Commission's package of measures for a more sustainable future, the EU Commission also brings a new aspect to this multi-layered discussion: the benefit of scientific progress for society and the environment. While the former discussion on an adequate regulation of GMOs has very much focussed on how to best address the risks arising from these organisms, this focus on potential benefits is new. And it seems, that potential benefits coming along with the application of new genomic techniques have a much higher priority than they had before.

Additionally, the prospect of a new GMO regulation in the EU brings up the question on how to best regulate genome edited plants in a way that also meets the EU's obligations under WTO law. A mere referral to the discussion in respect to the first generation of GMOs and the report of the WTO dispute settlement body from 2003 is not appropriate anymore, since genome edited plants differ substantially from transgenic GMO plants. These differences as well as the concerns on international trade implications of the CJEU's judgment prompted the present thesis. And since international trade and transboundary relations are to a large extent governed

[3] According to the EU Commission's proposal a plant obtained by new genomic techniques means a genetically modified plant obtained by targeted mutagenesis or cisgenes, or a combination thereof, on the condition that it does not contain any genetic material originating from outside the breeders'gene pool that temporarily may have been inserted during the development of the NGT plant", see European Commission (2023), p. 27 (Art. 3 No 2).

by the WTO law, this legal regime was chosen as the relevant standard of review. The Comprehensive Economic and Trade Agreement ('CETA') was added to the analysis because its impact on EU GMO law had already been discussed during the agreement's negotiation. The thesis is confined to the application of genome editing to plants since they play a major role in international trade and since EU GMO law is applicable to them.

The present work is divided into three parts:

The first part as a starting point gives an overview of the scientific background and displays the CJEU judgment and its context. The scientific background of genome editing techniques and of targeted mutagenesis techniques as a subgroup of genome editing techniques is outlined in Chap. 2. This includes the role of genome editing for plant breeding and agriculture, potential risks of these techniques and the European Commission's view on the risk potential of plants modified by new genomic techniques. Chapter 3 deals with the CJEU's judgment on targeted mutagenesis techniques, the corresponding procedure, and the reactions to the judgment by academia, industry and politics.

The second party analyses the EU GMO law in light of WTO law and CETA. Chapter 4 gives an overview of the EU GMO law with its authorisation procedure, labelling requirements and the possibility for Member States to opt-out from cultivation of genetically modified plants. Chapter 5 presents the relevant WTO rules, including the SPS Agreement, the TBT Agreement and GATT, as well as CETA. Chapter 6 then analyses the EU GMO law and its applicability to plants modified by targeted mutagenesis in light of the relevant WTO rules and CETA. This analysis is made on an abstract level. However, since an analysis of the national treatment principle as laid down in the GATT and TBT Agreement was not possible on a purely abstract level, a concrete example was chosen in this case.

The third part gives an outlook on the future regulation of genome edited plants in the EU and internationally. Chapter 7 presents the current developments at the EU level regarding a new regulatory framework for plants modified by targeted mutagenesis techniques and summarises the proposals that have been made on a future regulation by academia and the industry. The reform proposals are assessed in light of the results from the analysis in Chap. 6 and whether they can tackle legitimacy problems at the interface of EU GMO law and WTO law. Chapter 7 concludes by giving recommendations on a future regulation of genome edited plants in the EU.

Altogether, the present thesis deals with the regulation of scientific issues in a multi-level regulatory environment, bringing up, analysing and discussing similarities and discrepancies of different regulatory traditions concerning science.

Reference

European Commission (2023) Proposal for a Regulation of the European Parliament and of the Council on plants obtained by certain new genomic techniques and their food and feed, and amending Regulation (EU) 2017/625. COM(2023) 411 final, Brussels

Chapter 2
Scientific Background

Abstract The second chapter offers a scientific introduction to the basics of genetics and the functioning of genome editing techniques as well as an overview of their potential applications, especially in agriculture and the risks associated with the application of genome editing techniques. While genome editing techniques, particularly the CRISPR-Cas system, have great potential to significantly transform and improve global agriculture, the use of genome editing techniques also involves risks, the long-term effects of which have not yet been fully researched.

However, the European Commission has adopted the risk assessment by the European Food and Safety Authority that plants modified using targeted mutagenesis and cisgenesis techniques do not pose more risks than plants modified by conventional breeding methods.

2.1 Introduction

This chapter takes a look at the scientific principles of the different techniques used to genetically modify plants and of plant breeding techniques. This examination is necessary to understand the problems that arise for the regulation of genome edited plants under the legislation currently applicable in the European Union ('EU') and to be able to assess the EU Commission's proposal on a new set of rules for plants obtained by new genomic techniques ('NGT plants') in light of the EU's international trade obligations.

The present part does not claim to be a comprehensive presentation of the state of the art of genome editing techniques. While the analysis of this treatise is confined to genome editing in plants and accordingly also the scientific background presented, genome editing techniques are also applied in basic research, medicine and industrial biotechnology. Furthermore, it could also be applied to humans.[1]

[1] These different areas of application of genome editing techniques are briefly presented by Beck (2022), pp. 65–70.

E. A. L. Andersen, *Regulation of Biotechnological Risks in a Multi-Level System*, European Yearbook of International Economic Law 46,
https://doi.org/10.1007/978-3-032-02409-1_2

First, the functioning of genome editing techniques is described (2.1). Second, an overview of the application of genome editing techniques in agriculture is given, also addressing risk concerns associated with these techniques (2.2).

2.2 The Functioning of Genome Editing Techniques

Genome editing techniques rely on the basic principles of genetics which are presented first (2.2.1). In a second step, genetic mutations (2.2.2) and genome editing techniques to induce genetic mutations are described (2.2.3).

2.2.1 *Basic Principles of Genetics*

The genetic information of every living organism is stored in an organism's genome which corresponds to the entirety of an organism's genes.[2] Genes are segments of an organism's deoxyribonucleic acid ('DNA').[3] DNA consists of two strands of complementary nucleic acids that form a double helix. Both strands of nucleic acids are composed of nucleotides that carry a nitrogen-containing base. There are four bases: guanine, adenine, cytosine, and thymine. Guanine pairs with cytosine and adenine pairs with thymine to form the double strand.[4]

In the cell, DNA takes the form of chromosomes.[5] While most eukaryotes[6] are diploid, containing two identical copies of each of their chromosomes, plants are polyploid, containing multiple copies of each of their chromosomes.[7]

Due to its complementary structure DNA can replicate by separating its two nucleic acid strands which then serve as a template to generate a new complementary strand for each of the original strands.[8] This mechanism enables a cell to copy its genome and pass it on to new cells.[9] Also, this structure ensures that damage to

---

[2] *Cf.* "genome" in Lawrence (2011).

[3] Alberts et al. (2015), pp. 178, 182.

[4] For more details on the chemical structure of DNA, see Clark and Pazdernik (2016), pp. 4–6 and Alberts et al. (2015), pp. 175–178.

[5] Alberts et al. (2015), pp. 179–183.

[6] Eukaryotes are members of "one of the three domains or superkingdoms into which all living organisms are classified, the other two being the Bacteria and the Archaea. […] The eukaryotes comprise protozoans, algae, fungi, slime moulds, plants and animals.", see "eukaryote" and "Eukarya" in Lawrence (2011).

[7] Clark and Pazdernik (2016), p. 12.

[8] *Cf.* Alberts et al. (2015), pp. 177–178.

[9] For a detailed description of the mechanism of DNA replication, see Alberts et al. (2015), pp. 239–266; see also Alberts et al. (2019), pp. 199–215.

one DNA strand can be repaired by using the other strand as a template.[10] However, repair mechanisms using the complementary DNA strand do not function in the case of double-strand breaks where no template is left. In this case, the DNA is repaired either by *nonhomologous end joining* ('NHEJ') or by homologous recombination, also called *homology-directed repair* ('HDR').[11] NHEJ simply rejoins the broken ends of the DNA which generally results in the loss of nucleotides at the site of the double-strand break.[12] This mechanism is primarily used for the repair of double-strand breaks in mammalian somatic cells.[13,14] HDR repairs double-strand breaks using another stretch of homologous double-strand DNA as a template. Homologous are those parts of a double strand DNA that consist of very similar or identical nucleotide sequences.[15] Since this repair mechanism requires another homologous double-strand DNA, it primarily takes place just before cell division and after the DNA has already been replicated and can serve as a template.[16]

2.2.2 Genetic Mutations

Genetic mutations are heritable changes to an organism's genome (genotype[17]) that result in changes to the characteristics of an organism (phenotype[18]).[19] In most cases, mutations in the genome result from failures that occur when the genome is copied or repaired.[20]

---

[10] For a detailed description of the mechanisms of DNA repair, see Alberts et al. (2015), pp. 268–276; see also Alberts et al. (2019), pp. 215–222.

[11] Alberts et al. (2015), pp. 274–275.

[12] Alberts et al. (2015), p. 274.

[13] A somatic cell is "a body cell which will not produce gametes, as opposed to cells of the germ line", see "somatic" in Lawrence (2011).

[14] Alberts et al. (2015), p. 274.

[15] *Cf.* Alberts et al. (2015), pp. 276–277.

[16] See Alberts et al. (2019), p. 220.

[17] The genotype is the "genetic constitution of an individual cell or organism", see "genotype" in Alberts et al. (2015), p. 13 (Glossary).

[18] The phenotype is "the observable character (including both physical appearance and behavior) of a cell or organism", see "phenotype" in Alberts et al. (2015), p. 24 (Glossary).

[19] See "mutation" in Lawrence (2011); for the relation between phenotype and genotype and different types of mutations, see Alberts et al. (2015), pp. 486–487.

[20] Alberts et al. (2015), pp. 217–218.

2.2.3 Genome Editing

Genome editing techniques include *homing endonucleases* (also called *meganucleases*), *zinc finger nucleases* ('ZFNs'), *transcription activator-like effector nucleases* ('TALENs'), and *CRISPR-Cas* (CRISPR standing for Clustered Regularly Interspaced Short Palindromic Repeats). All these techniques have in common that they can insert mutations at specific sites of an organism's genome.[21] When used in plant breeding, they are also often referred to as *new (plant) breeding techniques* ('NPBTs' or 'NBTs'). Most of these genome editing techniques are also comprised by the term *new genomic techniques* ('NGTs') which is used by the EU Commission in its proposal on a new regulation for plants obtained by these new genomic techniques. The EU Commission understands this term as an umbrella term which describes "a variety of techniques that can alter the genetic material of an organism [in a more precise or targeted way than conventional breeding or established genomic techniques] and that have emerged or have been developed since 2001, when the [currently applicable] Union legislation on genetically modified organisms was adopted".[22] The EU Commission explicitly mentions targeted mutagenesis techniques and cisgenesis techniques, including intragenesis techniques as being comprised by the term of new genomic techniques.[23]

2.2.3.1 Introducing Mutations

Most genome editing techniques contain a nuclease that is used to introduce a double-strand break in the DNA of the target cell. This double strand break is then repaired by the cell's own repair mechanisms NHEJ or HDR.[24] Depending on the repair mechanism used, the technique is categorised as SDN-1, SDN-2, or SDN-3 (SDN standing for site-directed nucleases).[25]

SDN-1 techniques rely on NHEJ not providing a repair template and thereby inducing *random mutations* (changes, deletions, or insertions of a few base pairs) at a specific site.[26]

---

[21] High Level Group of Scientific Advisors (2017), p. 56; Walch-Solimena (2019), p. 2; see also the Glossary of scientific terminology provided by European Commission (2021), p. 61.

[22] European Commission (2023), p. 1 and footnote 1; see also the understanding of the European Food Safety Authority of the term *new genomic techniques*, https://www.efsa.europa.eu/en/topics/new-genomic-techniques

[23] European Commission (2023), p. 1.

[24] See above for the basic principles of genetics, p. 6.

[25] Agapito-Tenfen et al. (2018).

[26] See Agapito-Tenfen et al. (2018), p. 4; Beck (2022), pp. 57–59; these categories have been first introduced with regard to zinc finger nucleases by *Lusser et al*, see Joint Research Centre (2011), pp. 23–24; see also High Level Group of Scientific Advisors (2017), pp. 58–59.

SDN-2 techniques rely on HDR providing an exogenous DNA template to achieve a *desired mutation* (substitutions, deletions, or insertions of a few base pairs or more complex alterations) at the targeted site.[27]

SDN-3 techniques are not defined consistently in the scientific literature. They are considered to rely either both on NHEJ and on HDR or only on HDR. Furthermore, they are considered to be used either to insert large stretches of DNA[28] or to insert transgenes, meaning genetic material from non-crossable species,[29] at a specific site of the organism's DNA.[30]

The outcome of these three SDN techniques varies from small point mutations to large deletions or insertions, also of exogenous[31] DNA.[32]

Another mechanism is used by *oligonucleotide-directed mutagenesis* ('ODM') which does not induce a double-strand break at the target site, but only changes single nucleotides at the target site which are then incorporated into the organism's DNA by the cell's repair mechanisms.[33]

For the further analysis it is important to bear in mind the EU Commission's understanding of *targeted mutagenesis*, *cisgenesis* and *intragenesis* techniques since these techniques are addressed by the EU Commission's proposal on the regulation of NGTs.[34]

Targeted mutagenesis techniques comprise SDN-1, SDN-2, and ODM techniques to introduce modifications at precise locations of an organism's DNA and do not insert foreign material.[35]

---

[27] See Agapito-Tenfen et al. (2018), p. 4; Beck (2022), pp. 57–59; these categories have been first introduced with regard to zinc finger nucleases by *Lusser et al*, see Joint Research Centre (2011), pp. 23–24; see also High Level Group of Scientific Advisors (2017), pp. 58–59.

[28] See EFSA Panel on Genetically Modified Organisms (2020), p. 6.

[29] *Cf.* European Commission (2023), p. 1; a transgene is also described as "any gene transferred into an animal or plant artificially by the techniques of genetic engineering, such organisms being known as transgenic animals or plants. The transferred gene is usually from another species, but may also be a mutated version of a gene in the organism's own genome", see "transgene" in Lawrence (2011).

[30] See Agapito-Tenfen et al. (2018), p. 4; Beck (2022), pp. 57–59; these categories have been first introduced with regard to zinc finger nucleases by *Lusser et al*, see Joint Research Centre (2011), pp. 23–24; see also High Level Group of Scientific Advisors (2017), pp. 58–59.

[31] *Exogenous DNA* is DNA originating outside the plant which can be introduced naturally or by technological intervention, see "exogenous DNA" in European Food Safety Authority (2021), p. 39.

[32] *Cf.* European Food Safety Authority (2021), p. 12.

[33] For a comprehensive overview of the ODM mechanism, see Joint Research Centre (2021b), pp. 46–47; *cf.* also Joint Research Centre (2011), p. 24.

[34] See European Commission (2023), p. 1; the Court of Justice of the European Union also dealt with *targeted mutagenesis techniques* in its case C-528/16 – *Confédération paysanne et al.* which is displayed and analysed in detail in Chap. 3 below.

[35] See the definition for *targeted mutagenesis or site-directed mutagenesis techniques* as well as the definitions for *SDN-1*, *SDN-2* and *ODM* in the Glossary of scientific terminology provided for by European Commission (2021), p. 62; *cf.* also European Commission (2023), p. 16 (recital 2).

Cisgenesis techniques rely on SDN-2 techniques and use it to insert genetic material that is already present in the breeders' gene pool.[36]

Intragenesis techniques also rely on SDN-2 techniques, using it to insert a rearranged copy of genetic material composed of two or more DNA sequences already present in the breeders' gene pool.[37]

In contrast to these techniques, the term of *transgenesis* comprises techniques used to insert genetic material from outside the breeders' gene pool either randomly or at a targeted site.[38]

2.2.3.2 Targeting Specific Sites

The advantageous feature of genome editing techniques in comparison to conventional breeding techniques or transgenesis is their ability to target specific sites and induce mutations at these sites. The mechanism that genome editing techniques rely on to induce the double-strand break at a specific site differs. Some methods rely on endonucleases or restriction enzymes that have long recognition sequences. These are *inter alia* homing endonucleases, ZFNs and TALENs.[39] Another method is used by CRISPR-Cas which relies on an associated ribonucleic acid ('RNA') to target the desired site.[40]

2.2.3.3 Delivery of Genome Editing Components to the Cell

There exist several mechanisms to deliver the components of the genome editing techniques to the target cell.

One method is based on the Ti plasmid carried by *Agrobacterium tumefaciens*, a soil bacterium. This Ti plasmid is used because it possesses the ability to transfer specific segments of its DNA (the T-DNA region) to the plant DNA.[41] Accordingly, the necessary genetic information to express the relevant genome editing components can be inserted in this T-DNA region of the Ti plasmid and is then transferred to the plant's cell and inserted in its DNA.[42] The delivered components can then be expressed by the cell's own gene expression mechanisms and begin to induce the

---

[36] European Commission (2023), p. 16 (recital 2).

[37] European Commission (2023), p. 16 (recital 2).

[38] *Cf.* EFSA Panel on Genetically Modified Organisms (2012), p. 24; EFSA Panel on Genetically Modified Organisms (2020), p. 14; European Commission (2023), p. 16 (recital 2).

[39] See Clark and Pazdernik (2016), pp. 474, 556–558; see also Charpentier and Gross (2019), p. 3.

[40] See Clark and Pazdernik (2016), pp. 474–475, 560; see also Charpentier and Gross (2019), p. 4; for more advantages associated with the CRISPR-Cas technology, see also Walch-Solimena (2019), p. 2; Weigel (2019), p. 6.

[41] See Clark and Pazdernik (2016), p. 466.

[42] *Cf.* Clark and Pazdernik (2016), p. 468; *cf.* also Woo et al. (2015), p. 1162.

desired mutation.[43] This transgene inserted in the plant's DNA can be removed in the next generation by sexual crossing.[44] However, this is not feasible for plants that reproduce asexually, such as grape, potato, or banana.[45]

Other methods deliver the genome editing components as proteins, ribonucleoprotein complexes, or as messenger RNA by particle bombardment or other transfer ways to the plant's cell.[46] These methods do not insert transgenes into the plant's DNA.[47]

2.3 The Application of Genome Editing Techniques in Plant Breeding and Agriculture

The beginnings of plant breeding date back to the beginning of human civilisation when farmers conducted selective breeding by choosing crops with high yields for further breeding.[48] Selective breeding and the underlying mechanisms of heredity were studied by *Mendel* who systemised the procedure by using cross-pollination.[49] However, these methods of plant breeding are limited to the characteristics inherent in the genome of the plants that are crossed.[50] These limits were overcome by using chemical agents or radiation to randomly induce mutations in seeds and selecting the ones with favourable or desired traits.[51] This process is however very time-consuming until plants with heritable, novel traits are developed.[52] A faster mechanism to change a plant's genome has been provided by genetic engineering. The development of transgenesis techniques in the 1970 allowed for the inclusion of any gene into a plant's genome.[53] This technique was further developed and nowadays, transgenes or other mutations can even be induced in a plant's genome at specific sites by genome editing techniques. Many desirable traits that have been developed in the past are based on a knockout mutation which is easy to induce by genome

---

[43] For this mechanism see also Joint Research Centre (2021b), p. 20.

[44] Joint Research Centre (2021b), p. 20; Huang et al. (2016), p. 109.

[45] Woo et al. (2015), p. 1162.

[46] *Cf.* Joint Research Centre (2021b), p. 21; Clark and Pazdernik (2016), pp. 468–470; see also Huang et al. (2016), p. 109.

[47] For the use of ribonucleoprotein complexes, see Woo et al. (2015), pp. 1162, 1164; see also Huang et al. (2016), p. 109; Weigel (2019), p. 6; Zhang et al. (2019), pp. 786–787; see also the overview provided for by Puchta et al. (2022), p. 1726.

[48] Clark and Pazdernik (2016), p. 2; see also Vega Rodríguez et al. (2022), p. 5.

[49] Clark and Pazdernik (2016), p. 462.

[50] Clark and Pazdernik (2016), p. 462.

[51] Muller (1927); see also Clark and Pazdernik (2016), pp. 462–463.

[52] *Cf.* Clark and Pazdernik (2016), p. 463.

[53] Clark and Pazdernik (2016), p. 463; Walch-Solimena (2019), p. 2; van Belle et al. (2019), p. 29 (Figure 1).

editing techniques.[54] Also, genome editing makes it much easier to induce mutations in polyploid[55] plants in comparison to conventional breeding methods.[56] Accordingly, genome editing has the potential to greatly accelerate plant breeding.[57] Also, it is considered a tool to maintain genetic diversity in plants.[58]

The most popular genome editing technique is CRISPR-Cas since its RNA component can be altered easily which makes it very versatile.[59]

2.3.1 *Specific Applications of Genome Editing in Agriculture*

Genome editing techniques can be applied in plant breeding and agriculture.[60] While only some genome edited plants have been commercially released so far, many plants are currently developed.[61]

The first plant modified by ODM and commercially released in the US and Canada was CIBUS oilseed rape with herbicide tolerance.[62] Also, a soybean modified by TALEN to change the fatty acid composition has been commercially released in parts of the US.[63] A tomato modified by CRISPR-Cas with different nutritional contents has been commercially released in Japan.[64] Other genome edited plants that are nearly ready for commercialisation include oilseed rape, soybean, corn, rice, potatoes, tomatoes, wheat, oat, avocado, strawberries, mustard, salad, cannabis, and petunia.[65] They mostly contain mutations conferring herbicide and disease resistance, changing nutritional contents, generating higher yields, or improving storage conditions.[66] Some also contain mutations generating drought, cold or salt

---

[54] Weigel (2019), p. 6.

[55] Polyploid organisms are having more than one set of chromosomes per cell, see "polyploid" in Clark and Pazdernik (2016), p. 807.

[56] *Cf.* van Belle et al. (2019), p. 26; see also Hüdig et al. (2022), p. 2.

[57] Weigel (2019), p. 6.

[58] Weigel (2019), p. 6.

[59] See Clark and Pazdernik (2016), pp. 474–475, 560; see also Charpentier and Gross (2019), p. 4; for more advantages associated with the CRISPR-Cas technology, see also Walch-Solimena (2019), p. 2; Weigel (2019), p. 6; for a comprehensive overview of the CRISPR technique and its application to plants, see also Zhang et al. (2019); a short overview is provided by Zhang (2020).

[60] Hua et al. (2019); Weigel (2019), p. 6; for different applications of genome-editing techniques to plants, see also Beck (2022), pp. 65–67.

[61] See Huang et al. (2016), pp. 109–110; Joint Research Centre (2021a), p. 16; see also the overview by Hüdig et al. (2022).

[62] Gelinsky (2022), p. 2; see also Weigel (2019), p. 6.

[63] Gelinsky (2022), p. 4.

[64] Gelinsky (2022), p. 14.

[65] See Gelinsky (2022), pp. 1–22.

[66] Gelinsky (2022), pp. 1–22; see also the overview provided for by Menz et al. (2020), p. 4 and Figure 3 and by Joint Research Centre (2021a), p. 15 (tables 1 and 2).

tolerance, but these are only a few.[67] Also with regard to applications still in the research and development phase, it is striking that only a few applications aim at adapting plants to changing climatic conditions by conferring drought or salt tolerance.[68] Genome editing techniques can also be applied to plants to improve the quantity and quality of biofuel feedstocks.[69]

Another challenge for the application of genome editing to plants is missing knowledge of genomic sequences which is necessary for the effective use of genome editing techniques.[70]

2.3.2 *Risks and Concerns Related to the Application of Genome Editing Techniques to Plants*

The risks and concerns related to the application of genome editing techniques to plants are assessed very differently by scientists and other stakeholders.[71] In general, it is acknowledged that long-term experience on the risks of genome editing techniques is not yet available.[72] Due to this missing long-term experience, the risks associated with genetically modified ('GM') plants in general and the application of genome editing to plants are highly disputed.[73]

2.3.2.1 Risk Research on Conventional Genetic Engineering

Possible negative and unintended consequences that are associated with genetically modified plants relate to food safety, the environment and biodiversity.[74] They include horizontal gene transfer,[75] the development of herbicide or insecticide resis-

[67] Gelinsky (2022), pp. 1–22; for scientific publications on the application of genome-editing to enhance abiotic stress tolerance in plants, see Vats et al. (2019), p. 9; see also Lim et al. (2022).

[68] See Gelinsky (2022), pp. 23–54; on the development and research status of drought resistant plants, see also Hüdig et al. (2022), pp. 7–13.

[69] See e.g. Mohan et al. (2022); Lee et al. (2017).

[70] See e.g. with regard to sugarcane Mohan et al. (2022), p. 370.

[71] It should be noted that this part is only a non-exhaustive overview of the discussion on the risks that may be associated with the application of genome-editing techniques. The potential risks and the literature published on this subject are not assessed.

[72] See Nationale Akademie der Wissenschaften Leopoldina et al. (2019), p. 56.

[73] See Nationale Akademie der Wissenschaften Leopoldina et al. (2019), pp. 55–56; *cf.* also Beck (2022), p. 73 with further references.

[74] See e.g. the analysis by *Eckerstorfer et al.* on the environmental effects of genome-edited plants carrying different types of traits, including herbicide and disease resistance, Eckerstorfer et al. (2020).

[75] For an assessment of possible effects of GM maize on non-target organisms, see Wang et al. (2022); for an overview of possible effects see also EFSA Panel on Genetically Modified Organisms (2009) and EFSA Panel on Genetically Modified Organisms (2010).

tance in wild-type plants which necessitates the use of other and more herbicides or insecticides,[76] and the unknown long-term effects of genetically modified plants.[77] However, it is also noted that environmental concerns mentioned in the debate are not directly related to the genetic modification as such, but rather to the agricultural practices that come along with the cultivation of GM plants, such as monoculture or extensive herbicide and pesticide use.[78] Accordingly, most scientists and scientific associations do not ascribe specific risks to genetic modifications techniques per se; neither to techniques of conventional genetic engineering nor to new genome editing techniques.[79] More than two decades of research on genetic engineering in plants and possible consequences has shown that there are no specific risks linked to the modification technique as such, but rather to the product, regardless of the modification techniques.[80]

2.3.2.2 Technical Challenges Associated with the CRISPR-Cas System

Regardless of the risks associated with genome editing techniques, specific technical challenges are reported especially for the application of the CRISPR-Cas system being the prevalent genome editing technique so far. These challenges include off-target[81] and on-target effects,[82] genetic mosaicism, and the delivery of CRISPR components to the target organism.[83] It is not yet possible to conclusively assess whether these technical challenges lead to a higher risk.[84] With regard to off-target effects, it is however mentioned that traditional breeding methods induce a higher number of off-target mutations into an organism's DNA than precise modification techniques.[85]

[76] *Cf.* Clark and Pazdernik (2016), p. 485.

[77] See Kawall et al. (2020).

[78] See e.g. Vega Rodríguez et al. (2022), p. 6.

[79] See e.g. Nationale Akademie der Wissenschaften Leopoldina et al. (2019), p. 56.

[80] See Nationale Akademie der Wissenschaften Leopoldina et al. (2019), pp. 55–56; see also the conclusions drawn from the projects presented in this report: Bundesministerium für Bildung und Forschung (2014); see also High Level Group of Scientific Advisors (2017), p. 19.

[81] For the occurrence of *off-target effects*, see e.g. Sturme et al. (2022); Wang et al. (2021); Zhang et al. (2019), pp. 787–788; Höijer et al. (2022); see also Joint Research Centre (2021b), pp. 34–35; for the risks associated with off-target effects, see also the overview by Beck (2022), pp. 73–74.

[82] *On-target effects* are reported by Kosicki et al. (2018); Höijer et al. (2022).

[83] See Beck (2022), pp. 70–73 with further references.

[84] See Kadam et al. (2018), p. 23.

[85] See Nationale Akademie der Wissenschaften Leopoldina et al. (2019), p. 56 with further references; see also High Level Group of Scientific Advisors (2017), p. 89.

2.3.2.3 Risks Associated with Targeted Mutagenesis Techniques

Besides these technical challenges, it is often stated that the risks of the application of genome editing techniques are comparable to those of traditional breeding methods. This is reasoned by the equivalence of the functioning of genome editing techniques and traditional breeding methods.[86] Especially genome editing techniques categorised as SDN-1, SDN-2, or ODM (*targeted mutagenesis techniques*) are said to be very similar to natural mutation activity in the organism and conventional mutation breeding methods, except for their ability to induce the mutation at a predetermined site.[87]

In contrast to this assessment, it is also mentioned that traditional breeding builds on gradual changes of a plant's genome while genome editing techniques allow for abrupt and drastic changes of the plant's DNA. Consequently, experience gained from traditional breeding cannot simply be transferred to genome editing in plants.[88]

2.3.2.4 The European Commission's View on the Risk of Genome Edited Plants

The European Food Safety Authority ('EFSA') considers the potential off-target effects by SDN-1, SDN-2, or ODM techniques to be of the same character as the mutations induced by conventional breeding methods, including spontaneous mutations or those induced by mutagenesis techniques.[89] Furthermore, it is stated that off-target effects could be removed by backcrossing.[90]

This assessment has been adopted by the EU Commission stating that "EFSA did not identify new hazards specifically linked to the genomic modification produced via SDN-1, SDN-2 or ODM, compared with conventional breeding".[91] This assessment that certain genome editing techniques, specifically targeted mutagenesis techniques and cisgenesis do not carry more risks than conventional breeding techniques is also reflected in the EU Commission's proposal for a new regulation on plants obtained by certain new genomic techniques.[92]

---

[86] See Nationale Akademie der Wissenschaften Leopoldina et al. (2019), p. 56; see also Nationale Akademie der Wissenschaften Leopoldina (2021), https://www.leopoldina.org/en/topics/green-genetic-engineering/green-genetic-engineering-safety/

[87] Weigel (2019), p. 6; see also Huang et al. (2016), p. 110.

[88] Bauer-Panskus et al. (2020), p. 1.

[89] EFSA Panel on Genetically Modified Organisms (2020), p. 9 with further references; European Food Safety Authority (2021), p. 25; a different view is taken by Hüdig et al. (2022), p. 2; this view is also challenged by Testbiotech (2023).

[90] See EFSA Panel on Genetically Modified Organisms (2020), p. 10.

[91] European Commission (2021), pp. 29–30.

[92] See European Commission (2023), p. 1–2.

2.4 Conclusion

This chapter shows the functioning of genome editing techniques as well as potential applications of genome editing techniques in agriculture. While genome editing techniques and especially the CRISPR-Cas system have great potential to substantially change and improve worldwide agriculture, there are also risks associated with genome editing techniques whose long-term effects could not have been conclusively researched yet. These uncertainties associated with the risks of genome editing lead to difficulties regarding an adequate regulation of genetically modified plants which is also repeatedly evident in the context of this scientific work.

Despite these uncertainties, the EU Commission has adopted the assessment by EFSA that plants modified by targeted mutagenesis, cisgenesis and intragenesis techniques do not carry more risks than plants obtained by conventional breeding methods and has based its proposal on the regulation of NGT plants on this assessment.

References

Agapito-Tenfen SZ, Okoli AS, Bernstein MJ, Wikmark O-G, Myhr AI (2018) Revisiting risk governance of GM plants: the need to consider new and emerging gene-editing techniques. Front Plant Sci 9:1–16. https://doi.org/10.3389/fpls.2018.01874

Alberts B, Johnson A, Lewis J, Morgan D, Raff M, Roberts K, Walter P, Wilson J, Hunt T (2015) Molecular biology of the cell, 6th edn. Garland Science Taylor and Francis Group, New York

Alberts B, Hopkin K, Johnson A, Morgan D, Raff M, Roberts K, Walter P (2019) Essential cell biology, 5th edn. W.W. Norton & Company, New York

Bauer-Panskus A, Miyazaki J, Kawall K, Then C (2020) Risk assessment of genetically engineered plants that can persist and propagate in the environment. Environ Sci Eur 32:32. https://doi.org/10.1186/s12302-020-00301-0

Beck F (2022) Self-spreading biotechnology and international law: prevention, responsibility, and liability in a transboundary context, Beiträge zum ausländischen öffentlichen Recht und Völkerrecht, vol 316

Bundesministerium für Bildung und Forschung (2014) 25 Jahre BMBF-Forschungsprogramme zur biologischen Sicherheitsforschung: Umweltwirkungen gentechnisch veränderter Pflanzen. https://www.pflanzenforschung.de/application/files/9915/7355/9023/Biologische_Sicherheitsforschung.pdf

Charpentier E, Gross C (2019) The development and impact of genome editing technologies. In: Max Planck Society (ed) Discussion paper focusing on the scientific relevance of genome editing and on the ethical, legal and societal issues potentially involved, pp 3–5

Clark DP, Pazdernik NJ (2016) Biotechnology, 2nd edn. Elsevier AP Cell Press, Amsterdam

Eckerstorfer MF, Dolezel M, Greiter A, Miklau M, Heissenberger A, Steinbrecher RA (2020) Risk assessment of plants developed by new genetic modification techniques (nGMs): biosafety considerations for plants developed by genome editing and other new genetic modification techniques (nGMs) and considerations for their regulation. BfN-Skripten 592

EFSA Panel on Genetically Modified Organisms (2009) Scientific opinion on guidance for the risk assessment of genetically modified plants used for non-food or non-feed purposes. Scientific Opinion

EFSA Panel on Genetically Modified Organisms (2010) Scientific Opinion on the assessment of potential impacts of genetically modified plants on non-target organisms. Scientific Opinion, Parma. https://doi.org/10.2903/j.efsa.2010.1877

EFSA Panel on Genetically Modified Organisms (2012) Scientific opinion addressing the safety assessment of plants developed using Zinc Finger Nuclease 3 and other Site-Directed Nucleases with similar function. In: European Food Security Agency (ed) EFSA journal, vol 10, pp 1–31. https://doi.org/10.2903/j.efsa.2012.2943

EFSA Panel on Genetically Modified Organisms (2020) Applicability of the EFSA Opinion on site-directed nucleases type 3 for the safety assessment of plants developed using site-directed nucleases type 1 and 2 and oligonucleotide-directed mutagenesis. Scientific Opinion. https://doi.org/10.2903/j.efsa.2020.6299

European Commission (2021) Study on the status of new genomic techniques under Union law and in light of the Court of Justice ruling in Case C-528/16: Commission Staff Working Document. SWD(2021) 92 final, Brussels

European Commission (2023) Proposal for a Regulation of the European Parliament and of the Council on plants obtained by certain new genomic techniques and their food and feed, and amending Regulation (EU) 2017/625. COM(2023) 411 final, Brussels

European Food Safety Authority (2021) Overview of EFSA and European national authorities' scientific opinions on the risk assessment of plants developed through New Genomic Techniques. https://doi.org/10.2903/j.efsa.2021.6314

Gelinsky E (2022) Neue gentechnische Verfahren: Kommerzialisierungspipeline im Bereich Pflanzenzüchtung und Lizenzvereinbarungen

High Level Group of Scientific Advisors (2017) New techniques in Agricultural Biotechnology. Explanatory Note 02/2017, Brussels

Höijer I, Emmanouilidou A, Östlund R, van Schendel R, Bozorgpana S, Tijsterman M, Feuk L, Gyllensten U, den Hoed M, Ameur A (2022) CRISPR-Cas9 induces large structural variants at on-target and off-target sites in vivo that segregate across generations. Nat Commun 13:1–10

Hua K, Zhang J, Botella JR, Ma C, Kong F, Liu B, Zhu J-K (2019) Perspective on the application of genome-editing technologies in crop breeding. Mol Plant:1047–1059

Huang S, Weigel D, Beachy RN, Li J (2016) A proposed regulatory framework for genome-edited crops. Nat Genet 48:109–111

Hüdig M, Laibach N, Hein A-C (2022) Genome editing in crop plant research - alignment of expectations and current developments. Plants:1–27

Joint Research Centre (2011) New plant breeding techniques: state-of-the-art and prospects for commercial development. JRC - Scientific and Technical Reports

Joint Research Centre (2021a) Current and future market applications of new genomic techniques. JRC Science for Policy Report

Joint Research Centre (2021b) New genomic techniques: state-of-the-art review. JRC Technical Report

Kadam US, Shelake RM, Chavhan RL, Suprasanna P (2018) Concerns regarding 'off-target' activity of genome editing endonucleases. Plant Physiol Biochem 131:22–30. https://doi.org/10.1016/j.plaphy.2018.03.027

Kawall K, Miyazaki J, Bauer-Panskus A, Then C (2020) Overview of genome editing applications using SDN-1 and SDN-2 in regard to EU regulatory issues, 2020: New methods of genetic engineering (genome editing) and their potential impact on nature protection and the environment

Kosicki M, Tomberg K, Bradley A (2018) Repair of double-strand breaks induced by CRISPR-Cas9 leads to large deletions and complex rearrangements. Nat Biotechnol 36:765–771. https://doi.org/10.1038/nbt.4192

Lawrence E (ed) (2011) Henderson's dictionary of biology, 15th edn. Pearson education

Lee Y-G, Jin Y-S, Cha Y-L, Seo J-H (2017) Bioethanol production from cellulosic hydrolysates by engineered industrial Saccharomyces cerevisiae. Bioresour Technol 228:355–361

Lim C, Kang K, Shim Y, Yoo S-C, Paek N-C (2022) Inactivating transcription factor OsWRKY5 enhances drought tolerance through abscisic acid signaling pathways. Plant Physiol:1900–1916

Menz J, Modrzejewski D, Hartung F, Wilhelm R, Sprink T (2020) Genome edited crops touch the market: a view on the global development and regulatory environment. Front Plant Sci 11:1–17. https://doi.org/10.3389/fpls.2020.586027

Mohan C, Easterlin M, Yau Y-Y (2022) Gene editing technology for sugarcane improvement: opportunities and limitations. Sugar Tech 24:369–385

Muller HJ (1927) Artifical transmutation of the gene. Science 66:84–87. https://doi.org/10.1126/science.66.1699.84

Nationale Akademie der Wissenschaften Leopoldina (2021) How safe is green genetic engineering for the environment and human health? https://www.leopoldina.org/en/topics/green-genetic-engineering/green-genetic-engineering-safety/

Nationale Akademie der Wissenschaften Leopoldina, Union der Deutschen Akademien der Wissenschaften, Deutsche Forschungsgemeinschaft (2019) Towards a scientifically justified, differentiated regulation of genome edited plants in the EU. Statement, Halle (Saale). https://www.leopoldina.org/uploads/tx_leopublication/2019_Stellungnahme_Genomeditierte_Pflanzen_web.pdf

Puchta H, Jiang J, Wang K, Zhao Y (2022) Updates on gene editing and its applications. Plant Physiol 188:1725–1730

Sturme MHJ, van der Berg JP, Bouwman LMS, de Schrijver A, de Maagd RA, Kleter G, Battaglia-de Wilde E (2022) Occurrence and nature of off-target modifications by CRISPR-Cas genome editing in plants. Agric Sci Technol:192–201

Testbiotech (2023) Differences between new genetic engineering and conventional breeding (non-targeted mutagenesis). Testbiotech basic text 23-8-2023. https://www.testbiotech.org/sites/default/files/Differences_crispr_mutagenesis_august_2023.pdf

van Belle J, Schaart JG, van Loo R (2019) The logic of exempting CRISPR/Cas9-plants from strict GM approval under European Union GM regulation: a case study of genome editing in Camelina. In: Dürnberger C, Pfeilmeier S, Schleissing S (eds) Genome editing in agriculture: between precaution and responsibility. Nomos, Baden-Baden, pp 25–45

Vats S, Kumawat S, Kumar V, Patil G, Joshi T, Sonah H, Sharma TR, Deshmukh R (2019) Genome editing in plants: exploration of technological advancements and challenges. Cells:1–39

Vega Rodríguez A, Rodríguez-Oramas C, Sanjuán Velázquez E, Hardisson de la Torre A, Rubio Armendáriz C, Carrascos Iruzubieta C (2022) Myths and realities about genetically modified food: a risk-benefit analysis. Appl Sci:1–24

Walch-Solimena C (2019) Introduction and motivation for the discussion paper. In: Max Planck Society (ed) Discussion paper focusing on the scientific relevance of genome editing and on the ethical, legal and societal issues potentially involved, pp 1–3

Wang X, Tu M, Wang Y, Yin W, Zhang Y, Wu H, Gu Y, Li Z, Xi Z, Wang X (2021) Whole-genome sequencing reveals rare off-target mutations in CRISPR/Cas9-edited grapevine. Hortic Res 8:114. https://doi.org/10.1038/s41438-021-00549-4

Wang Y, Liu Q, Song X, Yang X, Han L, Romeis J, Li Y (2022) Unintended changes in transgenic maize cause no nontarget effects. Plants People Planet 4:392–402

Weigel D (2019) Genome editing in plants. In: Max Planck Society (ed) Discussion paper focusing on the scientific relevance of genome editing and on the ethical, legal and societal issues potentially involved, pp 6–8

Woo JW, Kim J, Kwon SI, Corvalán C, Cho SW, Kim H, Kim S-G, Kim S-T, Choe S, Kim J-S (2015) DNA-free genome editing in plants with preassembled CRISPR-Cas9 ribonucleoproteins. Nat Biotechnol 33:1162–1165

Zhang B (2020) CRISPR/Cas9: a robust genome-editing tool with versatile functions and endless application. Int J Mol Sci 21:1–3

Zhang Y, Malzahn AA, Sretenovic S, Yiping Q (2019) The emerging and uncultivated potential of CRISPR technology in plant science. Nat Plants 5:778–794

Chapter 3
The European Court of Justice's Decision on Genome Editing

Abstract This chapter discusses the decision of the Court of Justice of the European Union ('CJEU') in the case C-528/16 – Confédération paysanne et al. in which the CJEU classified organisms modified by targeted mutagenesis techniques as genetically modified organisms ('GMOs') under the GMO law of the European Union ('EU'). The Court based its decision on the process-based interpretation of the GMO definition laid down in Directive 2001/18/EC on the deliberate release into the environment of genetically modified organisms, highlighting that mutagenesis techniques result in genetic changes that do not occur naturally. The CJEU also ruled that targeted mutagenesis techniques do not fall under the mutagenesis exception in Annex I B of the Directive, thus falling within the Directive's scope. This decision has sparked debate about the adequacy of the currently applicable EU GMO law, particularly in relation to genome edited organisms, and raised concerns about its potential impact on international trade and the compatibility of EU GMO law with the EU's obligations under the law of the World Trade Organization and the Comprehensive Economic and Trade Agreement ('CETA') between Canada and the EU.

3.1 Introduction

The subject of this treatise arose out of a judgment of the Court of Justice of the European Union ('CJEU') in the case C-528/16 on a request for a preliminary ruling under Article 267 of the *Treaty on the Functioning of the European Union*[1] from the French Conseil d'État in the proceedings *Confédération paysanne et al. v Premier minister et al.*. These proceedings were primarily concerned with the applicability of *Directive 2001/18/EC of the European Parliament and of the Council of 12 March on the deliberate release into the environment of genetically modified*

[1] *Consolidated Version of the Treaty on the Functioning of the European Union* ('TFEU'), Official Journal of the European Union ('OJ EU') 2012, C326/47.

E. A. L. Andersen, *Regulation of Biotechnological Risks in a Multi-Level System*, European Yearbook of International Economic Law 46,
https://doi.org/10.1007/978-3-032-02409-1_3

organisms[2] ('Directive 2001/18/EC' or 'Deliberate Release Directive') on organisms obtained by techniques of targeted mutagenesis.[3] While the judgment also dealt with questions on the scope of *Council Directive 2002/53/EC of 13 June 2002 on the common catalogue of varieties of agricultural plant species*[4] ('Directive 2002/53/EC'), these questions are not relevant for the present thesis and therefore not analysed in detail.

The present chapter presents the initial proceedings before the French Court (3.2), the proceedings before the CJEU (3.3–3.4) and the CJEU's judgment (3.5) before the reactions to and consequences of the judgment are analysed (3.6–3.7).

3.2 Initial proceedings before the French Conseil d'État in 2016

The initial proceedings were taking place before the French Conseil d'État between 2015 and 2016. In these proceedings, Article D. 531-2 of the French *Code de l'environnement*[5] took centre stage. The claimants, namely *La Confédération Paysanne*, *Le reseau semence paysannes*, *Les amis de la terre France*, *Le collectif vigilance OGM et pesticides 16*, *Vigilance OG2M*, *CSFV 49*, *OGM dangers*, *Vigilance OGM 33* and *Federation nature et progress* (associations that defend the interests of small-scale farming and aim at environmental protection) had asked the Prime Minister to repeal Article D. 531-2 of the Code de l'environnement. A demand that the Prime Minister had implicitly rejected.[6] Therefore, the claimants by initiating court proceedings sought to annul this implicit decision of rejection by the Prime Minister.[7]

Article D. 531-2 2° a) states that the usage of mutagenesis techniques does not lead to a genetically modified organism ('GMO') as defined in Article L. 531-1 2°. Article D. 531-2 has been codified by a decree[8] as provided for by Article L. 531-2.

---

[2] *Directive 2001/18/EC of the European Parliament and the Council of 12 March 2001 on the deliberate release into the environment of genetically modified organisms and repealing Council Directive 90/220/EC* (consolidated version from 27 March 2021) ('Directive 2001/18/EC'), Official Journal of the European Communities ('OJ EC') 2001, L 106/1.

[3] CJEU, *Case C-528/16 - Confédération paysanne et al.* (25 July 2018), ECLI:EU:C:2018:583.

[4] *Council Directive 2002/53/EC of 13 June 2002 on the common catalogue of varieties of agricultural plant species* (consolidated version from 18 April 2004), OJ EC 2002, L193/1.

[5] *Code de l'environnement* (French Environmental Code), https://www.legifrance.gouv.fr/codes/id/LEGITEXT000006074220/

[6] *Cf.* Conseil d'État, *Décision No 388649 - Confédération paysanne et autres* (03.10.2016), FR:CECHR:2016:388649.20161003, paras 1–2; see also Confédération paysanne (2015).

[7] *Cf.* Conseil d'État, *Décision No 388649 - Confédération paysanne et autres* (03.10.2016), FR:CECHR:2016:388649.20161003, para 2; see also Confédération paysanne (2015).

[8] Décret n° 93-774 du 27 mars 1993 fixant la liste des techniques de modification génétique et les critères de classement des organisms génétiquement modifies, Article 2; this decree has been modified by Décret n° 2007-357 du 19 mars 2007 modifiant le décret n° 93-774 du 27 mars 1993 fixant

It entails a list that enumerates techniques that do not lead to a genetic modification or that have been subject to traditional use without any proven disadvantage for public health or the environment. Articles L. 531-1 et seq. Have been issued for the transposition of Directive 2001/18/EC into French law.[9]

The applicant associations raised procedural as well as substantive issues with regard to Article D. 531-2 of the Code de l'environnement.

On the procedural level, they contested the Prime Minister's competence to issue Article D. 531-2 and claimed irregularities during the legislative procedure. Both claims were rejected by the French Conseil d'État.[10]

On the merits, the complainants first asserted that Article D. 531-2 disregards Article 3 of the *Cartagena Protocol on Biosafety to the Convention on Biological Diversity*[11] ('Cartagena Protocol'). The French Conseil d'État rejected this claim since the complaining parties had failed to identify the precise obligations that would have been violated by Article D. 531-2 of the Code de l'environnement and to deliver sufficient details for an assessment of the merits.[12]

Second, the complainants claimed a violation of Article 2 of Directive 2001/18/EC since, contrary to what Article D. 531-2 states, the application of mutagenesis techniques would lead to a genetic modification.[13] The Court stated that organisms obtained by mutagenesis techniques *may* be regarded as GMOs and asked whether mutagenesis techniques and in particular the new techniques of directed mutagenesis may be regarded as one of the techniques listed in Annex I A of Directive 2001/18/EC. It concluded that this issue should be referred to the CJEU.[14]

As a third claim, the complaining parties asserted a violation of Article 4 of Directive 2002/53/EC since this Article only refers to Article 2 of Directive 2001/18/

---

la leste des techniques de modification génétique et les critères de classement des organisms génétiquement modifies; it has afterwards been repealed by Décret n° 2007-1467 du 12 octobre 2007 relatif au livre V de la partie réglementaire du code de l'environnement et modifiant certaines autres dispositions de ce code; see *Décret n°93-774 du 27 mars 1993 fixant la liste des techniques de modification génétique et les critères de classement des organismes génétiquement modifiés* (https://www.legifrance.gouv.fr/loda/article_lc/LEGIARTI000006931194/2007-03-20/#LEGIARTI000006931194)

[9] *Cf.* Conseil d'État, *Décision No 388649 - Confédération paysanne et autres* (03.10.2016), FR:CECHR:2016:388649.20161003, paras 6–7.

[10] Conseil d'État, *Décision No 388649 - Confédération paysanne et autres* (03.10.2016), FR:CECHR:2016:388649.20161003, paras 10–11.

[11] *Cartagena Protocol on Biosafety to the Convention on Biological Diversity* (adopted 29 January 2000, entered into force 11 September 2003) 2226 UNTS 208.

[12] Conseil d'État, *Décision No 388649 - Confédération paysanne et autres* (03.10.2016), FR:CECHR:2016:388649.20161003, para 12.

[13] Conseil d'État, *Décision No 388649 - Confédération paysanne et autres* (03.10.2016), FR:CECHR:2016:388649.20161003, para 13.

[14] Conseil d'État, *Décision No 388649 - Confédération paysanne et autres* (03.10.2016), FR:CECHR:2016:388649.20161003, para 13.

EC for the definition of a genetically modified organism but not to Article 3 of this Directive and its Annex I B.[15]

Finally, the claimants asserted that Article D. 531-2 is not in line with the precautionary principle as laid down in Article 5 of the French *Charte de l'environnement.*[16,17] To assess a possible violation, the French Conseil d'État first examined the applicable standard of review. Since Article D. 531-2 of the Code de l'environnement is a national measure of transposition of the Deliberate Release Directive the Court implicitly held that a challenge to the validity of this Article indirectly means a challenge to the Directive's validity itself. It, therefore, termed the assertion by the complainants as being one of potential (in)compatibility with European Union ('EU') law.[18] As a consequence, the French Conseil d'État first had to determine whether Articles 2 and 3 and Annex I B of Directive 2001/18/EC constitute full harmonisation measures. A question that it referred to the CJEU.[19]

In a second step, the Court elaborated on the risks of random mutagenesis technique, new targeted mutagenesis, and genome editing techniques as well as transgenesis techniques.[20] In this regard, the Court also outlined the different submissions that were brought forward by the respective parties. The applicant associations had submitted that it is possible to produce herbicide resistance by using the different forms of mutagenesis techniques. According to their submission, the use of such herbicide-resistant varieties poses a risk of significant damage to the environment and human and animal health. They further pointed to unintended effects with regard to the genome that may result from the in-vitro application of these techniques.[21]

On the contrary, the respondent Minister of Agriculture, Agri-Food and Forestry argued that the risks of damage to the environment and human and animal health are not the result of the varieties' properties obtained through genetic modification but

---

[15] Conseil d'État, *Décision No 388649 - Confédération paysanne et autres* (03.10.2016), FR:CECHR:2016:388649.20161003, para 14.

[16] Charte de l'environnement (French Environmental Charta) (https://www.legifrance.gouv.fr/contenu/menu/droit-national-en-vigueur/constitution/charte-de-l-environnement)

[17] Conseil d'État, *Décision No 388649 - Confédération paysanne et autres* (03.10.2016), FR:CECHR:2016:388649.20161003, para 15.

[18] Conseil d'État, *Décision No 388649 - Confédération paysanne et autres* (03.10.2016), FR:CECHR:2016:388649.20161003, paras 16–21; see also the considerations by Advocate General Bobek in his Opinion, *cf.* CJEU, *Case C-528/16 - Confédération paysanne et al.* (25 July 2018), ECLI:EU:C:2018:583, para 36.

[19] Conseil d'État, *Décision No 388649 - Confédération paysanne et autres* (03.10.2016), FR:CECHR:2016:388649.20161003, para 21; CJEU, *Case C-528/16 - Confédération paysanne et al.* (25 July 2018), ECLI:EU:C:2018:583, para 25.

[20] Conseil d'État, *Décision No 388649 - Confédération paysanne et autres* (03.10.2016), FR:CECHR:2016:388649.20161003, paras 23–29.

[21] Conseil d'État, *Décision No 388649 - Confédération paysanne et autres* (03.10.2016), FR:CECHR:2016:388649.20161003, paras 25–26.

of the farmers' cultivation practices. Furthermore, the unintended mutations could be eliminated by cross-breeding techniques.[22]

In its conclusion, the Court first dismissed the claim that the Deliberate Release Directive disregards the precautionary principle when it comes to the use of random mutagenesis techniques since these techniques have been used for several decades without any identified environmental or health risks.[23] With regard to the application of random in-vitro mutagenesis and directed mutagenesis techniques, the Court noted that it is impossible to determine with certainty the existence and significance of the alleged risks. It concluded that due to the non-existence of any evaluation or monitoring to date, the alleged risks, whether they result from the genetic modification used or from the plant's characteristics, are similar to those that could result from varieties obtained by transgenic techniques.[24] It added that the development of new genetic engineering techniques makes it possible to speed up the production of GMOs which correlates with an increased possibility of damage.[25] Due to these circumstances, the Court questioned the validity of the Deliberate Release Directive in light of the precautionary principle with regard to newly developed mutagenesis techniques. A question that the French Conseil d'État also referred to the CJEU. However, this question is dependent on the assessment of whether these new techniques of mutagenesis fall within or outside of the Directive's scope.[26]

Finally, the French Conseil d'État decided to suspend the proceedings and to refer the following questions to the CJEU:[27]

- Whether organisms obtained by mutagenesis constitute genetically modified organisms within the meaning of Article 2 of Directive 2001/18/EC although they are exempt by Article 3 and Annex I B to the Directive (as part of question 1)
- Whether mutagenesis techniques, in particular targeted mutagenesis techniques constitute techniques in the sense of Annex I A (as part of question 1)
- Whether Articles 2 and 3 of Directive 2001/18/EC in conjunction with its Annexes exempt only random mutagenesis or also targeted mutagenesis from the Directive's scope (as part of question 1)
- Whether varieties obtained by mutagenesis constitute genetically modified varieties within the meaning of Article 4 of Directive 2002/53/EC and would accord-

[22] Conseil d'État, *Décision No 388649 - Confédération paysanne et autres* (03.10.2016), FR:CECHR:2016:388649.20161003, paras 25–26.

[23] Conseil d'État, *Décision No 388649 - Confédération paysanne et autres* (03.10.2016), FR:CECHR:2016:388649.20161003, para 27.

[24] Conseil d'État, *Décision No 388649 - Confédération paysanne et autres* (03.10.2016), FR:CECHR:2016:388649.20161003, para 28.

[25] Conseil d'État, *Décision No 388649 - Confédération paysanne et autres* (03.10.2016), FR:CECHR:2016:388649.20161003, para 28.

[26] Conseil d'État, *Décision No 388649 - Confédération paysanne et autres* (03.10.2016), FR:CECHR:2016:388649.20161003, paras 29–30.

[27] Conseil d'État, *Décision No 388649 - Confédération paysanne et autres* (03.10.2016), FR:CECHR:2016:388649.20161003, para 31 and Décision Article 1er; CJEU, *Case C-528/16 - Confédération paysanne et al.* (25 July 2018), ECLI:EU:C:2018:583, para 25.

ingly not be exempted from that Directive or whether the exemption applicable under Directive 2001/18/EC also applies to Directive 2002/53/EC (question 2)
- Whether the exemption of mutagenesis from the scope of Directive 2001/18/EC constitutes a full harmonisation measure that Member States must abide by (question 3)
- Whether the precautionary principle calls into question a possible exemption of targeted mutagenesis techniques from the scope of Directive 2001/18/EC (question 4)

3.3 Proceedings Before the CJEU

After written submissions were filed by the Applicants, some EU Member States, the European Parliament, the Council, and the EU Commission, most of these parties presented their oral arguments at the hearing on 3 October 2017.[28]

The EU Commission in its submission stated that organisms modified by mutgenesis techniques constitute genetically modified organisms within the meaning of Article 2(2) of Directive 2001/18/EC and reasoned this by the fact that those organisms are exempted by Article 3 which would be pointless if they did not generally fall within the scope of application.[29] Furthermore, the EU Commission advocated for an exemption of new (targeted) mutagenesis techniques from the scope of Directive 2001/18/EC. It stated that the term "mutagenesis" in Annex I B was generic and that it already comprised different conventional mutagenesis techniques.[30] Also, the EU legislator in 2001 when adopting the Directive was not unaware of new technological developments in the field of genetic engineering and decided to adopt an open interpretation of the mutagenesis term.[31] According to the EU Commission this interpretation is also in line with the Directive's objectives to allow for the assessment of the potential risks posed by genetic modification techniques crossing the species barrier, such as transgenesis.[32]

The Council of the European Union in its submission did not present arguments on the status of mutagenesis techniques under Directive 2001/18/EC, but only stated its view on the third and fourth question referred to the CJEU.[33] Similarly, the European Parliament only submitted its view on the fourth question referred to the Court.[34]

---

[28] Opinion of Advocate General Bobek, *Case C-528/16 - Confédération paysanne et al.* (18 January 2018), ECLI:EU:C:2018:20, para 38; oral arguments were not presented by the Netherlands and Austrian Governments.

[29] European Commission (2017), paras 26–35.

[30] European Commission (2017), para 43.

[31] See European Commission (2017), paras 47–49.

[32] European Commission (2017), para 50.

[33] See Council of the European Union (2023).

[34] See European Parliament (2017).

Out of the Member States' submission, the submission from the Swedish Government was particularly interesting because it did not only elaborate on the safety of the different techniques and the EU framework as such[35] but also brought up the international law context of the Deliberate Release Directive, including the EU's obligations under the Cartagena Protocol and the *General Agreement on Tariffs and Trade*[36] ('GATT').[37] In this regard, it pointed to Article III of the GATT and the fact that organisms obtained by new mutagenesis techniques and those obtained by conventional mutagenesis techniques could be considered "like" products since they are identical and indistinguishable.[38] Furthermore, the Swedish Government found it difficult to argue that an exception enshrined in Article XX GATT is applicable.[39]

3.4 The Opinion of Advocate General Bobek

Advocate General Bobek delivered his Opinion on 28 January 2018.[40] He started his opinion by giving an overview of the facts, the procedure of the case, and the legal framework.[41] Concerning the first question, he offered some introductory remarks on the basic notions of the terms *mutagenesis* and *transgenesis* and the precautionary principle in EU law, before addressing the question in essence.[42] In his view organisms obtained by mutagenesis qualify as GMOs in the sense of Article 2(2) Directive 2001/18/EC provided these organisms fulfil the criteria set out in Article 2(2).[43] This "follows from the text, internal logic, and broader context of the GMO Directive".[44] He stated that Article 2(2) does explicitly not require the insertion of

---

[35] Swedish Government (2017), paras 7, pp. 35–38.

[36] *General Agreement on Tariffs and Trade 1994*, Annex 1 to the *Marrakesh Agreement establishing the World Trade Organization* (concluded 15 April 1994, entered into force 1 January 1995) 1867 UNTS 3; the *General Agreement on Tariffs and Trade 1994* incorporates the *General Agreement on Tariffs and Trade 1947* (concluded 30 October 1947) 55 UNTS 187.

[37] Swedish Government (2017), paras 29–32, pp. 39–42.

[38] CJEU, *Case C-528/16 - Confédération paysanne et al.* (25 July 2018), ECLI:EU:C:2018:583, Swedish Government's submission, para 40.

[39] CJEU, *Case C-528/16 - Confédération paysanne et al.* (25 July 2018), ECLI:EU:C:2018:583, Swedish Government's submission, paras 41–42.

[40] Opinion of Advocate General Bobek, *Case C-528/16 - Confédération paysanne et al.* (18 January 2018), ECLI:EU:C:2018:20.

[41] Opinion of Advocate General Bobek, *Case C-528/16 - Confédération paysanne et al.* (18 January 2018), ECLI:EU:C:2018:20, paras 1–38.

[42] Opinion of Advocate General Bobek, *Case C-528/16 - Confédération paysanne et al.* (18 January 2018), ECLI:EU:C:2018:20, paras 42–54.

[43] Opinion of Advocate General Bobek, *Case C-528/16 - Confédération paysanne et al.* (18 January 2018), ECLI:EU:C:2018:20, paras 56, 60, 66.

[44] Opinion of Advocate General Bobek, *Case C-528/16 - Confédération paysanne et al.* (18 January 2018), ECLI:EU:C:2018:20, para 60.

foreign DNA (standing for deoxyribonucleic acid) for an organism to qualify as genetically modified and that the wording of Article 3 and Annex I B implies that mutagenesis can be characterised as a technique of genetic modification.[45] To exempt organisms that do not fall within the Directive's scope would be illogical.[46] He further pointed out that the EU legislator could have foreseen an exclusion of mutagenesis "at the level of the definition itself" if it had wanted to exclude this technique of genetic modification.[47]

In a second step, the General Advocate then elaborated on the mutagenesis exemption itself.[48] He first summarised the different views taken by Member States and EU actors and then followed the approach taken by the European Commission: Organisms obtained by mutagenesis techniques are exempt from the obligations laid down in the Directive if these organisms fulfil the criteria set out in its Article 3(1) and especially in its Annex I B, namely the "Annex I B caveat".[49] According to this caveat, organisms obtained by mutagenesis are only exempt on the condition that the technique *does not involve the use of recombinant nucleic acid molecules or GMOs other than those produced by mutagenesis or cell fusion*. That caveat which was introduced in 2001 narrowed down the exemption and was aimed at taking into account the emergence of new mutagenesis techniques according to the Advocate General.[50] This however also shows that Article 3 and Annex I B should not serve as an exemption for all techniques of mutagenesis.[51] The Advocate General refered to the Applicant's submission and to that of the French Government which stated that only techniques considered safe in 2001 are exempt from the Directive's scope relying on recital 17 of the Directive and the precautionary principle.[52] He disagreed with these submissions since in his view "the legislature in 2001 clearly meant what it said in writing".[53] The EU did not intend to only exempt safe mutagenesis

---

[45] Opinion of Advocate General Bobek, *Case C-528/16 - Confédération paysanne et al.* (18 January 2018), ECLI:EU:C:2018:20, para 61.

[46] Opinion of Advocate General Bobek, *Case C-528/16 - Confédération paysanne et al.* (18 January 2018), ECLI:EU:C:2018:20, para 62 referring to and agreeing with the statement made by the European Commission.

[47] Opinion of Advocate General Bobek, *Case C-528/16 - Confédération paysanne et al.* (18 January 2018), ECLI:EU:C:2018:20, para 63.

[48] Opinion of Advocate General Bobek, *Case C-528/16 - Confédération paysanne et al.* (18 January 2018), ECLI:EU:C:2018:20, paras 68–106.

[49] Opinion of Advocate General Bobek, *Case C-528/16 - Confédération paysanne et al.* (18 January 2018), ECLI:EU:C:2018:20, paras 69–79.

[50] Opinion of Advocate General Bobek, *Case C-528/16 - Confédération paysanne et al.* (18 January 2018), ECLI:EU:C:2018:20, paras 80–81 referring to the observations made by the European Commission.

[51] Opinion of Advocate General Bobek, *Case C-528/16 - Confédération paysanne et al.* (18 January 2018), ECLI:EU:C:2018:20, para 82.

[52] Opinion of Advocate General Bobek, *Case C-528/16 - Confédération paysanne et al.* (18 January 2018), ECLI:EU:C:2018:20, para 88.

[53] Opinion of Advocate General Bobek, *Case C-528/16 - Confédération paysanne et al.* (18 January 2018), ECLI:EU:C:2018:20, para 89.

techniques from the Directive's scope as can be derived from its historical context and the internal logic of the Deliberate Release Directive.[54] He did not support the emphasis on recital 17 since this recital does not even mention mutagenesis techniques, and also do neither Article 3 nor Annex I B refer to recital 17.[55] These provisions do not mention *a long safety record* as justification or reason for the exemption.[56] Referring to the legislative process, the Advocate General pointed out that the mutagenesis exemption was introduced into the Directive independently of recital 17.[57] Furthermore, the legislative history as well as the statements by the EU Commission and the Council at the oral hearing confirm that there was no distinction between different mutagenesis techniques intended.[58] This is supported by the fact that the EU legislator expressly introduced distinctions where it wished to make such.[59]

With regard to the argument that the mutagenesis exemption does only comprise techniques that were considered safe at the time of the Directive's adoption in 2001, the Advocate General emphasised that the interpretation of law must be dynamic.[60] In his view, "a generic category labelled 'mutagenesis' should logically encompass all those techniques that are, at the given moment relevant for the case in question, understood as forming part of that category, including any new ones".[61] What the Applicants are asking for is not an interpretation of the Deliberate Release Directive but a judicial redrafting against the Directive's wording.[62] A task that should be carried out by the legislator and not by the Court according to the Advocate General's view.[63]

Concerning the third question, the Advocate General first disagreed with the Commission's view that this question is inadmissible. For him, this question seems relevant to the Applicant's request in the main proceedings to impose a moratorium

[54] Opinion of Advocate General Bobek, *Case C-528/16 - Confédération paysanne et al.* (18 January 2018), ECLI:EU:C:2018:20, paras 90–91.

[55] Opinion of Advocate General Bobek, *Case C-528/16 - Confédération paysanne et al.* (18 January 2018), ECLI:EU:C:2018:20, paras 92–93.

[56] Opinion of Advocate General Bobek, *Case C-528/16 - Confédération paysanne et al.* (18 January 2018), ECLI:EU:C:2018:20, para 93.

[57] Opinion of Advocate General Bobek, *Case C-528/16 - Confédération paysanne et al.* (18 January 2018), ECLI:EU:C:2018:20, para 94.

[58] Opinion of Advocate General Bobek, *Case C-528/16 - Confédération paysanne et al.* (18 January 2018), ECLI:EU:C:2018:20, para 95.

[59] Opinion of Advocate General Bobek, *Case C-528/16 - Confédération paysanne et al.* (18 January 2018), ECLI:EU:C:2018:20, para 96.

[60] Opinion of Advocate General Bobek, *Case C-528/16 - Confédération paysanne et al.* (18 January 2018), ECLI:EU:C:2018:20, 98, 100.

[61] Opinion of Advocate General Bobek, *Case C-528/16 - Confédération paysanne et al.* (18 January 2018), ECLI:EU:C:2018:20, para 101.

[62] Opinion of Advocate General Bobek, *Case C-528/16 - Confédération paysanne et al.* (18 January 2018), ECLI:EU:C:2018:20, para 104.

[63] Opinion of Advocate General Bobek, *Case C-528/16 - Confédération paysanne et al.* (18 January 2018), ECLI:EU:C:2018:20, para 105.

on herbicide-resistant varieties obtained by mutagenesis.[64] He argued in favour of a partial harmonisation. Thus, the exclusion of mutagenesis techniques from the Directive's scope simply shows that the EU legislature does not regulate these techniques at the EU level. Member States are free to subject organisms excluded from Directive 2001/18/EC to national regulation as long as they comply with their overall EU law obligations.[65]

Coming to the fourth question, the Advocate General determined the relevant time for a validity analysis, thereby challenging the view of the European Commission and the European Council "that the validity of a secondary law act is carried out, in principle, in the light of the facts and circumstances that prevailed at the time when that act was adopted".[66] He pleaded for "a constitutional duty for legislation to be relevant, in the sense of being technically and socially responsive, and, provided that it is necessary in view of later evolution, to be updated."[67] However, in the present case, such a duty does not have any effects on the validity of Articles 2 and 3 of and Annex I B to the Directive 2001/18/EC, according to the Advocate General.[68]

Lastly, the Advocate General dealt with the second question referred to the CJEU. He favoured an interpretation of Article 4(4) of Directive 2002/53/EC that is consistent with Directive 2001/18/EC and objected to a purely textual reading of Directive 2002/53/EC.[69] As reasons for such an interpretation, he named internal and external consistency of the Directive.[70]

3.5 The Judgment of the CJEU

In its decision, the CJEU classified all organisms modified by mutagenesis techniques, in particular by targeted mutagenesis techniques, as GMOs in the sense of Article 2(2) of Directive 2001/18/EC.[71] The Court implicitly followed a primarily

---

[64] Opinion of Advocate General Bobek, *Case C-528/16 - Confédération paysanne et al.* (18 January 2018), ECLI:EU:C:2018:20, paras 109–112.

[65] Opinion of Advocate General Bobek, *Case C-528/16 - Confédération paysanne et al.* (18 January 2018), ECLI:EU:C:2018:20, paras 117–124.

[66] Opinion of Advocate General Bobek, *Case C-528/16 - Confédération paysanne et al.* (18 January 2018), ECLI:EU:C:2018:20, paras 131–142.

[67] Opinion of Advocate General Bobek, *Case C-528/16 - Confédération paysanne et al.* (18 January 2018), ECLI:EU:C:2018:20, para 139.

[68] Opinion of Advocate General Bobek, *Case C-528/16 - Confédération paysanne et al.* (18 January 2018), ECLI:EU:C:2018:20, paras 143–152.

[69] Opinion of Advocate General Bobek, *Case C-528/16 - Confédération paysanne et al.* (18 January 2018), ECLI:EU:C:2018:20, paras 154–159.

[70] Opinion of Advocate General Bobek, *Case C-528/16 - Confédération paysanne et al.* (18 January 2018), ECLI:EU:C:2018:20, paras 160–165.

[71] CJEU, *Case C-528/16 - Confédération paysanne et al.* (25 July 2018), ECLI:EU:C:2018:583, paras 27–38.

process-based interpretation of the GMO definition laid down in Article 2(2) of Directive 2001/18/EC. It based its decision on several arguments: First, all mutagenesis techniques result in changes to the plant organism which, according to the referring court, do *not occur naturally*.[72] Second, the Directive's systematic supports this interpretation. Although mutagenesis techniques are not explicitly mentioned in Part 1 of Annex I A, it is clear from the expression *inter alia* in the introductory sentence of Part 1 of Annex I A that the list of techniques that result in a genetic modification is not exhaustive.[73] Furthermore, mutagenesis techniques have not been included in the exhaustive list of Part 2 of Annex I A to the Directive which entails techniques that do not result in a genetic modification.[74] That the use of mutagenesis techniques results in a genetic modification is also apparent from the explicit exclusion of mutagenesis techniques in Article 3(1) of Directive 2001/18/EC in conjunction with Annex I B.[75]

In a second step, the CJEU dealt with the actual interpretation of the *mutagenesis exception* listed in Annex I B of Directive 2001/18/EC. The CJEU found that targeted mutagenesis techniques do not fall within this exception and are thus covered by the scope of the Deliberate Release Directive.[76] The Court justified this finding with a narrow scope of application of Article 3(1) of Directive 2001/18/EC in conjunction with Annex I B.[77] In addition, not only the wording but also the context and objectives have to be taken into account when interpreting EU legislation.[78] Since Article 3(1) and Annex I B only generally refer to the term "mutagenesis", the term's wording itself does not provide any conclusive guidance.[79] The CJEU, therefore, had recourse to recital 17 of the Directive.[80] It noted that in the case at hand it had to rule on mutagenesis techniques which were only developed after the adoption of the Directive in 2001 and "in respect of which the risks for the environment

[72] CJEU, *Case C-528/16 - Confédération paysanne et al.* (25 July 2018), ECLI:EU:C:2018:583, paras 28–29.

[73] CJEU, *Case C-528/16 - Confédération paysanne et al.* (25 July 2018), ECLI:EU:C:2018:583, paras 33–35.

[74] CJEU, *Case C-528/16 - Confédération paysanne et al.* (25 July 2018), ECLI:EU:C:2018:583, para 36.

[75] CJEU, *Case C-528/16 - Confédération paysanne et al.* (25 July 2018), ECLI:EU:C:2018:583, para 37.

[76] CJEU, *Case C-528/16 - Confédération paysanne et al.* (25 July 2018), ECLI:EU:C:2018:583, paras 39–54.

[77] CJEU, *Case C-528/16 - Confédération paysanne et al.* (25 July 2018), ECLI:EU:C:2018:583, para 41.

[78] CJEU, *Case C-528/16 - Confédération paysanne et al.* (25 July 2018), ECLI:EU:C:2018:583, para 42.

[79] CJEU, *Case C-528/16 - Confédération paysanne et al.* (25 July 2018), ECLI:EU:C:2018:583, para 43.

[80] Recital 17 of Directive 2001/18/EC reads: "This Directive should not apply to organisms obtained through certain techniques of genetic modification which have conventionally been used in a number of applications and have a long safety record."

or human health have not thus far been established with certainty".[81] It refered to the statement of the Conseil d'État according to which "new techniques/methods of mutagenesis might prove to be similar to those which result from the production and release of a GMO through transgenesis".[82] From this, the CJEU concluded that the alteration of an organism by targeted mutagenesis techniques makes it possible to obtain the same effects as the alteration by transgenesis techniques which involve the introduction of foreign DNA.[83] Further, it concluded that these new techniques allow for the production of GMOs at a rate and in quantities that are much higher in comparison to the use of conventional mutagenesis techniques.[84] In light of these conclusions, the CJEU referred to recitals 4 and 5 of Directive 2001/18/EC[85] which require to control the risks of releasing GMOs.[86] Finally, the CJEU based its decision to apply the Directive to targeted mutagenesis techniques on the precautionary principle which is reflected in the Directive's recitals[87] as well as in Articles 1 and 4 of Directive 2001/18/EC.[88]

With regard to the second question, the CJEU also distinguished between new mutagenesis techniques and those mutagenesis techniques that "have conventionally been used in a number of applications".[89] Varieties obtained by the former fall within the scope of Article 4(4) of Directive 2002/53/EC; those obtained by the latter are exempt from its scope.[90] Although Article 4(4) of Directive 2002/53/EC

---

[81] CJEU, *Case C-528/16 - Confédération paysanne et al.* (25 July 2018), ECLI:EU:C:2018:583, para 47.

[82] CJEU, *Case C-528/16 - Confédération paysanne et al.* (25 July 2018), ECLI:EU:C:2018:583, para 48.

[83] CJEU, *Case C-528/16 - Confédération paysanne et al.* (25 July 2018), ECLI:EU:C:2018:583, para 48.

[84] *Cf.* CJEU, *Case C-528/16 - Confédération paysanne et al.* (25 July 2018), ECLI:EU:C:2018:583, para 48.

[85] Recital 4 of Directive 2001/18/EC reads: "Living organisms, whether released into the environment in large or small amounts for experimental purposes or as commercial products, may reproduce in the environment and cross national frontiers thereby affecting other Member States. The effects of such releases on the environment may be irreversible."; recital 5 of Directive 2001/18/EC reads: "The protection of human health and the environment requires that due attention be given to controlling risks from the deliberate release into the environment of genetically modified organisms (GMOs)".

[86] CJEU, *Case C-528/16 - Confédération paysanne et al.* (25 July 2018), ECLI:EU:C:2018:583, para 49.

[87] See recital 8 of Directive 2001/18/EC reading: "The precautionary principle has been taken into account in the drafting of this Directive and must be taken into account when implementing it".

[88] CJEU, *Case C-528/16 - Confédération paysanne et al.* (25 July 2018), ECLI:EU:C:2018:583, paras 50–53.

[89] CJEU, *Case C-528/16 - Confédération paysanne et al.* (25 July 2018), ECLI:EU:C:2018:583, paras 55–68.

[90] CJEU, *Case C-528/16 - Confédération paysanne et al.* (25 July 2018), ECLI:EU:C:2018:583, paras 67–68.

does not explicitly refer to the exemption laid down in Article 3(1) and Annex I B of Directive 2001/18/EC, it must be interpreted as covering these exemptions.[91]

Addressing the third question, the CJEU found that organisms obtained by conventional mutagenesis techniques may be subject to the obligations laid down in the Deliberate Release Directive as long as this complies with EU law.[92] Since these organisms are exempt from the scope of the Deliberate Release Directive, Member States are free to regulate them.[93] The Court hereby followed the considerations made by the Advocate General in his Opinion.[94]

Finally, the CJEU saw no need to answer the fourth question calling into question the validity of Articles 2 and 3 and Annex I B of Directive 2001/18/EC in light of the precautionary principle. This is because organisms obtained by new mutagenesis techniques fall within the scope of the Deliberate Release Directive and are thus not exempt from the obligations laid down therein.[95]

3.6 Comments on the CJEU's reasoning

Although the CJEU's judgement has raised a lot of criticism, it is seen as one of the most important judgements that has been issued in recent years in the field of plant biotechnology.[96] Before the judgment was issued, there was a lot of discussion on whether the regulatory approach of the EU GMO law is rather process- or product-based.[97] And there was disagreement on how to regulate organisms that have been altered by using new plant breeding techniques.[98] The judgement answered these questions but did not end the debate.

In general, it is said that the judgment fits in with the rather sceptical climate in the EU when it comes to genetic engineering.[99] From a scientific point of view, the

---

[91] CJEU, *Case C-528/16 - Confédération paysanne et al.* (25 July 2018), ECLI:EU:C:2018:583, paras 61, 65.

[92] CJEU, *Case C-528/16 - Confédération paysanne et al.* (25 July 2018), ECLI:EU:C:2018:583, para 82.

[93] CJEU, *Case C-528/16 - Confédération paysanne et al.* (25 July 2018), ECLI:EU:C:2018:583, paras 80–81.

[94] *Cf.* CJEU, Case C-528/16 – *Confédération paysanne et al.* (2018), Opinion of AG Bobek, ECLI:EU:C:2018:20, paras 115–124.

[95] CJEU, *Case C-528/16 - Confédération paysanne et al.* (25 July 2018), ECLI:EU:C:2018:583, paras 83–85.

[96] Brosset and Noiville (2019), pp. 197, 199; *cf.* Kahrmann and Leggewie (2018a), p. 497; Carreno and Dolle (2019), p. 96; see also Vogt (2018), p. 11; Vlaams Instituut voor Biotechnologie (2018), p. 2; Verband der Chemischen Industrie e.V. (2018).

[97] See for example Faltus (2019), p. 58; Kahrmann et al. (2017), pp. 178–180; *cf.* also Spranger (2018), p. 2929.

[98] *Cf.* Broll et al. (2019), p. 288; Vöneky (2019), p. 18; Abbott (2018); *Legal limbo* (2017); Dederer (2019b), pp. 77–78.

[99] *Cf.* Šimas and Schwedler (2018); Ladeur (2018), p. 198.

judgment is seen as a "major setback"[100] for the use and development of genome edited plants.[101] And, it is heavily criticised for leading to a regulatory situation that does not correctly reflect the current status of scientific knowledge.[102]

This view is countered by others underlining that the judgment is not "anti-science",[103] but only ensures that the objective and transparent risk assessment obligations laid down in the Deliberate Release Directive are complied with.[104] Therefore, from a legal point of view, the judgment is appraised as convincing and understandable.[105] Furthermore, the judgement is appreciated for upholding the precautionary principle.[106]

3.6.1 *Process- vs. Product-Based Approach*

In the context of Article 2(2) Directive 2001/18/EC,[107] it has been discussed for a while whether it entails a process- or a product-based approach.[108] There was hope for a final decision on this question,[109] but the CJEU did not explicitly decide in favour of one of these approaches. It rather implicitly opted for a process-based approach.[110] Such a process-based approach is acceptable from a juridical point of

[100] Callaway (2018).

[101] Callaway (2018); *cf.* Urnov et al. (2018), p. 800; Verband der Chemischen Industrie e.V. (2018).

[102] Hartung et al. (2018); Vlaams Instituut voor Biotechnologie (2018), p. 1; *cf.* EPSO Agricultural Technology Working Group (2019), p. 1; Urnov et al. (2018), p. 802; Central Commission on Biological Safety (2018), https://www.zkbs-online.de/ZKBS/EN/Meta/focus_topics/Genome_Editing/Genome_Editing_node.html; Cluster of Excellence on Plant Sciences (2018); Faltus (2019), p. 54; Schulman et al. (2020), p. 9.

[103] Garnett (2019), p. 349.

[104] Garnett (2019), pp. 349–350, 354–355; see also Spranger (2018), p. 2930 and Gelinsky and Hilbeck (2018), p. 56.

[105] Brosset and Noiville (2019), pp. 200, 208; Beck (2019), p. 253; Spranger (2018), p. 2929.

[106] *Cf.* Brosset and Noiville (2019), p. 208; Šimas and Schwedler (2018); see also Garnett (2019), p. 354 and Spranger (2018), p. 2930.

[107] Article 2(2) of Directive 2001/18/EC reads "genetically modified organism (GMO) means an organism […] in which the genetic material has been *altered* in a way that *does not occur naturally* by mating and/or natural recombination" (emphasis added).

[108] *Cf.* Kahrmann and Leggewie (2018b), p. 761 referring to the debate in Germany; Vöneky (2019), pp. 18–19 who also mentions a statement by the European Commission in which it seems to argue in favour of a process- and product-based approach; some do not speak of a process-/product-based approach but of whether the expression "which does not take place naturally" is considered in an absolute or in a relative manner, *cf.* Brosset and Noiville (2019), p. 202.

[109] Dederer (2019a), p. 241.

[110] Voigt (2018), p. 658; Kahrmann and Leggewie (2018a), p. 499; Beck (2019), p. 249; Dederer (2019b), p. 101; Dederer (2019a), p. 241.

view.[111] But since a product-based approach would have also been acceptable, the CJEU is criticised for not providing detailed reasoning for its decision.[112]

The German Science organisation *Leopoldina* and others criticise the process-based interpretation.[113] In their view it is incomprehensible to assess modified plants on the techniques that are used to obtain or alter them and not on the traits such plants are carrying.[114] It is the product itself that risks are linked to and not the process of alteration.[115]

A point that is also mentioned in this discussion is compliance with the *Nagoya Protocol on Access to Genetic Resources and the Fair and Equitable Sharing of Benefits Arising from their Utilization to the Convention on Biological Diversity.*[116] Such compliance requires disclosure of the genetic changes that were made which in turn calls for a careful handling of the "product- vs. process-based" question.[117]

3.6.2 The "Mutagenesis Exemption" Does Not Comprise Targeted Mutagenesis Techniques

The question of whether organisms obtained by targeted mutagenesis techniques fall within the exemption for mutagenesis techniques[118] lies at the heart of the CJEU's judgment. Before the CJEU's decision, it was unclear whether techniques of targeted mutagenesis fall within this exemption which only speaks of "mutagenesis" in general without further specifying this term. The CJEU decided that the term "mutagenesis" only includes those mutagenesis techniques that have been developed before the entry into force of the Deliberate Release Directive in 2001.[119]

The CJEU's reasoning is commented with regard to safety considerations (3.6.2.1) and detection problems (3.6.2.2). Comments are also made about the

---

[111] Kahrmann and Leggewie (2018b), p. 762; Kahrmann and Leggewie (2018a), p. 498; *cf.* Brosset and Noiville (2019), p. 200.

[112] Kahrmann and Leggewie (2018a), pp. 498–499; Kahrmann and Leggewie (2018b), p. 762; see also Faltus (2018), pp. 528–529, 530 and Voigt (2018), pp. 659–660.

[113] Vlaams Instituut voor Biotechnologie (2018), p. 1; this term is also used by Book (2019), p. 249 and Nationale Akademie der Wissenschaften Leopoldina et al. (2019), pp. 46, 58; *cf.* Hartung et al. (2018).

[114] *Cf. The Observer view on Europe's ban on gene-editing crops* (2018); see also Schulze-Lefert et al. (2018) and Central Commission on Biological Safety, https://www.zkbs-online.de/ZKBS/EN/Meta/focus_topics/Genome_Editing/Genome_Editing_node.html

[115] Nationale Akademie der Wissenschaften Leopoldina et al. (2019), p. 46; *cf.* Daniela Ruffell (2018), p. 3655.

[116] *Nagoya Protocol on Access to Genetic Resources and the Fair and Equitable Sharing of Benefits Arising from their Utilization to the Convention on Biological Diversity* (adopted 29 October 2010, entered into force 12 October 2014), UN Doc. UNEP/CBD/COP/DEC/X/1.

[117] Weigel (2019), p. 7.

[118] As laid down in Article 3(1) in conjunction with Annex I B to Directive 2001/18/EC.

[119] For the CJEU's judgement and its reasoning, see above p 28–31.

CJEU's approach of interpretation (3.6.2.3) and its allegedly unreflected acceptance of statements by the referring Conseil d'État (3.6.2.4).

3.6.2.1 Safety Considerations

According to many scientists, the CJEU's differentiation between techniques of conventional and targeted mutagenesis is not backed by scientific knowledge.[120] "Organisms that have undergone simple and targeted genome edits by means of precision breeding and which do not contain foreign genes are at least as safe as if they were derived from classical breeding techniques."[121] They mention that while conventional mutagenesis induces up to thousands of mutations in an organism without knowing their effects and consequences,[122] targeted mutagenesis techniques only induce one or a few mutations into an organism's DNA.[123] Since these methods are site-directed, breeders know exactly where the DNA is altered and which novel characteristics it carries.[124] In contrast, organisms altered by random mutagenesis need lengthy screening methods to find the mutations induced.[125] Therefore, these precise methods should even be considered safer than conventional mutagenesis techniques.[126]

These assertions concerning the safety of targeted mutagenesis techniques are challenged, especially by environmental NGOs and activists. According to them, techniques of targeted mutagenesis are not as precise as scientists or the seed industry claim them to be.[127] They point to the application of genome editing techniques in the medical field where many scientists call for a better understanding of these

[120] See for example Barrangou (2018), p. 251; Daniela Ruffell (2018), pp. 3654–3655; High Level Group of Scientific Advisors (2017), pp. 88–89, 95; *cf.* also Dederer (2019a), p. 245 with further references.

[121] Vlaams Instituut voor Biotechnologie (2018), pp. 1–2; see also Kahrmann and Leggewie (2018b), pp. 762–763 who also mention that even organisms altered by techniques of transgenesis do not carry higher risks for the environment than those altered by conventional breeding techniques; Voigt (2018), pp. 661–662 with further references; Broll et al. (2019), p. 289 with further references; Kahrmann and Leggewie (2018a), pp. 499–500; Central Commission on Biological Safety, https://www.zkbs-online.de/ZKBS/EN/Meta/focus_topics/Genome_Editing/Genome_Editing_node.html; EPSO Agricultural Technology Working Group (2019), pp. 1–2 referring to High Level Group of Scientific Advisors (2017); Nationale Akademie der Wissenschaften Leopoldina et al. (2019), p. 56; Halford (2020a), p. 21.

[122] *Cf.* Group of Chief Scientific Advisors (2018), p. 3.

[123] Weigel (2019), p. 6; Purnhagen et al. (2018), p. 800; *cf.* Hartung et al. (2018).

[124] Group of Chief Scientific Advisors (2018), p. 3; EPSO Agricultural Technology Working Group (2019), pp. 1–2; *cf.* Faltus (2019), p. 60; Schulman et al. (2020), p. 9.

[125] Group of Chief Scientific Advisors (2018), p. 3.

[126] Group of Chief Scientific Advisors (2018), p. 3 with further references; *cf.* also Schulze-Lefert et al. (2018) and Cluster of Excellence on Plant Sciences (2018).

[127] *Cf.* Michalopoulos (2019); see also Kawall et al. (2020), p. 24 giving examples of off- and on-target effects caused by genome editing techniques.

methods and their risks before applying them.[128] Advocates of genome editing techniques are criticised for neglecting the importance of understanding gene function in interaction with the environment and epigenetic regulation factors by solely focusing on the precision of these techniques.[129] Further, it is noted that genome editing techniques can also be used to overcome natural barriers. They are therefore different to conventional mutagenesis techniques.[130] Proponents of strict regulation of genome editing also call for more research on the risks and long-term effects of genetic engineering.[131] More research on the risk and long-term effects of genome editing techniques is also demanded by critics of the CJEU's decision.[132] However, such research requires field trials which are difficult to carry out under the existing regulatory conditions.[133]

3.6.2.2 Detection and Identification Problems

It is also stated that the CJEU's interpretation of the "mutagenesis exemption" might lead to detection and identification problems.[134] Organisms altered by targeted mutagenesis can be identical to organisms obtained by conventional mutagenesis and to organisms containing natural mutations.[135] While it might be possible to detect mutations induced by targeted mutagenesis, it will be impossible to prove whether such organisms have been altered by targeted or conventional mutagenesis or even by natural processes,[136] at least when using the established analytical tools.[137] It is therefore paradoxical to uphold a difference that is impossible to show.[138] This is particularly relevant since GMO-specific detection and identification methods are

---

[128] Gelinsky and Hilbeck (2018), p. 55 with further references.

[129] Gelinsky and Hilbeck (2018), p. 55.

[130] *Cf.* Carreno and Dolle (2019), p. 97 referring to Then and Tippe (2018).

[131] Gelinsky and Hilbeck (2018), p. 57.

[132] Nationale Akademie der Wissenschaften Leopoldina et al. (2019), pp. 60–63.

[133] See Nationale Akademie der Wissenschaften Leopoldina et al. (2019), pp. 61–62.

[134] In this context *Faltus* also criticises that the CJEU is not even addressing these problems, see Faltus (2019), p. 61.

[135] *The Observer view on Europe's ban on gene-editing crops* (2018); Michalopoulos (2019); Ladeur (2018), p. 199.

[136] For a detailed analysis of problems arising in the context of detection and identification of mutations induced by targeted mutagenesis see Broll et al. (2019), pp. 289–290; see also Carreno and Dolle (2019), p. 92 and Central Commission on Biological Safety, https://www.zkbs-online.de/ZKBS/EN/Meta/focus_topics/Genome_Editing/Genome_Editing_node.html; however, Kahrmann and Leggewie (2018a), p. 502 mention that such difficulties sometimes exist with regard to GMO altered by classical transgenesis as well.

[137] Grohmann et al. (2019), pp. 1–2 followed by a detailed analysis on the application of currently used detection and identification tools on genome edited plants and organisms and on possible other solutions.

[138] Ehrenhofer-Murray (2018).

a prerequisite for a GMO's approval.[139] As a consequence, it is unclear how applications for the approval of genome edited plants will be handled in the future.[140] As a second problem, and even if there was the possibility to detect changes induced by genome editing techniques, it would be difficult to quantify the level of GM material in feed or food which is however necessary for compliance with EU law.[141] Due to all these difficulties, some authors even assume the undetected entering of GM feed and food into the EU market.[142] Others predict that imports to the EU of crops of which gene-edited varieties exist might cease.[143]

This impossibility of detection and identification of gene-edited plants is challenged. Detection and identification of genome edited plants are possible by molecular and biochemical markers that plant breeders use to prove their intellectual property rights in disputes where others illegally use their varieties.[144] Furthermore, it is stated that the missing possibility to detect the usage of a technique does not necessarily exclude the technique's regulation. It is common for technology regulation to link its applicability to the usage of such techniques (and not to the outcome).[145]

3.6.2.3 Static vs. Dynamic Interpretation

Furthermore, the CJEU's differentiation between mutagenesis techniques that have been developed before and after the adoption of the Deliberate Release Directive is presented as "frozen" or "static".[146] While the CJEU reasons its decision with

---

[139] Vertreter der deutschen Agrar- und Ernährungswirtschaft (2019); Kahrmann and Leggewie (2018a), p. 502; Faltus (2019), p. 61; see also Halford (2020b), p. 3; relevant provisions are for example Arts. 4(2)(i) and 17(3)(i) of *Regulation (EC) No 1829/2003 of the European Parliament and of the Council of 22 September 2003 on genetically modified food and feed*, Official Journal of the European Union ('OJ EU') 2003, L268/1.

[140] Wasmer (2019), p. 4.

[141] For more details see Kahrmann and Leggewie (2018a), p. 502; see also Group of Chief Scientific Advisors (2018), p. 5.

[142] See Faltus (2019), pp. 61–62; *cf.* Kahrmann and Leggewie (2018a), p. 503; Group of Chief Scientific Advisors (2018), p. 5; Wasmer (2019), p. 1; see also Schulman et al. (2020), p. 9 mentioning possible consequences of these verifiability problems on *Directive (EU) 2015/412 of the European Parliament and of the Council of 11 March 2015 amending Directive 2001/18/EC as regards the possibility for the Member States to restrict or prohibit the cultivation of genetically modified organisms (GMOs) in their territory*, OJ EU 2015, L86/1.

[143] See Gocht et al. (2020), pp. 1, 4, 21–22.

[144] *Cf.* Informationsdienst Gentechnik (2020) referring to an instruction to identify plant varieties by molecular or biochemical markers that has been presented by the International Union for the Protection of New Varieties of Plants (UPOV) in November 2019, see International Union for the Protection of New Varieties of Plants (2020).

[145] Spranger (2018), p. 2930.

[146] *Cf.* Dederer (2019a), p. 240; Voigt (2018), p. 660; Beck (2019), p. 253; this differentiation is also mentioned by Seitz (2018), p. 762 who supports such a differentiation.

reference to recital 17 of Directive 2001/18/EC,[147] commentators do not understand why such an interpretation is supported by recital 17.[148] It is mentioned that recital 17, as well as recital 55 of Directive 2001/18/EC, enable a dynamic interpretation of this exemption.[149] Under a dynamic approach in line with recital 17, it would only be necessary to determine from what point on a technique is considered as having *a long safety record*.[150]

The same applies to the term *mutagenesis* which should rather be considered as a general term that is used in contrast to the term *transgenesis*. The legislator would have specified different techniques if it did not have considered the term as one that comprises a variety of different techniques.[151] This is especially true since the Directive has been changed five times since its adoption.[152]

Proponents of the CJEU's decision mention the absence of a definition for the term mutagenesis in the Directive and that it can be interpreted in a variety of ways.[153] They challenge the opinion that recital 17 is not linked to the *mutagenesis exemption* and welcome the Court's teleological interpretation. Recital 17 can be taken into account for the interpretation of the whole the Deliberate Release Directive including Article 3.[154] However, they admit that it remains unclear how the criteria of this recital should be applied.[155]

3.6.2.4 (Unreflected) Acceptance of Statements Made by the Conseil d'État

Some commentators identify the CJEU's unreflected acceptance of statements made by the Conseil d'État on the risks of gene-edited organisms as the underlying problem of the differentiation between different mutagenesis techniques.[156] They criticise that the CJEU did not ask for expert opinions on the potential risks of genome

---

147 CJEU, *Case C-528/16 - Confédération paysanne et al.* (25 July 2018), ECLI:EU:C:2018:583, paras 44–46.

148 See Kahrmann et al. (2017), p. 181.

149 As has also been stated by the Advocate General in his Opinion, see Opinion of Advocate General Bobek, *Case C-528/16 - Confédération paysanne et al.* (18 January 2018), ECLI:EU:C:2018:20, paras 98–105.

150 Dederer (2019a), pp. 241–242; similar questions are posed by Kahrmann and Leggewie (2018a), p. 501; see also Zimny et al. (2019), p. 54 and Beck (2019), p. 253.

151 Faltus (2018), pp. 529–530.

152 *Cf.* Kahrmann and Leggewie (2018a), p. 501.

153 Brosset and Noiville (2019), p. 203.

154 Brosset and Noiville (2019), p. 205; *cf.* also Spranger (2018), p. 2929.

155 *Cf.* Brosset and Noiville (2019), pp. 208–209 which also mention consequences that could arise out of the Court not mentioning criteria for the application of recital 17.

156 Dederer (2019a), p. 242; Kahrmann and Leggewie (2018b), p. 762; *cf.* Voigt (2018), pp. 662–663.

edited organisms.[157] However, in this context, it is also mentioned that taking for granted facts presented by the referring court is common to the preliminary ruling procedure. While the CJEU can request expert opinions it barely did so in the past.[158]

3.6.3 *The Precautionary Principle*

To support its interpretation, the CJEU also had recourse to the precautionary principle.

On the one hand, this is welcomed by proponents of the judgment.[159] According to their view, it is logical to subject organisms obtained by targeted mutagenesis techniques to the Directive's provision because these techniques are new.[160] They criticise a "so-called 'evidence-based approach'"[161] that, in their view, is favoured by advocates of an unregulated application of new breeding techniques.[162]

On the other hand, the CJEU is criticised for not even addressing whether the precautionary principle is applicable at all in the present case. Nor does the CJEU consider the criteria it has developed for the principle's application.[163] While for some it appears that the Court based its decision on merely hypothetical risks,[164] others speculate that the CJEU did not directly deal with the applicability of the precautionary principle because it did not consider the the Deliberate Release Directive to be a protective measure in itself.[165] It could be possible that the CJEU opted for an application of the Directive to ensure the application of the precautionary principle in the process of risk assessment of each single GMO.[166]

---

157 *Cf.* Dederer (2019a), p. 242 with further considerations on how the CJEU should have proceeded in this case; see also Voigt (2018), p. 662 and Faltus (2018), p. 530.

158 Kahrmann and Leggewie (2018a), p. 498; *cf.* Purnhagen et al. (2018), p. 799; for critical considerations on the specifics of the preliminary ruling procedure in this case see Beck (2019), p. 251; see also a comment on this aspect by Advocate General Bobek in his Opinion, Opinion of Advocate General Bobek, *Case C-528/16 - Confédération paysanne et al.* (18 January 2018), ECLI:EU:C:2018:20, para 130.

159 *Cf.* Spranger (2018), p. 2930.

160 *Cf.* Brosset and Noiville (2019), p. 208.

161 Gelinsky and Hilbeck (2018), p. 53.

162 Gelinsky and Hilbeck (2018), p. 53.

163 Dederer (2019a), p. 242 with reference to ECJ, *Case C-236/1 – Monsanto Agricoltura Italia et al.* (2003), ECLI:EU:C:2003:431; CJEU, *Case C-333/08 – Commission vs France* (2010), ECLI:EU:C:2010:44 and CJEU, *Case C-282/15 – Queisser Pharma* (2017), ECLI:EU:C:2017:26; see also Beck (2019), p. 252; Faltus (2019), p. 60; *cf.* Faltus (2018), p. 530.

164 Seitz (2018), pp. 762–763.

165 Beck (2019), p. 252.

166 Beck (2019), p. 252.

3.7 Practical Implications of the CJEU's Judgment

3.7.1 Implications for Research in the Field of Biotechnology

Many commentators mention the possible effects of the CJEU's judgment on research in the field of new biological breeding techniques.[167] There is a fear that subjecting organisms obtained by targeted mutagenesis techniques to a "long and expensive regulatory process[es]"[168] will banish small and medium-sized European seed-breeding companies as well as investors from the EU market.[169] It is stated that nobody invests in a technology that cannot be used commercially or that cannot have advantages for society.[170] This in turn could lead to job losses in this sector and, in the longer term, to a brain drain effect since European researchers who want to work with the latest techniques will go abroad for job opportunities.[171]

Furthermore, critics mention the limitations for classical crossbreeding that are caused by the CJEU's judgement due to the restricted availability of genetic varieties from third countries that are free from genetic modifications.[172]

Due to these possible implications, it is also criticised that there was and is no possibility for scientists to take part in court proceedings before the CJEU.[173]

However, it is also mentioned that laboratory work of researchers within the framework of their scientific freedom is still possible and that the EU and its Member States provide substantial funding for genetic engineering research.[174]

---

[167] *Cf.* Schulze-Lefert et al. (2018); for further details on the problems arising in the context of field trials see Nationale Akademie der Wissenschaften Leopoldina et al. (2019), pp. 46, 48, 60–62; Wight (2018), p. 15.

[168] Vlaams Instituut voor Biotechnologie (2018), p. 3.

[169] Vlaams Instituut voor Biotechnologie (2018), p. 3; Group of Chief Scientific Advisors (2018), p. 5; *cf.* Vertreter der deutschen Agrar- und Ernährungswirtschaft (2019); Daniela Ruffell (2018), p. 3656; see also Nationale Akademie der Wissenschaften Leopoldina et al. (2019), p. 62 stating that "the majority of research and development projects with new breeding methods in Germany and Europe have already been discontinued in the sector as a result of the ECJ ruling"; for an example see Gabrielczyk (2019), https://european-biotechnology.com/up-to-date/backgrounds-stories/story/cjeu-ruling-triggers-exodus-of-eu-plant-research.html

[170] *Cf.* Callaway (2018); Hartung et al. (2018); Wight (2018), pp. 15–16; see also the statements of Bayern and BASF summarized by Eriksson et al. (2019), p. 1680 and Gabrielczyk, https://european-biotechnology.com/up-to-date/backgrounds-stories/story/cjeu-ruling-triggers-exodus-of-eu-plant-research.html, who reports on a reduction of private and public funding in the field of research on new breeding methods.

[171] Vlaams Instituut voor Biotechnologie (2018), p. 3; *cf.* Barrangou (2018), p. 251; Halford (2020a), p. 21; Faltus (2018), p. 533; EPSO Agricultural Technology Working Group (2019), p. 4; Carreno and Dolle (2019), p. 98; Schulze-Lefert et al. (2018); Nationale Akademie der Wissenschaften Leopoldina et al. (2019), p. 61.

[172] *Cf.* Nationale Akademie der Wissenschaften Leopoldina et al. (2019), p. 63; Vertreter der deutschen Agrar- und Ernährungswirtschaft (2019).

[173] Ladeur (2018), p. 198.

[174] Gelinsky and Hilbeck (2018), p. 57.

3.7.2 Implications for European Agriculture

While genome editing techniques might not be the only answer to current challenges in agriculture, the judgment is nevertheless said to "hinder progress in sustainable agriculture".[175] New plant breeding techniques, including targeted mutagenesis techniques, are essential for the development of sustainable and climatically adapted agricultural practices.[176] European farmers will not get the possibility to use plants that are more nutritious and adapted to climate change.[177] The judgment is even described as "irresponsible in the face of the world's current far-reaching agricultural challenges"[178] and it is questioned whether the Court's ruling really serves to protect the environment which is one of the Directive's objectives.[179] Furthermore, it is said to stand in the way of using targeted mutagenesis techniques to ensure worldwide food security.[180]

These views are challenged by those who remind of the fact that most genetically modified ('GM') plants do not address sustainable agricultural practices but at present mostly carry herbicide or insecticide resistance and thereby even increase the usage of pesticides. The modifications necessary for drought or cold resistance or salt stress are complex and often not yet possible to realise.[181]

3.7.3 Implications for International Trade and the EU's Obligations Under WTO Law and CETA

A major concern for many commentators are the judgment's implications for global trade and the economy.

---

175 Nationale Akademie der Wissenschaften Leopoldina et al. (2019), p. 46; Vlaams Instituut voor Biotechnologie (2018), p. 2; Urnov et al. (2018), p. 800; *cf.* EPSO Agricultural Technology Working Group (2019), pp. 1–2.

176 *Cf.* Vertreter der deutschen Agrar- und Ernährungswirtschaft (2019); *The Observer view on Europe's ban on gene-editing crops* (2018); Hartung et al. (2018); see also Kahrmann and Leggewie (2018a), p. 500; Schulman et al. (2020), p. 10 and Weigel (2019), p. 8 who is pointing out advantages of using genome editing to generate new plant varieties; Group of Chief Scientific Advisors (2018), pp. 5–6 providing examples of potential applications; an overview is also provided by Nationale Akademie der Wissenschaften Leopoldina et al. (2019), pp. 53–55.

177 *Cf.* Hartung et al. (2018); see the example mentioned by Nigel Halford, Principal Research Scientist at Rothamsted Research, UK mentioned in an interview with the Genetic Literacy Project, *cf.* Genetic Literacy Project, Halford (2020b), p. 3; Carreno and Dolle (2019), p. 98.

178 Vlaams Instituut voor Biotechnologie (2018); see also Kahrmann and Leggewie (2018b), p. 763.

179 Kahrmann and Leggewie (2018a), p. 500.

180 Carreno and Dolle (2019), p. 97; Group of Chief Scientific Advisors (2018), p. 6 also raising concerns that developing countries might continue to follow EU authorisation practices and therefore might not benefit from genome edited crops and plants; Schulze-Lefert et al. (2018); *cf.* Halford (2020a), p. 21; Urnov et al. (2018), p. 800.

181 Gelinsky and Hilbeck (2018), pp. 56–57.

First, subjecting organisms obtained by targeted mutagenesis to the EU's regulatory framework is a competitive disadvantage for these industries.[182] Only a few multinational companies have the financial means to undergo complex and expensive approval procedures for their breeds.[183] This will benefit cash crops since development and approval costs will not be covered by the market for minor crops.[184] This "promotes further monopolisation in already concentrated plant breeding and seed markets".[185] It is predicted that Europe will lose its biotech industry since companies are not going to invest in technologies without the possibility to use them commercially.[186] In the longer run, the EU will thereby lose its chance to generate new jobs and economic growth.[187] Especially, smaller companies and start-ups which often use CRISPR due to its low costs are hit by the CJEU's judgment.[188] Such companies could have been interested in using the technology for ecological solutions, but will probably not use it anymore due to high costs for approval procedures of genetically modified plants.[189]

Second, negative impacts on trade could also be caused by the impossibility to identify whether organisms have been obtained by targeted mutagenesis in contrast to conventional mutagenesis.[190] This is a requirement for the approval of GMOs that cannot be fulfilled by companies applying for authorisation.[191] This impossibility of differentiation is also problematic since organisms obtained by targeted mutagenesis are not considered GMOs and are not labelled as such in other jurisdictions. This could lead to import barriers and will certainly have consequences for international trade.[192] Some even predict that the missing possibility to identify whether certain

[182] Vlaams Instituut voor Biotechnologie (2018), p. 2; Hartung et al. (2018); *cf.* Halford (2020a), p. 21; Wasmer (2019), p. 5.

[183] Urnov et al. (2018), pp. 801–802; see also *The Observer view on Europe's ban on gene-editing crops* (2018), mentioning costs of £30 m to obtain approval for GM crops in Europe; Barrangou (2018), p. 251; Faltus (2018), p. 531.

[184] *Cf.* Daniela Ruffell (2018), p. 3656; Nationale Akademie der Wissenschaften Leopoldina et al. (2019), p. 63; Schulman et al. (2020), p. 9.

[185] Nationale Akademie der Wissenschaften Leopoldina et al. (2019), pp. 46, 48 according to which a high market share of small and medium-sized seed breeding companies could help counter this process of monopolisation.

[186] Genetic Literacy Project, Halford (2020b), p. 3; *cf.* Barrangou (2018), p. 251; see also Garnett (2019), p. 354; Callaway (2018).

[187] *Cf.* The European Association for Bioindustries (2018).

[188] Urnov et al. (2018), p. 802; on this issue see also the considerations by Ehrenhofer-Murray (2018), p. 573.

[189] Ladeur (2018), p. 200.

[190] Vertreter der deutschen Agrar- und Ernährungswirtschaft (2019); Voigt (2018), p. 655 referring to Joint Research Centre (2011), pp. 69–70; this is also acknowledged by proponents of the judgment, see Brosset and Noiville (2019), p. 210.

[191] Vertreter der deutschen Agrar- und Ernährungswirtschaft (2019); Faltus (2018), p. 531.

[192] *Cf.* EPSO Agricultural Technology Working Group (2019), pp. 3–4; Central Commission on Biological Safety, https://www.zkbs-online.de/ZKBS/EN/Meta/focus_topics/Genome_Editing/Genome_Editing_node.html; Purnhagen et al. (2018), p. 800; Eriksson et al. (2019), pp. 1678–1679;

changes to an organism's DNA have been introduced by genome editing techniques or other techniques could lead to a cessation of imports for those crops for which a gene-edited variety is available, for example, soy or maize.[193] This could not only have economic but also environmental consequences.[194]

Economic consequences could also arise out of the fact that genetically modified products have to be labelled, and the EU consumers are rather sceptical towards GM products.[195]

The negative consequences of the judgment on international trade have also been discussed in the *Committee on Sanitary and Phytosanitary Measures* ('SPS Committee')[196] under the auspices of the *World Trade Organization* ('WTO'). Several States where genome edited plants are grown raised concerns about the asynchronous regulation of such organisms. These States implicitly point toward violations of WTO law that could arise out of the applicability of the EU GMO law to genome edited organisms.[197] The EU's regulatory approach could therefore soon come under WTO scrutiny.[198] Also, the US Secretary of Agriculture criticised the judgment directly after it was published for hindering innovation. He called for global efforts to ensure a science- and risk-based regulation of GMOs.[199] In this context also implications for the *Comprehensive Economic and Trade Agreement*[200] between Canada and the EU ('CETA') are mentioned since Canada does not consider organisms altered by genome editing techniques as genetically modified.[201]

Concerns raised by critics especially relate to the likeness of gene-edited plants and those developed by conventional mutagenesis since only the former are subject

---

Schulman et al. (2020), p. 9; Daniela Ruffell (2018), p. 3657; Vertreter der deutschen Agrar- und Ernährungswirtschaft (2019).

[193] Gocht et al. (2020), pp. 1, 4, 21–22; see also Wasmer (2019), p. 5.

[194] See the study by Gocht et al. (2020).

[195] Carreno and Dolle (2019), p. 97; *cf.* Zimny et al. (2019), p. 55.

[196] The SPS Committee is the forum where WTO members discuss issues related to the implementation of the SPS Agreement and potential trade concerns, see World Trade Organization, https://www.wto.org/english/tratop_e/sps_e/work_and_doc_e.htm; the SPS Committee has been established on the basis of Article 12 of the *Agreement on the Application of Sanitary and Phytosanitary Measures*, Annex 1 to the Marrakesh Agreement establishing the World Trade Organization (concluded 15 April 1994, entered into force 1 January 1995) 1867 UNTS 3.

[197] *Cf.* Committee on Sanitary and Phytosanitary Measures (2018); this debate is also mentioned by Dederer (2019a), p. 244, Carreno and Dolle (2019), p. 100; Wasmer (2019), p. 5; Nationale Akademie der Wissenschaften Leopoldina et al. (2019), p. 69 and Eriksson et al. (2019), pp. 1679–1680; the incompatibility with WTO law is challenged by Spranger (2018), p. 2930; see also Spranger (2019).

[198] Carreno and Dolle (2019), p. 99; possible regulatory constraints imposed by WTO law are also discussed by Dederer (2019b), pp. 101–104.

[199] See U.S. Department of Agriculture (2018); the statement is also mentioned by Carreno and Dolle (2019), p. 98.

[200] *Comprehensive Economic and Trade Agreement between Canada, of the one part, and the European Union and its Member States, of the other part* (14 January 2017), OJ EU 2017, L 11/23 (CETA).

[201] Carreno and Dolle (2019), p. 99.

to authorisation and labelling requirements.[202] This could constitute an unjustified differentiation. Also, authorisation procedures for specific gene-edited plants could be unduly delayed or authorisation requirements could be too strict.[203]

The Swedish Board of Agriculture has asked the European Commission to analyse possible effects of the CJEU's judgment under WTO law.[204]

3.8 Conclusion

While the CJEU's decision that organisms modified by targeted mutagenesis techniques are comprised by the EU GMO law brought legal clarity, it did not end the debate on the adequacy of the EU GMO law and its applicability to genome edited organisms. Especially the plant breeding industry, but also many scientists call for less strict regulations of genome edited plants. While the Court's reasoning is reasonable from a legal point of view, it displays a rather conservative and careful approach. This is consistent and worthy of support in view of the Court's lack of factual and legal powers to conclusively assess the scientific questions at issue in this case. The CJEU is not the right body to make far-reaching decisions regarding the deregulation of genome editing procedures, the long-term effects of which simply cannot yet be known. By deciding this way, the Court passes on the question of an adequate regulation of genome edited organisms to the Union legislator which is responsible for these issues. It is not the CJEU's task to assess the risks of new biotechnological methods and decide about their regulation, but the task of the European legislator.

One point that was repeatedly raised in this debate is the possibility of negative implications of the CJEU's judgement for international trade. One practical question in this context is whether the applicability of the EU GMO law to genome edited plants (as a consequence of the judgement) is in line with WTO law and CETA. Especially the different treatment of genome edited plants and traditionally bred plants could possibly violate WTO regulations and CETA. The Court's judgement has thus also given rise to this scientific study.

As a reaction to the CJEU's judgement many called for a reform of the EU GMO law. A call that has been taken up by the EU Commission which issued a proposal on a regulation of genome edited plants in July 2023.[205]

---

[202] Nationale Akademie der Wissenschaften Leopoldina et al. (2019), p. 69.

[203] Nationale Akademie der Wissenschaften Leopoldina et al. (2019), p. 69.

[204] Swedish Board of Agriculture (2018), pp. 4–5.

[205] For the proposal by the EU Commission, see Chap. 7 below.

References

Literature

Abbott A (2018) European court suggests relaxed gene-editing rules. Nature. https://doi.org/10.1038/d41586-018-01013-5
Barrangou R (2018) CRISPR craziness: a response to the EU Court ruling. CRISPR J 1:251–252. https://doi.org/10.1089/crispr.2018.29025.edi
Beck F (2019) All about that risk? A (re-)assessment of the CJEU's reasoning in the "genome editing" case. Europäische Zeitschrift für Umwelt- und Planungsrecht 17:246–255
Broll H, Braeuning A, Lampen A (2019) European Court of Justice decision for genome editing: consequences on food/feed risk assessment and detection. Food Control 104:288–291. https://doi.org/10.1016/j.foodcont.2019.05.002
Brosset E, Noiville C (2019) Droit des biotechnologies. Cahiers Droit Sci Technol 8:197–212. https://doi.org/10.4000/cdst.866
Callaway E (2018) EU law deals blow to CRISPR crops: top court's ruling threatens research on gene-edited plants. Nature 560:16
Carreno I, Dolle T (2019) The Court of Justice of the European Union's judgment on mutagenesis and international trade: a case of GMO, mutagenesis and international trade. Global Trade Customs J 14:91–101
Central Commission on Biological Safety (2018) Genome editing - impact of European Court of Justice (ECJ) judgment on plant breeding. https://www.zkbs-online.de/ZKBS/EN/Meta/focus_topics/Genome_Editing/Genome_Editing_node.html
Cluster of Excellence on Plant Sciences (2018) Stellungnahme des Exzellenzclusters für Pflanzenwissenschaften CEPLAS zum EuGH-Urteil/Mutagenese. Press release
Committee on Sanitary and Phytosanitary Measures (2018) International Statement on agricultural applications of precision biotechnology: communication from Argentina, Australia, Brazil, Canada, The Dominican Republic, Guatemale, Honduras, Paraguay, The United States of America and Uruguay. G/SPS/GEN/1658/Rev.3
Confédération paysanne (2015) Communiqué commun: recours en Conseil d'Etat/VrTH. Press release
Council of the European Union (2023) Written submission in the CJEU proceedings C-528/16. https://www.infogm.org/IMG/pdf/conseil_ue_francais.pdf
Daniela Ruffell (2018) The EU Court of Justice extends the GMO Directive to gene-edited organisms: Interview with Dr. Stefan Jansson and Dr. Ralf Wilhelm. FEBSPRESS:3653–3657
Dederer H-G (2019a) Genomeditierung ist Gentechnik. Europäische Zeitschrift für Umwelt- und Planungsrecht 17:236–245
Dederer H-G (2019b) Options for the regulation of genome edited plants - framing the issues. In: Dürnberger C, Pfeilmeier S, Schleissing S (eds) Genome editing in agriculture: between precaution and responsibility. Nomos, Baden-Baden, pp 77–122
Ehrenhofer-Murray A (2018) Chance verpasst: ein rückwärtsgewandtes Urteil des EuGH zu Genomeditierten Organismen. BIOspektrum 24:573. https://doi.org/10.1007/s12268-018-0959-9
EPSO Agricultural Technology Working Group (2019) On the ECJ Ruling regarding mutagenesis and the genetically modified organisms directive: statement, Brussels. https://epsoweb.org/download/epso-statement-on-ecj-ruling-regarding-mutagenesis-and-gmo/
Eriksson D, Kershen D, Nepomuceno A, Pogson BJ, Prieto H, Purnhagen K, Smyth S, Wesseler J, Whelan A (2019) A comparison of the EU regulatory approach to directed mutagenesis with that of other jurisdictions, consequences for international trade and potential steps forward. New Phytol 222:1673–1684
European Commission (2017) Written submission in the CJEU proceedings C-528/16. Original in French. https://www.infogm.org/IMG/pdf/commission_europeenne_francais.pdf

European Parliament (2017) Written submission in the CJEU proceeding C-528/16. https://www.infogm.org/IMG/pdf/parlement_ue_francais.pdf

Faltus T (2018) Mutagene(se) des Gentechnikrechts. Zeitschrift für Umweltrecht 2018:524–534

Faltus T (2019) Recht der Genomeditierung in Pflanzenzucht und Humanmedizin - Regulierung der grünen und roten Genomeditierung nach dem Mutagenese-Urteil des EuGH und den ersten vermeintlichen Keimbahneingriffen. In: Faltus T (ed) Ethik, Recht und Kommunikation des Genome Editings, pp 54–77

Gabrielczyk T (2019) CJEU ruling triggers exodus of EU plant research. https://european-biotechnology.com/up-to-date/backgrounds-stories/story/cjeu-ruling-triggers-exodus-of-eu-plant-research.html

Garnett K (2019) Hold your pipettes: The European Court of Justice's findings in Confédération Paysanne & Others stirs GMOtions. Rev Eur Comp Int Environ Law 28:349–355. https://doi.org/10.1111/reel.12291

Gelinsky E, Hilbeck A (2018) European Court of Justice ruling regarding new genetic engineering methods scientifically justified: a commentary on the biased reporting about the recent ruling. Environ Sci Eur 30:52–60. https://doi.org/10.1186/s12302-018-0182-9

Gocht A, Consmüller N, Thom F, Grethe H (2020) Economic and environmental consequences of the ECJ genome editing judgement in agriculture. Thünen Working Paper 150. https://doi.org/10.3220/WP1595233767000

Grohmann L, Keilwagen J, Duensing N, Dagand E, Hartung F, Wilhelm R, Bendiek J, Sprink T (2019) Detection and identification of genome editing in plants: challenges and opportunities. Front Plant Sci 10:1–8. https://doi.org/10.3389/fpls.2019.00236

Group of Chief Scientific Advisors (2018) A scientific perspective on the regulatory status of products derived from gene editing and the implications for the GMO directive

Halford N (2020a) Top of the Crops: Has the EU got it wrong on genetically modified and gene edited crops? Features Health. Actuary:20–21

Halford N (2020b) Viewpoint: Europe missed the GMO revolution. Sensible regulation could ensure they don't miss out on CRISPR gene editing. Genetic Literacy Project

Hartung F, Wilhelm R, Rogowski P (2018) On the ECJ Ruling regarding mutagenesis and the Genetically Modified Organisms Directive. First reaction, Brussels. https://epsoweb.org/wp-content/uploads/2018/11/18_07_26_EPSO_ECJ-Ruling-regarding-mutagenesis-and-GMO_First-reaction.pdf

High Level Group of Scientific Advisors (2017) New techniques in agricultural biotechnology. Explanatory note 02/2017, Brussels

Informationsdienst Gentechnik (2020) *Neue gentechnisch veränderte Sorten lassen sich nachweisen*, https://www.keine-gentechnik.de/nachricht/33971/

International Union for the Protection of New Varieties of Plants (2020) Guidance on the Use of Biochemical and Molecular Markers in the Examination of Distinctness, Uniformity and Stability (DUS). Document TGP/15/3. https://www.upov.int/edocs/tgpdocs/en/tgp_15.pdf

Joint Research Centre (2011) New plant breeding techniques: state-of-the-art and prospects for commercial development. JRC - Scientific and Technical Reports

Kahrmann J, Leggewie G (2018a) CJEU's Ruling Makes Europe's GMO Legislation Ripe for Reformation. Europäische Zeitschrift für Umwelt- und Planungsrecht 16:497–504

Kahrmann J, Leggewie G (2018b) Gentechnikrechtliches Grundsatzurteil des EuGH und die Folgefragen für das deutsche Recht. Natur und Recht 40:761–765. https://doi.org/10.1007/s10357-018-3429-8

Kahrmann J, Bömeke O, Leggewie G (2017) Aged GMO Legislation Meets New Genome Editing Techniques. Europäische Zeitschrift für Umwelt- und Planungsrecht 15:176–182

Kawall K, Miyazaki J, Bauer-Panskus A, Then C (2020) Overview of genome editing applications using SDN-1 and SDN-2 in regard to EU regulatory issues, 2020: New methods of genetic engineering (genome editing) and their potential impact on nature protection and the environment

Ladeur K-H (2018) Die Entscheidung des EuGH zur Anwendung des geltenden Gentechnikrechts auf CRISPR/Cas9-Verfahren v. 25.7.2018 – eine Entscheidung gegen technologische Innovation! Zeitschrift zum Innovations- und Technikrecht:198–201
Michalopoulos S (2019) Industry shocked by EU Court decision to put gene editing technique under GM law. EURACTIV
N.N (2017) Legal limbo. Nature 542:392. https://doi.org/10.1038/542392a
N.N (2018) The Observer view on Europe's ban on gene-editing crops: observer editorial. The Observer
Nationale Akademie der Wissenschaften Leopoldina, Union der Deutschen Akademien der Wissenschaften, Deutsche Forschungsgemeinschaft (2019) Towards a scientifically justified, differentiated regulation of genome edited plants in the EU. Statement, Halle (Saale), Bonn, Mainz, https://www.leopoldina.org/uploads/tx_leopublication/2019_Stellungnahme_Genomeditierte_Pflanzen_web.pdf
Purnhagen KP, Kok E, Kleter G, Schebesta H, Visser RGF, Wesseler J (2018) EU court casts new plant breeding techniques into regulatory limbo. Nat Biotechnol 36:799–800. https://doi.org/10.1038/nbt.4251
Schulman AH, Oksman-Caldentey K-M, Teeri TH (2020) European Court of Justice delivers no justice to Europe on genome-edited crops. Plant Biotechnol J 18:8–10. https://doi.org/10.1111/pbi.13200
Schulze-Lefert P, Coupland G, Tsiantis M (2018) Statement from the directors of the Max Planck Institute for Plant Breeding Research on the recent decision of the European Court of Justice regarding gene-edited organisms. Press release
Seitz C (2018) Modifiziert oder nicht? - Regulatorische Rechtsfragen zur Genoptimierung durch neue biotechnologische Verfahren. Europäische Zeitschrift für Wirtschaftsrecht 18:757–764
Šimas L, Schwedler C (2018) Judgment of the Court of Justice of the European Union of July 25, 2018, in Case C-528/16 Confédération paysanne and Others. https://www.wilmerhale.com/en/insights/client-alerts/20180806-judgment-of-the-court-of-justice-of-the-european-union-of-july-25-2018-in-case-c52816-conf%C3%A9d%C3%A9ration-paysanne-and-others#
Spranger MT (2018) Neue Techniken und Europäisches Gentechnikrecht. Neue Juristische Woche 71:2929–2930
Spranger TM (2019) Memorandum on the international trade law implications of the judgment of the European Court of Justice in case C-528/16. Commissiond by the Federal Agency for Nature Conservation (BfN), Bonn
Swedish Board of Agriculture (2018) Follow-up from PAFF-meeting on September 11, 2018 (Dnr. 5.1.21-124/18)
Swedish Government (2017) Written submission in the CJEU proceedings C-528/16. Original in French. https://www.infogm.org/IMG/pdf/gvt_suede_francais.pdf
The European Association for Bioindustries (EuropaBio) (2018) Court ruling could lock out the benefits of genome editing from Europe. Press release, Brussels
Then C, Tippe R (2018) Genome Editing: Increasing monopolisation in agriculture and breeding: Patents can also impact conventional breeding. Testbiotech Background 29-06-2018. https://www.testbiotech.org/sites/default/files/Background%20Patents%20%26%20Genome%20Editing.pdf
U.S. Department of Agriculture (2018) Secretary Perdue Statement on ECJ Ruling on Genome Editing. Release No. 0155.18, Washington. https://www.usda.gov/media/press-releases/2018/07/27/secretary-perdue-statement-ecj-ruling-genome-editing
Urnov FD, Ronald PC, Carroll D (2018) A call for science-based review of the European court's decision on gene-edited crops. Nat Biotechnol 36:800–802. https://doi.org/10.1038/nbt.4252
Verband der Chemischen Industrie e.V. (2018) ECJ judgement on genome editing blocks innovation. Press release
Vertreter der deutschen Agrar- und Ernährungswirtschaft (2019) Verbändestellungnahme zum Urteil des Europäischen Gerichtshofes zu neuen Züchtungsmethoden. https://www.

vci.de/dib/positionen/verbaendestellungnahme-urteil-europaeischer-gerichtshof-neue-zuechtungsmethoden.jsp
Vlaams Instituut voor Biotechnologie (2018) Regulating genome edited organisms as GMOs has negative consequences for agriculture, society and economy. https://www.mpg.de/13748566/position-paper-crispr.pdf
Vogt W (2018) An editing mistake: European court makes a bad decision on gene editing. Western Farm Press, p 11
Voigt B (2018) Anmerkung Genomeditierung = Gentechnik. Zeitschrift für Lebensmittelrecht 5:654–663
Vöneky S (2019) Legal framework. In: Max Planck Society (ed) Discussion paper focusing on the scientific relevance of genome editing and on the ethical, legal and societal issues potentially involved, pp 17–22
Wasmer M (2019) Roads forward for European GMO policy-uncertainties in wake of ECJ judgment have to be mitigated by regulatory reform. Front Bioeng Biotechnol 7:132. https://doi.org/10.3389/fbioe.2019.00132
Weigel D (2019) Genome editing in plants. In: Max Planck Society (ed) Discussion paper focusing on the scientific relevance of genome editing and on the ethical, legal and societal issues potentially involved, pp 6–8
Wight AJ (2018) Strict EU ruling on gene-edited crops squeezes science. Nature 563:15–16. https://doi.org/10.1038/d41586-018-07166-7
World Trade Organization, *The SPS Committee*, https://www.wto.org/english/tratop_e/sps_e/work_and_doc_e.htm
Zimny T, Sowa S, Tyczewska A, Twardowski T (2019) Certain new plant breeding techniques and their marketability in the context of EU GMO legislation – recent developments. New Biotechnol 51:49–56

Jurisprudence: Court of Justice of the European Union (Former European Court of Justice)

CJEU (2010) *Case C-333/08 – Commission vs France*
CJEU (2017) *Case C-282/15 – Queisser Pharma*
CJEU (2018) *Case C-528/16 - Confédération paysanne et al.*
ECJ (2003) *Case C-236/1 – Monsanto Agricoltura Italia et al.*
Opinion of Advocate General Bobek (2018) *Case C-528/16 - Confédération paysanne et al.*

Jurisprudence: Domestic Courts

Conseil d'État (2016) *Décision No 388649 - Confédération paysanne et autres*

Chapter 4
The Regulation of Genetically Modified Plants in the European Union

Abstract This chapter outlines the current legislatory framework for genetically modified organisms ('GMOs') in the European Union ('EU'), including authorisation procedures, labelling requirements, and a so-called opt-out mechanism. The key regulation is Directive 2001/18/EC on the deliberate release into the environment of genetically modified organisms, supplemented by Regulation (EC) No 1829/2003 on genetically modified food and feed and Regulation (EC) No 1830/2003 concerning the traceability and labelling of genetically modified organisms and the traceability of food and feed products produced from genetically modified organisms. The EU employs a step-by-step approach, gradually releasing GMOs based on prior risk assessments. It also emphasises the precautionary principle. This chapter explains the authorisation process for GMOs which requires applications to meet the conditions set by EU law, as well as the EU's comprehensive labelling regulations to strengthen consumer rights. Additionally, an opt-out mechanism allows EU member states to restrict or ban GMO cultivation within their territory when certain criteria are met.

4.1 Introduction

As has been decided by the Court of Justice of the European Union ('CJEU') in *Confédération paysanne et al.*, the European Union ('EU') regulatory framework for the deliberate release and placing on the market of genetically modified organisms ('GMOs') and products thereof is applicable to all techniques of genetic modification that have been developed since 2001. This necessarily comprises all genome editing techniques. Accordingly, genome edited plants are governed by the EU GMO law. To understand the consequences arising out of this judgement, the EU legal framework regulating GMOs is examined.

E. A. L. Andersen, *Regulation of Biotechnological Risks in a Multi-Level System*, European Yearbook of International Economic Law 46,
https://doi.org/10.1007/978-3-032-02409-1_4

4.2 The Regulatory Framework

The regulatory framework for genetically modified organisms in the European Union is characterised by the mixture of a horizontal and vertical regulatory approach.[1]

Directive 2001/18/EC of the European Parliament and of the Council of 12 March 2001 on the deliberate release into the environment of genetically modified organisms[2] ('Directive 2001/18/EC' or 'Deliberate Release Directive') which is at the heart of the EU GMO law, follows a horizontal approach.[3] This Directive is accompanied by *Regulation (EC) No 1829/2003 of the European Parliament and of the Council of 22 September 2003 on genetically modified food and feed*[4] ('Regulation 1829/2003' or 'GM Food and Feed Regulation') following a vertical approach.[5] Both legislative acts are complemented by *Regulation (EC) No 1830/2003 of the European Parliament and of the Council of 22 September 2003 concerning the traceability and labelling of genetically modified organisms and the traceability of food and feed products produced from genetically modified organisms*[6] ('Regulation 1830/2003') which again incorporates a horizontal approach.[7] Additionally, there is *Directive 2009/41/EC of the European Parliament and of the Council of 6 May 2009 on the contained use of genetically modified micro-organisms*[8] ('Directive 2009/41/EC'). The regulatory framework is complemented by other legislative acts of the EU further defining and specifying different aspects of the Directives and Regulations.[9]

---

[1] Voß (2006), pp. 167–171.

[2] *Directive 2001/18/EC of the European Parliament and the Council of 12 March 2001 on the deliberate release into the environment of genetically modified organisms and repealing Council Directive 90/220/EC* (consolidated version from 27 March 2021) ('Directive 2001/18/EC'), Official Journal of the European Communities ('OJ EC') 2001, L 106/1.

[3] *Cf.* Voß (2006), pp. 168–170.

[4] *Regulation (EC) No 1829/2003 2003 of the European Parliament and of the Council of 22 September 2003 on genetically modified food and feed* (consolidated version from 27 March 2021) ('Regulation 1829/2003'), Official Journal of the European Union ('OJ EU') 2003, L 268/1.

[5] *Cf.* Voß (2006), p. 168.

[6] *Regulation (EC) No 1830/2003 2003 of the European Parliament and of the Council of 22 September 2003 concerning the traceability and labelling of genetically modified organisms and the traceability of food and feed products produced from genetically modified organisms* (consolidated version from 26 July 2019) ('Regulation 1830/2003'), OJ EU 2003, L 268/24.

[7] Voß (2006), p. 168.

[8] *Directive 2009/41/EC of the European Parliament and of the Council of 6 May 2009 on the contained use of genetically modified micro-organisms* ('Directive 2009/41/EC'), OJ EU 2009, L 125/75.

[9] See e.g. *Commission Implementing Regulation (EU) No 503/2013 of 3 April 2013 on applications for authorisation of genetically modified food and feed in accordance with Regulation (EC) No 1829/2003 of the European Parliament and of the Council and amending Commission Regulations (EC) No 641/2004 and (EC) No 1981/2006* ('Implementing Regulation 503/2013'), OJ EU 2013, L 157/1; *Directive (EU) 2015/412 of the European Parliament and of the Council of 11 March*

Furthermore, the *European Food Safety Authority*[10] ('EFSA') plays a central role in the authorisation procedure for genetically modified food and feed.[11]

4.2.1 Scope of Application

The EU legislation regulating genetically modified ('GM') plants contains a technology-related, so-called process-based approach, meaning its applicability is linked to the specific technique used to alter a plant.[12]

The central definition is laid down in Article 2(2) of Directive 2001/18/EC which reads:

> [For the purposes of this Directive:] 'genetically modified organism (GMO)' means an organism [...] in which the genetic material has been altered in a way that does not occur naturally by mating and/or nature recombination;
>
> Within the terms of this definition:
>
> (a) genetic modification occurs at least through the use of the techniques listed in Annex I A, part 1;
>
> (b) the techniques listed in Annex I A, part 2, are not considered to result in genetic modification;

Furthermore, Article 3(1) of Directive 2001/18/EC exempts organisms obtained by the techniques listed in Annex I B from its scope. Annex I B lists the *mutagenesis technique* which does, however, not include the technique of targeted mutagenesis according to the Court of Justice of the European Union.[13]

This definition is also incorporated by Regulation 1829/2003 and Regulation 1830/2003.[14]

2015 amending Directive 2001/18/EC as regards the possibility for the Member States to restrict or prohibit the cultivation of GMOs in their territory ('Directive 2015/412'), OJ EU 2015, L 68/1; *Regulation (EC) No 178/2002 of the European Parliament and of the Council of 28 January 2002 laying down the general principles and requirements of food law, establishing the European Food Safety Authority and laying down procedures in matters of food safety* (consolidated version from 26 May 2021) ('Regulation 178/2002'), OJ EC 2002, L 31/1.

[10] See the official website of the European Food Safety Authority, https://www.efsa.europa.eu/en.

[11] For further details on EFSA's role during the authorisation procedure see below, Sect. 4.2.5.

[12] *Cf.* Voß (2006), p. 227; Agapito-Tenfen et al. (2018), p. 2; on the contrary, *Eriksson* outlines why the regulatory approach in EU GMO law is process- and product-based, see Eriksson (2018), pp. 1–2.

[13] For the CJEU's judgment on targeted mutagenesis techniques see above Chap. 3, p. 28.

[14] See Article 2 No. 5 of Regulation 1820/2003 and Article 3 No. 1 of Regulation 1830/2003.

4.2.2 *"Step by Step" Approach*

The EU GMO framework is characterised by a "step by step" approach.[15] According to this principle, "the containment of GMOs is reduced and the scale of release increased gradually, step by step, but only if evaluation of the earlier steps in terms of protection of human health and the environment indicates that the next step can be taken".[16] Accordingly, three release steps can be taken under the EU GMO regime: (1) contained use, (2) experimental releases in form of field trials and, (3) placing on the market of GMOs as or in products.[17] However, it is not mandatory to pass through all these stages. Instead, applicants can also only apply for an authorisation for placing on the market.[18] But, the safety of a GM plant or product as proven in laboratory research and field trials is a mandatory prerequisite for authorisation for placing on the market and must be demonstrated by the applicant.[19]

This "step by step" approach has been articulated by the Organisation for Economic Co-operation and Development ('OECD') to collect data on the safety and performance of GMOs and to predict their performance in less confined stages of development.[20] It is an expression of the precautionary principle.[21]

4.2.3 *The Precautionary Principle's Role in EU GMO Law*

The EU GMO law is characterised by the precautionary principle which is a central principle of EU environmental law.[22,23] Directive 2001/18 explicitly mentions the precautionary principle in its Articles 1 and 4(1). And, also the GM Food and Feed Regulation by its reference to the principles laid down in *Regulation (EC) No 178/2002 2002 of the European Parliament and of the Council of 28 January 2002 laying down the general principles and requirements of food law, establishing the*

---

[15] See recitals 24 and 25 of Directive 2001/18/EC; see also Agapito-Tenfen et al. (2018), p. 2.

[16] Recital 24 of Directive 2001/18/EC.

[17] Dederer (2019), pp. 79–80; *cf.* also Voigt and Münichsdorfer (2019), p. 142.

[18] See Voigt and Münichsdorfer (2019), p. 142; see also Voß (2006), p. 247.

[19] See the information required for an application for placing on the market as laid down in Annex III A and B of Directive 2001/18/EC.

[20] Organisation for Economic Co-operation and Development (1986), pp. 8, 29; *cf.* Voß (2006), p. 245.

[21] Voß (2006), p. 245.

[22] The precautionary principle is expressly included in Article 191(2) *Treaty on the Functioning of the European Union* (consolidated version) ('TFEU'), OJ EU 2012, C 326/47; for an overview of the precautionary principle in EU law, see van Calster and Reins (2018), pp. 28–33.

[23] See also Dederer (2019), p. 97.

European Food Safety Authority and laying down procedures in matters of food safety[24] ('Regulation 178/2002') incorporates the precautionary principle.[25]

Furthermore, different elements of the EU GMO legislation, such as the "step by step" approach,[26] the approval reservation before releasing GMOs into the environment and the case-by-case assessment of applications[27] can be considered an expression of the precautionary principle.[28] Also, the precautionary principle finds expression in every single authorisation decision taken by the European Commission or a Member State's competent authority.[29]

4.2.4 Implications of the Cartagena Protocol on the EU GMO Law

The EU is a party to the Cartagena Protocol on Biosafety to the Convention on Biological Diversity[30] ('Cartagena Protocol').[31] The Cartagena Protocol has been partly implemented into EU law by Regulation (EC) No 1946/2003 on transboundary movements of genetically modified organisms[32] ('Regulation 1946/2003'). This Regulation adopts the definition of Directive 2001/18/EC for a GMO and thereby fits into the EU GMO law framework.[33] Furthermore, it complements the existing legislation which primarily concerns the intra-EU use and release of GMOs with rules for the transboundary movement of GMOs. By acceding to the Cartagena Protocol, the EU has reaffirmed its commitment to precautionary action in the field of biotechnology, especially with regard to the conservation and sustainable use of biological diversity.[34]

---

[24] See footnote 9.

[25] See Article 7 of Regulation 178/2002.

[26] For the "step by step" approach see above, Sects. 4.2.2.

[27] For details on the authorisation procedures see below, Sect. 4.3.

[28] *Cf.* Voß (2006), p. 243.

[29] *Cf.* Voß (2006), p. 243.

[30] *Cartagena Protocol on Biosafety to the Convention on Biological Diversity* (adopted 29 January 2000, entered into force 11 September 2003) 2226 UNTS 208.

[31] See Secretariat of the Convention on Biological Diversity (2022); see also Council Decision 2002/628/EC of 25 June 2002 concerning the conclusion, on behalf of the European Community, of the Cartagena Protocol on Biosafety, OJ EC 2002, L 201/48.

[32] *Regulation (EC) No 1946/2003 of the European Parliament and of the Council of 15 July 2003 on transboundary movements of genetically modified organisms* ('Regulation 1946/2003'), OJ EU 2003, L 287/1.

[33] See Article 3(2) of Regulation 1946/2003.

[34] See Article 1 Cartagena Protocol and Article 1 of Regulation 1946/2003.

4.2.5 The Role of the European Food Safety Authority

The European Food Safety Authority has been established by Regulation 178/2002. Such an institution became necessary because scientific matters in relation to food and feed safety became more and more complex and the previous system of the EU for scientific and technical support on these matters was no longer able to respond to the increasing demands.[35] To improve the system of scientific and technical support in this field, EFSA was designed to be an independent scientific point of reference in risk assessment and an independent scientific source of advice, information and risk communication.[36] Nevertheless, the system of risk assessment on the one hand and risk management on the other was uphold.[37]

In accordance with these regulatory and political targets, EFSA's task is to provide scientific advice and scientific and technical support for the Community's legislation and policies in all fields which have a direct or indirect impact on food and feed safety, including human nutrition, animal health and welfare, as well as plant health. EFSA provides independent information on all matters within these fields and communicate on risks.[38] Furthermore, it provides scientific opinions on products other than food and feed relating to genetically modified organisms as defined by Directive 2001/18/EC.[39] The scientific opinions provided for by EFSA serve as the scientific basis for the drafting and adoption of Community measures in the fields falling within EFSA's mission.[40]

EFSA's institutional framework comprises a Management Board, an Executive Director, an Advisory Forum as well as a Scientific Committee and Scientific Panels.[41] The Scientific Committee and the permanent Scientific Panels are responsible for providing the scientific opinions of the Authority.[42] At the moment, there are eleven scientific panels, one dealing with all matters in the field of GMOs.[43]

For an adequate representation of the EU Member States' interests, the management board of EFSA comprises one representative and an alternate representative of each Member State.[44] This management board is also responsible to appoint the scientific members of the Scientific Committee and the Scientific Panels which are independent scientific experts.[45]

---

[35] See Regulation 178/2002, recital 33.

[36] See Regulation 178/2002, recitals 34, 35.

[37] See Regulation 178/2002, recital 35.

[38] See Article 22(2), (5) of Regulation 178/2002.

[39] See Article 22(5) and 23 of Regulation 178/2002.

[40] See Article 22(6) of Regulation 178/2002.

[41] See Article 24 of Regulation 178/2002.

[42] See Article 28(1) of Regulation 178/2002.

[43] See Article 28(4) of Regulation 178/2002.

[44] See Article 25(1) of Regulation 178/2002.

[45] See Article 28(3), (4) of Regulation 178/2002, see also Article 28(5)–(5b) of Regulation 178/2002 on the selection and appointment procedure of Scientific Committee and Scientific Panel members.

4.3 Authorisation Procedures for Placing on the Market of GM Plants

4.3.1 General Framework

The placing on the market of GM plants as such, as or in products is subject to the authorisation by a competent national authority or the European Commission.[46] Accordingly, an application must be filed to obtain approval. The placing on the market of GM plants is authorised where the application complies with the requirements laid down in the Deliberate Release Directive or the GM Food and Feed Regulation. The authorisation procedures are conducted on a case-by-case basis assessing each application individually.[47]

The authorisation procedure is characterised by a modified *ex officio* examination.[48] The applicant has to submit all necessary information for the authorisation decision which the competent authority checks for conformity with the relevant requirements in EU law.[49] However, the competent national authority can ask the applicant to provide further information and also has the possibility, even obligation, to conduct its own examination of the facts.[50]

4.3.1.1 "One Door – One Key" Principle

To avoid conflicts between authorisation procedures under the Deliberate Release Directive with its horizontal approach and under the sectoral product-specific regulations, the so-called "one door – one key" principle applies.[51] Under this principle, Directive 2001/18/EC does not apply to GMOs as or in products that are authorised by sectoral Union legislation which provides equivalents to the Directive's requirements.[52] The GM Food and Feed Regulation constitutes such sectoral legislation which provides equivalents to the Deliberate Release Directive's requirements and therefore excludes the applicability of the Directive.[53] Accordingly, for the placing on the market of GM plants used as/or in food or feed only one authorisation procedure is necessary which is governed by Regulation 1829/2003.[54]

---

[46] See Article 19(1) and (2) of Directive 2001/18/EC and Articles 7 and 19 of Regulation 1829/2003.

[47] See recitals 18 and 19 of Directive 2001/18/EC; for a critical assessment of the case by case approach, see Voß (2006), pp. 247–249.

[48] Voß (2006), pp. 264, 276.

[49] *Cf.* Voß (2006), pp. 264–266.

[50] *Cf.* Voß (2006), p. 265.

[51] *Cf.* Voß (2006), pp. 171–172; see also Commission of the European Communities (1996), p. 2.

[52] See Article 12 of Directive 2001/18/EC.

[53] See also Voß (2006), p. 188 with further references.

[54] *Cf.* also Voigt and Münichsdorfer (2019), p. 143.

4.3.1.2 Risk Assessment and Risk Management

The authorisation procedure for the placing on the market of GMOs in the EU is divided into the stage of risk assessment and the stage of risk management.[55] The risk assessment is either conducted by the national competent authority (Part C applications under Directive 2001/18/EC) or by EFSA (Part C applications under Directive 2001/18/EC in case of objections[56] and applications under Regulation 1829/2003).[57] The risk management decision, meaning the approval or rejection of an application, is then taken either by the national competent authority or by the European Commission.

4.3.2 Regulatory Objectives Pursued by the Authorisation Procedures

The regulatory objectives pursued by the authorisation procedures laid down in the Deliberate Release Directive and the GM Food and Feed Regulation can be deduced from the general objectives of these instruments as well as from its Annexes and the EFSA guidelines further elaborating on the potential effects of GM plants. The presentation of the comprehensive guidelines published by EFSA[58] is necessary for the subsequent analysis under the law of the World Trade Organisation and the *Comprehensive Economic and Trade Agreement*[59] in Chap. 6.

---

[55] See Articles 14 and 15 of Directive 2001/18/ and Articles 6, 7, 18 and 19 of Regulation 1829/2003; *cf.* also Dederer (2019), p. 85; for risk assessment and risk management as elements of risk analysis, see also Caswell (2000), pp. 666–667; Codex Alimentarius Commission (2007), p. 44.

[56] "If during the authorisation process of the GM product, objections on the risk assessment are raised and maintained by another Member State, then the Commission may consult EFSA for an independent risk assessment for human and animal health and the environment. Under Directive 2001/18/EC (Article 28.1) EFSA is consulted only on the maintained objections of the Member States, and is not supposed to carry out a full environmental risk assessment. However, on its own initiative the Authority considers it important to conduct a full environmental risk assessment according to the standards as laid down in the Guidance Document.", EFSA Panel on Genetically Modified Organisms (2010b), p. 12.

[57] According to *Voigt* and *Münichsdorfer*, the community procedure is applied for all Part C applications under Directive 2001/18, *cf.* Voigt and Münichsdorfer (2019), p. 156; the centralised risk assessment and risk management procedure was introduced by Directive 2001/18/EC and Regulation 1829/2003, see Eriksson (2019), p. 570.

[58] For an overview of EFSA's publications concerning the risk assessment of GMOs, see Waigmann et al. (2012); see also Agapito-Tenfen et al. (2018), pp. 5–6.

[59] *Comprehensive Economic and Trade Agreement between Canada, of the one part, and the European Union and its Member States, of the other part* (14 January 2017), OJ EU 2017, L 11/23.

4.3.2.1 Purposes Pursued by the Authorisation Procedures Laid Down in Directive 2001/18/EC

4.3.2.1.1 Purposes Listed in Directive 2001/18/EC

The Deliberate Release Directive aims at the protection of human health and the environment when GMOs are deliberately released into the environment and placed on the market as or in products.[60] Potential adverse effects of GMOs on human health or the environment are further specified in Annex II C.3.1.b. They include "effects on the dynamics of populations of species in the receiving environment and the genetic diversity of each of these populations leading to a potential decline in biodiversity", "altered susceptibility to pathogens facilitating the dissemination of infectious diseases or creating new reservoirs or vectors", "compromising prophylactic or therapeutic medical, veterinary, or plant protection treatments, for example by transfer of genes conferring resistance to antibiotics used in human or veterinary medicine", "effects on biogeochemistry (biogeochemical cycles), including carbon and nitrogen recycling through changes in soil decomposition of organic material", "disease affecting humans, including allergenic or toxic reactions" and "disease affecting animals and plants, including toxic, and, in the case of animals, allergenic reactions".[61]

Further areas of risk are listed in Annex II D.2. and include "persistence and invasiveness of the GM plant, including plant-to-plant gene transfer", "plant to micro-organisms gene transfer", "interactions of the [GM plant] with target organisms", "interactions of the [GM plant] with non-target organisms", "impacts of the specific cultivation, management and harvesting techniques", "effects on biogeochemical processes" and "effects on human and animal health".[62]

According to Annex III B I.B.3., information on these risk areas is required to be submitted by applicants seeking approval for the deliberate release of GM plants. Therefore, all the aforementioned adverse effects of GM plants are to be identified and evaluated in an environmental risk assessment[63] that has to be conducted to

---

[60] See recitals 5, 24, 25, 42, 43, 47 and Articles 1 and 4(1) of Directive 2001/18/EC.

[61] For all negative effects mentioned see Annex II C.3.1.b. of Directive 2001/18/EC; Annex II C.3. has been amended to its current form on the basis of EFSA Panel on Genetically Modified Organisms (2010a), see recital 5 of *Commission Directive 2018/350 of 8 March 2018 amending Directive 2001/18/EC of the European Parliament and of the Council as regards the environmental risk assessment of genetically modified organisms* ('Commission Directive 2018/350'), OJ EU 2018, L 67/30.

[62] These risks are listed for genetically modified higher plants which mean all plants that belong to the taxonomic group Spermatophytae (Gymnospermae and Angiospermae), see Annex II D.2., para 1 of Directive 2001/18/EC; they have also been incorporated in the Directive to update the Directive based on the EFSA Guidance, see recital 8 of Commission Directive 2018/350; the present analysis is confined to authorisation procedures for plants falling within this group, see Chap. 1.

[63] See Annex II A of Directive 2001/18/EC; *cf.* also EFSA Panel on Genetically Modified Organisms (2010a), pp. 11, 13.

obtain approval for their deliberate release.[64] The environmental risk assessment does not only assess direct or immediate effects but also indirect or delayed effects of the GM plant on human health and the environment.[65]

The areas of risk and potential adverse effects connected to them are further elaborated on in the *Guidance on the environmental risk assessment of genetically modified plants*[66] ('ERA Guidance') and in the *Scientific Opinion on Guidance for the risk assessment of genetically modified plants used for non-food or non-feed purposes*[67] issued by the EFSA Panel on Genetically Modified Organisms.

The potential adverse effects shall be linked to any changes in the characteristics of an organism, linked to the genetic modification, in comparison to the characteristics of a chosen non-genetically modified comparator.[68]

4.3.2.1.2 Further Guidance by EFSA on the Purposes Pursued

The ERA Guidance by EFSA includes a problem formulation for all seven areas of risk listed in Annex II D.2 of Directive 2001/18/EC. This problem formulation is a description of the risk areas including potential adverse effects. These problem formulations are shortly summarised in the following.

4.3.2.1.2.1 Persistence and Invasiveness Including Plant-to-Plant Gene Flow

For the first area of risk, EFSA mentions two types of adverse effects. "First, enhanced fitness[69] of the GM plant or of transgenic (introgressed) wild relatives within production systems may make them more persistent, exacerbating weed problems that may need to be controlled by more complex weed control strategies, which themselves might cause environmental harm."[70] And "[s]econd, enhanced

[64] See Articles 4(3), 6(2), 7(3), and 13(2) of Directive 2001/18/EC.

[65] See Annex II A of Directive 2001/18/EC.

[66] EFSA Panel on Genetically Modified Organisms (2010a).

[67] EFSA Panel on Genetically Modified Organisms (2009).

[68] *Cf.* Annex III C.3.1.a. and b. of Directive 2001/18/EC.

[69] "Fitness is defined as the number of seeds (or propagules) produced per seed sown, and includes the whole life cycle of the plant (Crawley et al., 1993). In some studies, only components of fitness are measured – frequently this is fecundity (Snow et al., 2003). If other vital rates are unchanged (which is an assumption that should be substantiated), an increase in fecundity will lead to an increase in fitness. Enhanced fitness can be defined as a characteristic of an individual or subpopulation of individuals that consistently contribute more offspring to the subsequent generation (Wilkinson and Tepfer, 2009). Fitness will vary depending upon the environmental context (including anthropogenic influences like mowing), particularly upon the presence of inter and intra-specific competitors, herbivores and pathogens, and the abiotic conditions. The variation in fitness according to biotic and abiotic conditions is often referred to as the 'genotype by environment interaction'. It is therefore appropriate that an appropriate range of environmental conditions are considered.", EFSA Panel on Genetically Modified Organisms (2010a), footnote 18.

[70] EFSA Panel on Genetically Modified Organisms (2010a), p. 40.

fitness of transgenic feral plants, or of transgenic (introgressed) wild relatives in semi-natural or natural habitats may reduce the diversity/abundance of valued flora and fauna. For instance, native plant species may be displaced, which in turn might affect species that use those plants as food, shelter, etc. Alternatively, and depending on which plant and which transgenes are involved, gene flow to wild relatives may decrease the fitness of hybrid offspring."[71]

4.3.2.1.2.2 Plant to Micro-Organisms Gene Transfer

Potential adverse effects for human and animal health and the environment in this risk area might arise out of horizontal gene transfer ('HGT'). "HGT can be initiated by uptake of cell free DNA from the environment, which may also include DNA derived from GM plants. After initial HGT from plant to micro-organism, the horizontally transferred genes may be further spread to other micro-organisms"[72] since "[m]icro-organisms, especially bacteria, are capable of exchanging genetic material directly between each other and even across species boundaries using different mechanisms i.e. conjugation, transduction or transformation."[73] Also, plant to micro-organisms gene transfer could have indirect effects on biogeochemical cycles.[74]

4.3.2.1.2.3 Interactions of GM Plants with Target Organisms

Adverse effects that might arise in this area of risk are the development of resistance of the target organism[75] and undesired changes in the interaction between the GM plant and target organisms.[76] Such effects might lead to further adverse consequences since "resistance development may compromise other pest control products, can destabilise pest control strategies, and may lead to increased pesticide use. As a consequence, it might lead to changes of cultivation management and might result in an increased environmental impact."[77]

---

[71] EFSA Panel on Genetically Modified Organisms (2010a), p. 40.

[72] EFSA Panel on Genetically Modified Organisms (2010a), p. 50.

[73] EFSA Panel on Genetically Modified Organisms (2010a), p. 50.

[74] EFSA Panel on Genetically Modified Organisms (2010a), p. 52.

[75] "Target organisms (TO) are organisms on which specifically designed characteristics of a GM plant are intended to act and are generally pests or pathogens of the plant.", EFSA Panel on Genetically Modified Organisms (2010a), p. 52 and footnote 26.

[76] EFSA Panel on Genetically Modified Organisms (2010a), pp. 52–53.

[77] EFSA Panel on Genetically Modified Organisms (2010a), p. 52.

4.3.2.1.2.4 Interactions of GM Plants with Non-target Organisms

Potential adverse effects can also arise from interactions of GM plants with non-target organisms.[78] These include "adverse effects on biodiversity[79] and its functioning at several levels, through interactions with populations of other species associated with or sympatric with the GM plant."[80] "Since the environment (including biodiversity) is to be protected from harm according to protection goals set out by EU legislation,[81] the protection of species richness and ecological functions [as well as the overall functionality of the ecosystems] should be considered in the [environmental risk assessment]."[82] "For sustainable land use, the scope is to maintain a certain level of biodiversity, providing essential ecological services, including biological control of pests and diseases, nutrient fixing and cycling, decomposition of plant materials, maintenance of soil quality and fertility, and structural stability. Therefore, the criterion of functional biodiversity is deemed important in this context, since preserving the functional biodiversity may guarantee the quality of production systems (e.g. agro-ecosystems) and ensure their sustainability. Applicants shall consider whether a GM plant and its use are directly and/or indirectly (e.g. through food web interactions, scale of adoption) potentially harmful to species guilds involved in ecosystem functions. The different features of the GM plant are considered the novel stressor since environmental impacts can be a consequence of changes to the GM plant, to its management as well as the effects of the introduced traits."[83]

Also, potential adverse effects on soil functioning and soil biodiversity fall within this area of risk.[84]

[78] This part of the EFSA Guidance includes the main findings of the EFSA *Scientific Opinion on the assessment of potential impacts of genetically modified plants on non-target organisms*, *cf.* EFSA Panel on Genetically Modified Organisms (2010b), p. 1.

[79] Biodiversity "covers both species richness and agro-eco functions providing ecosystem services", EFSA Panel on Genetically Modified Organisms (2010a), p. 56; "Ecosystems services include all services provided by ecosystems, e.g. production of food, fuel, fibre and medicines, regulation of water, air and climate, maintenance of soil fertility, cycling of nutrients. Ecosystems services are characterised by the fact that humans benefit directly from these natura assets and processes", see EFSA Panel on Genetically Modified Organisms (2010b), p. 8.

[80] EFSA Panel on Genetically Modified Organisms (2010a), p. 55.

[81] For protection goals as set out by EU legislation, see EFSA Panel on Genetically Modified Organisms (2010b), p. 10.

[82] EFSA Panel on Genetically Modified Organisms (2010a), pp. 56, 69.

[83] EFSA Panel on Genetically Modified Organisms (2010a), p. 56.

[84] EFSA Panel on Genetically Modified Organisms (2010b), p. 9.

4.3.2.1.2.5 Impacts of the Specific Cultivation, Management and Harvesting Techniques

As impacts of specific cultivation, management and harvesting techniques, the EFSA Guidance mentions environmental harm and greater adverse effects on biodiversity.[85] It also mentions impacts on soil structure and soil biodiversity as well as on greenhouse gas emissions and the overall energy balance.[86] Also, biogeochemical cycles and their functioning might be affected by specific cultivation, management and harvesting techniques related to GMOs.[87]

4.3.2.1.2.6 Effects on Biogeochemical Processes

Potential adverse effects in this area of risk might include effects on soil fertility, nutrient transformations and food webs as well as on ecosystem functioning.[88]

4.3.2.1.2.7 Effects on Human and Animal Health

EFSA, in its Guidance, outlines as potential adverse effects on human health, "the risk to persons working with the GM plant, coming into contact with it or exposed to products such as pollen or dust from processed plants."[89] Furthermore, with regard to GM plant applications for non-food or non-feed purposes that fall within the ambit of the Deliberate Release Directive, it refers to its *Scientific Opinion on Guidance for the risk assessment of genetically modified plants used for non-food or non-feed purposes.*[90] In this Opinion, one "focus of the evaluation for human and animal safety is on the risks resulting from oral exposure through the accidental intake (through inadvertent entry in the food and feed chain via admixture or gene flow or through accidental consumption in the field)",[91] but adverse effects can also arise from contact with GM plants.[92] This includes potential dermal, ocular and inhalatory exposure.[93] Adverse effects in this area of risk may occur due to toxic or allergenic characteristics of the GM plant.[94]

---

[85] EFSA Panel on Genetically Modified Organisms (2010a), pp. 71, 72, 77.

[86] EFSA Panel on Genetically Modified Organisms (2010a), p. 71.

[87] EFSA Panel on Genetically Modified Organisms (2010a), pp. 71, 77.

[88] *Cf.* EFSA Panel on Genetically Modified Organisms (2010a), pp. 80, 81.

[89] *Cf.* EFSA Panel on Genetically Modified Organisms (2010a), p. 83.

[90] EFSA Panel on Genetically Modified Organisms (2009).

[91] EFSA Panel on Genetically Modified Organisms (2009), p. 4.

[92] *Cf.* EFSA Panel on Genetically Modified Organisms (2009), p. 4.

[93] *Cf.* EFSA Panel on Genetically Modified Organisms (2009), p. 20.

[94] *Cf.* EFSA Panel on Genetically Modified Organisms (2009), pp. 21–26.

4.3.2.2 Purposes Pursued by the Authorisation Procedures Laid Down in Regulation 1829/2003

The GM Food and Feed Regulation aims to ensure "a high level of protection of human life and health, animal life and welfare, environment and consumer interests in relation to genetically modified food and feed".[95] Accordingly, it introduces additional objectives to those pursued by Directive 2001/18.[96] The assurance of such a high level is to be assessed during the authorisation process where an applicant must demonstrate that its application satisfies these requirements.[97] The single application requirements also aim at avoiding adverse effects on biological diversity,[98] and the adverse effects listed in Annex II.C.3.b of Directive 2001/18/EC.[99]

4.3.3 Application

To receive authorisation for the placing on the market of GM plants under the Deliberate Release Directive, applicants must submit a notification to the competent authority of the Member State where the GM plant is to be placed on the market for the first time.[100] The information required for the notification is specified in Article 13(2), (3) and Annexes II, III, IV and VII of Directive 2001/18. This includes *inter alia* an environmental risk assessment carried out in accordance with the requirements laid down in Annex II,[101] a monitoring plan[102] as well as labelling and packaging proposals[103] and results from previous experimental releases.[104]

Applications for the placing on the market of GM food and feed in the sense of Regulation 1829/2003[105] also have to be submitted to the competent authority which

[95] Article 1(a) Regulation 1829/2003; see also Recital 9 to and Articles 4(1) and 16(1) of Regulation 1829/2003.

[96] Scott (2003), p. 217.

[97] See Articles 4(3), 5(4)(c) and (e), 5(5), 6(3)(b) and (c) and 6(4) as well as Articles 16(3), 17(3)(e), 17(5) and 18(4) of Regulation 1829/2003.

[98] *Cf.* Article 5(3)(c) of Regulation 1829/2003 in conjunction with Annexes II and III to the Cartagena Protocol.

[99] See Articles 5(5)(a), 6(3)(c), 6(4), 17(5)(a), 18(4) of Regulation 1829/2003; see also recital 7 of Implementing Regulation 503/2013; for the objectives listed in Annex II.C.3.b. of Directive 2001/18/EC, see above, Sect. 4.3.2.1.

[100] See Article 13(1) of Directive 2001/18/EC.

[101] See Article 13(2)(b) of Directive 2001/18/EC.

[102] See Article 13(2)(e) of Directive 2001/18/EC.

[103] See Article 13(2)(f) and (g) of Directive 2001/18/EC.

[104] See Article 13(3) of Directive 2001/18/EC.

[105] Meaning GMOs for food or feed use, food or feed containing or consisting of GMOs, food or feed produced from GMOs or, food containing ingredients produced from GMOs, see Articles 3 and 5 of Regulation 1829/2003.

forwards it to EFSA.[106] The applications shall *inter alia* include technical data on the GMO and corresponding scientific studies, a labelling proposal in case of possible ethical or religious concerns, detection methods, specific conditions for use and handling, and the information required by Annexes III and IV of Directive 2001/18/EC, conclusions of the environmental risk assessment carried out in accordance with Annex II of Directive 2001/18/EC and, a monitoring plan in accordance with Annex VII of Directive 2001/18/EC.[107]

4.3.4 Risk Assessment

4.3.4.1 For the Placing on the Market of GM Plants Under Directive 2001/18/EC

The risk assessment for the placing on the market of GM plants not intended for food or feed purposes is in principle carried out by the competent national authority.[108] Within 90 days from the receipt of the application,[109] the competent national authority prepares an assessment report, examining the application for compliance with the Deliberate Release Directive.[110] In case, the competent authority concludes that the GM plant in question can be placed on the market, it sends its assessment report to the European Commission which forwards it to the Member States.[111] The Commission and the other Member States may ask for further information, comment or present reasoned objections to the placing on the market of the respective GM plant.[112] Outstanding issues shall be solved within 105 days after the assessment report has been circulated.[113] In the case that objections by another national authority or the European Commission cannot be solved and are maintained, the Commission may consult EFSA which then carries out a full risk assessment on its own.[114]

---

[106] See Articles 5(2) and 17(2) of Regulation 1829/2003.

[107] See Articles 5 and 17 of Regulation 1829/2003; the information required by the Annexes to Directive 2001/18 are only necessary in the case of applications for GMOs for food or feed use, or for food or feed containing or consisting of GMOs, see Article 5(5) and 17(5) of Regulation 1829/2003.

[108] See Article 14 of Directive 2001/18/EC.

[109] This does not include the time needed by the applicant to provide further information as requested by the competent authority, see Article 14(4) of Directive 2001/18/EC.

[110] See Article 14(1), (2) of Directive 2001/18/EC.

[111] See Article 14(2) of Directive 2001/18/EC.

[112] See Article 15(1) of Directive 2001/18/EC.

[113] See Article 15(1) of Directive 2001/18/EC.

[114] See Articles 18(1) and 28 of Directive 2001/18/EC; EFSA Panel on Genetically Modified Organisms (2010b), p. 12.

4.3.4.2 For the Placing on the Market of GM Plants Under Regulation 1829/2003

For the placing on the market of GM plants falling within the scope of the GM Food and Feed Regulation, the risk assessment is carried out at the European level by EFSA.[115] However, EFSA may require the competent national authorities to carry out environmental or health risk assessments as provided for by Articles 6(3)(b), (c) and 18(3)(b), (c) of Regulation 1829/2003.[116] Where the applicant seeks the authorisation for cultivation, an environmental risk assessment by the competent national authority is mandatory, in addition to EFSA's risk assessment.[117] Furthermore, the *European Union Reference Laboratory for Genetically Modified Food and Feed*[118] ('EURL GMFF') carries out testing and validation of the detection and identification methods submitted by the applicant.[119]

The risk assessment by EFSA is carried out following the principles laid down in Annex II of Directive 2001/18/EC. Also, EFSA has published several guidance documents on its environmental risk assessment.[120]

After the risk assessment has been carried out, EFSA gives an opinion on its risk assessment[121] within 6 months from the receipt of a valid application.[122] This does not include time periods that the applicant takes to provide further information.[123] EFSA's opinion is forwarded to the Commission and the Member States.[124]

[115] See Articles 6 and 18 of Regulation 1829/2003.

[116] See also Voigt and Münichsdorfer (2019), p. 160, Figure 5.7.

[117] See Articles 6(3)(c) and 18(3)(c) of Regulation 1829/2003; *cf.* Voigt and Münichsdorfer (2019), p. 160.

[118] "The European Union Reference Laboratory for Genetically Modified Food and Feed (EURL GMFF) performs the scientific assessment and validation of detection methods for GM Food and Feed as part of the EU authorisation procedure. It also assists National Reference Laboratories (NRL) for GMO control in the EU Member States. The EURL GMFF is supported by the ENGL, the European Network of GMO Laboratories, and hosted by the Joint Research Centre (JRC) of the European Commission.", see European Commission (n.d.-b), https://gmo-crl.jrc.ec.europa.eu/; see also Article 32 and the Annex to Regulation 1829/2003.

[119] See Articles 6(3)(d) and 18(3)(d) of Regulation 1829/2003.

[120] For an overview on the guidance documents relevant for genetically modified plants see above, Sects. 4.3.2.1.1–4.3.2.1.2; see also Waigmann et al. (2012); the risk assessment is also outlined by Agapito-Tenfen et al. (2018), pp. 5–6.

[121] "Including a report describing its assessment of the food/feed and stating the reasons for its opinion and the information on which this opinion is based, including the opinions of the competent authorities when consulted", see Articles 6(6) and 18(6) of Regulation 1829/2003.

[122] See Articles 6(1) and 18(1) of Regulation 1829/2003.

[123] See Articles 6(1), (2) and 18(1), (2) of Regulation 1829/2003.

[124] See Articles 6(6) and 18(6) of Regulation 1829/2003.

4.3.5 *Risk Management*

For the placing on the market of GM plants not intended for food or feed purposes, the risk management is in principle carried out by the competent national authority.[125] In the case that the European Commission or other Member States raise objections to the national assessment report that cannot be solved, the risk management decision is taken by the European Commission following the Community procedure laid down in *Regulation (EU) No 182/2011 of the European Parliament and of the Council of 16 February 2011 laying down the rules and general principles concerning mechanisms for control by Member States of the Commission's exercise of implementing powers*[126] ('Regulation 182/2011').[127]

Under Regulation 1829/2003, the risk management decision for the placing on the market of GM food and feed is taken by the European Commission. It is also taken following the comitology procedure provided for by Regulation 182/2011.[128]

4.3.5.1 Comitology Procedure

According to the comitology procedure, the European Commission is assisted by a committee when deciding on the authorisation of the placing on the market of GM plants. For part C notifications under Directive 2001/18/EC that are decided upon on the Union level, the *Regulatory Committee 2001/18/EC*[129] is responsible. For applications submitted under the GM Food and Feed Regulation, the *Standing Committee on Plants, Animals, Food and Feed*[130] ('SCoPAFF') with its section on GM food and feed and environmental risks is responsible.

In case, the competent committee delivers a positive opinion on the Commission's proposal,[131] the European Commission shall adopt the draft implementing act.[132] In case, the competent committee delivers a negative opinion, the draft implementing

---

[125] See Article 15(2), (3) of Directive 2001/18/EC.

[126] *Regulation (EU) No 182/2011 of the European Parliament and of the Council of 16 February 2011 laying down the rules and general principles concerning mechanisms for control by Member States of the Commission's exercise of implementing powers* ('Regulation 182/2011'), OJ EU 2011, L 55/13.

[127] Article 18 in conjunction with Article 30(2) Directive 2001/18 refers to the comitology procedure laid down in Regulation 182/2011.

[128] See Articles 7(3) and 19(3) in conjunction with Article 35(2) of Regulation 1829/2003.

[129] See European Commission (n.d.-c), https://ec.europa.eu/food/horizontal-topics/committees/other-committees/regulatory-committee-200118ec_en.

[130] See European Commission (n.d.-f), https://food.ec.europa.eu/horizontal-topics/committees/paff-committees/genetically-modified-food-and-feed-and-environmental-risk_en.

[131] The Commission's proposal is a draft implementing act proposing either the approval or rejection of an application.

[132] See Article 5(2) of Regulation 182/2011.

act shall not be adopted.[133] In case the competent committee does not deliver an opinion, the Commission shall not adopt the draft implementing act.[134] However, since a decision (in form of an implementing act) is deemed necessary in the case of GMO authorisation, the Commission's proposal is submitted to the Appeal Committee (as provided for by Article 5(4), subpara. 3 of Regulation 182/2011).

The Appeal Committee acts under the procedure provided for by Article 6 of Regulation 182/2011. Where a positive or negative opinion is given, the European Commission shall act accordingly.[135] Where no opinion is given, it is within the European Commission's discretion to adopt the draft implementing act.[136]

4.3.5.2 Approval Decisions Since 2015

Since the entry into force of the Deliberate Release Directive and the GM Food and Feed Regulation, bringing with it the centralised authorisation procedure, no opinion has been delivered by the *Regulatory Committee 2001/18/EC* or the SCoPAFF, but all draft implementing acts were transferred to the respective Appeal Committee.[137] Also, the Appeal Committee did not take any decision.[138] Reasons that were given by the Member States for not adopting or rejecting the Commission's drafts include the following: there is no agreed national position, a negative public opinion, political reasons, lack of a 90-day toxicity study, lack of a long-term feeding study, the risk assessment is deemed insufficient, interactions between single events have not been sufficiently assessed, the general surveillance plan is not satisfactory, the precautionary principle, there is no finalised opinion of the national scientific committee, the Regulation on GM food and feed is not considered the right legal basis to authorise products other than food and feed containing and consisting of GMOs,[139] the national risk assessment has not yet been finalised, the national GM-free strategy, scientific reasons, lack of comprehensive data on long-

---

[133] See Article 5(3) of Regulation 182/2011.

[134] This can be taken from the transitional provisions in Article 13(1)(c) Regulation 182/2011 and the fact that both Directive 2001/18/EC and Regulation 1829/2003 refer to Article 5 of Decision 1999/468/EC.

[135] See Article 6(3), subpara. 1 and 3 of Regulation 182/2011.

[136] See Article 6(3), subpara. 2 of Regulation 182/2011.

[137] See Tables 4.1 and 4.2, Sect. 4.3.5.2 the tables display the authorisation process since 2015 because the meetings documents of the SCoPAFF and the Appeal Committee are publicly available from 2015 on; a document by the European Commission however states that there has been no opinion on the Commission's drafts since the entry into force of Regulation 1829/2003, see European Commission (2015), p. 2; this is also noted by Eriksson (2019), p. 570 with further references and by Klika et al. (2013), p. 327.

[138] See Tables 4.1 and 4.2 in Annex to this chapter, p. 78.

[139] This reason is mentioned because the Commission in Article 2(c) of the draft implementing acts that are based on Regulation 1829/2003 proposes the authorisation of GM plants not only for food and feed purposes, but also for other uses (except for cultivation), see addendum to Tables 4.3 and 4.4 in Annex, this chapter, p. 78 for the Commission Implementing Decisions.

term potential impacts of GMOs, existing uncertainties in risk assessment, safety concerns for the environment, the risk of harm to the national agri-food industry, that human-aided propagation cannot be excluded, that a potential spread of pollen and cross-pollination cannot be excluded, the social utility of these GMOs is unclear, ethical concerns, that a plant-to-plant gene transfer cannot be excluded.

Accordingly, it has always been the European Commission that adopted the draft implementing act in the end. An authorisation is granted for a maximum of 10 years.[140]

4.3.6 Safeguard and Emergency Measures

Article 23 Directive of 2001/18/EC allows EU Member States to restrict or prohibit the use and/or sale of a GMO or a GM product after authorisation when the Member State has detailed grounds to consider that the GMO constitutes a risk to human health or the environment. This restriction or prohibition must be based on new or additional information that has been published since the authorisation and affect the environmental risk assessment or reassessment of existing information on the basis of new or additional scientific knowledge. The European Commission and the other Member States must be immediately informed of such a decision and the reasons must be made available.[141] A decision on the restriction or prohibition is taken by the European Commission and all Member States following the comitology procedure.[142,143]

Also, the GM Food and Feed Regulation allows for modifying or suspending an authorisation where authorised GM products constitute a serious risk to human health, animal health or the environment.[144] Such suspension or modification shall be done in accordance with the procedure provided for by Articles 53 and 54 of Regulation 178/2002.

---

[140] See Article 15(4), subpara. 1 Directive 2001/18 and Articles 7(5) and 19(5) of Regulation 1829/2003.

[141] See Article 23(1), subpara. 3 of Directive 2001/18/EC.

[142] For the comitology procedure as part of the risk management phase see above, Sect. 4.3.5.1.

[143] See Article 23(2), subpara. 1 in conjunction with Article 30(2) of Directive 2001/18/EC.

[144] See Article 34 of Regulation 1829/2003.

4.4 Labelling Requirements When Placing GM Plants on the Market

GM plants when placed on the market in the EU must be labelled as such. The EU's labelling regime is said to be one of the most extensive labelling regimes worldwide.[145] It does apply to GMOs or GM products irrespective of their origin in or outside of the EU.[146]

4.4.1 Objectives Pursued by the EU Labelling Requirements

The labelling requirements laid down in the Deliberate Release Directive and Regulations 1829/2003 and 1830/2003 pursue the objective of consumer and risk information.[147] They shall ensure that operators and consumers can "exercise their freedom of choice in an effective manner".[148] Furthermore, the labelling requirements laid down in Article 13(2)(a)(i)–(iv) serve the objective of consumer health protection.[149]

4.4.2 Labelling Requirements for GM Food

Food containing or consisting of GMOs, or food produced from or containing ingredients produced from GMOs shall be labelled in accordance with Article 13 of Regulation 1829/2003.[150] The labelling shall indicate that the foodstuff is genetically modified, has been produced from genetically modified ingredients or contains genetically modified ingredients.[151] Furthermore, the labelling shall indicate where food is different from its conventional counterpart concerning composition, nutritional characteristics, intended use or implications for the health of certain sections of the population or where food may give rise to ethical or religious concerns.[152]

---

145 *Cf.* Voigt and Münichsdorfer (2019); see also Baumüller (2004), pp. 34–35; Broeders et al. (2012), p. 1.

146 See also Voigt and Münichsdorfer (2019), p. 185.

147 See recitals 17, 20 and 21 of Regulation 1829/2003; for an extensive analysis of the objectives pursued by the labelling requirements laid down in Directive 2001/18/EC, see Burchardi (2007), pp. 209–220.

148 See recitals 4 and 11 of Regulation 1830/2003; see also Article 1 of Regulation 1829/2003; *cf.* also Dederer (2019), pp. 86–87.

149 *Cf.* Burchardi (2007), pp. 118, 247–248.

150 See Article 12(1) of Regulation 1829/2003.

151 See Article 13(1)(a)–(e) of Regulation 1829/2003.

152 See Article 13(2)(a), (b) of Regulation 1829/2003.

4.4.3 Labelling Requirements for GM Feed

Regulation 1829/2003 also lays down labelling requirements for GMOs for feed use, feed containing or consisting of GMOs and, feed produced from GMOs.[153] GMOs for feed use or feed containing or consisting of GMOs shall be labelled as "genetically modified (name of organism)".[154] Feed produced from GMOs shall carry the label "produced from genetically modified (name of organism)".[155] And also with regard to GM feed, differences to the conventional counterpart with regard to composition, nutritional characteristics, intended use or, implications for the health of certain species or categories of animals shall be indicated on the label.[156] Also, any characteristic of the feed that may give rise to ethical or religious concerns shall be indicated.[157]

4.4.4 Labelling Requirements for GMOs Other Than Food and Feed

GMOs as or in products must be labelled as such when placed on the market.[158] The applicant is obliged to propose labelling in accordance with the requirements laid down in Annex IV of Directive 2001/18/EC in its notification.[159] The final labelling that must be displayed on the product is specified by the competent national authority in its written consent.[160] The labelling must include the statement "This product contains genetically modified organisms".[161]

The labelling requirements for products consisting or containing GMOs are also laid down in Article 4(6) of Regulation 1830/2003.

---

[153] See Articles 24(1) and 15(1) of Regulation 1829/2003.

[154] See Article 25(2)(a) of Regulation 1829/2003.

[155] See Article 25(2)(b) of Regulation 1829/2003.

[156] See Article 25(2)(c) of Regulation 1829/2003.

[157] See Article 25(2)(d) of Regulation 1829/2003.

[158] See Article 21(1) of Directive 2001/18/EC.

[159] See Article 13(1)(f) of Directive 2001/18/EC.

[160] See Article 19(3)(e) of Directive 2001/18/EC.

[161] See Annex IV A.8 of Directive 2001/18/EC.

4.4.5 *Exemptions to the Mandatory Labelling Requirements: Tolerance Threshold*

For some cases, the EU labelling requirements for GMOs do not apply to traces of authorised GMOs in proportions no higher than 0.9% or lower. These cases comprise products intended for direct processing,[162] foodstuff containing material which contains, consists of or is produced from GMOs,[163] or feedstuff containing material which contains, consists of or is produced from GMOs.[164] Furthermore, the presence of GMO traces must be adventitious or technically unavoidable.[165]

4.4.6 *Voluntary GM-Free Label*

There is no Union-wide GM-free label. Such labelling is regulated at the Member State level, but not all Member States have introduced legislation regulating the use of GM-free labels.[166]

4.5 Possibility to Opt-Out from Cultivation

Article 26b of Directive 2001/18/EC offers Member States the possibility to restrict or prohibit the cultivation of GMOs during the authorisation procedure or after the GMOs have been authorised in the EU.[167] To restrict the territorial scope of a GMO authorisation, a Member State may request that the authorisation for cultivation is not granted for its territory.[168] Where the applicant adjusts the territorial scope of its initial application or does not react to the request, the geographical scope of the authorisation is adjusted accordingly.[169] Where the applicant confirms the initial scope of its application and does not adjust the geographical scope in accordance with the Member State's request, the Member State may only restrict or prohibit the cultivation of the GMO within its territory based on the grounds laid down in Article

[162] See Article 21(3) of Directive 2001/18/EC.

[163] See Article 12(2) of Regulation 1829/2003.

[164] See Article 24(2) of Regulation 1829/2003.

[165] See Article 21(3) of Directive 2001/18/EC and Articles 12(2), (3) and 24(2), (3) of Regulation 1829/2003; see also Article 4(7), (8) of Regulation 1830/2003; for an interpretation of "adventitious or technically unavoidable" in Regulation 1829/2003, see Schäfer (2005), pp. 6–7.

[166] For an overview see Voigt and Münichsdorfer (2019), p. 186.

[167] For the legislative history of this provision, see Monien (2016), pp. 103–105; see also Palme (1997), paras 42–43.

[168] See Article 26b(1) of Directive 2001/18/EC.

[169] See Article 26b(2) of Directive 2001/18/EC.

26b(3) of Directive 2001/18/EC. Also, where a Member State wants to restrict or prohibit the cultivation of a GMO within its territory after the GMO has already been authorised, it must base its measure on these grounds. Grounds laid down in para. 3 include environmental policy objectives, town and country planning, land use, socioeconomic impacts, avoidance of GMO presence in other products, agricultural policy objectives or public policy.[170] However, the Member State's invocation of one or more of the grounds laid down in para. 3 must not conflict with the environmental risk assessment carried out under the Deliberate Release Directive or the GM Food and Feed Regulation.

Up to now, no demand for the restriction or prohibition of a GMO's cultivation within a Member States' territory has been based on Article 26b of Directive 2001/18/EC. All demands have been based on the transitional measures laid down in Article 26c of Directive 2001/18/EC.[171]

Another proposal by the European Commission to amend the GM Food and Feed Regulation giving Member States the possibility to restrict or prohibit the use of GM food and feed on their territory[172] failed in the European Parliament.[173]

4.6 The Regulatory Framework for Plants Obtained by Conventional Breeding Methods

Since one point often raised after the CJEU's judgement on targeted mutagenesis techniques was the different regulation of plants altered by targeted and conventional mutagenesis techniques, the regulatory framework for plants obtained by conventional breeding techniques shall be outlined in brief.

Plant varieties that can be marketed in the EU are listed in the *Common catalogue of varieties of agricultural plant species* ('Common Catalogue'), compiled based on national variety catalogues.[174] *Council Directive 2002/53/EC of 13 June 2002 on the common catalogue of varieties of agricultural plant species*[175]

---

[170] For a more detailed analysis of the grounds provided for by Article 26b(3) of Directive 2001/18/EC, see Monien (2016), pp. 106–108.

[171] See European Commission (n.d.-d), https://food.ec.europa.eu/plants/genetically-modified-organisms/gmo-authorisation/gmo-authorisations-cultivation/restrictions-geographical-scope-gmo-applicationsauthorisations-eu-countries-demands-and-outcomes_en.

[172] European Commission (2015); see also European Parliamentary Research Service (2025); this proposal is also discussed by Monien (2016), pp. 111–112.

[173] See European Parliament (2015).

[174] See Article 1(2) of *Council Directive 2002/53/EC of 13 June 2002 on the common catalogue of varieties of agricultural plant species* (consolidated version from 18 April 2004) ('Directive 2002/53/EC'), OJ EC 2002, L193/1; see also *Marketing of seeds of agricultural crops. Summaries of EU Legislation*, https://eur-lex.europa.eu/EN/legal-content/summary/marketing-of-seeds-of-agricultural-crops.html.

[175] See footnote 174.

('Directive 2002/53/EC') lays down the rules for including agricultural plant varieties in the common catalogue. According to Article 4(1) of Directive 2002/53/EC, a variety shall only be included in a Member States' variety catalogue if it is *distinct, (sufficiently) uniform* and *stable* (the so-called DUS criteria).[176] Furthermore, the variety must be of satisfactory value for cultivation and use.[177] These characteristics shall be evidenced by official examinations, including growing trials before a variety is accepted to a national catalogue.[178] The variety registration in the national catalogue shall be valid for 10 years according to Article 12(1) of Directive 2002/53/EC. A variety that is accepted to one of the national variety registers is also published in the common catalogue and can be marketed throughout the EU.[179]

Additionally, there is specific legislation for different groups of plant varieties.[180]

4.7 Summary

This chapter presents the currently applicable GMO law in the EU and in particular the authorisation procedure, labelling requirements and the so-called opt-out mechanism. The central regulatory instrument is Directive 2001/18/EC. This Directive is supplemented by Regulation 1829/2003 and Regulation 1830/2003. The competent authority at EU level is the European Food Safety Authority.

The EU GMO law contains a technology-based, so-called process-based approach, i.e. the applicability is linked to the specific technology used to modify an organism. The central definition is laid down in Article 2 (2) of Directive 2001/18/EC.

EU GMO law is characterised by a step-by-step approach. According to this approach, GMOs are released step by step, but only if the assessment of the previous steps with regard to the protection of human health and the environment shows

[176] *Cf.* also Habets et al. (2019), p. 9; the requirements for a plant variety to be considered distinct, uniform and stable are laid down in Article 5 of Directive 2002/53/EC.

[177] See Articles 4(1) and 5(4) of Directive 2002/53/EC.

[178] See Article 7(1) of Directive 2002/53/EC.

[179] *Cf.* Habets et al. (2019), p. 10; see also *Marketing of seeds of agricultural crops. Summaries of EU Legislation*, https://eur-lex.europa.eu/EN/legal-content/summary/marketing-of-seeds-of-agricultural-crops.html.

[180] See e.g. *Council Directive 66/401/EEC of 14 June 1966 on the marketing of fodder plant seed* (consolidated version from 01 February 2022), OJ EC 1966, 132; *Council Directive 66/402/EEC of June 1966 on the marketing of cereal seed* (consolidated version from 01 February 2022), OJ EC 1966, 143; *Council Directive 2002/57/EC of 13 June 2002 on the marketing of seed of oil and fibre plants* (consolidated version from 16 February 2020), OJ EC 2002, L 193/74; *Council Directive 2002/56/EC of 13 June 2002 on the marketing of seed potatoes* (consolidated version from 16 February 2020), OJ EC, L 193/60; *Council Directive 2002/54/EC of 13 June 2002 on the marketing of beet seed* (consolidated version from 01 April 2017), OJ EC 2002, L 193/12; for further legislation on plant reproductive material see European Commission (n.d.-e), https://food.ec.europa.eu/plants/plant-reproductive-material/legislation/specific-legislation_en.

that the next step can be taken. This step-by-step approach is also an expression of the precautionary principle, a central principle of EU environmental law.

This chapter presents three important regulatory instruments of EU GMO law: authorisation procedures, labelling requirements and the so-called opt-out mechanism.

The placing on the market of genetically modified plants as such, as a product or in products is subject to authorisation by a competent national authority or the European Commission. The general authorisation requirement serves the protection of human and animal health as well as the environment. The release or placing on the market of genetically modified plants is authorised if the application meets the requirements of Directive 2001/18/EC or Regulation 1829/2003. The authorisation procedures are carried out on a case-by-case basis. The risk assessment and authorisation decision are carried out either by the national authority or at EU level by EFSA and the European Commission. In the case of an authorisation decision by the EU Commission, the decision is made in the so-called comitology procedure, which regularly leads to lengthy decision-making processes due to the specific structure of the procedure, in which the Member States do not make a clear decision but leave this to the Commission.

Labelling regulations are another regulatory instrument of EU GMO law. If GM plants are placed on the market in the EU, they must be labelled as such. The EU's labelling regulations apply to GMOs regardless of their origin within or outside the EU. The aim of the labelling regulations is to inform consumers about the risks associated with GMOs. They are intended to ensure that businesses and consumers can effectively exercise their freedom of choice. In addition, the labelling requirements also partly serve the protection of consumer health.

Directive 2001/18/EC allows Member States to restrict or prohibit the cultivation of GMOs during the authorisation procedure or after authorisation of the GMOs in the EU, the so-called opt-out mechanism. However, so far no use has been made of this option laid down in Article 26b of Directive 2001/18/EC.

In contrast to GMOs, plants obtained through conventional breeding are significantly less regulated in the EU. In order to be marketed in the EU, conventionally bred plants must be included in the Common Catalogue which is compiled on the basis of the national catalogues of varieties. Directive 2002/53/EC lays down the rules for the inclusion of agricultural plant varieties in the common catalogue. Accordingly, a variety is only included in the catalogue of a Member State if it fulfils the so-called DUS criteria. In addition, the variety must have sufficient value for cultivation and use.

This shows why it is decisive for the marketing of a plant and its (economic) value whether it qualifies as GMO or not. Accordingly, a GM plant must recoup the high costs incurred for its authorisation and marketing. This is only likely to be worthwhile if the plant has a high economic benefit. Social benefits, on the other hand, are less likely to play a role in this calculation.

Appendix

Annex (Tables 4.1 and 4.2)

For the respective **EFSA Opinions** and **Commission Implementing Decisions**, see Table 4.3. For the **summaries of the SCoPAFF Meetings**, see (European Commission). For the **summaries of the Appeal Committee Meetings**, see (European Commission).

Addendum (Tables 4.3 and 4.4)

For the respective assessment reports, EFSA Opinions and Commission Implementing Decisions, see Table 4.4.

Table 4.1 Authorisation procedures under Regulation 1829/2003

Products containing, consisting of, or produced from	EFSA		European Commission		
	Application [a]	Opinion published	SCoPAFF (decision +/o/-)	Appeal Committee (decision +/o/-)	Decision
GM Cotton					
Cotton MON 15985 [b]	22.05.2008	28.07.2014	16.03.2015 (o)	31.03.2015 (o)	24.04.2015
Cotton 281-24-236 × 3006-210-23 × MON 88913 (DAS-24236-5×DAS-21Ø23-5×MON-88913-8)	19.03.2009	19.04.2016	08.07.2016 (o)	15.09.2016 (o)	04.07.2017
Cotton GHB614 × LLcotton25 × MON 15985	18.02.2011	20.04.2018	03.12.2018 (o)	14.01.2019 (o)	26.07.2019
Cotton GHB119 (BCS-GHØØ5-8)	07.04.2011	21.10.2016	27.03.2017 (o)	16.05.2017 (o)	04.07.2017
Cotton GHB614 × T304-40 × GHB119	08.10.2014	25.07.2018	16.12.2020 (o)	26.02.2021 (o)	17.08.2021
Cotton GHB811 (BCS-GH811-4)	11.10.2018	16.08.2021	17.12.2021 (o)	10.02.2022 (o)	31.03.2022
GM Maize					
Maize Bt11 × MIR162 × MIR604 × GA21 and subcombinations	04.03.2009	07.12.2015	25.04.2016 (o)	92.06.2016 (o)	16.09.2016
Maize NK603 × T25 [b]	21.05.2010	15.07.2015	19.10.2015 (o)	10.11.2015 (o)	04.12.2015
Maize Bt11 × MIR162 × 1507 × GA21 and subcombinations	10.08.2010	11.07.2018	14.01.2019 (o)	22.02.2019 (o)	26.07.2019

(continued)

Table 4.1 (continued)

Products containing, consisting of, or produced from	EFSA		European Commission		
	Application [a]	Opinion published	SCoPAFF (decision +/o/-)	Appeal Committee (decision +/o/-)	Decision
Maize DAS-40278-9	11.11.2010	05.12.2016	27.03.2017 (o)	16.05.2017 (o)	04.07.2017
Maize 1507 × 59122 × MON 810 × NK603 and sub-combinations	03.02.2011	28.11.2017	23.04.2018 (o)	15.05.2018 (o)	03.08.2018
Maize 5307 (SYN-Ø53Ø7-1)	07.04.2011	05.05.2015	03.12.2018 (o)	14.01.2019 (o)	26.07.2019
Maize Bt11 × 59122 × MIR604 × 1507 × GA21 and subcombinations	07.07.2011	26.08.2016	27.01.2017 (o)	27.03.2017 (o)	04.07.2017
Maize Bt11 × MIR162 × MIR604 × 1507 × 5307 × GA21 and subcombinations	16.12.2011	05.04.2019	16.09.2019 (o)	11.10.2019 (o)	28.11.2019
Maize MON 87427 (MON-87427-7) [b]	21.06.2012	19.06.2015	14.09.2015 (o)	10.11.2015 (o)	04.12.2015
MON 89034 × 1507 × NK603 × DAS-40278-9 and subcombinations	11.01.2013	16.01.2019	12.07.2019 (o)	16.09.2019 (o)	28.11.2019
Maize MON 89034 × 1507 × MON 88017 × 59122 × DAS-40278-9 and subcombinations	06.02.2013	14.01.2019	12.07.2019 (o)	16.09.2019 (o)	28.11.2019
Maize MON 87427 × MON 89034 × NK603	13.09.2013	01.08.2017	16.01.2018 (o)	26.02.2018 (o)	03.08.2018
Maize MON 87427 × MON 89034 × 1507 × MON 88017 × 59122 and subcombinations	26.11.2013	01.08.2017	11.09.2018 (o)	22.10.2018 (o)	19.12.2018
Maize 4114 (DP-ØØ4114-3)	27.11.2014	24.05.2018	14.01.2019 (o)	22.02.2019 (o)	26.07.2019
Maize MON 87411 (MON-87411-9)	10.02.2015	28.06.2018	14.01.2019 (o)	22.02.2019 (o)	26.07.2019

Maize MON 87403 (MON-874Ø3-1)	26.06.2015	28.03.2018	03.12.2018 (o)	14.01.2019 (o)	26.07.2019
Maize 1507 × MIR162 × MON810 × NK603 and subcombinations	18.12.2015	13.01.2021	17.05.2021 (o)	06.07.2021 (o)	17.08.2021
Maize MON 87427 × MON 89034 × MIR162 × NK603 and subcombinations	18.02.2016	08.07.2019	15.09.2020 (o)	12.11.2020 (o)	22.01.2021
Maize MZHG0JG (SYN-ØØØJG-2)	27.09.2016	14.11.2018	30.04.2019 (o)	05.06.2019 (o)	28.11.2019
Maize MON 87427 × MON 87460 × MON 89034 × MIR162 × NK603 and subcombinations	30.11.2016	08.08.2019	15.09.2020 (o)	12.11.2020 (o)	22.01.2021
Maize MON 87427 × MON 87460 × MON 89034 × 1507 × MON 87411 × 59122 and subcombinations	21.02.2017	19.01.2021	08.06.2021 (o)	22.07.2021 (o)	17.08.2021
Maize MZIR098 (SYN-ØØØ98-3)	02.05.2017	26.06.2020	16.12.2020 (o)	26.02.2021 (o)	17.08.2021
Maize MON 87427 × MON 89034 × MIR162 × MON 87411 and subcombinations	24.05.2017	07.11.2019	07.10.2020 (o)	03.12.2020 (o)	22.01.2021
Maize DP4114 × MON 810 × MIR604 × NK603 and subcombinations	08.05.2018	07.03.2022	16.05.2022 (?)	-	-
Maize NK603 × T25 × DAS-40278-9 and its sub-combination T25 × DAS-40278-9	13.12.2019	13.12.2021	01.04.2022 (o)	26.04.2022 (o)	19.05.2022
GM Soybean					
Soybean 305423 × 40-3-2 (DP-3Ø5423-1 × MON-Ø4Ø32-6)	24.09.2007	18.08.2016	14.09.2017 (o)	19.10.2017 (o)	21.12.2017

(continued)

Table 4.1 (continued)

Products containing, consisting of, or produced from	EFSA		European Commission		
	Application [a]	Opinion published	SCoPAFF (decision +/o/-)	Appeal Committee (decision +/o/-)	Decision
Soybean MON 87769 × MON 89788	30.07.2010	08.10.2015 12.05.2021 (complementary statement)	16.02.2022 (o)	05.04.2022 (o)	19.05.2022
Soybean DAS-68416-4	25.01.2011	16.03.2017	12.06.2017 (o)	12.07.2017 (o)	21.12.2017
Soybean FG72	24.06.2011	16.07.2015	18.11.2015 (o)	11.01.2016 (o)	22.07.2016
Soybean MON 87705 × MON 89788	17.08.2011	16.07.2015	18.11.2015 (o)	11.01.2016 (o)	22.07.2016
Soybean DAS-44406-6	16.02.2012	21.03.2017	17.07.2017 (o)	14.09.2017 (o)	21.12.2017
Soybean MON 87708 × MON 89788	29.03.2012	18.06.2015	18.11.2015 (o)	11.01.2016 (o)	22.07.2016
Soybean SYHT0H2 (SYN-ØØØH2-5)	08.08.2012	20.01.2020	15.09.2020 (o)	12.11.2020 (o)	22.01.2021
Soybean DAS-81419-2	13.05.2013	05.12.2016	17.05.2021 (o)	06.07.2021 (o)	17.08.2021
Soybean FG72 × A5547-127	10.12.2013	06.04.2017	17.07.2017 (o)	14.09.2017 (o)	21.12.2017
Soybean MON 87751 (MON-87751-7)	08.10.2014	02.08.2018	07.03.2019 (o)	11.04.2019 (o)	26.07.2019

Soybean MON 87705 × MON 87708 × MON89788	16.09.2015	18.05.2020	15.09.2020 (presentation by EFSA) Vote pending	–	–
Soybean GMB151 (BCS-GM151-6)	09.10.2018	19.04.2021	20.01.2022 (o)	03.03.2022 (o)	31.03.2022
Soybean DAS-81419-2 × DAS-44406-6	02.03.2016	20.11.2020	17.05.2021 (o)	06.07.2021 (o)	17.08.2021
Soybean MON 87751 × MON 87701 × MON 87708 × MON 89788	23.12.2015	11.11.2019	07.10.2020 (o)	03.12.2020 (o)	22.01.2021
Soybean MON 87708 × MON 89788 × A5547-127	03.11.2016	05.07.2019	09.12.2019 (o)	23.01.2020 (o)	28.09.2020

[a] The application date is displayed in the respective EFSA Opinion
[b] Authorisation for the plant as such and not for products containing, consisting of, or produced from the GM plant

Table 4.2 Authorisation procedures under Directive 2001/18/EC

	National Competent Authority		EFSA	European Commission		
	Application	Assessment report	Opinion	SCoPAFF/Regulatory Committee 2001/18/EC (decision +/o/-)	Appeal Committee (decision +/o/-)	Decision
Carnation (*Dianthus caryophyllus L.*, line 26407) genetically modified for flower colour	17.03.2009	30.06.2009	12.12.2014	16.03.2015 (o)	31.03.2015 (o)	24.04.2015
Carnation (Dianthus caryophyllus L., line 25958) genetically modified for flower colour	17.03.2009	30.06.2009	12.12.2014	16.03.2015 (o)	31.03.2015 (o)	24.04.2015
Carnation (*Dianthus caryophyllus L.*, line FLO-40685-2) (FLORIGENE®Moonvista™)	21.10.2013	17.04.2014	19.04.2016	18.10.2018 (o)	07.12.2018 (o)	26.07.2019
Carnation (*Dianthus caryophyllus L.*, line SHD-27531-4)	13.03.2013	15.07.2013	10.11.2014	25.04.2016 (o)	02.06.2016 (o)	22.11.2016
Maize 1507 (DAS-Ø15Ø7-1) seeds [a]	No information	No information	No information	27.01.2017 (o)	27.03.2017 (o)	–
Maize Bt11 (SYN-BTØ11-1) seeds [a]	No information	No information	No information	27.01.2017 (o)	27.03.2017 (o)	–

[a] There is no information about the Commission's decision on the two maize seed varieties that passed the Appeal Committee in 2017

Table 4.3 Authorisation procedures under Regulation 1829/2003

	EFSA Opinion	European Commission decision
COTTON		
Cotton MON 15985	Scientific Opinion on applications (EFSA-GMO-UK-2008-57 and EFSA-GMO-RX-MON15985) for the placing on the market of insect-resistant genetically modified cotton MON 15985 for food and feed uses, import and processing, and for the renewal of authorisation of existing products produced from cotton MON 15985, both under Regulation (EC) No 1829/2003 from Monsanto (https://efsa.onlinelibrary.wiley.com/doi/epdf/10.2903/j.efsa.2014.3770, last accessed 13 August 2022)	*Commission Implementing Decision (EU) 2015/685 of 24 April 2015 authorising the placing on the market of genetically modified cotton MON 15985 (MON-15985-7) and renewing the authorisation for existing genetically modified cotton MON 15985 (MON-15985-7) products pursuant to Regulation (EC) No 1829/2003 of the European Parliament and of the Council*, OJ EU 2015, L 112/11
Cotton 281-24-236 × 3006-210-23 × MON 88913 (DAS-24236-5×DAS-21Ø23-5×MON-88913-8)	Scientific Opinion on an application by DowAgrosciences LLC (EFSA-GMO-NL-2009-68) for placing on the market of cotton 281-24-23633006-210-233MON 88913 for food and feed uses, import and processing under Regulation (EC) No 1829/2003 (https://efsa.onlinelibrary.wiley.com/doi/epdf/10.2903/j.efsa.2016.4430, last accessed 13 August 2022)	*Commission Implementing Decision (EU) 2017/1211 of 4 July 2017 authorising the placing on the market of products containing, consisting of, or produced from genetically modified cotton 281-24-236 × 3006-210-23 × MON 88913 (DAS-24236-5 × DAS-21Ø23-5 × MON-88913-8) pursuant to Regulation (EC) No 1829/2003 of the European Parliament and of the Council*, OJ EU 2017, L 173/38
Cotton GHB614 × LLcotton25 × MON 15985	Assessment of genetically modified cotton GHB6143 × LLCotton25 × MON 15985 for food and feed uses, under Regulation (EC) No 1829/2003 (application EFSA-GMO-NL-2011-94) (https://efsa.onlinelibrary.wiley.com/doi/epdf/10.2903/j.efsa.2018.5213, last accessed 13 August 2022)	*Commission Implementing Decision (EU) 2019/1302 of 26 July 2019 authorising the placing on the market of products containing, consisting of or produced from genetically modified cotton GHB614 × LLCotton25 × MON 15985 pursuant to Regulation (EC) No 1829/2003 of the European Parliament and of the Council*, OJ EU 2019, L 204/54

(continued)

Table 4.3 (continued)

	EFSA Opinion	European Commission decision
Cotton GHB119 (BCS-GHØØ5-8)	Scientific opinion on application (EFSA-GMO-NL-2011-96) for the placing on the market of genetically modified insect-resistant and herbicide-tolerant cotton GHB119,for food and feed uses, import and processing under Regulation (EC) No 1829/2003 from Bayer CropScience AG (https://efsa.onlinelibrary.wiley.com/doi/epdf/10.2903/j.efsa.2016.4586, last accessed 13 August 2022)	*Commission Implementing Decision (EU) 2017/1208 of 4 July 2017 authorising the placing on the market of products containing, consisting of, or produced from genetically modified cotton GHB119 (BCS-GHØØ5-8) pursuant to Regulation (EC) No 1829/2003 of the European Parliament and of the Council on genetically modified food and feed*, OJ EU 2017, L 173/23
Cotton GHB614 × T304-40 × GHB119	Assessment of genetically modified cotton GHB6143 × T304403 × GHB119 for food and feed uses, import and processing under Regulation (EC) No 1829/2003 (application EFSA-GMO-NL-2014-122) (https://efsa.onlinelibrary.wiley.com/doi/epdf/10.2903/j.efsa.2018.5349, last accessed 13 August 2022)	*Commission Implementing Decision (EU) 2021/1389 of 17 August 2021 authorising the placing on the market of products containing, consisting of or produced from genetically modified cotton GHB614 × T304-40 × GHB119 pursuant to Regulation (EC) No 1829/2003 of the European Parliament and of the Council*, OJ EU 2021, L 300/29
Cotton GHB811 (BCS-GH811-4)	Assessment of genetically modified cotton GHB811 for food and feed uses, under Regulation (EC) No 1829/2003(application EFSA-GMO-ES-2018-154) (https://efsa.onlinelibrary.wiley.com/doi/epdf/10.2903/j.efsa.2021.6781, last accessed 13 August 2022)	*Commission Implementing Decision (EU) 2022/530 of 31 March 2022 authorising the placing on the market of products containing, consisting of or produced from genetically modified cotton GHB811 (BCS-GH811-4), pursuant to Regulation (EC) No 1829/2003 of the European Parliament and of the Council*, OJ 2022, L 105/45

MAIZE		
Maize Bt11 × MIR162 × MIR604 × GA21 and subcombinations	Scientific Opinion on an application by Syngenta (EFSA-GMO-DE-2009-66) for placing on the market of herbicide tolerant and insect resistant maize Bt11 × MIR162 × MIR604 × GA21 and subcombinations independently of their origin for food and feed uses, import and processing under Regulation (EC) No 1829/2003 (https://efsa.onlinelibrary.wiley.com/doi/epdf/10.2903/j.efsa.2015.4297, last accessed 13 August 2022)	*Commission Implementing Decision (EU) 2016/1685 of 16 September 2016 authorising the placing on the market of products containing, consisting of, or produced from genetically modified maize Bt11 × MIR162 × MIR604 × GA21, and genetically modified maizes combining two or three of the events Bt11, MIR162, MIR604 and GA21, and repealing Decisions 2010/426/EU, 2011/892/EU, 2011/893/EU and 2011/894/EU*, OJ 2016, L 254/22
Maize NK603 × T25	Scientific Opinion on an application (EFSA-GMO-NL-2010-80) for the placing on the market of herbicide-tolerant genetically modified maize NK603 × T25 for food and feed uses, import and processing under Regulation (EC) No 1829/2003 from Monsanto (https://efsa.onlinelibrary.wiley.com/doi/epdf/10.2903/j.efsa.2015.4165, last accessed 13 August 2022)	*Commission Implementing Decision (EU) 2015/2279 of 4 December 2015 authorising the placing on the market of products containing, consisting of, or produced from genetically modified maize NK603 × T25 (MON-ØØ6Ø3-6 × ACS-ZMØØ3-2) pursuant to Regulation (EC) No 1829/2003 of the European Parliament and of the Council*, OJ EU 2015, L 322/58
Maize Bt11 × MIR162 × 1507 × GA21 and subcombinations	Assessment of genetically modified maize Bt11 × MIR162 × 1507 × GA21 and three subcombinations independently of their origin, for food and feed uses under Regulation (EC) No 1829/2003 (application EFSA-GMO-DE-2010-86) (https://efsa.onlinelibrary.wiley.com/doi/epdf/10.2903/j.efsa.2018.5309, last accessed 13 August 2022)	*Commission Implementing Decision (EU) 2019/1305 of 26 July 2019 authorising the placing on the market of products containing, consisting of or produced from genetically modified maize Bt11 × MIR162 × 1507 × GA21 and sub-combinations Bt11 × MIR162 × 1507, MIR162 × 1507 × GA21 and MIR162 × 1507 pursuant to Regulation (EC) No 1829/2003 of the European Parliament and of the Council*, OJ EU 2019, L 204/69

(continued)

Table 4.3 (continued)

	EFSA Opinion	European Commission decision
Maize DAS-40278-9	Scientific Opinion on an application by DOW AgroSciences LLC (EFSA-GMO-NL-2010-89) for placing on the market the genetically modified herbicide-tolerant maize DAS-40278-9for food and feed uses, import and processing under Regulation (EC) No 1829/2003 (https://efsa.onlinelibrary.wiley.com/doi/epdf/10.2903/j.efsa.2016.4633, last accessed 13 August 2022)	*Commission Implementing Decision (EU) 2017/1212 of 4 July 2017 authorising the placing on the market of products containing, consisting of, or produced from genetically modified maize DAS-40278-9, pursuant to Regulation (EC) No 1829/2003 of the European parliament and of the Council on genetically modified food and feed*, OJ EU 2017, L 173/43
Maize 1507 × 59122 × MON 810 × NK603 and sub-combinations	Assessment of genetically modified maize1507 × 59122 × MON810 × NK603 and subcombinations, for food and feed uses, under Regulation (EC) No 1829/2003 (application EFSA-GMO-NL-2011-92) (https://efsa.onlinelibrary.wiley.com/doi/epdf/10.2903/j.efsa.2017.5000, last accessed 13 August 2022)	*Commission Implementing Decision (EU) 2018/1110 of 3 August 2018 authorising the placing on the market of products containing, consisting of, or produced from genetically modified maize 1507 × 59122 × MON 810 × NK603, and genetically modified maize combining two or three of the single events 1507, 59122, MON 810 and NK603, and repealing Decisions 2009/815/EC, 2010/428/EU and 2010/432/EU*, OJ EU 2018, L 203/13
Maize 5307 (SYN-Ø53Ø7-1)	Scientific Opinion on application (EFSA-GMO-DE-2011-95) for the placing on the market of genetically modified maize 5307 for food and feed uses, import and processing under Regulation (EC) No 1829/2003 from Syngenta Crop Protection AG (https://efsa.onlinelibrary.wiley.com/doi/epdf/10.2903/j.efsa.2015.4083, last accessed 13 August 2022)	*Commission Implementing Decision (EU) 2019/1303 of 26 July 2019 authorising the placing on the market of products containing, consisting of or produced from genetically modified maize 5307 (SYN-Ø53Ø7-1), pursuant to Regulation (EC) No 1829/2003 of the European Parliament and of the Council on genetically modified food and feed*, OJ EU 2019, L 204/60

Maize Bt11 × 59122 × MIR604 × 1507 × GA21 and subcombinations	Scientific Opinion on an application by Syngenta (EFSA-GMO-DE-2011-99) for the placing on the market of maize Bt11 × 59122 × MIR604 × 1507 × GA21 and twenty subcombinations, which have not been authorised previously independently of their origin, for food and feed uses, import and processing under Regulation (EC) No 1829/2003 (https://efsa.onlinelibrary.wiley.com/doi/epdf/10.2903/j.efsa.2016.4567, last accessed 13 August 2022)	*Commission Implementing Decision (EU) 2017/1209 of 4 July 2017 authorising the placing on the market of products containing, consisting of, or produced from genetically modified maize Bt11 × 59122 × MIR604 × 1507 × GA21, and genetically modified maize combining two, three or four of the events Bt11, 59122, MIR604, 1507 and GA21 pursuant to Regulation (EC) No 1829/2003 of the European parliament and of the Council on genetically modified food and feed*, OJ EU 2017, L 173/28
Maize Bt11 × MIR162 × MIR604 × 1507 × 5307 × GA21 and subcombinations	Assessment of genetically modified maize Bt11 × MIR162 × MIR604 × 1507 × 5307 × GA21 and subcombinations, for food and feed uses, under Regulation (EC) No 1829/2003 (application EFSA-GMO-DE-2011-103) (https://efsa.onlinelibrary.wiley.com/doi/epdf/10.2903/j.efsa.2019.5635, last accessed 13 August 2022)	*Commission Implementing Decision (EU) 2019/2087 of 28 November 2019 authorising the placing on the market of products containing, consisting of or produced from genetically modified maize Bt11 × MIR162 × MIR604 × 1507 × 5307 × GA21 and genetically modified maize combining two, three, four or five of the single events Bt11, MIR162, MIR604, 1507, 5307 and GA21 pursuant to Regulation (EC) No 1829/2003 of the European Parliament and of the Council*, OJ EU 2019, L 316/94
Maize MON 87427 (MON-87427-7)	Scientific Opinion on the application (EFSA-GMO-BE-2012-110) for the placing on the market of tissue-selective herbicide-tolerant genetically modified maize MON 87427 for food and feed uses, import and processing under Regulation (EC) No 1829/2003 from Monsanto (https://efsa.onlinelibrary.wiley.com/doi/epdf/10.2903/j.efsa.2015.4130, last accessed 13 August 2022)	*Commission Implementing Decision (EU) 2015/2281 of 4 December 2015 authorising the placing on the market of products containing, consisting of, or produced from genetically modified maize MON 87427 (MON-87427-7) pursuant to Regulation (EC) No 1829/2003 of the European Parliament and of the Council*, OJ EU 2015, L 322/67

(continued)

Table 4.3 (continued)

	EFSA Opinion	European Commission decision
MON 89034 × 1507 × NK603 × DAS-40278-9 and subcombinations	Assessment of genetically modified maize MON 89034 × 1507 × NK603 × DAS-40278-9 and subcombinations independently of their origin for food and feed uses, import and processing, under Regulation (EC) No 1829-2003 (application EFSA-GMO-NL-2013-112) (https://efsa.onlinelibrary.wiley.com/doi/epdf/10.2903/j.efsa.2019.5522, last accessed 13 August 2022)	*Commission Implementing Decision (EU) 2019/2085 of 28 November 2019 authorising the placing on the market of products containing, consisting of or produced from genetically modified maize MON 89034 × 1507 × NK603 × DAS-40278-9 and sub-combinations MON 89034 × NK603 × DAS-40278-9, 1507 × NK603 × DAS-40278-9 and NK603 × DAS-40278-9 pursuant to Regulation (EC) No 1829/2003 of the European Parliament and of the Council*, OJ EU 2019, L 316/80
Maize MON 89034 × 1507 × MON 88017 × 59122 × DAS-40278-9 and subcombinations	Assessment of genetically modified maize MON 89034 × 1507 × MON 88017 × 59122 × DAS-40278-9and subcombinations independently of their origin for food and feed uses, import and processing under Regulation (EC) No 1829/2003 (application EFSA-GMO-NL-2013-113) (https://efsa.onlinelibrary.wiley.com/doi/epdf/10.2903/j.efsa.2019.5521, last accessed 13 August 2022)	*Commission Implementing Decision (EU) 2019/2086 of 28 November 2019 authorising the placing on the market of products containing, consisting of or produced from genetically modified maize MON 89034 × 1507 × MON 88017 × 59122 × DAS-40278-9 and genetically modified maize combining two, three or four of the single events MON 89034, 1507, MON 88017, 59122 and DAS-40278-9 pursuant to Regulation (EC) No 1829/2003 of the European Parliament and of the Council*, OJ EU 2019, L 316/87

Maize MON 87427 × MON 89034 × NK603	Scientific Opinion on application EFSA-GMO-BE-2013-117for authorisation of genetically modified maize MON 87427 × MON 89034 × NK603 and subcombinations independently of their origin, for food and feed uses, import and processing submitted under Regulation (EC) No1829/2003 by Monsanto Company (https://efsa.onlinelibrary.wiley.com/doi/epdf/10.2903/j.efsa.2017.4922, last accessed 13 August 2022)	*Commission Implementing Decision (EU) 2018/1111 of 3 August 2018 authorising the placing on the market of products containing, consisting of, or produced from genetically modified maize MON 87427 × MON 89034 × NK603 (MON-87427-7 × MON-89Ø34-3 × MON-ØØ6Ø3-6) and genetically modified maize combining two of the events MON 87427, MON 89034 and NK603, and repealing Decision 2010/420/EU*, OJ EU 2018, L 203/20 *Commission Implementing Decision (EU) 2021/60 of 22 January 2021 authorising the placing on the market of products containing, consisting of or produced from genetically modified maize MON 87427 × MON 89034 × MIR162 × NK603 and genetically modified* *maize combining two or three of the single events MON 87427, MON 89034, MIR162 and NK603, and repealing Implementing Decision (EU) 2018/1111 pursuant to Regulation (EC) No 1829/2003 of the European Parliament and of the Council*, OJ EU 2021, L 26/5

(continued)

Table 4.3 (continued)

	EFSA Opinion	European Commission decision
Maize MON 87427 × MON 89034 × 1507 × MON 88017 × 59122 and subcombinations	Scientific Opinion on application EFSA-GMO-BE-2013-118for authorisation of genetically modified maize MON 87427 × MON 89034 × 1507 × MON 88017 × 59122and subcombinations independently of their origin, for food and feed uses, import and processing submitted under Regulation (EC) No 1829/2003 by Monsanto Company (https://efsa.onlinelibrary.wiley.com/doi/epdf/10.2903/j.efsa.2017.4921, last accessed 13 August 2022)	*Commission Implementing Decision (EU) 2018/2046 of 19 December 2018 authorising the placing on the market of products containing, consisting of or produced from genetically modified maize MON 87427 × MON 89034 × 1507 × MON 88017 × 59122, and genetically modified maize combining two, three or four of the single events MON 87427, MON 89034, 1507, MON 88017 and 59122 and repealing Decision 2011/366/EU*, OJ EU 2018, L 327/70
Maize 4114 (DP-ØØ4114-3)	Assessment of genetically modified maize 4114 for food and feed uses, under Regulation (EC) No 1829/2003 (application EFSA-GMO-NL-2014-123) (https://efsa.onlinelibrary.wiley.com/doi/epdf/10.2903/j.efsa.2018.5280, last accessed 13 August 2022)	*Commission Implementing Decision (EU) 2019/1304 of 26 July 2019 authorising the placing on the market of products containing, consisting of or produced from genetically modified maize 4114 (DP-ØØ4114-3), pursuant to Regulation (EC) No 1829/2003 of the European Parliament and of the Council*, OJ EU 2019, L 204/65
Maize MON 87411 (MON-87411-9)	Assessment of genetically modified maize MON 87411 for food and feed uses, import and processing, under Regulation (EC) No 1829/2003 (application EFSA-GMO-NL-2015-124) (https://efsa.onlinelibrary.wiley.com/doi/epdf/10.2903/j.efsa.2018.5310, last accessed 13 August 2022)	*Commission Implementing Decision (EU) 2019/1308 of 26 July 2019 authorising the placing on the market of products containing, consisting of or produced from genetically modified maize MON 87411 (MON-87411-9), pursuant to Regulation (EC) No 1829/2003 of the European Parliament and of the Council*, OJ EU 2019, L 204/85

Maize MON 87403 (MON-874Ø3-1)	Assessment of genetically modified maize MON 87403 for food and feed uses, import and processing, under Regulation (EC) No 1829/2003 (applicationEFSA-GMO-BE-2015-125) (https://efsa.onlinelibrary.wiley.com/doi/epdf/10.2903/j.efsa.2018.5225, last accessed 13 August 2022)	*Commission Implementing Decision (EU) 2019/1307 of 26 July 2019 authorising the placing on the market of products containing, consisting of or produced from genetically modified maize MON 87403 (MON-874Ø3-1), pursuant to Regulation (EC) No 1829/2003 of the European Parliament and of the Council*, OJ EU 2019, L 204/81
Maize 1507 × MIR162 × MON810 × NK603 and subcombinations	Assessment of genetically modified maize 1507 × MIR162 × MON810 × NK603 and subcombinations, for food and feed uses, under Regulation (EC) No 1829/2003(application EFSA-GMO-NL-2015-127) (https://efsa.onlinelibrary.wiley.com/doi/epdf/10.2903/j.efsa.2021.6348, last accessed 13 August 2022)	*Commission Implementing Decision (EU) 2021/1388 of 17 August 2021 authorising the placing on the market of products containing, consisting of or produced from genetically modified maize 1507 × MIR162 × MON810 × NK603 and genetically modified maize combining two or three of the single events 1507, MIR162, MON810 and NK603, pursuant to Regulation (EC) No 1829/2003 of the European Parliament and of the Council*, OJ EU 2021, L 300/22
Maize MON 87427 × MON 89034 × MIR162 × NK603 and subcombinations	Assessment of genetically modified maize MON 87427 × MON 89034 × MIR 162 × NK 603 and subcombinations, for food and feed uses, under Regulation(EC) No 1829/2003 (application EFSA-GMO-NL-2016-131) (https://efsa.onlinelibrary.wiley.com/doi/epdf/10.2903/j.efsa.2019.5734, last accessed 13 August 2022)	*Commission Implementing Decision (EU) 2021/60 of 22 January 2021 authorising the placing on the market of products containing, consisting of or produced from genetically modified maize MON 87427 × MON 89034 × MIR162 × NK603 and genetically modified maize combining two or three of the single events MON 87427, MON 89034, MIR162 and NK603, and repealing Implementing Decision (EU) 2018/1111 pursuant to Regulation (EC) No 1829/2003 of the European Parliament and of the Council*, OJ EU 2021, L 26/5

(continued)

Table 4.3 (continued)

	EFSA Opinion	European Commission decision
Maize MZHG0JG (SYN-ØØØJG-2)	Assessment of genetically modified maize MZHG0JG for food and feed uses, import and processing under Regulation (EC) No 1829/2003 (applicationEFSA-GMO-DE-2016-133) (https://efsa.onlinelibrary.wiley.com/doi/epdf/10.2903/j.efsa.2018.5469, last accessed 13 August 2022)	*Commission Implementing Decision (EU) 2019/2080 of 28 November 2019 authorising the placing on the market of products containing, consisting of or produced from genetically modified maize MZHG0JG (SYN-ØØØJG-2), pursuant to Regulation (EC) No 1829/2003 of the European Parliament and of the Council*, OJ EU 2019, L 316/51
Maize MON 87427 × MON 87460 × MON 89034 × MIR162 × NK603 and subcombinations	Assessment of genetically modified maize MON 87427 × MON 87460 × MON 89034 × MIR162 × NK603 and subcombinations, for food and feed uses, under Regulation(EC) No 1829/2003 (application EFSA-GMO-NL-2016-134) (https://efsa.onlinelibrary.wiley.com/doi/epdf/10.2903/j.efsa.2019.5774, last accessed 13 August 2022)	*Commission Implementing Decision (EU) 2021/61 of 22 January 2021 authorising the placing on the market of products containing, consisting of or produced from genetically modified maize MON 87427 × MON 87460 × MON 89034 × MIR162 × NK603 and* *genetically modified maize combining two, three or four of the single events MON 87427, MON 87460, MON 89034, MIR162 and NK603, pursuant to Regulation (EC) No 1829/2003 of the European Parliament and of the Council*, OJ EU 2021, L 26/12
Maize MON 87427 × MON 87460 × MON 89034 × 1507 × MON 87411 × 59122 and subcombinations	Assessment of genetically modified maize MON 87427 × MON 87460 × MON 89034 × 1507 × MON 87411 × 59122 and subcombinations, for food and feed uses, under Regulation (EC) No 1829/2003 (applicationEFSA-GMO-NL-2017-139) (https://efsa.onlinelibrary.wiley.com/doi/epdf/10.2903/j.efsa.2021.6351, last accessed 13 August 2022)	*Commission Implementing Decision (EU) 2021/1394 of 17 August 2021 authorising the placing on the market of products containing, consisting of or produced from genetically modified maize MON 87427 × MON 87460 × MON 89034 × 1507 × MON 87411 × 59122* *and genetically modified maize combining two, three, four or five of the single events MON 87427, MON 87460, MON 89034, 1507, MON 87411 and 59122, pursuant to Regulation (EC) No 1829/2003 of the European Parliament and of the Council*, OJ EU 2021, L 300/60

Maize MZIR098 (SYN-ØØØ98-3)	Assessment of genetically modified maize MZIR098 for food and feed uses, under Regulation (EC) No 1829/2003 (application EFSA-GMO-DE-2017-142) (https://efsa.onlinelibrary.wiley.com/doi/epdf/10.2903/j.efsa.2020.6171, last accessed 13 August 2022)	*Commission Implementing Decision (EU) 2021/1390 of 17 August 2021 authorising the placing on the market of products containing, consisting of or produced from genetically modified maize MZIR098 (SYN-ØØØ98-3), pursuant to Regulation (EC) No 1829/2003 of the European Parliament and of the Council*, OJ EU 2021, L 300/35
Maize MON 87427 × MON 89034 × MIR162 × MON 87411 and subcombinations	Assessment of genetically modified maize MON 87427 × MON 89034 × MIR162 × MON 87411 and subcombinations, for food and feed uses, under Regulation(EC) No 1829/2003 (application EFSA-GMO-NL-2017-144) (https://efsa.onlinelibrary.wiley.com/doi/epdf/10.2903/j.efsa.2019.5848, last accessed 13 August 2022)	*Commission Implementing Decision (EU) 2021/65 of 22 January 2021 authorising the placing on the market of products containing, consisting of or produced from genetically modified maize MON 87427 × MON 89034 × MIR162 × MON 87411 and genetically modified maize combining two or three of the single events MON 87427, MON 89034, MIR162 and MON 87411 pursuant to Regulation (EC) No 1829/2003 of the European Parliament and of the Council*, OJ EU 2021, L 26/37
Maize DP4114 × MON 810 × MIR604 × NK603 and subcombinations	Assessment of genetically modified maize DP4114 × MON810 × MIR604 × NK603 and subcombinations, for food and feed uses, under Regulation (EC) No 1829/2003(application EFSA-GMO-NL-2018-150) (https://efsa.onlinelibrary.wiley.com/doi/epdf/10.2903/j.efsa.2022.7134, last accessed 13 August 2022)	No decision until now

(continued)

Table 4.3 (continued)

	EFSA Opinion	European Commission decision
Maize NK603 × T25 × DAS-40278-9 and its sub-combination T25 × DAS-40278-9	Assessment of genetically modified maize NK603 × T25 × DAS-40278-9 and subcombinations, for food and feed uses, under Regulation (EC) No 1829/2003 (application EFSA-GMO-NL-2019-164) (https://efsa.onlinelibrary.wiley.com/doi/epdf/10.2903/j.efsa.2021.6942, last accessed 13 August 2022)	*Commission Implementing Decision (EU) 2022/797 of 19 May 2022 authorising the placing on the market of products containing, consisting of or produced from genetically modified maize NK603 × T25 × DAS-40278-9 and its sub-combination T25 × DAS-40278-9, pursuant to Regulation (EC) No 1829/2003 of the European Parliament and of the Council*, OJ EU 2022, L 141/116
SOYBEANS		
Soybean 305423 × 40-3-2 (DP-3Ø5423-1 × MON-Ø4Ø32-6)	Scientific Opinion on an application by Pioneer(EFSA-GMO-NL-2007-47) for the placing on the market of the herbicide-tolerant, high-oleic acid, genetically modified soybean 305423340-3-2 for food and feed uses, import and processing under Regulation (EC) No 1829/2003 (https://efsa.onlinelibrary.wiley.com/doi/epdf/10.2903/j.efsa.2016.4566, last accessed 13 August 2022)	*Commission Implementing Decision (EU) 2017/2448 of 21 December 2017 authorising the placing on the market of products containing, consisting of, or produced from genetically modified soybean 305423 × 40-3-2 (DP-3Ø5423-1 × MON-Ø4Ø32-6) pursuant to Regulation (EC) No 1829/2003 of the European Parliament and of the Council on genetically modified food and feed*, OJ EU 2017, L 346/6

Soybean MON 87769 × MON 89788	Scientific Opinion on an application (EFSA-GMO-NL-2010-85) for the placing on the market of MON 87769 × MON 89788 soybean, genetically modified to contain stearidonic acid and be tolerant to glyphosate for food and feed uses, import and processing under Regulation (EC) No 1829/2003 from Monsanto (no full risk assessment has been conducted) (https://efsa.onlinelibrary.wiley.com/doi/epdf/10.2903/j.efsa.2015.4256, last accessed 13 August 2022) Statement complementing the EFSA Scientific Opinion on application (EFSA-GMO-NL-2010-85) for authorisation of food and feed containing, consisting of and produced from genetically modified soybean MON 877693MON 89788 (https://efsa.onlinelibrary.wiley.com/doi/epdf/10.2903/j.efsa.2021.6589, last accessed 13 August 2022)	*Commission Implementing Decision (EU) 2022/798 of 19 May 2022 authorising the placing on the market of products containing, consisting of or produced from genetically modified soybean MON 87769 × MON 89788 pursuant to Regulation (EC) No 1829/2003 of the European Parliament and of the Council*, OJ EU 2022, L 141/123
Soybean DAS-68416-4	Scientific Opinion on an application by Dow AgroSciences LLC (EFSA-GMO-NL-2011-91) for the placing on the market of genetically modified herbicide-tolerant soybeanDAS-68416-4 for food and feed uses, import and processing under Regulation (EC) No 1829/2003 (https://efsa.onlinelibrary.wiley.com/doi/epdf/10.2903/j.efsa.2017.4719, last accessed 13 August 2022)	*Commission Implementing Decision (EU) 2017/2449 of 21 December 2017 authorising the placing on the market of products containing, consisting of, or produced from genetically modified soybean DAS-68416-4, pursuant to Regulation (EC) No 1829/2003 of the European Parliament and of the Council on genetically modified food and feed*, OJ EU 2017, L 346/12

(continued)

Table 4.3 (continued)

	EFSA Opinion	European Commission decision
Soybean FG72	Scientific Opinion on an application (EFSA-GMO-BE-2011-98) for the placing on the market of herbicide-tolerant genetically modified soybean FG72 for food and feed uses, import and processing under Regulation (EC) No 1829/2003 from Bayer CropScience (https://efsa.onlinelibrary.wiley.com/doi/epdf/10.2903/j.efsa.2015.4167, last accessed 13 August 2022)	*Commission Implementing Decision (EU) 2016/1215 of 22 July 2016 authorising the placing on the market of products containing, consisting of, or produced from genetically modified soybean FG72 (MST-FGØ72-2) pursuant to Regulation (EC) No 1829/2003 of the European Parliament and of the Council*, OJ EU 2015, L 199/16
Soybean MON 87705 × MON 89788	Scientific Opinion on an application (Reference EFSA-GMO-NL-2011-100) for the placing on the market of the herbicide-tolerant, increased oleic acid genetically modified soybean MON 87705 × MON 89788 for food and feed uses, import and processing under Regulation (EC) No 1829/2003 from Monsanto (https://efsa.onlinelibrary.wiley.com/doi/epdf/10.2903/j.efsa.2015.4178, last accessed 13 August 2022)	*Commission Implementing Decision (EU) 2016/1217 of 22 July 2016 authorising the placing on the market of products containing, consisting of, or produced from genetically modified soybean MON 87705 × MON 89788 (MON-877Ø5-6 × MON-89788-1) pursuant to Regulation (EC) No 1829/2003 of the European Parliament and of the Council*, OJ EU 2016, L 199/28
Soybean DAS-44406-6	Scientific opinion on an application by Dow AgroSciences LLC (EFSA-GMO-NL-2012-106) for the placing on the market of genetically modified herbicide-tolerant soybeanDAS-44406-6 for food and feed uses, import and processing under Regulation (EC) No 1829/2003 (https://efsa.onlinelibrary.wiley.com/doi/epdf/10.2903/j.efsa.2017.4738, last accessed 13 August 2022)	*Commission Implementing Decision (EU) 2017/2450 of 21 December 2017 authorising the placing on the market of products containing, consisting of, or produced from genetically modified soybean DAS-44406-6, pursuant to Regulation (EC) No 1829/2003 of the European Parliament and of the Council on genetically modified food and feed*, OJ EU 2017, L 346/16

Soybean MON 87708 × MON 89788	Scientific Opinion on application (EFSA-GMO-NL-2012-108) for the placing on the market of the herbicide-tolerant genetically modified soybean MON 87708 × MON 89788 for food and feed uses, import and processing under Regulation (EC) No 1829/2003 from Monsanto (https://efsa.onlinelibrary.wiley.com/doi/epdf/10.2903/j.efsa.2015.4136, last accessed 13 August 2022)	*Commission Implementing Decision (EU) 2016/1216 of 22 July 2016 authorising the placing on the market of products containing, consisting of, or produced from genetically modified soybean MON 87708 × MON 89788 (MON-877Ø8-9 × MON-89788-1) pursuant to Regulation (EC) No 1829/2003 of the European Parliament and of the Council*, OJ EU 2016, L 199/22
Soybean SYHT0H2 (SYN-ØØØH2-5)	Assessment of genetically modified soybean SYHT0H2 for food and feed uses, import and processing, under Regulation (EC) No 1829/2003 (application EFSA-GMO-DE-2012-111) (https://efsa.onlinelibrary.wiley.com/doi/epdf/10.2903/j.efsa.2020.5946, last accessed 13 August 2022)	*Commission Implementing Decision (EU) 2021/64 of 22 January 2021 authorising the placing on the market of products containing, consisting of or produced from genetically modified soybean SYHT0H2 (SYN-ØØØH2-5), pursuant to Regulation (EC) No 1829/2003 of the European Parliament and of the Council*, OJ EU 2021, L 26/31
Soybean DAS-81419-2	Scientific Opinion on an application by Dow AgroSciences (EFSA-GMO-NL-2013-116) for placing on the market of genetically modified insect-resistant soybean DAS-81419-2 for food and feed uses, import and processing under Regulation (EC) No 1829/2003 (https://efsa.onlinelibrary.wiley.com/doi/epdf/10.2903/j.efsa.2016.4642, last accessed 13 August 2022)	*Commission Implementing Decision (EU) 2021/1386 of 17 August 2021 authorising the placing on the market of products containing, consisting of or produced from genetically modified soybean DAS-81419-2 pursuant to Regulation (EC) No 1829/2003 of the European Parliament and of the Council*, OJ EU 2021, L 300/10

(continued)

Table 4.3 (continued)

	EFSA Opinion	European Commission decision
Soybean FG72 × A5547-127	Scientific opinion on application EFSA-GMO-NL-2013-120 for authorisation of genetically modified soybean FG72 × A5547-127 for food and feed uses, import and processing submitted in accordance with Regulation (EC)No 1829/2003 by Bayer CropScience LP and M.S. Technologies LLC (https://efsa.onlinelibrary.wiley.com/doi/epdf/10.2903/j.efsa.2017.4744, last accessed 13 August 2022)	*Commission Implementing Decision (EU) 2017/2451 of 21 December 2017 authorising the placing on the market of products containing, consisting of, or produced from genetically modified soybean FG72 × A5547-127, pursuant to Regulation (EC) No 1829/2003 of the European Parliament and of the Council on genetically modified food and feed*, OJ EU 2017, L 346/20
Soybean MON 87751 (MON-87751-7)	Assessment of genetically modified soybean MON 87751 for food and feed uses under Regulation (EC) No 1829/2003(application EFSA-GMO-NL-2014-121) (https://efsa.onlinelibrary.wiley.com/doi/epdf/10.2903/j.efsa.2018.5346, last accessed 13 August 2022)	*Commission Implementing Decision (EU) 2019/1309 of 26 July 2019 authorising the placing on the market of products containing, consisting of or produced from genetically modified soybean MON 87751 (MON-87751-7), pursuant to Regulation (EC) No 1829/2003 of the European Parliament and of the Council*, OJ 2019, L 204/90
Soybean MON 87705 × MON 87708 × MON89788	Assessment of genetically modified soybean MON 87705 × MON 87708 × MON 89788, for food and feed uses, under Regulation (EC) No 1829/2003 (applicationEFSA-GMO-NL-2015-126) (https://efsa.onlinelibrary.wiley.com/doi/epdf/10.2903/j.efsa.2020.6111, last accessed 13 August 2022)	No decision until now
Soybean GMB151 (BCS-GM151-6)	Assessment of genetically modified soybean GMB151 for food and feed uses, under Regulation (EC) No 1829/2003 (application EFSA-GMO-NL-2018-153) (https://efsa.onlinelibrary.wiley.com/doi/epdf/10.2903/j.efsa.2021.6424, last accessed 13 August 2022)	*Commission Implementing Decision (EU) 2022/531 of 31 March 2022 authorising the placing on the market of products containing, consisting of or produced from genetically modified soybean GMB151 (BCS-GM151-6) pursuant to Regulation (EC) No 1829/2003 of the European Parliament and of the Council*, OJ EU 2022, L 105/51

Soybean DAS-81419-2 × DAS-44406-6	Scientific Opinion on application EFSA-GMO-NL-2016-132 for authorisation of genetically modified of insect-resistant and herbicide-tolerant soybean DAS-81419-23DAS-44406-6 for food and feed uses, import and processing submitted in accordance with Regulation (EC)No 1829/2003 by Dow Agrosciences LCC (https://efsa.onlinelibrary.wiley.com/doi/epdf/10.2903/j.efsa.2020.6302, last accessed 13 August 2022)	*Commission Implementing Decision (EU) 2021/1387 of 17 August 2021 authorising the placing on the market of products containing, consisting of or produced from genetically modified soybean DAS-81419-2 × DAS-44406-6, pursuant to Regulation (EC) No 1829/2003 of the European Parliament and of the Council*, OJ EU 2017, L 300/16
Soybean MON 87751 × MON 87701 × MON 87708 × MON 89788	Assessment of genetically modified soybean MON 87751 × MON 87701 × MON 87708 × MON 89788 for food and feed uses, under Regulation (EC) No 1829/2003(application EFSA-GMO-NL-2016-128) (https://efsa.onlinelibrary.wiley.com/doi/epdf/10.2903/j.efsa.2019.5847, last accessed 13 August 2022)	*Commission Implementing Decision (EU) 2021/66 of 22 January 2021 authorising the placing on the market of products containing, consisting of or produced from genetically modified soybean MON 87751 × MON 87701 × MON 87708 × MON 89788, pursuant to Regulation (EC) No 1829/2003 of the European Parliament and of the Council*, OJ EU 2021, L 26/44
Soybean MON 87708 × MON 89788 × A5547-127	Assessment of genetically modified soybean MON87708 × MON 89788 × A5547-127, for food and feed uses, under Regulation (EC) No 1829/2003 (application EFSA-GMO-NL-2016-135) (https://efsa.onlinelibrary.wiley.com/doi/epdf/10.2903/j.efsa.2019.5733, last accessed 13 August 2022)	*Commission Implementing Decision (EU) 2020/1360 of 28 September 2020 authorising the placing on the market of products containing, consisting of or produced from genetically modified soybean MON 87708 × MON 89788 × A5547-127, pursuant to Regulation (EC) No 1829/2003 of the European Parliament and of the Council*, OJ EU 2020, L 316/1

Table 4.4 Authorisation procedures under Directive 2001/18/EC

	Assessment report national competent authority	EFSA Opinion	European Commission decision
Carnation (*Dianthus caryophyllus L.*, line 26407) genetically modified for flower colour	Dutch Competent Authority, Notification C/NL/09/02 (https://webgate.ec.europa.eu/fip/GMO_Registers/files/csnifs/C-NL-09-02_AssessmentReport.pdf?dt=20220608043214, last accessed 13 August 2022)	Scientific Opinion on a notification (reference C/NL/09/02) for the placing on the market of the genetically modified carnation IFD-26407-2 with a modified colour, for import of cut flowers for ornamental use, under Part C of Directive 2001/18/EC from Florigene (https://efsa.onlinelibrary.wiley.com/doi/epdf/10.2903/j.efsa.2014.3935, last accessed 13 August 2022)	*Commission Implementing Decision (EU) 2015/694 of 24 April 2015 concerning the placing on the market, in accordance with Directive 2001/18/EC of the European Parliament and of the Council, of a carnation (Dianthus caryophyllus L., line 26407) genetically modified for flower colour*, OJ EU 2015, L 112/52
Carnation (Dianthus caryophyllus L., line 25958) genetically modified for flower colour	Dutch Competent Authority, Notification C/NL/09/01 (https://webgate.ec.europa.eu/fip/GMO_Registers/files/csnifs/C-NL-09-01_AssessmentReport.pdf?dt=20220608043214, last accessed 13 August 2022)	Scientific Opinion on a notification (reference C/NL/09/01) for the placing on the market of the genetically modified carnation IFD-25958-3 with a modified colour, for import of cut flowers for ornamental use, under Part C of Directive 2001/18/EC from Florigene (https://efsa.onlinelibrary.wiley.com/doi/epdf/10.2903/j.efsa.2014.3934, last accessed 13 August 2022)	*Commission Implementing Decision (EU) 2015/692 of 24 April 2015 concerning the placing on the market, in accordance with Directive 2001/18/EC of the European Parliament and of the Council, of a carnation (Dianthus caryophyllus L., line 25958) genetically modified for flower colour*, OJ EU 2015, L 112/44

Carnation (*Dianthus caryophyllus L.*, line FLO-40685-2) (FLORIGENE®Moonvista™)	Dutch Competent Authority, NOTIFICATION C/NL/13/02 (https://webgate.ec.europa.eu/fip/GMO_Registers/files/csnifs/C-NL-13-02-Assessment-Report.pdf?dt=20220608043214, last accessed 13 August 2022)	Part C notification (reference C/NL/13/02) from Suntory Holdings Limited for the import, distribution and retailing of carnation FLO-40685-2 cut flowers with modified petal colour for ornamental use (https://efsa.onlinelibrary.wiley.com/doi/epdf/10.2903/j.efsa.2016.4431, last accessed 13 August 2022)	*Commission Implementing Decision (EU) 2019/1300 of 26 July 2019 as regards the placing on the market of a genetically modified carnation (Dianthus caryophyllus L., line FLO-40685-2)*, OJ EU 2019, L 204/46
Carnation (*Dianthus caryophyllus L.*, line SHD-27531-4)	Dutch Competent Authority, NOTIFICATION C/NL/13/01 (https://webgate.ec.europa.eu/fip/GMO_Registers/files/csnifs/C-NL-13-01-AssessmentReport.pdf?dt=20220608043214, last accessed 13 August 2022)	Scientific Opinion on objections of a Member State to a notification (Reference C/NL/13/01) for the placing on the market of the genetically modified carnation SHD-27531-4 with a modified colour, for import of cut flowers for ornamental use, under Part C of Directive 2001/18/EC from Suntory Holdings Limited (https://efsa.onlinelibrary.wiley.com/doi/epdf/10.2903/j.efsa.2014.3878, last accessed 13 August 2022)	*Commission Implementing Decision (EU) 2016/2050 of 22 November 2016 as regards the placing on the market of a genetically modified carnation (Dianthus caryophyllus L., line SHD-27531-4)*, OJ EU 2016, L 318/13

References

Agapito-Tenfen SZ, Okoli AS, Bernstein MJ, Wikmark O-G, Myhr AI (2018) Revisiting risk governance of GM plants: the need to consider new and emerging gene-editing techniques. Front Plant Sci 9:1–16. https://doi.org/10.3389/fpls.2018.01874

Baumüller H (2004) Domestic import regulations for genetically modified organisms and their compatibility with WTO rules. Asian Biotechnol Dev Rev 6:33–42

Broeders SRM, de Keersmaecker SCJ, Roosens NHC (2012) How to deal with the upcoming challenges in GMO detection in food and feed. J Biomed Biotechnol:1–11. https://doi.org/10.1155/2012/402418

Burchardi J-E (2007) Die Vereinbarkeit der europäischen Vorschriften zur Kennzeichnung gentechnisch veränderter Lebensmittel mit dem Welthandelsrecht. Rechtsfragen der Globalisierung. Duncker & Humblot, Berlin

Caswell JA (2000) An evaluation of risk analysis as applied to agricultural biotechnology (with a case study of GMO labeling). In: Transitions in agbiotech: economics of strategy and policy, Chapter 36, pp 665–674

Codex Alimentarius Commission (2007) Procedural manual, 17th edn

Commission of the European Communities (1996) Report on the review of Directive 90/220/EEC in the context of the Commission's communication on biotechnology and the white paper. COM(96) 630 final, Brussels. https://eur-lex.europa.eu/legal-content/EN/TXT/PDF/?uri=CELEX:51996DC0630&from=DE

Dederer H-G (2019) Options for the regulation of genome edited plants - framing the issues. In: Dürnberger C, Pfeilmeier S, Schleissing S (eds) Genome editing in agriculture: between precaution and responsibility. Nomos, Baden-Baden, pp 77–122

EFSA Panel on Genetically Modified Organisms (2009) Scientific Opinion on guidance for the risk assessment of genetically modified plants used for non-food or non-feed purposes. Scientific Opinion

EFSA Panel on Genetically Modified Organisms (2010a) Guidance on the environmental risk assessment of genetically modified plants. Scientific Opinion, Parma. https://doi.org/10.2903/j.efsa.2010.1879

EFSA Panel on Genetically Modified Organisms (2010b) Scientific Opinion on the assessment of potential impacts of genetically modified plants on non-target organisms. Scientific Opinion, Parma. https://doi.org/10.2903/j.efsa.2010.1877

Eriksson D (2018) Recovering the original intentions of risk assessment and management of genetically modified organisms in the European Union. Front Bioeng Biotechnol 6:1–4. https://doi.org/10.3389/fbioe.2018.00052

Eriksson D (2019) The evolving EU regulatory framework for precision breeding. Theor Appl Genet 132:569–573. https://doi.org/10.1007/s00122-018-3200-9

European Commission (2015) Proposal for a Regulation of the European Parliament and of the Council amending Regulation (EC) No 1829/2003 as regards the possibility for the Member States to restrict or prohibit the use of genetically modified food and feed on their territory. COM(2015) 177 final. https://www.europarl.europa.eu/RegData/docs_autres_institutions/commission_europeenne/com/2015/0177/COM_COM(2015)0177_EN.pdf

European Commission (n.d.-b) European Union Reference Laboratory for Genetically Modified Food and Feed (EURL GMFF). Main website. https://gmo-crl.jrc.ec.europa.eu/

European Commission (n.d.-c) Regulatory Committee 2001/18/EC: agendas and summary reports. https://ec.europa.eu/food/horizontal-topics/committees/other-committees/regulatory-committee-200118ec_en

European Commission (n.d.-d) Restrictions of geographical scope of GMO applications/authorisations: EU countries demands and outcomes. Overview. https://food.ec.europa.eu/plants/genetically-modified-organisms/gmo-authorisation/gmo-authorisations-cultivation/restrictions-geographical-scope-gmo-applicationsauthorisations-eu-countries-demands-and-outcomes_en

European Commission (n.d.-e) Specific legislation on plant reproductive material. Overview. https://food.ec.europa.eu/plants/plant-reproductive-material/legislation/specific-legislation_en
European Commission (n.d.-f) Standing Committee on Plants, Animals, Food and Feed (Section for Genetically Modified Food and Feed and Environmental Risks): agendas and summary reports. https://food.ec.europa.eu/horizontal-topics/committees/paff-committees/genetically-modified-food-and-feed-and-environmental-risk_en
European Parliament (2015) Parliament rejects national GMO bans proposal. Press release
European Parliamentary Research Service (2025) Member States' possibility to 'opt out' from GM food and feed import authorisations: at a glance. Plenary - 22 October 2015
Habets M, van Hove L, van Est R (2019) Genome editing in plants and crops: towards a modern biotechnology policy focused on differences in risks and broader considerations. The Hague
Klika C, Kim J, Versluis E (2013) Why science cannot tame politics: the new EU comitology rules and the centralised authorisation procedure of GMOs. Eur J Risk Regul 4:327–334
Marketing of seeds of agricultural crops. Summaries of EU Legislation. https://eur-lex.europa.eu/EN/legal-content/summary/marketing-of-seeds-of-agricultural-crops.html
Monien J (2016) § 8 The New Opt-Out Rule - new challenges in the legal multi-level system of the usage of GMOs. In: Härtel I, Budzinowski R (eds) Food security, food safety, food quality: current developments and challenges in European Union law, 1st edn. Nomos Verlagsgesellschaft mbH & Co. KG, Baden-Baden, pp 103–113
Organisation for Economic Co-operation and Development (1986) Recombinant DNA safety considerations: safety considerations for industrial, agricultural and environmental applications of organisms derived by recombinant DNA techniques
Palme C (1997) EG-Richtlinie "Freisetzung" Einleitung. In: Eberbach WH, Lange P, Ronellenfitsch M (eds) Recht der Gentechnik und Biomedizin: GenTR/BioMedR, vol 3, 114th edn. C.F. Müller, Heidelberg
Schäfer A (2005) Ausgewählte Probleme der Auslegung der neuen EG-Verordnungen bei genetisch veränderten Lebensmitteln. In: Lebensmittelchemische Gesellschaft (ed) Neue EU-Regelungen für gentechnisch veränderte Lebensmittel und Futtermittel: eAspekte zur Umsetzung in die Praxis; Recht, Überwachung, Probenahme, Analytik. Behr, Hamburg, pp 1–10
Scott J (2003) European regulation of GMOs and the WTO. Columbia J Eur Law 9:213–240
Secretariat of the Convention on Biological Diversity (2022) Cartagena protocol on biosafety: ratification list. https://www.cbd.int/doc/lists/cpb-ratifications.pdf
van Calster G, Reins L (2018) EU environmental law. Elgar European law. Edward Elgar, Cheltenham
Voigt B, Münichsdorfer A (2019) Regulation of genome editing in plant biotechnology: European Union. Chapter 5. In: Dederer H-G, Hamburger D (eds) Regulation of genome editing in plant biotechnology: a comparative analysis of regulatory frameworks of selected countries and the EU. Springer, Cham, pp 137–238
Voß U (2006) Die Novelle der Freisetzungsrichtlinie - Richtlinie 2001/18/EG. Schriftenreihe Recht, Ethik und Ökonomie der Biotechnologie, vol 16. Nomos, Baden-Baden
Waigmann E, Paoletti C, Davies H, Perry J, Kärenlampi S, Kuiper H (2012) Risk assessment of Genetically Modified Organisms (GMOs). Special Issue. https://doi.org/10.2903/j.efsa.2012.s1008

Chapter 5
The EU's Obligations Under WTO Law and CETA

Abstract This chapter provides an overview of the regulatory framework of the World Trade Organisation ('WTO') and the Comprehensive Economic and Trade Agreement ('CETA') between the European Union ('EU') and Canada. Both systems aim to promote free trade and reduce trade barriers, limiting the sovereignty of states to take measures that fall under their respective agreements. While the WTO Agreements do not explicitly regulate genetically modified organisms ('GMOs'), there are lengthy discussions of how to best regulate GMOs under the WTO regime which came up especially in the early 2000s when the WTO Dispute Settlement Body was concerned with a dispute concerning the EU's regulation of GMOs at that time. Since Canada was also involved in this dispute and since the different regulation of GMOs in Canada and the EU is constantly debated, CETA has established a dialogue process for biotech-related issues between the EU and Canada.

5.1 Introduction

The *World Trade Organization* ('WTO') is the main institution when it comes to regulating international economic and trade relations between States. In addition to the law established by the WTO itself, there are many regional trade agreements, such as the *North American Free Trade Agreement* ('NAFTA') or the *Association of Southeast Asian Nations* ('ASEAN').[1] The *Comprehensive Economic and Trade Agreement*[2] ('CETA'), as a *mega-regional trade agreement*, marks a new era of

This chapter has last been updated in December 2023.

[1] For other examples of regional trade agreements, see Herdegen (2020), para 5.

[2] *Comprehensive Economic and Trade Agreement (CETA) between Canada, of the one part, and the European Union and its Member States, of the other part* ('CETA'), Official Journal of the European Union ('OJ EU') 2017, L 11/23.

E. A. L. Andersen, *Regulation of Biotechnological Risks in a Multi-Level System*, European Yearbook of International Economic Law 46,
https://doi.org/10.1007/978-3-032-02409-1_5

regional trade relations between States.[3] It goes further than the "standard" regional trade agreements since it does not only address traditional concerns of trade policy, such as tariffs and quantitative restrictions but also to a large extent aims at a reduction of non-tariff barriers and the liberalisation of investment flows. Also, it addresses areas that have not been addressed by regional trade agreements so far.[4] Thereby, it goes beyond the relations that exist between Canada and the European Union ('EU') in the WTO framework.[5] With its geopolitical impact, it is also meant to largely influence the international economic order.[6]

Accordingly, CETA as a mega-regional trade agreement somehow is the next step in the development of globalisation which began with the reduction of tariffs and quantitative measures under *the General Agreement on Tariffs and Trade 1947*[7] ('GATT 1947'), soon comprising also non-tariff barriers which are also to a large extent addressed by the WTO and its agreements.[8] CETA now goes even further by aiming at a total harmonisation of economic conditions. Also, CETA serves as one mean for the EU to overcome hurdles regarding multilateral negotiations at the WTO.[9]

The present chapter outlines the legal framework against which the EU regulations governing the release and placing on the market of genetically modified organisms ('GMOs') are measured. First, the law of the WTO with its Dispute Settlement Body ('DSB') and the relevant agreements are presented (Sect. 5.2), followed by an overview of the legal framework established by CETA (Sect. 5.3). Thereby, this chapter together with the third chapter on EU GMO regulations lays the foundation for the analysis following in the fifth chapter which forms the centrepiece of the entire work. In the following, it is therefore in particular analysed how the WTO system and CETA differ from the EU regulatory system, especially with regard to precautionary considerations as a mean to justify regulatory measures. And, how regulation of biotechnological risks has been assessed so far in the context of the WTO regime and CETA.

5.2 WTO Law

5.2.1 Introduction

The foundations for the current WTO regime were laid down in the aftermath of World War II. After challenging times in the first half of the twentieth century, multilateral agreements and international organisations were seen as guarantees for

[3] *Cf.* Stoll et al. (2016), p. 8; Stoll (2017), pp. 3–4.

[4] *Cf.* Stoll (2017), p. 5; for further details, see Stoll (2017), pp. 6–10.

[5] *Cf.* Stoll (2017), p. 5.

[6] *Cf.* Griller et al. (2017a), p. 3.

[7] *General Agreement on Tariffs and Trade* (concluded 30 October 1947) 55 UNTS 187.

[8] *Cf.* Cottier and Baumann (2017), p. 56.

[9] *Cf.* Commission of the European Communities (2006), p. 8; see also Hummer (2018), para 12.

peace and prosperity. This did not only lead to the establishment of the United Nations system, but States also wanted to strengthen their cooperation in the field of international trade by opening markets and reducing trade barriers. While the establishment of an *International Trade Organization* ('ITO') failed, there was another agreement negotiated, intended to be provisional until the ITO's establishment: *The General Agreement on Tariffs and Trade 1947*.[10] This general agreement replaced the failed ITO and constituted one pillar of international trade for half a century until the WTO was established in 1995.

5.2.2 *The WTO System*

The WTO is based on the *Marrakesh Agreement Establishing the World Trade Organization*[11] ('WTO Agreement'). According to Article II:1 of the WTO Agreement, the WTO serves as a

> common institutional framework for the conduct of trade relations among its Members in matters related to the agreements and associated legal instruments.

These agreements and associated legal instruments are binding upon all WTO Member States (so-called "single undertaking"[12]). They are listed in Annexes 1, 2 and 3 to the WTO Agreement and are referred to as *Multilateral Agreements*.[13] Among these Multilateral Agreements are the *General Agreement on Tariffs and Trade 1994*[14] ('GATT') which incorporates and succeeds the GATT 1947, the *Agreement on the Application of Sanitary and Phytosanitary Measures*[15] ('SPS Agreement' or 'SPS'), the *Agreement on Technical Barriers to Trade*[16] ('TBT Agreement' or 'TBT') and the *Agreement on Agriculture*[17] ('Agriculture Agreement'), but also others concerned with specific areas of international trade, such as intellectual property or trade in services.

---

[10] See on the details of the process leading to GATT and the failure of an International Trade Organization Lowenfeld (2008), Ch. 3.1–3.2.

[11] *Marrakesh Agreement establishing the World Trade Organization* (concluded 15 April 1994; entered into force 1 January 1995) 1867 UNTS 3 ('WTO Agreement').

[12] Davey (2005), p. 57.

[13] See Article II:2 WTO Agreement.

[14] *General Agreement on Tariffs and Trade 1994*, Annex 1 to the WTO Agreement, see footnote 11.

[15] *Agreement on the Application of Sanitary and Phytosanitary Measures* ('SPS Agreement' or 'SPS'), Annex 1 to the WTO Agreement, see footnote 11.

[16] *Agreement on Technical Barriers to Trade* ('TBT Agreement' or 'TBT'), Annex 1 to the WTO Agreement, see footnote 11.

[17] *Agreement on Agriculture*, Annex 1 to the WTO Agreement, see footnote 11.

Annex 2 contains the *Understanding on Rules and Procedures Governing the Settlement of Disputes*[18] ('Dispute Settlement Understanding' or 'DSU') which provides the WTO Member States with a Dispute Settlement System and establishes the DSB.[19]

The agreements and legal instruments listed in Annex 4, referred to as *Plurilateral Agreements*, are only binding upon those Members that have agreed so.[20]

5.2.2.1 The World Trade Organization (WTO)

The WTO is tasked to

> facilitate the implementation, administration and operation, and further the objectives, of this Agreement [the WTO Agreement] and of the Multilateral Agreements[21]

and to provide a forum for negotiations between the Member States concerning their multilateral trade relations in general and under the Agreements annexed to the WTO Agreement.[22] Furthermore, the WTO administers the Dispute Settlement Understanding and the *Trade Policy Review Mechanism* ('TPRM') which is laid down in Annex 3 to the WTO Agreement.[23]

To fulfil these tasks, the WTO is equipped with the *Secretariat of the WTO*, headed by the Director-General, the *Ministerial Conference* as the supreme body and the *General Council*, with the *Council for Trade in Goods*, the *Council for Trade in Services* and the *Council for Trade-Related Aspects of Intellectual Property Rights*, as well as with several Committees.[24] The *Ministerial Conference* and the *General Council* are composed of representatives of all WTO Member States. The *Ministerial Conference* meets twice every year and has the authority to take decisions on all matters under any of the Multilateral Agreements.[25] In between these meetings, the *General Council* is responsible to carry out the functions of the WTO and meets as appropriate.[26] It also convenes as the DSB and as the *Trade Policy Review Body* which carries out TPRM procedures.[27]

---

[18] *Understanding on Rules and Procedures Governing the Settlement of Disputes* ('Dispute Settlement Understanding' or 'DSU'), Annex 2 to the WTO Agreement, see footnote 11.

[19] For further details on the WTO DSB see below, Sect. 5.2.2.1.1.

[20] See Article II:3 WTO Agreement.

[21] See Article III:1 WTO Agreement.

[22] See Article III:2 WTO Agreement.

[23] See Arts. III:3 and III:4 WTO Agreement.

[24] See Arts. IV and VI WTO Agreement.

[25] See Article IV:1 WTO Agreement; for decision-making of this body see Article XI WTO Agreement; for further details on the working mode of the Ministerial Conference and the outcome of the Ministerial Conferences held between 1996 and 2003, see Davey (2005), pp. 60–63.

[26] See Article IV:2 WTO Agreement; for decision-making of this body see Article XI WTO Agreement.

[27] Davey (2005), p. 64.

The WTO has legal personality and enjoys privileges and immunities necessary for the exercise of its functions vis-à-vis its Member States.[28]

5.2.2.1.1 WTO Dispute Settlement System

The Dispute Settlement System, resolving disputes between the WTO Member States, has been considered one of the greatest achievements of the WTO system until its current crisis started.[29] It is the DSB's objective to provide security and predictability within the WTO system.[30] To fulfil this objective, the Dispute Settlement Body is tasked with the preservation of the rights and obligations of Members under the covered agreements, and with the clarification of the existing provisions of those agreements by customary rules of interpretation of public international law.[31]

The Dispute Settlement Body is established by the Dispute Settlement Understanding. The provisions of the DSU as well as the consultation and dispute settlement provisions of the Agreements covered by the DSU are administered by the Dispute Settlement Body.[32]

Under the Dispute Settlement Understanding, Member States shall first enter into consultations before requesting the establishment of a panel to resolve their dispute.[33] The procedures that panels shall follow for the settlement of disputes are laid down in Annex 3 to the DSU. A panel delivers its final conclusion in form of a report which is first considered by the Member States and shall then be adopted by the DSB.[34] Parties to the dispute that object to a panel report shall give their reasons in written form to explain their objection.[35] The parties also have the possibility to appeal panel reports.[36] Therefore, a standing Appellate Body ('AB') is established by the DSB.[37] An Appellate Body report shall be adopted by the DSB and shall be unconditionally accepted by the parties to the dispute. However, the parties still may express their views on the AB report.[38]

The relevant customary rules of treaty interpretation that the DSB may apply to resolve disputes are laid down in Articles 31 and 32 of the *Vienna Convention on the*

[28] See Article VIII WTO Agreement.

[29] See below, Sect. 5.2.2.1.3.

[30] See Article 3.2 DSU.

[31] See Article 3.2 DSU.

[32] See Article 2.1 DSU.

[33] See Article 4 DSU.

[34] See Article 16 DSU.

[35] See Article 16.2 DSU.

[36] See Article 16.4 DSU.

[37] See Article 17.1 DSU.

[38] See Article 17.14 DSU; for an overview of the elements and stages of the dispute settlement process, see Stoll (2014), paras 23–36.

Law of Treaties[39] ('VCLT').[40] In this regard, the Appellate Body stressed that a treaty's text and its ordinary meaning are at the core of treaty interpretation.[41] To deduce the term's ordinary meaning, dictionaries are a helpful tool, but should not be the only one.[42] The ordinary meaning also has to be ascertained in the term's context and in light of the treaty's object and purpose.[43]

The DSU applies to all disputes that are brought to the DSB under the agreements listed in Annexes 1 and 2 to the DSU by the WTO Member States.[44] Its jurisdiction is compulsory according to Article 6.1 DSU and exclusive according to Article 23.2 DSU.[45]

Also, it has been clarified that not only a Member States application of measures can be scrutinised by the DSB but also its legislation as such.[46] This has been reasoned on grounds of judicial economy and the DSB's objective to provide for security and predictability in trade relations.[47] Also, Article XVI:4 WTO Agreement is brought forward in this regard.[48]

While the DSU does not provide for a formal *stare decisis*,[49] previous decisions of other Panels and the Appellate Body are frequently taken into account. This practice has also been acknowledged by the Appellate Body.[50]

Furthermore, Panels have the right to seek technical advice or to consult experts to obtain their opinion on certain aspects of the respective dispute.[51] They may even request an advisory report from a group of experts following the rules laid down in

---

[39] *Vienna Convention on the Law of Treaties* ('VCLT') (adopted 22 May 1969, entered into force 27 January 1980) 1155 UNTS 331.

[40] As provided for by Article 3.2 DSU; see also WTO Appellate Body, *Japan - Taxes on Alcoholic Beverages* (4 October 1996b), WT/DS8/AB/R, WT/DS10/AB/R, WT/DS11/AB/R, 10.

[41] *Cf.* WTO Appellate Body, *Japan - Taxes on Alcoholic Beverages* (4 October 1996b), WT/DS8/AB/R, WT/DS10/AB/R, WT/DS11/AB/R, 11–12.

[42] WTO Appellate Body, *China - Measures Affecting Trading Rights and Distribution Services for Certain Publications and Audiovisual Entertainment Products* (21 December 2009), WT/DS363/AB/R, para 348 with further references.

[43] WTO Appellate Body, *China - Measures Affecting Trading Rights and Distribution Services for Certain Publications and Audiovisual Entertainment Products* (21 December 2009), WT/DS363/AB/R, para 348 with further references.

[44] See Article 1 DSU.

[45] See also van den Bossche and Zdouc (2022), pp. 177–178.

[46] See van den Bossche and Zdouc (2022), pp. 181–182.

[47] See van den Bossche and Zdouc (2022), p. 182 referring to WTO Appellate Body, *United States - Sunset Review of Anti-Dumping Duties on Corrosion-Resistant Steel Flat Products from Japan* (15 December 2003), WT/DS244/AB/R, para 82.

[48] Davey (2005), p. 81 referring to WTO Panel, *United States - Sections 301–310 of the Trade Act of 1974* (22 December 1999), WT/DS152/R, paras 7.41–7.42.

[49] Henckels (2006), p. 299.

[50] WTO Appellate Body, *Japan - Taxes on Alcoholic Beverages* (4 October 1996b), WT/DS8/AB/R, WT/DS10/AB/R, WT/DS11/AB/R, 14.

[51] See Article 13 DSU.

Appendix 4 to the DSU. In this respect, Article 11.2 SPS also recommends Panels to seek expert advice in disputes involving scientific or technical issues.

5.2.2.1.2 Interpretation of the WTO Agreements' Provisions in Light of Public International Law

While Articles 31 and 32 VCLT are not directly applicable to the WTO agreements,[52] they apply to WTO law due to their customary nature.[53] According to custom codified in Article 31(3)(c) VCLT, any relevant rules of international law applicable in the relations between the parties shall be taken into account. This does not give a treaty interpreter the mere possibility to do so, but mandates for taking into account relevant rules of international law.[54] However, only those rules that are *applicable in the relations between the parties* are comprised by Article 31(3)(c) VCLT. Accordingly, only those rules of public international law that apply to all WTO Member States fall within Article 31(3)(c) VCLT.[55] This does however not prevent the Dispute Settlement Bodies to rely on relevant rules of international law if it deems such rules informative according to the Panel in *EC – Biotech*.[56] This has been approved by the Appellate Body stating that Article 31(3)(c) VCLT ensures a provision's interpretation in accordance with its normative environment. Accordingly, a WTO Panel when confronted with international rules that are not binding upon all WTO Member States should try to find a balance between the international obligations of an individual Member State and the interest of a consistent interpretation of WTO law amongst all WTO Members. This is necessary to respect the multilateral context of the WTO.[57]

---

[52] Not all State parties to the WTO are also parties to the VCLT, see World Trade Organization (n.d.-a) and *Vienna Convention on the Law of Treaties* (n.d.).

[53] See WTO Appellate Body, *United States - Standards for Reformulated and Conventional Gasoline* (29 April 1996a), WT/DS2/AB/R, 17 and WTO Appellate Body, *Japan - Taxes on Alcoholic Beverages* (4 October 1996b), WT/DS8/AB/R, WT/DS10/AB/R, WT/DS11/AB/R, 10; see also Article 3.2 DSU.

[54] van den Bossche and Zdouc (2022), p. 205.

[55] See WTO Panel, *European Communities - Measures Affecting the Approval and Marketing of Biotech Products* (29 September 2006), WT/DS291/R, WT/DS292/R, WT/DS293/R, para 7.68.

[56] See WTO Panel, *European Communities - Measures Affecting the Approval and Marketing of Biotech Products* (29 September 2006), WT/DS291/R, WT/DS292/R, WT/DS293/R, para 7.93; see also van den Bossche and Zdouc (2022), pp. 206–207.

[57] *Cf.* WTO Appellate Body, *European Communities and Certain Member States - Measures Affecting Trade in Large Civil Aircraft* (18 May 2011), WT/DS316/AB/R, para 845.

5.2.2.1.3 Crisis of the WTO's Dispute Settlement System

While the DSB is considered crucial for the WTO's success in governing international trade relations, the WTO Appellate Body currently is technically inoperable. This crisis of the WTO's dispute settlement mechanism has been looming over the last few years and finally culminated in a dispute primarily between the EU and the United States ('US') on the modalities of the selection process for two positions that became vacant in June and December 2017.[58] In August 2017, a third position unexpectedly became vacant and the member whose term had expired in June 2017 continued to serve in the appeal procedures where he had been involved as a sitting member in accordance with Rule 15 of the *Appellate Body's Working Procedures*.[59,60] In the next meeting of the DSB, the US no longer reasoned its refusal to appoint new AB Members with modalities of the selection procedure but with the continued service of a former AB Member without authorisation by the DSB. While the US welcomed the continued performance of a former Member, it criticised that this continuance had been authorised by the Appellate Body and not by the DSB which was responsible for the appointments of Appellate Body Members according to Article 17.2 DSU.[61] The US position on this matter has to be seen in the greater context of its position on the Appellate Body and the DSB in general. The US asserts that the Appellate Body is exceeding its mandate within the WTO system.[62]

In 2018 and 2019, various WTO members in different constellations issued proposals to address the US concerns regarding the dispute settlement system.[63] They were all rejected by the US.[64] An informal process on Appellate Body matters with New Zealand's WTO ambassador as facilitator was initiated in January 2019 and continued until December 2019. But it did not bring the US blockade to an end.[65] In February 2020, the US Trade Representative issued a report on the Appellate Body asserting the Appellate Body's failure to apply the WTO agreements in a consistent manner thereby diminishing US rights and adding to US obligations.[66]

---

[58] For details see van den Bossche and Zdouc (2022), pp. 316–320; Lehne (2019), pp. 13–17.

[59] WTO Appellate Body (2010).

[60] *Cf.* Lehne (2019), pp. 17–18.

[61] *Cf.* WTO Dispute Settlement Body (2017), 5.5, 7.3, 7.11; see also Lehne (2019), p. 19.

[62] *Cf.* Lehne (2019), pp. 21–24 referring to statements the US has made between 2017 and 2018 in different fora; see also van den Bossche and Zdouc (2022), pp. 318–319; see also Davey (2005), pp. 81–85 on problems arising out of the WTO's institutional design.

[63] See van den Bossche and Zdouc (2022), pp. 320–321.

[64] See van den Bossche and Zdouc (2022), pp. 320–324.

[65] *Cf.* Lehne (2019), pp. 26–27 summarizing the status of the process until July 2019; the last report of the informal process was discussed at the WTO's General Council Meeting from 9 to 10 December 2019, see World Trade Organization (2020a), paras 5.1–5.202.

[66] Office of the United States Trade Representative (2020a), Introduction; Office of the United States Trade Representative (2020b); the report was also presented and discussed at the WTO's General Council Meeting on 3 March 2020, see World Trade Organization (2020b), paras 11.1–11.56.

As of today, only one out of seven Appellate Body Members is in office.[67] This renders the Appellate Body inoperable since three members are necessary to review cases according to Article 17.1 DSU.[68] All but one of the panel reports were appealed into the void since October 2020. They were not adopted by the DSB and, accordingly, did not become legally binding. For the time being, this has put the legally binding adjudication of disputes in the WTO context to an end.[69]

In the meantime, the European Union and 18 other WTO Member States[70] have established a *Multi-Party Interim Appeal Arbitration Arrangement pursuant to Article 25 DSU* ('MPIA') that was notified to the WTO by end of April 2020.[71] In their notification, the participating Members indicate their intention to resort to arbitration under Article 25 DSU in cases of appeal procedures as long as the Appellate Body is inoperable.[72] As of today, there are 26 WTO Members party to the MPIA.[73]

At the 12th Ministerial Conference in June 2022, the WTO Member States have acknowledged the challenges and concerns with respect to the Appellate Body. They have committed themselves to address those challenges and concerns in order to have "a fully and well-functioning dispute settlement system accessible to all Members by 2024."[74]

5.2.2.2 The EU and the World Trade Organization

The European Communities ('EC') which have been replaced by the EU are founding members of the WTO.[75] Also, all EU Member States are members of the WTO.[76] This is because the European Communities when acceding to the WTO did not have the competencies to accede to the WTO on its own. The competencies to conclude the WTO Agreement and the multilateral agreements were divided between Member

[67] See World Trade Organization (2020d), para 1; see also Article 17.1 DSU.

[68] See also World Trade Organization (2019).

[69] van den Bossche and Zdouc (2022), pp. 319–320.

[70] Australia, Brazil, Canada, China, Chile, Colombia, Costa Rica, Guatemala, Hong Kong (China), Iceland, Mexico, New Zealand, Norway, Pakistan, Singapore, Switzerland, Ukraine and Uruguay.

[71] World Trade Organization (2020c).

[72] World Trade Organization (2020c), p. 2; for an overview of cases litigated by the MPIA, see Multi-Party Interim Appeal Arbitration Arrangement (MPIA), Website created by the Geneva Trade Platform, https://wtoplurilaterals.info/plural_initiative/the-mpia/.

[73] See Multi-Party Interim Appeal Arbitration Arrangement (MPIA), Website created by the Geneva Trade Platform, https://wtoplurilaterals.info/plural_initiative/the-mpia/.

[74] World Trade Organization (2022), para 4.

[75] See Article XI WTO Agreement.

[76] See World Trade Organization (n.d.-a) and European Commission (n.d.).

States and the European Communities.[77] Since the *Treaty of Lisbon*[78] entered into force, the EU has exclusive competencies concerning all actions falling within the area of common commercial policy which also comprises WTO law.[79] Accordingly, the European Commission represents all EU Member States at the WTO and is acting for the EU and on behalf of its Member States vis-à-vis the WTO.[80] This also comprises the negotiation of trade agreements and the representation in disputes before the WTO DSB.[81]

But, the effect of WTO law within the EU's legal order remains a special one. In general, the European Union is bound by the international treaties it has concluded according to Article 216(2) of the *Treaty on the Functioning of the European Union*[82] ('TFEU').[83] Those treaties have direct effect in Union law and take precedence over secondary law. Accordingly, secondary Union law and national law of the EU Member States have to be interpreted in line with the international treaties the EU has entered into.[84]

This is different in regard to WTO law. While the EU and the EU's Member States are bound by WTO law according to international law and the doctrine of *pacta sunt servanda* as laid down in Art. 26 VCLT,[85] WTO law does not have direct effect in EU law according to the jurisprudence of the Court of Justice of the European Union ('CJEU').[86] This is due to the structure and nature of WTO law.[87] Therefore, neither WTO law nor the DSB's reports serve as a standard of review for the CJEU when scrutinising acts by EU institutions.[88]

However, WTO law is directly applicable to acts by the EU Member States and their acts can be examined against WTO law.[89] This is consequent since the EU is liable vis-á-vis other WTO parties for WTO law violations of its Member States.[90]

Also, the EU can be held responsible for its institutions' and its Member States' acts before the WTO DSB. Article XVI:4 WTO Agreement prescribes that each

---

[77] Heidfeld (2012), pp. 122–123.

[78] *Treaty of Lisbon amending the Treaty on European Union and the Treaty establishing the European Community*, OJ EU 2007, C 306/1.

[79] See Articles 3(1)(e), 206 and 207 of the *Treaty on the Functioning of the European Union* ('TFEU'), OJ EU 2012, C 326/47; see also Heidfeld (2012), pp. 121, 133; Streinz et al. (2008), p. 128.

[80] European Parliament (2021), p. 4.

[81] European Parliament (2021), p. 4.

[82] See footnote 79.

[83] *Cf.* Vöneky and Beylage-Haarmann (2020), para 26.

[84] *Cf.* Mögele (2018), para 59.

[85] Vöneky and Beylage-Haarmann (2020), para 26; see also Mögele (2018), para 73.

[86] Mögele (2018), para 65; see also Heidfeld (2012), pp. 138–146.

[87] For further details see Mögele (2018), pp. 65–66.

[88] See Heidfeld (2012), pp. 138–139 and footnote 446 summarising the CJEU's jurisprudence in this matter and giving further references.

[89] See for a detailed analysis Heidfeld (2012), pp. 150–163.

[90] Heidfeld (2012), pp. 157–159.

Member State shall ensure the conformity of its laws, regulations and administrative procedures with its obligations under the WTO system.

5.2.3 *GATT*

The GATT 1947 which was initially designed as an interim agreement until the ITO would have been established, is the centrepiece of the current WTO system.[91] Intended as a provisional agreement, it was further developed during eight trade rounds taking place between 1947 and 1995.[92] While the first rounds only brought about changes concerning tariffs, the Kennedy and Tokyo Round already addressed other trade barriers. The eighth round, the Uruguay Round, included major changes to the framework of the GATT system by establishing the WTO and by setting up a network of agreements concerned with trade in services, intellectual property, agricultural products and textiles, with non-tariff barriers to trade and with the settlement of trade disputes.[93] On this occasion, the GATT 1947 was formally terminated and the new GATT (1994) was established, consisting of the pre-existing GATT 1947, new understandings on several GATT provisions and the Marrakesh Protocol to the GATT (1994).

According to a general interpretative note to Annex 1A to the WTO Agreement, the GATT provisions are subordinate to the provisions of another agreement listed in Annex 1A to the WTO Agreement in the event and to the extent of a conflict arising between these provisions.

5.2.3.1 Basic Principles

The principles underlying the GATT are the principle of non-discrimination and the principle of liberalisation. The principle of non-discrimination of *like products* is expressed in the most-favoured-nation principle and the national treatment principle. The principle of liberalisation finds expression in the GATT's aim to eliminate and reduce tariffs and non-tariff barriers to trade.[94]

The principle of most-favoured-nation treatment obliges states to grant trade advantages given to one contracting state party to all other state parties, too. The principle is laid down in Article I:1 GATT, but also finds expression in several other provisions of the GATT, such as Arts. V, IX:1, XIII:1 and XVII:1. It includes the prohibition of *de jure* as well as *de facto* discrimination.[95] The principle of most-

[91] *Cf.* van den Bossche and Zdouc (2022), pp. 87–90.

[92] See World Trade Organization (n.d.-d); *cf.* also van den Bossche and Zdouc (2022), pp. 90–93.

[93] See for details Herdegen (2016), Ch. XI.2 and World Trade Organization (n.d.-d).

[94] *Cf.* Herdegen (2016), Ch. XIV.1.

[95] van den Bossche and Zdouc (2022), pp. 341–342.

favoured-nation treatment only applies to *like products*.[96] Exceptions to the principle are made in cases of customs unions and free-trade areas[97] and for developing countries.[98]

The principle of national treatment prohibits the discrimination between imported and domestic products to ensure equal competitive conditions between these products. It is laid down in Article III GATT. This Article is further specified in Annex I of the GATT. While Article III:1 GATT enshrines the basic notion of the national treatment principle, Article III:2 GATT codifies the national treatment principle with regard to internal charges, such as taxes. Article III:4 GATT lays down the national treatment principle for laws, regulations and requirements.[99]

In addition to these two principles, the GATT contains provisions that directly remove custom duties and other non-tariff barriers to trade. This also includes the general prohibition on quantitative restrictions laid down in Article XI:1 GATT. As has been stated by the Appellate Body in *China – Raw Materials*, Article XI:1 GATT comprises measures that limit the quantity or amount of the import or export of a product.[100]

5.2.3.2 The Concept of *Like Products*

One important concept under GATT is that of *like product* which is incorporated in several provisions, such as Arts. I:1, III:2, III:4, VI:1, XI:2 GATT. However, the concept's meaning varies with regard to the different provisions.[101] With regard to Arts. III:2 and III:4 GATT, the Appellate Body has stated that like products within the meaning of Article III:2 GATT are also comprised by Article III:4 GATT which is broader in its scope.[102] Therefore, the conditions which have been established in law in terms of Article III:2 GATT also apply to Article III:4 GATT. These conditions as established by case law are (1) the products' properties, nature, and quality, (2) the products' end uses in a given market, (3) the consumers' tastes and habits, and (4) the products' tariff classification.[103] One decisive component that has to be

---

[96] Herdegen (2016), Ch. XIV.2.a; for the concept of *like products*, see below, Sect. 5.2.3.2.

[97] See Article XXIV:4-XXIV:12 GATT.

[98] *Cf.* Herdegen (2016), Ch. XIV.2.b.

[99] For a detailed overview on Article III GATT see van den Bossche and Zdouc (2022), pp. 378–437.

[100] WTO Appellate Body, *China - Measures Related to the Exportation of Various Raw Materials* (30 January 2012a), WT/DS394/AB/R, WT/DS395/AB/R, WT/DS398/AB/R, para 320.

[101] Herdegen (2016), Ch. XIV.2.a.

[102] *Cf.* WTO Appellate Body, *European Communities - Measures Affecting Asbestos and Asbestos-Containing Products* (12 March 2001), WT/DS135/AB/R, para 99; Herdegen (2016), Ch. XIV.3.c.

[103] *Report by the Working Party on Border Tax Adjustments* (1970), para 18; see also WTO Appellate Body, *Canada - Certain Measures Concerning Periodicals* (30 June 1997), WT/DS31/AB/R, para 20; WTO Appellate Body, *Japan - Taxes on Alcoholic Beverages* (4 October 1996b), WT/DS8/AB/R, WT/DS10/AB/R, WT/DS11/AB/R, 20–21; WTO Panel, *Mexico - Tax Measures on Soft Drinks and Other Beverages* (7 October 2005), WT/DS308/R, para 8.29.

observed in the determination of *likeness*, especially concerning the second and third criterion, is the competitive relationship between the compared products.[104]

5.2.3.3 General Exceptions Under GATT

Article XX GATT lays down exceptions that apply to all obligations under GATT in contrast to specific exceptions that only apply to specific provisions (e.g. Article III:8 GATT). Article XX GATT contains a "chapeau" which all exceptions have to comply with and several grounds for exception that cover different situations. According to the chapeau, measures must not be "applied in a manner which would constitute a means of arbitrary or unjustifiable discrimination between countries where the same conditions prevail, or a disguised restriction on international trade".[105] This chapeau has been qualified as an expression of the principle of good faith by the WTO Appellate Body that aims at balancing the different rights and obligations of the Member States under the GATT Agreement.[106] Exceptions to the GATT obligations are *inter alia* allowed for the protection of public morals (Article XX(a)), human, animal or plant life or health (Article XX(b)), national treasures of artistic, historic or archaeological value (Article XX(f)), or in relation to the conservation of exhaustible natural resources (Article XX(g)).

5.2.3.4 Specific Exceptions Under GATT

While some provisions themselves already contain specific exceptions, there are three other forms for Member States to justify non-compliance with GATT obligations. First, Article XXI GATT allows the Member States to justify their non-compliance with the protection of security interests. Second, Member States are allowed to take emergency measures for the protection of their domestic industries under Article XIX GATT. This safeguard clause is accompanied by the *Agreement on Safeguards*[107] which lays down special procedural requirements for the invocation of Article XIX GATT measures.[108] And third, Article IX:3 WTO Agreement offers the possibility to waive obligations under the WTO Agreement or any of the other multilateral agreements for one or more State Parties. This can only be done in situations with exceptional circumstances and by a three-quarters majority of the Member States.

---

[104] *Cf.* Herdegen (2016), Ch. XIV.3.b; van den Bossche and Zdouc (2022), p. 422.

[105] See Article XX GATT.

[106] *Cf.* WTO Appellate Body, *United States - Import Prohibition of Certain Shrimp and Shrimp Products* (12 October 1998b), WT/DS58/AB/R, 158–159.

[107] *Agreement on Safeguards*, Annex 1A to the WTO Agreement, see footnote 11.

[108] For a further overview, see van den Bossche and Zdouc (2022), pp. 689–716.

5.2.4 *The Agreement on the Application of Sanitary and Phytosanitary Measures*

The SPS Agreement lays down a framework that allows the Member States to apply measures for the protection of human, animal or plant life or health. It has been established as an outgrowth of Article XX(b) GATT, but clearly goes beyond this provision.[109] It applies to sanitary and phytosanitary measures which are further defined in Annex A(1) of the SPS Agreement.

5.2.4.1 General Obligations

According to Article 2.2, SPS measures shall only be applied

> to the extent necessary to protect human, animal or plant life or health, [shall be] based on scientific principles and [shall not be] maintained without sufficient scientific evidence, except as provided for in paragraph 7 of Article 5.

Furthermore, they shall

> not arbitrarily or unjustifiably discriminate between Members where identical or similar conditions prevail [...][and] shall not be applied in a manner which would constitute a disguised restriction on international trade.

according to Article 2.3 SPS Agreement.

5.2.4.2 The Role of International Standards, Guidelines or Recommendations

5.2.4.2.1 Article 3 SPS Agreement

Article 3.2 SPS Agreement contains an assumption that sanitary and phytosanitary measures are in compliance with the provisions of the SPS Agreement and the GATT when these conform to international standards, guidelines or recommendations. Such international standards, guidelines and recommendations are further specified in Annex A(3) and include those developed by the *Codex Alimentarius Commission* ('CAC') for food safety, by the *World Organisation for Animal Health*[110] ('WOAH') for animal health and by the Secretariat of or regional organizations working within the framework of the *International Plant Protection Convention*[111] ('IPPC') for plant health. Included are also standards developed by

---

[109] Prévost and van den Bossche (2005), p. 243; see also Cheyne (2008), p. 56.

[110] The *World Organisation for Animal Health* succeeded the *International Office of Epizootics* ('IOE') in 2003.

[111] *International Plant Protection Convention* ('IPPC') (entered into force 3 April 1952), 150 UNTS 67.

other relevant organisations and identified by the *Committee on Sanitary and Phytosanitary Measures* ('SPS Committee')[112] concerning matters that are not covered by the three organisations listed in Annex A(3).[113] The introduction of a higher level of protection than envisaged by the relevant standards, guidelines or recommendations is only possible when such a higher level of protection is scientifically justified or is in compliance with Arts. 5.1–5.8 SPS Agreement.[114] Where no international standards, guidelines or recommendations exist, Member States are free to choose their level of protection in accordance with the SPS Agreement.[115]

5.2.4.2.2 Context for the Interpretation of SPS Provisions

Furthermore, the international standards, guidelines and recommendations by the CAC, the IOE and those established within the framework of the IPPC can be taken into account as context in the sense of Article 31 VCLT when interpreting the SPS Agreement's provisions.[116] According to Article 31(2) VCLT, the context of a treaty comprises its preamble and annexes. The SPS Agreement's preamble recognizes "the important contribution that international standards, guidelines and recommendations make" for the establishment of the SPS Agreement.[117] Furthermore, international standards, guidelines and recommendations are mentioned as the basis for a harmonised system of sanitary and phytosanitary measures among WTO Members.[118] Also, these organisations are constantly referred to as the "standard-setting organisations for the SPS Agreement".[119] And they played an important role during the negotiating process.[120]

---

[112] For information on the Committee on Sanitary and Phytosanitary Measures see below, Sect. 5.2.4.5.

[113] *Cf.* Landwehr (2007), para 7.

[114] *Cf.* Article 3.3 SPS; see also Prévost and van den Bossche (2005), pp. 276–277.

[115] *Cf.* Landwehr (2007), para 9.

[116] For a similar case see WTO Appellate Body, *European Communities - Customs Classification of Frozen Boneless Chicken Cuts* (12 September 2005), WT/DS269/AB/R, WT/DS286/AB/R, paras 197–199 where the Appellate Body qualified the decision by the GATT Contracting Parties "to use the Harmonized System as the basis for […] WTO Schedules" as an agreement in the sense of Article 31(2)(a) VCLT and therefore as context in the sense of Article 31(2) VCLT; however, the WTO Panel in *EC – Biotech* has denied the application of international standards, guidelines and recommendations as context of Annex A(1) of the SPS Agreement, see WTO Panel, *European Communities - Measures Affecting the Approval and Marketing of Biotech Products* (29 September 2006), WT/DS291/R, WT/DS292/R, WT/DS293/R, para 7.300.

[117] *Cf.* Preamble, para 5 of the SPS Agreement.

[118] See Preamble, paras 5, 6, Articles 3.1, 3.4, Annex A(3) of the SPS Agreement.

[119] See e.g. the WTO introduction to the SPS Agreement: World Trade Organization (n.d.-b).

[120] *Cf.* Prévost and van den Bossche (2005), pp. 240–241.

5.2.4.3 Science-Based Obligations: Article 5 SPS

Article 5 SPS lays down the framework that the Member States have to comply with when determining their level of protection and establishing sanitary and phytosanitary measures. According to Article 5.1 SPS, every SPS measure must be based on an appropriate risk assessment, the requirements of which are further specified in Article 5.2. SPS. When determining the concrete SPS measure, Member States shall take into account several economic factors listed in Article 5.3 SPS Agreement and the objective of minimizing negative trade effects (Article 5.4 SPS Agreement). This also includes not applying measures that are more trade-restrictive than required to achieve the appropriate level of protection (Article 5.6 SPS Agreement). Furthermore, Article 5.7 SPS Agreement allows for provisional SPS measures where relevant scientific evidence is insufficient in contrast to the obligation laid down in Article 2.2 SPS Agreement. Whether this Article is a reflection of the precautionary principle as applied in EU law is disputed.[121]

5.2.4.4 Other Obligations

Further requirements for control, inspection and approval procedures are laid down in Article 8 SPS Agreement and its Annex C.

Lastly, the SPS Agreement aims at the harmonisation of the Member States' sanitary and phytosanitary protection levels by requiring Member States to accept the sanitary or phytosanitary measures as equivalent when these levels appropriately reflect the former's standards of protection (Article 4 SPS Agreement).

5.2.4.5 The Committee on Sanitary and Phytosanitary Measures

The SPS Agreement in its Article 12 also establishes the SPS Committee. It functions as a regular forum for consultation between the WTO Member States and "*shall carry out the functions necessary to implement the provisions of [the SPS] Agreement*".[122] It shall promote the further harmonisation of SPS measures between Member States and therefore shall "*develop a procedure to monitor the process of international harmonization and the use of international standards, guidelines or recommendations*".[123] The SPS Committee is composed of representatives of all WTO Member States and takes its decisions by consensus.[124]

---

[121] For a discussion of the precautionary principle's reflection in Article 5.7 SPS see Chap. 6, p. 192.

[122] See Article 12.1 SPS Agreement.

[123] See Article 12.4 SPS Agreement.

[124] Prévost and van den Bossche (2005), p. 342; see also Article 12.1 SPS.

5.2.5 *The Agreement on Technical Barriers to Trade*

The TBT Agreement applies to technical regulations and standards, as defined in Annex 1(1) and (2) of the TBT Agreement, that relate to product characteristics and production processes and methods, such as packaging, marking or labelling requirements. While such regulations and standards help to improve the efficiency of production and to facilitate international trade in such products, the purpose of the TBT Agreement is that such regulations "do not create unnecessary obstacles to international trade".[125] Since such product-related rules are less trade invasive than SPS measures, the provisions of the TBT Agreement are less strict than those of the SPS Agreement.[126] Technical standards in contrast to technical regulations are non-binding.[127] The TBT Agreement furthermore comprises conformity assessment procedures as defined in Annex 1(3) to the TBT Agreement.

5.2.5.1 General Obligations

The TBT Agreement in its Article 2.1 lays down the national treatment principle.[128] According to the WTO Appellate Body, this provision does not solely aim for trade liberalization but already incorporates the balance between free trade on the one hand and the pursuit of legitimate interests on the other, as can be derived from the agreement's preamble.[129] Such balance is also expressed in Article 2.2 TBT Agreement which states that

> technical regulations shall not be more trade-restrictive than necessary to fulfil a legitimate objective, taking account of the risks non-fulfilment would create

It calls for a test of proportionality according to the WTO Appellate Body.[130] Legitimate objectives are listed in Article 2.2 itself, but also in Article 5.4 TBT Agreement.[131]

According to Article 2.4 TBT Agreement

> Members shall use [relevant international standards], or the relevant parts of them, as a basis for their technical regulations.

---

[125] Preamble para 5 of the TBT Agreement.

[126] *Cf.* Herdegen (2016), Ch. XVI.1.

[127] *Cf.* Herdegen (2016), Ch. XVI.1.

[128] For the national treatment principle laid down in GATT see above, Sect. 5.2.3.1.

[129] *Cf.* WTO Appellate Body, *United States - Measures Affecting the Production and Sale of Clove Cigarettes* (4 April 2012b), WT/DS406/AB/R, para 109; Herdegen (2016), Ch. XVI.2.

[130] *Cf.* WTO Appellate Body, *United States - Measures concerning the Importation, Marketing and Sale of Tuna and Tuna Products* (16 May 2012c), WT/DS381/AB/R, para 322; Herdegen (2016), Ch. XVI.3.

[131] Herdegen (2016), Ch. XVI.3.

International standards are considered "relevant" if they are established by international bodies whose standardization activity is widely recognized and which are open to all WTO Member States.[132] Where international standards do not exist or where a Member State's measures are not in compliance with such standards and the measure may have a significant effect on the trade of other Members, a Member State has to fulfil certain notification obligations and has to give other Member States the possibility to comment on such measures.[133] Such procedures do however not apply where urgent problems to safety, health, environmental protection or national security arise.[134]

5.2.5.2 Committee on Technical Barriers to Trade

A *Committee on Technical Barriers to Trade* ('TBT Committee') is established by Article 13 TBT Agreement. This Committee serves as a forum for Member States to discuss matters related to the TBT Agreement and to exchange views on the implementation of the Agreement. Furthermore, Member States and observers can raise *specific trade concerns* ('STCs'), i.e. specific laws, regulations or procedures from the other Member States that affect their trade.[135]

5.2.6 Relationship Between the SPS Agreement, the TBT Agreement and the GATT

The relationship between the SPS Agreement and other WTO agreements, such as the TBT Agreement and the GATT is not entirely clear which is due to the agreement's negotiating history.[136] Apparently, the SPS Agreement has the narrowest scope, concerning only sanitary and phytosanitary risks.[137]

The provisions of the SPS Agreement prevail over the TBT Agreement's provisions to the extent that the relevant measures fall within the SPS Agreement's scope.[138] But, the rights of Member States under the TBT Agreement are not affected by the SPS Agreement with regard to measures that do not fall within the scope of the SPS Agreement.[139]

---

[132] *Cf.* Herdegen (2016), Ch. XVI.3 with further references.

[133] As laid down in Article 2.9 TBT Agreement.

[134] See Article 2.10 TBT Agreement.

[135] For further details see World Trade Organization (n.d.-c).

[136] For details, see Gruszczynski (2018), p. 4.

[137] Peel (2006), pp. 1014–1015.

[138] See Article 1.5 TBT Agreement.

[139] See Article 1.4 SPS Agreement.

Furthermore, according to Article 2.4 SPS Agreement, measures that are in conformance with the SPS Agreement shall be presumed to comply with the obligations laid down in the GATT Agreement. Also, the *General interpretative note to Annex 1A* to the WTO Agreement states that "[i]n the event of conflict between a provision of the [GATT]and a provision of another [WTO] agreement [...], the provision of the other agreement shall prevail to the extent of the conflict." Accordingly, where a measure falls within the SPS Agreement's scope, an examination of this measure's compatibility with the GATT is not necessary anymore. Either, it complies with the SPS Agreement, and accordingly also with the GATT. Or, it violates the SPS Agreement and an examination under the GATT is not necessary due to judicial economy.[140]

In contrast, the TBT Agreement does not contain an equivalent to Article 2.4 SPS Agreement but remains silent on its relationship to the GATT Agreement. Therefore, the *General interpretative note to Annex 1A* to the WTO Agreement also applies to the relationship between the GATT and the TBT Agreement. Accordingly, the TBT Agreement takes precedence over the GATT in the event of a conflict between provisions of the two agreements as has also been stated by the Panel in *US – Tuna II*.[141]

5.2.7 WTO Measures Addressing Multiple Regulatory Purposes

A measure applied by a WTO member state can come within the ambit of more than one of the WTO agreements. In such a case, the question arises under which Agreement to scrutinize the measure. It is possible to simply consider the SPS Agreement as *lex specialis* to the TBT Agreement and the GATT, thus considering every measure falling within the SPS Agreement's ambit to fall outside the scope of the other two agreements.[142] However, the WTO Panel in the *EC – Biotech* Case decided that a measure can have multiple regulatory purposes and can thus fall within the ambit of multiple WTO agreements.[143] The regulation is then considered an SPS measure to the extent it covers SPS purposes and a TBT measure to the extent it covers TBT purposes.[144]

---

[140] *Cf.* Seibert-Fohr (2007), paras 44–46.

[141] WTO Panel, *United States - Measures concerning the Importation, Marketing and Sale of Tuna and Tuna Products* (15 September 2011), WT/D381/R, 7.46; see also the analysis of the relationship between the TBT Agreement and the GATT by Burchardi (2007), pp. 236–239.

[142] See the example given by Scott (2009), p. 19.

[143] *Cf.* WTO Panel, *European Communities - Measures Affecting the Approval and Marketing of Biotech Products* (29 September 2006), WT/DS291/R, WT/DS292/R, WT/DS293/R, paras 7.165–7.171.

[144] *Cf.* WTO Panel, *European Communities - Measures Affecting the Approval and Marketing of Biotech Products* (29 September 2006), WT/DS291/R, WT/DS292/R, WT/DS293/R, paras

5.2.8 *Biotechnology Under WTO Law*

Biotechnology did not play a role during the Uruguay Round and no WTO agreement was dedicated explicitly to biotechnology. However, issues concerning biotechnology, especially in the agricultural context, have come up every now and then since the founding of the WTO. At the turn of the millennium, the topic was particularly in the focus of the contracting parties. First, discussions on the international trade of GMOs under the framework of the *Convention on Biological Diversity*[145] ('CBD') resulted in discussions by the Member States on whether and how the WTO Agreements cover biotechnological issues (a.). Second, there arose a dispute between the EU, on the one side, and the US, Canada and Argentina, on the other side, concerning a *de facto* moratorium on approvals of genetically modified products by the EU (b.). This dispute also brought up the question of the relationship between WTO law and the *Cartagena Protocol on Biosafety to the Convention on Biological Diversity*[146] ('Cartagena Protocol') (c.).

5.2.8.1 Proposal for Working Party on Biotechnology in the WTO

During preparations for the 1999 Ministerial Conference of the WTO in Seattle, Canada proposed to establish a Working Party on Biotechnology under the auspices of the WTO.[147] It would have been mandated "to consider adequacy and effectiveness of existing [WTO] rules [in regard to biotechnology] [and] the capacity of WTO Members to implement these rules effectively".[148] It should have examined how trade in biotechnology is covered by the existing WTO rules and whether the WTO Agreements adequately cover biotechnological issues.[149] Another proposal was submitted by Japan. But, no Working Group on GMOs was ever established.[150] Also, the proposal by Canada was seen as an obstacle to the negotiations for the Cartagena Protocol that were taking place at the same time.[151]

7.165–7.171; see also Scott (2009), pp. 19–20 who also points to possible difficulties that might arise when scrutinising a measure under two different agreements; Gruszczynski (2018), pp. 23–24.

[145] *Convention on Biological Diversity* ('CBD') (adopted 5 June 1992, entered into force 29 December 1993) 1760 UNTS 79.

[146] *Cartagena Protocol on Biosafety to the Convention on Biological Diversity* ('Cartagena Protocol') (adopted 29 January 2000, entered into force 11 September 2003) 2226 UNTS 208.

[147] General Council (1999).

[148] General Council (1999), para 1.

[149] General Council (1999), para 6.

[150] See also Böckenförde (2004), pp. 100–101.

[151] *Cf.* Böckenförde (2004), p. 100.

5.2.8.2 WTO Dispute: EC Biotech

From 2003 to 2006, the WTO Dispute Settlement Body had to decide on the compatibility of *European Communities'* measures affecting the approval and marketing of biotechnological products with WTO law.[152] The US, Canada and Argentina first requested consultations with the EC under Article 4 of the DSU, Article XXII GATT, Article 11 of the SPS Agreement, Article 19 of the Agreement on Agriculture and Article 14 of the TBT Agreement. They asserted violations of the SPS Agreement, the TBT Agreement, the Agreement on Agriculture and the GATT. These agreements were allegedly violated by a *de facto* moratorium concerning the approval of biotechnology products introduced by the EC since 1998. Furthermore, the claimants challenged measures taken by several EC Member States which allegedly maintained marketing and import bans on biotechnology products that had already been approved by the EC for marketing and import.[153] The consultations between the EC, the US, Canada and Argentina were joined by Australia, Brazil, Chile, Colombia, India, Mexico, New Zealand and Peru and were held jointly.[154] After the consultations had failed,[155] the US, Canada and Argentina all requested the establishment of a panel as provided for by Article 6.1 DSU.[156] The DSB in accordance with Article 9.1 DSU and with the parties' agreement established a single panel to examine the dispute which was composed on 4 March 2004.[157] The Panel six times postponed the issuance of its report which was actually due in August 2004.[158] The interim report was released to the parties in February 2006.[159] The final report was issued and circulated to the WTO Member States in September 2006.[160] It was adopted in November 2006.[161]

---

[152] See WTO Panel, *European Communities - Measures Affecting the Approval and Marketing of Biotech Products* (29 September 2006), WT/DS291/R, WT/DS292/R, WT/DS293/R.

[153] See WTO Dispute Settlement Body (2003b); WTO Dispute Settlement Body (2003a); WTO Dispute Settlement Body (2003c).

[154] See WTO Dispute Settlement Body (2003f); WTO Dispute Settlement Body (2003e); WTO Dispute Settlement Body; *cf.* also WTO Dispute Settlement Body (2003d).

[155] WTO Panel, *European Communities - Measures Affecting the Approval and Marketing of Biotech Products* (29 September 2006), WT/DS291/R, WT/DS292/R, WT/DS293/R, 1.2, 1.5, 1.8.

[156] WTO Dispute Settlement Body (2003h); WTO Dispute Settlement Body (2003i); WTO Dispute Settlement Body (2003g).

[157] WTO Dispute Settlement Body (2003j), para 69; see also WTO Dispute Settlement Body (2004a); for an overview of the circumstances leading to the conflict and of the dispute's initiation by the US see also Boisson de Chazournes and Mbengue (2004), pp. 289–291; Cheyne (2008), pp. 52–53.

[158] WTO Dispute Settlement Body (2004b); WTO Dispute Settlement Body (2004c); WTO Dispute Settlement Body (2004d); WTO Dispute Settlement Body (2005a); WTO Dispute Settlement Body (2005b); WTO Dispute Settlement Body (2005c); WTO Dispute Settlement Body (2006a).

[159] WTO Panel, *European Communities - Measures Affecting the Approval and Marketing of Biotech Products* (29 September 2006), WT/DS291/R, WT/DS292/R, WT/DS293/R, 1.18.

[160] WTO Dispute Settlement Body (2006b).

[161] WTO Dispute Settlement Body (2006c), p. 8.

The dispute concerned first "the operation and applicability by the European Communities of its regime for approval of biotech products; and [second] certain measures adopted and maintained by EC member States prohibiting or restricting the marketing of biotech products."[162] The relevant legal framework at the time of the complaint comprised *Directive 2001/18/EC of the European Parliament and the Council of 12 March 2001 on the deliberate release into the environment of genetically modified organisms*[163] ('Directive 2001/18/EC' or 'Deliberate Release Directive') and its predecessor *Council Directive 90/220/EEC of 23 April 1990 on the deliberate release into the environment of genetically modified organisms*[164] ('Directive 90/220/EEC') as well as *Regulation (EC) 258/97 of the European Parliament and of the Council of 27 January 1997 concerning novel foods and novel food ingredients*[165] ('Regulation 258/97').[166]

5.2.8.2.1 The Panel's Findings

In its findings, the Panel first elaborates on procedural and general matters. These are amongst others *Amicus curiae* briefs, the Panel's consultation of individual scientific experts and international organisations, and challenges that the Panel faced in the conduct of the proceedings.[167]

In this context, it also addresses the relevance of other international law rules for the interpretation of the WTO agreements at issue in this dispute.[168] These are the CBD and its Cartagena Protocol as well as the precautionary principle.

Concerning the relevance of the CBD and the Cartagena Protocol, the EC brought forward a statement by the Appellate Body in *US – Gasoline* that WTO agreements

---

[162] WTO Panel, *European Communities - Measures Affecting the Approval and Marketing of Biotech Products* (29 September 2006), WT/DS291/R, WT/DS292/R, WT/DS293/R, 2.1.

[163] *Directive 2001/18/EC of the European Parliament and the Council of 12 March 2001 on the deliberate release into the environment of genetically modified organisms and repealing Council Directive 90/220/EC* (consolidated version from 27 March 2021) ('Directive 2001/18/EC'), Official Journal of the European Communities ('OJ EC') 2001, L 106/1.

[164] *Council Directive 90/220/EEC of 23 April 1990 on the deliberate release into the environment of genetically modified organisms* (latest consolidated version from 28 June 1997), OJ EC 1990, L 117/15.

[165] *Regulation (EC) No 258/97 of the European Parliament and of the Council of 27 January 1997 concerning novel foods and novel food ingredients* (latest consolidated version from 07 August 2009), OJ EC 1997, L 43/1 (no longer in force).

[166] WTO Panel, *European Communities - Measures Affecting the Approval and Marketing of Biotech Products* (29 September 2006), WT/DS291/R, WT/DS292/R, WT/DS293/R, para 2.3.

[167] WTO Panel, *European Communities - Measures Affecting the Approval and Marketing of Biotech Products* (29 September 2006), WT/DS291/R, WT/DS292/R, WT/DS293/R, paras 7.10–7.11, 7.12–7.32, 7.37–7.46.

[168] WTO Panel, *European Communities - Measures Affecting the Approval and Marketing of Biotech Products* (29 September 2006), WT/DS291/R, WT/DS292/R, WT/DS293/R, paras 7.49–7.96.

should not be read in clinical isolation from public international law.[169] It also mentioned the Appellate Body Report in *US – Shrimp*[170] according to which WTO provisions could also be interpreted by reference to treaties which are not binding upon all parties to a dispute.[171] Therefore, and although the CBD and the Cartagena Protocol were not binding upon all parties to the present dispute, these instruments should be considered by the Panel in its interpretation of WTO provisions.[172] The EC further mentioned connections between the Cartagena Protocol and the SPS Agreement and that they should be seen as complementary. Also, the negotiators of the Protocol were aware of the existing WTO obligations and could hardly have intended inconsistencies of both international regimes.[173] The US disagreed with the EC's view and emphasised that the Cartagena Protocol cannot be considered as a rule of international law in the sense of Article 31(3)(c) VCLT.[174] Furthermore, the US referred to the Cartagena Protocol's Preamble explicitly stating that it does not change rights and obligations under any existing international agreement.[175] Lastly, the US claimed that the EC had not sufficiently shown how the Cartagena Protocol or the precautionary principle are relevant for the interpretation of WTO provisions at stake in the present dispute.[176] Canada also mentioned the Protocol's Preamble as a reason for not taking the Cartagena Protocol into account.[177] And it stated that international agreements can only be taken into account under Article 31(3)(c) VCLT if all WTO members are party to the agreement.[178]

The Panel in its findings determines what is meant by "the parties" in Article 31(3)(c) VCLT and comes to the conclusion that Article 31(3)(c) VCLT only

---

[169] WTO Panel, *European Communities - Measures Affecting the Approval and Marketing of Biotech Products* (29 September 2006), WT/DS291/R, WT/DS292/R, WT/DS293/R, para 7.49 referring to WTO Appellate Body, *United States - Standards for Reformulated and Conventional Gasoline* (29 April 1996a), WT/DS2/AB/R, 17.

[170] WTO Appellate Body, *United States - Import Prohibition of Certain Shrimp and Shrimp Products* (12 October 1998b), WT/DS58/AB/R.

[171] WTO Panel, *European Communities - Measures Affecting the Approval and Marketing of Biotech Products* (29 September 2006), WT/DS291/R, WT/DS292/R, WT/DS293/R, para 7.52.

[172] WTO Panel, *European Communities - Measures Affecting the Approval and Marketing of Biotech Products* (29 September 2006), WT/DS291/R, WT/DS292/R, WT/DS293/R, para 7.53.

[173] WTO Panel, *European Communities - Measures Affecting the Approval and Marketing of Biotech Products* (29 September 2006), WT/DS291/R, WT/DS292/R, WT/DS293/R, paras 7.54–7.55.

[174] WTO Panel, *European Communities - Measures Affecting the Approval and Marketing of Biotech Products* (29 September 2006), WT/DS291/R, WT/DS292/R, WT/DS293/R, para 7.58.

[175] WTO Panel, *European Communities - Measures Affecting the Approval and Marketing of Biotech Products* (29 September 2006), WT/DS291/R, WT/DS292/R, WT/DS293/R, para 7.59.

[176] WTO Panel, *European Communities - Measures Affecting the Approval and Marketing of Biotech Products* (29 September 2006), WT/DS291/R, WT/DS292/R, WT/DS293/R, para 7.59.

[177] WTO Panel, *European Communities - Measures Affecting the Approval and Marketing of Biotech Products* (29 September 2006), WT/DS291/R, WT/DS292/R, WT/DS293/R, para 7.61.

[178] WTO Panel, *European Communities - Measures Affecting the Approval and Marketing of Biotech Products* (29 September 2006), WT/DS291/R, WT/DS292/R, WT/DS293/R, para 7.60.

encompasses those international instruments which are binding upon all parties of the treaty that is being interpreted. In the case at hand, this means that only instruments binding upon all WTO members can be taken into account for the interpretation of the relevant WTO provisions.[179] Since the US is not a party to the CBD and the Cartagena Protocol and also Canada and Argentina are not parties to the Cartagena Protocol, these instruments must not be considered in the dispute.[180]

With regard to the EC's argument that the "precautionary principle has by now become a fully-fledged and general principle of international law",[181] the Panel notes that the precautionary principle could be taken into account under Article 31(3)(c) VCLT if it constituted a general principle of international law.[182] However, the Panel does not consider it necessary to resolve the disputed question of the precautionary principle's legal status in international law since the principle is not necessary to dispose of the legal claims in the present dispute.[183]

After having made these general observations, the Panel gives an overview of the measures at issue and the relevant EC approval procedures[184] and examines whether these approval procedures fall within the scope of the SPS Agreement.[185] It qualifies Directive 90/220, Directive 2001/18 and Regulation 258/97 as SPS measures. As such, they are subject to the provisions of the SPS Agreement.[186]

The Panel then examines the complaints about a general EC moratorium. A large part of that examination concerns the existence of such a moratorium as alleged by the complaining parties.[187] It finds that there was a *de facto* moratorium on approvals in effect in the EC between 1999 and 2003 under Directive 90/220/EEC and

---

[179] WTO Panel, *European Communities - Measures Affecting the Approval and Marketing of Biotech Products* (29 September 2006), WT/DS291/R, WT/DS292/R, WT/DS293/R, para 7.68.

[180] WTO Panel, *European Communities - Measures Affecting the Approval and Marketing of Biotech Products* (29 September 2006), WT/DS291/R, WT/DS292/R, WT/DS293/R, paras 7.74–7.75.

[181] WTO Panel, *European Communities - Measures Affecting the Approval and Marketing of Biotech Products* (29 September 2006), WT/DS291/R, WT/DS292/R, WT/DS293/R, para 7.78.

[182] WTO Panel, *European Communities - Measures Affecting the Approval and Marketing of Biotech Products* (29 September 2006), WT/DS291/R, WT/DS292/R, WT/DS293/R, para 7.67.

[183] WTO Panel, *European Communities - Measures Affecting the Approval and Marketing of Biotech Products* (29 September 2006), WT/DS291/R, WT/DS292/R, WT/DS293/R, para 7.89 with reference to WTO Appellate Body, *EC Measures Concerning Meat and Meat Products (Hormones)* (16 January 1998a), WT/DS26/AB/R, WT/DS48/AB/R, paras 123–124.

[184] WTO Panel, *European Communities - Measures Affecting the Approval and Marketing of Biotech Products* (29 September 2006), WT/DS291/R, WT/DS292/R, WT/DS293/R, paras 7.97–7.146.

[185] WTO Panel, *European Communities - Measures Affecting the Approval and Marketing of Biotech Products* (29 September 2006), WT/DS291/R, WT/DS292/R, WT/DS293/R, paras 7.147–7.437.

[186] WTO Panel, *European Communities - Measures Affecting the Approval and Marketing of Biotech Products* (29 September 2006), WT/DS291/R, WT/DS292/R, WT/DS293/R, para 7.436.

[187] WTO Panel, *European Communities - Measures Affecting the Approval and Marketing of Biotech Products* (29 September 2006), WT/DS291/R, WT/DS292/R, WT/DS293/R, paras 7.457–7.1285.

Directive 2001/18/EC as well as under Regulation 258/97.[188] Further, the Panel decides to make findings on this general EC moratorium although the moratorium might have ceased to exist after panel proceedings were instituted.[189]

In its analysis of the moratorium's compatibility with the SPS Agreement, the Panel does not qualify the general *de facto* moratorium as an SPS measure in the sense of Articles 5.1, 5.6, 5.5 and 2.2 SPS Agreement.[190] Further, the Panel decides that Article 2.3 SPS Agreement is not violated by the *de facto* moratorium since a violation of Article 2.3 SPS Agreement is premised on a violation of Article 5.5 SPS Agreement according to the complainants' submission.[191] Also, Article 7 in conjunction with Annex B(1) of the SPS Agreement is not violated by the general *de facto* moratorium since the moratorium does not qualify as an SPS regulation in the sense of Annex B(1) of the SPS Agreement.[192]

The Panel then examines a violation of Article 8 in conjunction with Annex C(1)(a) and (b) SPS Agreement.[193]

It qualifies Annex C(1)(a) of the SPS Agreement as a good faith obligation which allows Member States "to take the time that is reasonably needed to determine with adequate confidence whether their relevant SPS requirements are fulfilled, at least if these requirements are WTO-consistent".[194] It finds that the term "undertaken and completed without undue delay" has to be interpreted in the way that approval procedures be undertaken with no unjustifiable loss of time.[195] For the determination of

---

[188] WTO Panel, *European Communities - Measures Affecting the Approval and Marketing of Biotech Products* (29 September 2006), WT/DS291/R, WT/DS292/R, WT/DS293/R, paras 7.1272, 7.1285.

[189] WTO Panel, *European Communities - Measures Affecting the Approval and Marketing of Biotech Products* (29 September 2006), WT/DS291/R, WT/DS292/R, WT/DS293/R, para 7.1312.

[190] WTO Panel, *European Communities - Measures Affecting the Approval and Marketing of Biotech Products* (29 September 2006), WT/DS291/R, WT/DS292/R, WT/DS293/R, paras 7.1393, 7.1405, 7.1419, 7.1440.

[191] WTO Panel, *European Communities - Measures Affecting the Approval and Marketing of Biotech Products* (29 September 2006), WT/DS291/R, WT/DS292/R, WT/DS293/R, para 7.1447.

[192] WTO Panel, *European Communities - Measures Affecting the Approval and Marketing of Biotech Products* (29 September 2006), WT/DS291/R, WT/DS292/R, WT/DS293/R, paras 7.1445–7.1463.

[193] A violation of Article 8 and Annex C(1)(a) was only asserted by the US and Canada, see WTO Panel, *European Communities - Measures Affecting the Approval and Marketing of Biotech Products* (29 September 2006), WT/DS291/R, WT/DS292/R, WT/DS293/R, para 7.1466; a violation of Article 8 and Annex C(1)(b) was only asserted by the US, see WTO Panel, *European Communities - Measures Affecting the Approval and Marketing of Biotech Products* (29 September 2006), WT/DS291/R, WT/DS292/R, WT/DS293/R, para 7.1571; however, Canada integrates a violation of Annex C(1)(b) in its claim on a violation of Annex C(1)(a), *cf.* WTO Panel, *European Communities - Measures Affecting the Approval and Marketing of Biotech Products* (29 September 2006), WT/DS291/R, WT/DS292/R, WT/DS293/R, paras 7.1472–7.1473, 7.1475.

[194] WTO Panel, *European Communities - Measures Affecting the Approval and Marketing of Biotech Products* (29 September 2006), WT/DS291/R, WT/DS292/R, WT/DS293/R, para 7.1498.

[195] WTO Panel, *European Communities - Measures Affecting the Approval and Marketing of Biotech Products* (29 September 2006), WT/DS291/R, WT/DS292/R, WT/DS293/R, para 7.1495.

whether a delay is undue, it is not the time aspect that is decisive but whether there is a legitimate reason or justification for a delay.[196] This has to be determined on a case-by-case basis, including relevant facts and circumstances and also taking into account the Agreement's object and purpose of minimizing negative trade effects.[197] Contrary to Canada's submission, missing scientific evidence for a measure does not necessarily lead to an undue delay.[198] Furthermore, the Panel notes that "without undue delay" comprises both the undertaking and completion of approval procedures.[199] In its examination of the concrete case at hand, the Panel first considers whether possible reasons mentioned by the EC for the general moratorium could have justified any delays that might have occurred.[200] Both reasons, namely the lack of EC legislation on traceability and labelling of GMOs and GMO-derived products and pending new regulations on labelling and traceability on the one hand and the incompleteness of scientific knowledge on GMOs and GMO-derived products, on the other hand, are not considered adequate to justify delays in the EC's approval procedures.[201] Since already one application that has been unduly delayed due to the general de facto moratorium leads to a violation of Annex C(1)(a), it is sufficient for the applicants to demonstrate the existence of undue delay in only one case.[202] The Panel randomly chooses an approval procedure concerning MS8/RF3 oilseed rape that has been brought forward by both the US and Canada.[203] It finds that the Commission by not sufficiently trying to cast a vote on this application without legitimate reasons has unjustifiably delayed this approval procedure and that this delay was a consequence of the general de facto moratorium.[204] Thus, the Panel

[196] WTO Panel, *European Communities - Measures Affecting the Approval and Marketing of Biotech Products* (29 September 2006), WT/DS291/R, WT/DS292/R, WT/DS293/R, para 7.1469.

[197] WTO Panel, *European Communities - Measures Affecting the Approval and Marketing of Biotech Products* (29 September 2006), WT/DS291/R, WT/DS292/R, WT/DS293/R, paras 7.1497, 7.1499.

[198] WTO Panel, *European Communities - Measures Affecting the Approval and Marketing of Biotech Products* (29 September 2006), WT/DS291/R, WT/DS292/R, WT/DS293/R, para 7.1500.

[199] WTO Panel, *European Communities - Measures Affecting the Approval and Marketing of Biotech Products* (29 September 2006), WT/DS291/R, WT/DS292/R, WT/DS293/R, para 7.1501.

[200] WTO Panel, *European Communities - Measures Affecting the Approval and Marketing of Biotech Products* (29 September 2006), WT/DS291/R, WT/DS292/R, WT/DS293/R, paras 7.1506–7.1530.

[201] WTO Panel, *European Communities - Measures Affecting the Approval and Marketing of Biotech Products* (29 September 2006), WT/DS291/R, WT/DS292/R, WT/DS293/R, paras 7.1518, 7.1529, 7.1530.

[202] WTO Panel, *European Communities - Measures Affecting the Approval and Marketing of Biotech Products* (29 September 2006), WT/DS291/R, WT/DS292/R, WT/DS293/R, paras 7.1504, 7.1568.

[203] WTO Panel, *European Communities - Measures Affecting the Approval and Marketing of Biotech Products* (29 September 2006), WT/DS291/R, WT/DS292/R, WT/DS293/R, para 7.1533.

[204] WTO Panel, *European Communities - Measures Affecting the Approval and Marketing of Biotech Products* (29 September 2006), WT/DS291/R, WT/DS292/R, WT/DS293/R, paras 7.1550–7.1565.

finds that the European Communities have violated Article 8 in conjunction with Annex C(1)(a) of the SPS Agreement.[205]

Lastly, the Panel examines a violation of Article 8 in conjunction with Annex C(1)(b) of the SPS Agreement brought forward by the US and a violation of Article 10.1 SPS Agreement brought forward by Argentina. In both cases, it finds that the complainants have not sufficiently demonstrated a violation of the respective provisions.[206]

Regarding the general de facto moratorium, the Panel therefore only finds a violation of Article 8 in conjunction with Annex C(1)(a) of the SPS Agreement.

After having analysed the general de facto moratorium, the Panel examines the applicants' claims concerning product-specific measures. With regard to the claimants' assertion of a violation of Articles 5.1, 5.5 and 5.6 SPS Agreement by the product-specific measures, the Panel finds that the product-specific moratoria applied by the EC do not constitute SPS measures and therefore, Articles 5.1, 5.5 and 5.6 SPS Agreement are not applicable.[207] Furthermore, the Panel rejects violations of Articles 2.2 and 2.3 SPS Agreement alleged by Canada since they are premised on a violation of Articles 5.5 and 5.6 SPS Agreement.[208] Also, a violation of Article 7 and Annex B(1) brought forward by the US is rejected.[209]

The Panel only finds a violation of Annex C(1)(a), first clause by most of the product-specific moratoria.[210]

A violation of Annex C(1)(a), second clause, claimed by Argentina, is rejected. The Panel finds that Annex C(1)(a), second clause entails the national treatment obligation but does not make findings on the likeness of imported biotech products and domestic non-biotech products. Instead, it finds that Argentina has not

[205] WTO Panel, *European Communities - Measures Affecting the Approval and Marketing of Biotech Products* (29 September 2006), WT/DS291/R, WT/DS292/R, WT/DS293/R, paras 7.1569–7.1570.

[206] See WTO Panel, *European Communities - Measures Affecting the Approval and Marketing of Biotech Products* (29 September 2006), WT/DS291/R, WT/DS292/R, WT/DS293/R, paras 7.1604, 7.1627.

[207] WTO Panel, *European Communities - Measures Affecting the Approval and Marketing of Biotech Products* (29 September 2006), WT/DS291/R, WT/DS292/R, WT/DS293/R, paras 7.1700, 7.1705, 7.1712–7.1714, 7.1721–7.1722, 7.1727–7.1729, 7.1740–7.1743, 7.1748–7.1750.

[208] WTO Panel, *European Communities - Measures Affecting the Approval and Marketing of Biotech Products* (29 September 2006), WT/DS291/R, WT/DS292/R, WT/DS293/R, paras 7.1757–7.1758, 7.1760, 7.1765–7.1766.

[209] WTO Panel, *European Communities - Measures Affecting the Approval and Marketing of Biotech Products* (29 September 2006), WT/DS291/R, WT/DS292/R, WT/DS293/R, paras 7.1776–7.1778.

[210] See WTO Panel, *European Communities - Measures Affecting the Approval and Marketing of Biotech Products* (29 September 2006), WT/DS291/R, WT/DS292/R, WT/DS293/R, paras 7.2390–7.2391 and table on p. 843.

submitted sufficient evidence that imported biotech products have been accorded less favourable treatment because of their origin.[211]

Alleged violations of Annex C(1)(b), (c) and (e) are also rejected.[212]

A violation of Article III:4 GATT as alleged by Canada and Argentina is not examined by the Panel for reasons of judicial economy[213] and because Argentina has not sufficiently shown that the different treatment of imported biotech products and domestic non-biotech products is depending on the imported products' origin.[214]

The claims brought forward by Canada and Argentina concerning a violation of the TBT Agreement's provisions are not considered by the Panel since these were brought forward as alternative claims in case a violation of the SPS Agreement is not found.[215]

In a further part, the Panel examines the claimants' allegations that nine safeguard measures[216] applied by six EC Member States are inconsistent with WTO law,[217] namely with the SPS Agreement, the GATT and the TBT Agreement.[218] The

---

[211] WTO Panel, *European Communities - Measures Affecting the Approval and Marketing of Biotech Products* (29 September 2006), WT/DS291/R, WT/DS292/R, WT/DS293/R, paras 7.2418–7.2419.

[212] WTO Panel, *European Communities - Measures Affecting the Approval and Marketing of Biotech Products* (29 September 2006), WT/DS291/R, WT/DS292/R, WT/DS293/R, paras 7.2474, 7.2487, 7.2498.

[213] WTO Panel, *European Communities - Measures Affecting the Approval and Marketing of Biotech Products* (29 September 2006), WT/DS291/R, WT/DS292/R, WT/DS293/R, para 7.2505.

[214] WTO Panel, *European Communities - Measures Affecting the Approval and Marketing of Biotech Products* (29 September 2006), WT/DS291/R, WT/DS292/R, WT/DS293/R, para 7.2514.

[215] WTO Panel, *European Communities - Measures Affecting the Approval and Marketing of Biotech Products* (29 September 2006), WT/DS291/R, WT/DS292/R, WT/DS293/R, paras 7.2524, 7.2526–7.2527.

[216] "Where a biotech product has been approved for Community-wide marketing under Directives 90/220 or 2001/18, or Regulation 258/97, member States ordinarily may not prohibit or restrict trade in, or use of, that product on their respective territories, provided the conditions attached to the marketing approval are being met. Exceptionally, however, member States may provisionally adopt safeguard measures which prohibit or restrict trade in, or use of, biotech products which have been granted Community-wide marketing approval. Pursuant to Article 16 of Directive 90/220, a member State may provisionally restrict or prohibit the use and or sale of a product in its territory where it has 'justifiable reasons to consider that a product which has been properly notified and has received written consent [...] constitutes a risk to human health or the environment'.", WTO Panel, *European Communities - Measures Affecting the Approval and Marketing of Biotech Products* (29 September 2006), WT/DS291/R, WT/DS292/R, WT/DS293/R, paras 7.2530–7.2531; for the possibility to apply safeguard measures, see also above Chap. 4, p. 70.

[217] These safeguard measures are taken by Austria with regard to T25 maize, Bt-176 maize and MON810 maize; by France with regard to MS1/RF1 oilseed rape (EC-161) and Topas oilseed rape; by Germany with regard to Bt-176 maize; by Greece with regard to Topas oilseed rape; by Italy with regard to BT-11 maize (EC-163), MON810 maize, MON809 maize and T25 maize; and by Luxembourg with regard to Bt-176 maize, see WTO Panel, *European Communities - Measures Affecting the Approval and Marketing of Biotech Products* (29 September 2006), WT/DS291/R, WT/DS292/R, WT/DS293/R, para 7.2534.

[218] WTO Panel, *European Communities - Measures Affecting the Approval and Marketing of Biotech Products* (29 September 2006), WT/DS291/R, WT/DS292/R, WT/DS293/R, paras

legal basis for these safeguard measures was Article 16 of Directive 90/220/EEC (later replaced by Article 23 of Directive 2001/18/EC) and Article 12 of Regulation 258/97. The Panel finds that the Commission has not taken any decision on these measures although assessments by EC scientific committees have found no new risks with regard to the specific products to which safeguard measures were applied.[219]

In its analysis, the Panel first finds that all safeguard measures challenged constitute SPS measures in the sense of Annex A(1) and Article 1.1 SPS Agreement.[220]

The Panel then assesses whether the safeguard measures applied by the EC Member States are consistent with Article 5.1 SPS Agreement. It finds that the risk assessment required by Article 5.1 SPS Agreement is one in the sense of Annex A(4),[221] but that a Member State does not necessarily have to carry out a risk assessment on its own.[222] Therefore, also the risk assessments conducted by the "lead CA"[223] and by the EC scientific committees qualify as risk assessments for the application of safeguard measures.[224] Furthermore, the Panel notes that SPS measures must be based on a risk assessment in the sense that there is a rational relationship between a risk assessment and the SPS measure. This means, that "the results of the risk assessment must 'sufficiently warrant' or 'reasonably support' the SPS measure at issue".[225] Whether there is a valid risk assessment and whether the safeguard measures have been based on that risk assessment, has to be determined for each safeguard measure separately according to the Panel.[226] Concerning the

7.2538–7.2544.

[219] WTO Panel, *European Communities - Measures Affecting the Approval and Marketing of Biotech Products* (29 September 2006), WT/DS291/R, WT/DS292/R, WT/DS293/R, para 7.2536.

[220] See WTO Panel, *European Communities - Measures Affecting the Approval and Marketing of Biotech Products* (29 September 2006), WT/DS291/R, WT/DS292/R, WT/DS293/R, paras 7.2610, 7.2662, 7.2702, 7.2749, 7.2774, 7.2813, 7.2854, 7.2891, 7.2922.

[221] WTO Panel, *European Communities - Measures Affecting the Approval and Marketing of Biotech Products* (29 September 2006), WT/DS291/R, WT/DS292/R, WT/DS293/R, para 7.3023.

[222] WTO Panel, *European Communities - Measures Affecting the Approval and Marketing of Biotech Products* (29 September 2006), WT/DS291/R, WT/DS292/R, WT/DS293/R, para 7.3024.

[223] The lead CA is "the CA [competent authority] of the member State to which the product application was originally submitted", WTO Panel, *European Communities - Measures Affecting the Approval and Marketing of Biotech Products* (29 September 2006), WT/DS291/R, WT/DS292/R, WT/DS293/R, para 7.3026.

[224] WTO Panel, *European Communities - Measures Affecting the Approval and Marketing of Biotech Products* (29 September 2006), WT/DS291/R, WT/DS292/R, WT/DS293/R, para 7.3027.

[225] WTO Panel, *European Communities - Measures Affecting the Approval and Marketing of Biotech Products* (29 September 2006), WT/DS291/R, WT/DS292/R, WT/DS293/R, para 7.3028 with reference to WTO Appellate Body, *EC Measures Concerning Meat and Meat Products (Hormones)* (16 January 1998a), WT/DS26/AB/R, WT/DS48/AB/R, paras 193–194.

[226] WTO Panel, *European Communities - Measures Affecting the Approval and Marketing of Biotech Products* (29 September 2006), WT/DS291/R, WT/DS292/R, WT/DS293/R, para 7.3029.

individual safeguard measures, the Panel finds that no Member State has carried out an individual risk assessment for any of these measures.[227]

But since there have been risk assessments carried out by the lead CA and EC scientific committees with regard to each of these measures which qualify as risk assessments in the sense of Article 5.1 and Annex A(4) SPS Agreement,[228] the Panel examines whether the individual safeguard measures have been based on these risk assessments. While it admits that risk assessments reflecting divergent opinions can serve as a basis for different SPS measures this is not the case here. The risk assessments carried out by the lead CA and the EC scientific committees do not warrant the safeguard measures taken by the Member States.[229] Furthermore, the Panel finds that a precautionary approach does not relieve the Member States from their obligation to carry out a risk assessment.[230] Thus, the Panel decides that all safeguard measures applied by six EC Member States are inconsistent with Article 5.1 SPS Agreement.[231]

It then examines each safeguard measure's consistency with Article 5.7 SPS Agreement. In case, the measures would be consistent with Article 5.7, Article 5.1 SPS Agreement would not be applicable.[232] In its analysis, the Panel first rejects the EC's argument that insufficiency of scientific evidence, as one requirement of Article 5.7 SPS Agreement, has to be assessed with reference to a Member State's appropriate level of protection.[233] Furthermore, it finds that the relevant point in time for the existence of insufficient scientific evidence is at the time of a measure's adoption.[234] Accordingly, the Panel finds for all nine safeguard measures that insufficiency of scientific evidence could not be shown at the time of adoption of the

---

[227] See WTO Panel, *European Communities - Measures Affecting the Approval and Marketing of Biotech Products* (29 September 2006), WT/DS291/R, WT/DS292/R, WT/DS293/R, paras 7.3046, 7.3051, 7.3080, 7.3096, 7.3101, 7.3122, 7.3132, 7.3152, 7.3172, 7.3190, 7.3206.

[228] WTO Panel, *European Communities - Measures Affecting the Approval and Marketing of Biotech Products* (29 September 2006), WT/DS291/R, WT/DS292/R, WT/DS293/R, para 7.3054.

[229] WTO Panel, *European Communities - Measures Affecting the Approval and Marketing of Biotech Products* (29 September 2006), WT/DS291/R, WT/DS292/R, WT/DS293/R, paras 7.3059–7.3064, 7.3085–7.3086, 7.3106–7.3107, 7.3127–7.3128, 7.3137–7.3138, 7.3157–7.3158, 7.3177–7.3178, 7.3195–7.3196, 7.3211–7.3212.

[230] WTO Panel, *European Communities - Measures Affecting the Approval and Marketing of Biotech Products* (29 September 2006), WT/DS291/R, WT/DS292/R, WT/DS293/R, paras 7.3065–7.3067.

[231] See WTO Panel, *European Communities - Measures Affecting the Approval and Marketing of Biotech Products* (29 September 2006), WT/DS291/R, WT/DS292/R, WT/DS293/R, paras 7.3069, 7.3085, 7.3106, 7.3127, 7.3137, 7.3157, 7.3177, 7.3195, 7.3211.

[232] WTO Panel, *European Communities - Measures Affecting the Approval and Marketing of Biotech Products* (29 September 2006), WT/DS291/R, WT/DS292/R, WT/DS293/R, para 7.3217.

[233] WTO Panel, *European Communities - Measures Affecting the Approval and Marketing of Biotech Products* (29 September 2006), WT/DS291/R, WT/DS292/R, WT/DS293/R, para 7.3246.

[234] WTO Panel, *European Communities - Measures Affecting the Approval and Marketing of Biotech Products* (29 September 2006), WT/DS291/R, WT/DS292/R, WT/DS293/R, para 7.3253.

safeguard measures.[235] Therefore, the requirements for Article 5.7 SPS Agreement are not met and Article 5.1 is applicable.[236]

Furthermore, the Panel sees no need to examine possible violations of Articles 5.6, 5.5 and 2.3 SPS Agreement as alleged by Canada and Argentina for the reason that the safeguard measures cannot be maintained in the present form due to their inconsistency with Article 5.1 SPS Agreement.[237] But it finds that the inconsistency with Article 5.1 also leads to a violation of Article 2.2 SPS Agreement.[238]

Since the safeguard measures fall within the SPS Agreement, the Panel does not consider alleged violations of the TBT Agreement brought forward by Canada and Argentina.[239] Also, it does not examine alleged violations of Article III:4 GATT and Article XI:1 GATT for reasons of judicial economy.[240]

In summary, the Panel decided that the general *de facto* moratorium resulted in a violation of Article 8 and Annex C of the SPS Agreement due to the EC's failure to complete individual authorisation procedures without undue delay.[241] Furthermore, the Panel found that nine safeguard measures taken by Member States were not in compliance with the obligations laid down in Article 5 of the SPS Agreement.[242] The Panel also emphasised that it did not decide on whether biotech products, in general, are safe or not,[243] it did not decide on the question of likeness of biotech and non-biotech products, it did not decide on the general legitimacy of the EC pre-marketing approval system and whether the approval procedures established by the

[235] See WTO Panel, *European Communities - Measures Affecting the Approval and Marketing of Biotech Products* (29 September 2006), WT/DS291/R, WT/DS292/R, WT/DS293/R, paras 7.3260, 7.3273, 7.3286, 7.3300, 7.3314, 7.3327, 7.3341, 7.3356, 7.3369.

[236] See WTO Panel, *European Communities - Measures Affecting the Approval and Marketing of Biotech Products* (29 September 2006), WT/DS291/R, WT/DS292/R, WT/DS293/R, paras 7.3261, 7.3274, 7.3287, 7.3301, 7.3315, 7.3328, 7.3342, 7.3357, 7.3370.

[237] WTO Panel, *European Communities - Measures Affecting the Approval and Marketing of Biotech Products* (29 September 2006), WT/DS291/R, WT/DS292/R, WT/DS293/R, paras 7.3377, 7.3384 and 7.3405.

[238] WTO Panel, *European Communities - Measures Affecting the Approval and Marketing of Biotech Products* (29 September 2006), WT/DS291/R, WT/DS292/R, WT/DS293/R, para 7.3396.

[239] WTO Panel, *European Communities - Measures Affecting the Approval and Marketing of Biotech Products* (29 September 2006), WT/DS291/R, WT/DS292/R, WT/DS293/R, paras 7.3412–7.3413.

[240] WTO Panel, *European Communities - Measures Affecting the Approval and Marketing of Biotech Products* (29 September 2006), WT/DS291/R, WT/DS292/R, WT/DS293/R, paras 7.3422, 7.3429.

[241] WTO Panel, *European Communities - Measures Affecting the Approval and Marketing of Biotech Products* (29 September 2006), WT/DS291/R, WT/DS292/R, WT/DS293/R, paras 8.6–8.7.

[242] WTO Panel, *European Communities - Measures Affecting the Approval and Marketing of Biotech Products* (29 September 2006), WT/DS291/R, WT/DS292/R, WT/DS293/R, paras 8.8–8.10.

[243] In this regard it was speculated whether the claims were expressly kept narrow in order to avoid findings on the safety of GMOs, *cf.* Cheyne (2008), p. 54.

EC are WTO-consistent and it did not decide on the findings by the EC scientific committees in their safety evaluations of specific biotech products.[244]

5.2.8.2.2 Assessment of the WTO Dispute

The report from the DSB clearly shows that the WTO system was not designed for the regulation of biotechnological risks. While the DSB very carefully analyses whether the risks that come along with genetically modified organisms are comprised by Annex A I to the SPS Agreement, the DSB's approach to the SPS Agreement's scope is too broad. In contrast to the Panel's findings, the EU authorisation procedures can only be considered as SPS measures to some extent. Since the SPS Agreement does not adequately address biodiversity and environmental protection, the authorisation procedures to the extent they serve these purposes cannot be qualified as SPS measures.[245]

Although the Panel did not directly decide on the role of the precautionary principle in the WTO system, it did to some extent indirectly. Its findings on Article 5.7 SPS together with other reports by the Appellate Body support the view that the precautionary principle as it is laid down in EU law is reflected in the SPS Agreement.[246] The finding that precautionary measures are to some extent allowed by the SPS Agreement is also important in view of the Panel's findings on the relationship of WTO law and the Cartagena Protocol which incorporates the precautionary principle. The formal precedence of WTO law which was found by the Panel significantly diminishes the role of the Cartagena Protocol in the field of international plant biotechnology regulation.

In the end, the Panel's findings on alleged violations of WTO law are rather unspectacular. Expectations that the Panel report would clarify crucial questions in the context of biotechnology regulation under WTO law could not be fulfilled. In particular, the legitimacy of the EU's pre-market authorisation procedures has not been analysed since it was not called into question by the claimant States.

[244] WTO Panel, *European Communities - Measures Affecting the Approval and Marketing of Biotech Products* (29 September 2006), WT/DS291/R, WT/DS292/R, WT/DS293/R, para 8.3.

[245] For a detailed analysis of the authorisation procedures and whether they can be considered as SPS measures, see below Chap. 6, p. 168.

[246] For a detailed analysis how the precautionary principle as laid down in EU law is reflected in Article 5.7 SPS, see below Chap. 6, p. 192.

5.2.8.2.3 Reactions to the Panel Report

In general, the dispute that the Panel was concerned with in *EC – Biotech* is described as a multi-faceted and complex one.[247] On the one hand, it shows regulatory differences between WTO members in the context of science and governance,[248] but also growing differences at the interface of international trade law and the regulation of agricultural biotechnology.[249] On the other hand, it is concerned with basic questions in the context of science and governance under the WTO regime, especially under the SPS Agreement. These are questions on the proper reaction in cases of "not-knowing"[250] and on the role of social, economic and political factors in governance and regulatory decision-making.[251] The Panel's findings are considered to "have the potential to work important changes in the relationship between the SPS Agreement and environmental regulatory regimes, both domestic[ally] and international[ly]".[252] They may "have [...] opened a Pandora's Box of unintended consequences for the delicate balance between free trade and national sanitary and phytosanitary protection".[253]

5.2.8.2.3.1 Subject of Examination

It is noted that the Panel only examined compliance with the SPS Agreement and refrained from making findings with regard to compliance with the TBT Agreement, GATT and the Agriculture Agreement.[254] This is mostly for reasons of judicial economy, although violations of these agreements were brought forward by the complainants. As a consequence, fundamental questions concerning the GATT were not discussed, namely whether a different treatment of biotech and conventional products, as accorded by the EC, can be justified by small physical differences. Also, whether a different treatment is relevant under WTO law, even if the measure does not de jure—and perhaps not even de facto—discriminate against foreign products. And, under which circumstances such different treatment could be justified by Article XX GATT.[255] However, the Panel's findings on the SPS Agreement's scope are considered one of the most extraordinary and most far-reaching.[256] Since it was

---

[247] Davies (2007), p. 250; *cf.* also Gruber (2004), p. 39.

[248] Footer (2007), p. 281; however, *Footer* also notes that the differences appear especially at the risk management stage, rather than at the stage of risk assessment, *cf.* Footer (2007), pp. 287–289; see also Levidow (2007), p. 118; Cheyne (2008), p. 63.

[249] *Cf.* Footer (2007), p. 281.

[250] See Davies (2007), pp. 249, 251–252.

[251] *Cf.* Footer (2007), p. 282.

[252] Peel (2006), p. 1009.

[253] Prévost (2007), pp. 67, 71.

[254] Prévost (2007), p. 71; see also Anderson and Jackson (2012), pp. 167–168; Cheyne (2008), p. 56; Conrad (2007), p. 234.

[255] Conrad (2007), p. 234.

[256] Peel (2006), p. 1009.

the first time that the applicability of the SPS Agreement was at stake, the report is said to have an impact on future disputes in the context of the SPS Agreement.[257]

Important to note with regard to the Panel's report is that it was not concerned with *Regulation (EC) No 1829/2003 on genetically modified food and feed*[258] ('Regulation 1829/2003') and *Regulation (EC) No 1830/2003 concerning the traceability and labelling of genetically modified organisms and the traceability of food and feed products produced from genetically modified organisms*[259] ('Regulation 1830/2003'). However, there were assumptions that labelling provisions could be scrutinised by the WTO in the near future.[260] An assumption that has not yet proven to be true. But one should not underestimate the report's relevance for informal bilateral consultations set up to resolve disputes arising under the SPS Agreement's scope.[261]

5.2.8.2.3.2 Extensive Interpretation of the SPS Agreement's Scope

While the Panel outlined the criterion of a *rational relationship* as the decisive one to qualify the approval procedures as SPS measures, the Panel is criticised for not further defining this criterion.[262] Especially *Conrad* notes that the Panel chose a "'better safe than sorry'-approach"[263] by relying on several possibilities provided in Annex A to qualify approval procedures as SPS measures.[264] Also, other scholars are rather sceptical about the very broad interpretation of the Panel.[265] They mention the diffuse risks related to GMOs, especially in the environmental context, which lead to difficulties when qualifying measures in the context of GMOs as SPS measures.[266] While the SPS Agreement does not adequately deal with those risks, the TBT Agreement is proposed as a more suitable instrument to deal with environmental concerns.[267] Furthermore, the negotiation history is mentioned in favour of a

---

[257] Conrad (2007), p. 235.

[258] *Regulation (EC) No 1829/2003 on genetically modified food and feed* (consolidated version from 27 March 2021) ('Regulation 1829/2003'), Official Journal of the European Union ('OJ EU') 2003, L 268/1.

[259] *Regulation (EC) No 1830/2003 concerning the traceability and labelling of genetically modified organisms and the traceability of food and feed products produced from genetically modified organisms* (consolidated version from 26 July 2019) ('Regulation 1830/2003'), OJ EU 2003, L 268/24.

[260] Sander and Sasdi (2006), p. 141; *cf.* also Conrad (2007), pp. 233, 246.

[261] *Cf.* Prévost (2007), p. 69.

[262] Conrad (2007), pp. 238, 239.

[263] Conrad (2007), p. 240.

[264] Conrad (2007), p. 240.

[265] For extensive elaborations on the Panel's findings in this regard, see Peel (2006), pp. 1021–1024; see also Levidow and Bonneuil (2013), pp. 2–3.

[266] Conrad (2007), pp. 241–245; *cf.* Peel (2006), p. 1017.

[267] *Cf.* Peel (2006), pp. 1019–1021; Conrad (2007), p. 244, footnote 51.

narrow scope of the SPS Agreement.[268] Such a narrow scope is also supported by the notion of the precautionary approach in other international environmental agreements which is different from the SPS Agreement's approach.[269] A broad scope, therefore, is said to possibly "contribute to 'fragmentation' of international law in the health and environmental area, by facilitating complainants' framing of disputes in SPS terms so as to attract the more stringent requirements of the WTO SPS regime".[270] It is questionable whether the Panel was aware of its interpretation's far-reaching implications with regard to the interface of trade and the environment.[271]

5.2.8.2.3.3 The Panel's Understanding of Scientific Uncertainty and Precaution in the Context of the SPS Agreement

The Panel's findings with regard to the obligations laid down in the SPS Agreement are taken differently. It is noted that the Panel made few findings with regard to substantive law, but the focus rather laid on procedural obligations.[272] Its findings concerning Article 5.7 SPS Agreement are to some extent welcomed. The Panel implicitly acknowledged that "some measure of scientific uncertainty is an ever-present phenomenon"[273] and it left open the possibility to qualify what constitutes scientific evidence today as insufficient tomorrow.[274] However, the Panel's findings on Article 5.7 SPS are also criticised. To require Member States to conduct a new risk assessment to demonstrate the inadequacy of an earlier risk assessment would render Article 5.7 SPS Agreement inutile.[275] In this context, it is also criticised that while the Panel noted that the risk assessment required by Article 5.7 SPS Agreement is different from the kind of risk assessment envisaged by Annex A(4), it did not give further explanations on what kind of risk assessment is required.[276] Also, it is mentioned that the Panel's notion of risk assessment constitutes the narrowest application of this term within the SPS Agreement so far and would support the US "'science-based risk assessment' narrative".[277] Criticism is also raised with regard to a strict division between the stages of risk assessment and risk management.[278]

---

[268] Peel (2006), pp. 1016, 1018 with reference to Motaal (2004).

[269] *Cf.* Peel (2006), pp. 1016–1018.

[270] Peel (2006), pp. 1012, 1013.

[271] Peel (2006), p. 1021.

[272] Cheyne (2008), p. 61; see also Levidow and Bonneuil (2013), p. 5.

[273] Kogan (2007), p. 152.

[274] Kogan (2007), p. 153.

[275] Henckels (2006), p. 296; see also Perez (2007), pp. 272–273.

[276] Perez (2007), pp. 272–273.

[277] Levidow and Bonneuil (2013), p. 7; *Peel* notes in this respect that "[g]iven the increasingly stringent approach that panels and the Appellate Body have adopted in recent case law construing the scientific evidence requirements of the SPS Agreement, the precautionary tenor of much national and international regulation of biotechnology may make it particularly susceptible to WTO challenge", see Peel (2006), p. 1025.

[278] *Cf.* Cheyne (2008), pp. 62–63; Perez (2007), p. 278.

This "unnecessarily exclude[s] the subjective concerns of individual Member States".[279] "Uncertainties raised in scientific studies [...] might be relevant to the decision of how to respond to a risk assessment even if they do not substitute for one".[280]

Connected with the Panel's findings on Article 5.7 SPS Agreement are its findings on the precautionary principle which are criticised since the Panel refuses to give statements on the principle's status under the WTO regime[281] and in public international law,[282] respectively.[283] Furthermore, it is noted that the Panel "missed an opportunity"[284] to examine the relationship between Article 5.7 SPS Agreement and the precautionary principle. Other relevant multilateral environmental agreements and their notion of the precautionary principle should have been taken into account.[285] However, the Panel failed to elaborate on the interconnectedness of international instruments.[286] It thereby isolates WTO law and furthers the fragmentation of public international law.[287]

5.2.8.3 The WTO and the Cartagena Protocol on Biosafety

The relationship between WTO law and the Cartagena Protocol has always been the subject of debate.[288] To scrutinise government action in the field of biotechnology under WTO law and the SPS Agreement is seen as problematic in light of the more specific rules laid down in the Cartagena Protocol.[289] Whether the Cartagena Protocol's approach to precautionary government action is in line with the SPS Agreement's obligations seems to be disputed and depends on the interpretation of the Protocol's precautionary approach.[290]

---

[279] Cheyne (2008), p. 63.

[280] Cheyne (2008), p. 63; this is also supported by the Appellate Body, see Sander and Sasdi (2006), p. 142 with reference to WTO Appellate Body, *EC Measures Concerning Meat and Meat Products (Hormones)* (16 January 1998a), WT/DS26/AB/R, WT/DS48/AB/R, para 187.

[281] Perez (2007), p. 272.

[282] Kogan (2007), p. 153.

[283] For criticism on the Panel's findings with regard to the precautionary principle, *cf.* Cheyne (2008), pp. 61–62.

[284] Henckels (2006), p. 303.

[285] Henckels (2006), p. 303.

[286] Henckels (2006), pp. 278, 280; see also Conrad (2007), pp. 241–245.

[287] Riffel (2018), paras 5, 7–8.

[288] For extensive elaborations on the relationship of the WTO regime and the Cartagena Protocol, see e.g. Böckenförde (2004); Qureshi (2000); Schoenbaum (2000); see also Hahn (2008), pp. 196–198; Sheldon and Josling (2002), p. 11.

[289] See Böckenförde (2004), p. 100; see also Kerr (2014), p. 224.

[290] See Schoenbaum (2000), p. 862 stating that the Cartagena Protocol "explicitly adopts the precautionary principle for the [import] regulation of FFP-LMOs [...]. This undoubtedly will result in future conflict with the SPS Agreement, which allows the precautionary principle only for prelimi-

However, when scrutinised by the WTO DSB, the WTO rules take precedence over the Cartagena Protocol in the field of plant biotechnology regulation.[291] The Panel in *EC – Biotech* ruled that the Cartagena Protocol must not be applied when interpreting WTO rules since it does not fall within Article 31(3)(c) VCLT.[292]

Nevertheless, the Cartagena Protocol's rules cannot simply be swept under the carpet but must be given due account. The Appellate Body in *Large Civil Aircraft* pointed towards the intention of Article 31(3)(c) VCLT to ensure coherence of the interpretation of international agreements in line with their normative environments.[293] Accordingly, the international obligations of an individual Member State should be taken into account when interpreting WTO law, also where they are not binding upon all WTO Member States.[294]

With regard to the Cartagena Protocol, this is also important because States cannot bring disputes concerning biotechnology trade issues before a dispute settlement system of the Cartagena Protocol. The Protocol does not establish a binding dispute settlement mechanism.[295]

Nevertheless, the formal precedence of WTO law significantly diminishes the role of the Cartagena Protocol in the field of international plant biotechnology regulation.

Since the Cartagena Protocol is said to address biotechnological risks more adequately, it is suggested to align both agreements with regard to the definitions and procedures employed.[296]

5.2.8.4 Conclusion

Whether and how the WTO agreements cover regulations of genetically modified plants cannot yet be conclusively determined here. The WTO Panel has assumed a very broad scope of application of the SPS Agreement. A finding that cannot be fully endorsed. Furthermore, the Panel did not make any findings on whether genetically modified plants are covered by the TBT Agreement or GATT. Also, it is

---

nary regulatory decisions."; a different view is taken by *Böckenförde* who does not see a conflict of both agreements, see Böckenförde (2004), pp. 374–379.

[291] See also Biber-Klemm et al. (2011), p. 303.

[292] WTO Panel, *European Communities - Measures Affecting the Approval and Marketing of Biotech Products* (29 September 2006), WT/DS291/R, WT/DS292/R, WT/DS293/R, paras 7.74–7.75; while 173 States are parties to the Protocol, Argentina, Canada and the US as major players in the field of plant biotechnology are not, see Secretariat of the Convention on Biological Diversity (2022).

[293] *Cf.* WTO Appellate Body, *European Communities and Certain Member States - Measures Affecting Trade in Large Civil Aircraft* (18 May 2011), WT/DS316/AB/R, 845.

[294] *Cf.* WTO Appellate Body, *European Communities and Certain Member States - Measures Affecting Trade in Large Civil Aircraft* (18 May 2011), WT/DS316/AB/R, 845.

[295] *Cf.* Kerr (2014), p. 225; see also Hahn (2008), p. 198.

[296] Biber-Klemm et al. (2011), p. 305.

questionable to exclude the Cartagena protocol when answering the question of whether the EU regulations on genetically modified plants are compatible with WTO law. Since the EU is a party to the Cartagena protocol and the CBD it is not only bound by WTO law, but also by these two agreements. Therefore, the regulations of both international regimes have to be aligned.

The present work in this chapter below attempts to make a more comprehensive assessment of EU regulations on genetically modified plants, and especially genome edited plants, under the WTO framework which is still lacking. It remains to be seen whether the WTO agreements can adequately address the scientific issues that arise in the regulation of GMOs

5.3 CETA

5.3.1 Introduction

CETA establishes a free trade area on the territory of Canada and the EU as specified in Arts. 1.3 and 1.4 CETA. As a "WTO-plus" agreement, it reconfirms, improves and complements the WTO rules that also govern trade relations between Canada and the EU which are both WTO members.[297] CETA adds to WTO rules in a country-specific manner and by establishing additional mechanisms such as enhanced regulatory cooperation.[298] Hereby, it aims at increasing regulatory compatibility to remove differences that could present obstacles to bilateral trade.[299] Its conformity with WTO law is guaranteed by Arts. XXIV GATT and Article V *General Agreement on Trade in Services*[300] to which a cross-reference can be found in Article 1.4 CETA.[301] Also, WTO obligations of the EU and Canada are to a large part incorporated into CETA. The parties affirm their rights and obligations under the WTO Agreement in Article 1.5 CETA.

But why is such a bilateral free trade agreement necessary when trade relations between Canada and the EU are already governed by WTO law? There are several grounds mentioned for this additional cooperation.[302] Trade negotiations between WTO members are characterised by difficulties: the complexity of topics, conflicting interests and a decision-making process that is based on consensus which complicates effective decision-making.[303] Furthermore, the reduction of non-tariff

[297] *Cf.* Griller et al. (2017b), p. vii; Vranes (2017), p. 47.

[298] Griller et al. (2017b), p. vii; Vranes (2017), p. 49; for details on "enhanced regulatory cooperation" see Sect. 5.3.3.5; *cf.* also Stoll et al. (2016), p. 12.

[299] See also Griller et al. (2017a), p. 4 referring to a statement by Thomas Hirst.

[300] *General Agreement on Trade in Services*, Annex 1B to the WTO Agreement, see footnote 11.

[301] See also Vranes (2017), pp. 48–49.

[302] See Griller et al. (2017a), pp. 4–5.

[303] *Cf.* Griller et al. (2017a), p. 4; see also Petersmann (2017a), p. 18.

barriers which are in most cases the reason for obstacles to international trade is difficult to achieve in a multilateral context. Overcoming such non-tariff barriers often requires cooperative strategies on a bilateral level.[304] The aim to remove such barriers makes up a large part of CETA.[305]

The negotiation and signature process was accompanied by heavy disputes and criticism not only with regard to the question of EU Member State involvement.[306] There were also fears that the investment framework installed by CETA could discriminate against Europeans and violate fundamental principles of EU law[307] and that regulatory standards in the EU, such as the precautionary principle, are not adequately addressed throughout the agreement and have to adapt to Canadian regulatory standards.[308] In this regard, it was acknowledged that CETA entails environmental aspects,[309] but that these are not on an equal footing with trade and investment aspects.[310]

From an economic perspective, CETA is said to have a higher impact on Canada than on the EU since the EU is already Canada's second-largest trade partner but not the other way around.[311] It may also help Canada to counterbalance the US influence on its economy.[312] But also for the EU, CETA turned into an important project and it spent major effort in making this project work despite obstacles by the EU Member States and society.[313]

Furthermore, CETA as a mega-regional trade agreement is hoped to set global standards on trade issues that spill over to other agreements. This should prevent other rising economic powers such as China from fundamentally influencing such standards.[314] As such, CETA can serve as a regulatory alliance against China or other Asian countries.

---

[304] *Cf.* Griller et al. (2017a), p. 5; see also Stoll (2017), p. 7.

[305] *Cf.* Vranes (2017), p. 47.

[306] See below Sects. 5.3.2.1–5.3.2.2.

[307] *Cf.* Schill (2017), pp. 114–115; Croisant (2019); Arcuri et al. (2020); see also Petersmann (2017b) and *Nettesheim* who notes that the whole CETA framework, especially its harmonising effects, could circumvent democratic processes, Nettesheim (2017), pp. 20–21.

[308] For the precautionary principle in the context of CETA, see Stoll et al. (2016), pp. 12–17; see also Stoll (2017), p. 9 where he acknowledges that the precautionary principle is implicitly reflected in CETA in the context of environmental and labour standards; *cf.* also *Nettesheim* who notes that it is possible that the CETA provisions are no longer comprised by EU trade policy, but rather reach far beyond the border having harmonising effects in the contracting party's State(s), see Nettesheim (2017), p. 20.

[309] Vranes (2017), p. 49; *cf.* Stoll (2017), p. 9.

[310] *Cf.* Stoll et al. (2016), pp. 5, 14.

[311] *Cf.* Griller et al. (2017a), p. 7.

[312] *Cf.* Griller et al. (2017a), p. 11.

[313] *Cf.* Griller et al. (2017a), p. 12; see also below.

[314] *Cf.* Griller et al. (2017a), p. 8; see also Fahey (2017), p. 295 on the role of CETA for global governance.

CETA falls within the scope of treaty law as laid down in Article 38(1)(a) of the *Statute of the International Court of Justice*.[315] Accordingly, the customary rules on treaty interpretation laid down in the VCLT are applicable.[316]

5.3.2 *The Beginnings of CETA*

5.3.2.1 Negotiation History

After a joint study[317] examining the costs and benefits of pursuing a closer economic partnership was conducted by Canada and the European Union, the Council of the European Union authorised the European Commission to open negotiations for CETA in April 2009.[318] The launch of trade negotiations was announced at the Canada-EU Summit 2009. CETA was officially negotiated between May 2009 and August 2014, before it was legally reviewed until February 2016.[319] After the Council of the European Union had adopted its decision to sign CETA,[320] it was signed by Canada and the EU on 30 October 2016.[321] The European Parliament gave its consent in February 2017.[322] And, CETA has been provisionally applied since September 2017 with regard to all parts that fall within the exclusive competence of the EU.[323] The Agreement can fully enter into force after ratification by all 27 EU Member States and formal conclusion by the Council of the European Union.[324] As of today, 15 Member States have notified the Council of the European Union of

[315] *Statute of the International Court of Justice* (adopted 26 June 1945) 15 UNCIO 355.

[316] See Article 1 VCLT.

[317] Government of Canada and European Commission (n.d.).

[318] Council of the European Union (2013), p. 1.

[319] See Federal Ministry for Economic Affairs and Energy (n.d.) and Government of Canada (2018); see also European Commission (2016a), p. 1.

[320] *Council Decision (EU) 2017/37 of 28 October 2016 on the signing on behalf of the European Union of the Comprehensive Economic and Trade Agreement (CETA) between Canada, of the one part, and the European Union and its Member States, of the other part* ('Council Decision 2017/37'), OJ EU 2017, L11/1; Council of the European Union (2016c).

[321] Government of Canada (2018).

[322] See Council Decision 2017/37; see also European Parliament (2017b); European Parliament (2017a).

[323] *Notice concerning the provisional application of the Comprehensive Economic and Trade Agreement (CETA) between Canada, of the one part, and the European Union and its Member States, of the other part* (2017); see also *Council Decision (EU) 2017/38 of 28 October 2018 on the provisional application of the Comprehensive Economic and Trade Agreement (CETA) between Canada, of the one part, and the European Union and its Member States, of the other part* ('Council Decision 2017/38'), OJ EU 2017, L 11/1080.

[324] See Federal Ministry for Economic Affairs and Energy (n.d.) and Government of Canada (2018); see also European Commission (2016a), p. 1; European Parliamentary Research Service (2017).

their ratification.[325] The signature of CETA was accompanied by the signature of a *Strategic Partnership Agreement between the European Union and its Member States, of the one part, and Canada, of the other part.*[326]

The conclusion of CETA almost failed because of the opposition of the Wallonian parliament which prevented Belgium from signing CETA.[327] This blockade was solved by an internal agreement between the Federal Government of Belgium and the governments of the federated entities. This agreement included the request for an opinion from the CJEU "regarding the compatibility of certain aspects of CETA with the European Treaties, in particular with regards to Opinion 2/15."[328] With its request to the CJEU, Belgium sought an opinion on the question of whether "Section F ('Resolution of investment disputes between investors and states') of Chapter Eight ('Investment') of [CETA] [is] compatible with the [European] Treaties, including with fundamental rights".[329] The CJEU in its opinion concluded that Section F of Chapter eight is compatible with EU primary law.[330]

As a reaction to major resistance by some EU Member States to the signature of CETA, the *Joint Interpretative Instrument on the Comprehensive Economic and Trade Agreement (CETA) between Canada and the European Union and its Member States*[331] was released which can serve as an interpretative document according to customary international law as laid down in Article 31(2)(b) VCLT.[332]

5.3.2.2 Legal Nature of CETA and Its Provisional Application

Before its signature, there was substantial dispute about the legal nature of CETA. This dispute was related to the EU's competencies to conclude such an agreement in its entirety without the involvement of Member States' parliaments. While the European Commission considered the agreement to fall under the EU's

---

[325] See Council of the European Union, https://www.consilium.europa.eu/en/documents-publications/treaties-agreements/agreement/?id=2016017; for the United Kingdom CETA ceased to apply from 01 January 2021, see Government of the United Kingdom (n.d.).

[326] Council of the European Union (2016a); for more information, see European Union External Action (n.d.).

[327] Rankin (2016); *Belgium Walloons block key EU Ceta trade deal with Canada* (2016a).

[328] Federale Overheidsdienst, Kingdom of Belgium (2017), p. 1.

[329] CJEU, *Opinion 1/17 - EU-Canada CET Agreement* (30 April 2019), ECLI:EU:C:2019:341, para 1; Belgium in its request questioned the compatibility of the envisaged ISDS mechanism with the autonomy of the EU legal order, with the general principle of equal treatment and the requirement of effectiveness and with the right of access to an independent tribunal, see CJEU, *Opinion 1/17 - EU-Canada CET Agreement* (30 April 2019), ECLI:EU:C:2019:341, paras 46–69.

[330] CJEU, *Opinion 1/17 - EU-Canada CET Agreement* (30 April 2019), ECLI:EU:C:2019:341, para 245.

[331] *Joint Interpretative Instrument of the Comprehensive Economic and Trade Agreement (CETA) between Canada and the European Union and its Member States*, OJ EU 2017, L 11/3.

[332] For a short summary of the Joint Interpretative Instrument, see van der Loo (2016), p. 2.

exclusive competencies and aimed at concluding an "EU-only" agreement,[333] Member States were opposing this view and were calling for the involvement of national parliaments.[334] In the end and for political reasons, the European Commission proposed CETA as a mixed agreement to the Council of the European Union.[335]

Whether an international agreement can be concluded by the EU only or together with its Member States depends on the agreement's scope and the areas of competence covered.

On the one hand, the EU can act autonomously and only has to abide by the procedures provided for in the *Treaty on European Union*[336] ('TEU') and TFEU when exercising its exclusive external competencies.[337]

The EU's exclusive external competencies are laid down in Title V of the TEU and Part V of the TFEU and comprise amongst others the *Common Security and Foreign Policy* ('CSFP') and the *Common Commercial Policy* ('CCP').[338] In addition, the EU has implied external competencies where it has exercised internal powers and needs to act on the external plane to achieve the objective pursued by its internal action.[339]

On the other hand, there are cases where the conclusion of a so-called mixed agreement is mandatory.[340] This is the case where some parts of an international agreement fall within the exclusive competence of the EU while other parts fall within the exclusive competence of the Member States.[341]

Such a mixed agreement is also possible in the case of shared competence[342] when the competencies of the EU and the Member States overlap and they can act both autonomously or jointly with regard to the conclusion of an international

---

[333] *Cf.* European Commission (2016c), p. 4; see also the statement by former EU Trade Commissioner Cecilia Malmström in European Commission (2016b).

[334] See Vincenti (2016).

[335] European Commission (2016b); on the dispute as to whether CETA falls within the exclusive competences of the EU or of the EU and its Member States, see Kleimann and Kübek (2016), pp. 9–10; see also Fahey (2017), pp. 296–297; on the pitfalls of mixed agreements for EU trade policy and corresponding recommendations on a new strategy to improve the effectiveness of EU trade policy, see Wahl and Prete (2016).

[336] *Consolidated Version of the Treaty on European Union* ('TEU'), OJ EU 2012, C 326/13.

[337] *Cf.* Craig and de Búrca (2020), p. 364.

[338] For an overview see Craig and de Búrca (2020), pp. 108–112; Schütze (2018), pp. 271–273; see also *Schütze* on the relationship between the external competences laid down in the TFEU and TEU, Schütze (2018), pp. 277–279.

[339] For an overview on the establishment of these implied external powers in the ECJ's jurisprudence and its possible codification in EU primary law, see Craig and de Búrca (2020), pp. 111–112; Schütze (2018), pp. 273–277, 281–284; Kleimann and Kübek (2016), pp. 6–7.

[340] Schütze (2018), p. 299.

[341] See Figure 8.3 in Schütze (2018), p. 299.

[342] See Arts. 2(2) and 4 of the TFEU.

agreement.[343] But, in the case of shared competencies, the conclusion of a mixed agreement is only facultative.[344]

As of today, CETA has not been ratified by all EU Member States but is only applied provisionally as provided for by Article 218(5) TFEU and Article 30.7 CETA and, as decided by the Council of the European Union.[345] This provisional application does not comprise the entirety of CETA provisions but only those that fall within the EU's exclusive competence.[346] In this dimension, CETA is binding upon the EU institutions and the EU Member States according to Article 216(2) TFEU. Which parts of the Agreement fall within the Union's exclusive competence and which parts fall within the Member States' competence is disputed among Member States and EU Commission.[347] CETA fully enters into force after all EU Member States notify the Council that they have completed their internal ratification procedures.[348]

5.3.2.3 Consequences of Non-ratification by the Member States

Since so far only 17 Member States out of 27 have notified the Council of the European Union of their ratification of CETA,[349] the question of the consequences of a non-ratification by some or one Member State(s) arises.

In general, the non-ratification by some or one Member State(s) would lead to a so-called "incomplete" mixed agreement.[350] As such, only Member States that have ratified the agreement would be bound by all its provisions. Member States that have not ratified the agreement would only be bound by the provisions that fall within the exclusive competencies of the EU.[351] However, CETA, as a bilateral mixed agreement, can only enter into force after "the Parties exchange written

[343] Schütze (2018), pp. 298–300; according to Article 2(2) TFEU, the Union and the Member States may legislate and adopt legally binding acts in the area of shared competence. The Member States shall exercise their competence to the extent that the Union has not exercised its competence. The Member States shall again exercise their competence to the extent that the Union has decided to cease exercising its competence.

[344] Schütze (2018), p. 299 referring to Rosas (1998), pp. 125–148; see also van der Loo and Wessel (2017), pp. 736–737.

[345] See Council Decision 2017/38; this provisional application is a frequently used instrument in international law, see Kleimann and Kübek (2016), pp. 15.

[346] See Recital 4 of Council Decision 2017/38; however, this is not required by past Member States' practice or EU primary law according to *Kleimann/Kübek*, see Kleimann and Kübek (2016), p. 17.

[347] See e.g. Nettesheim (2016), p. 3568.

[348] See the overview of the EU-Canada Comprehensive Economic and Trade Agreement (CETA) provided for by the European Commission, https://ec.europa.eu/trade/policy/in-focus/ceta/ceta-explained/.

[349] See the ratification details provided for by the Council of the European Union, https://www.consilium.europa.eu/en/documents-publications/treaties-agreements/agreement/?id=2016017.

[350] See van der Loo and Wessel (2017), pp. 740–741.

[351] *Cf.* van der Loo and Wessel (2017), p. 741.

notifications certifying that they have completed their respective internal requirements", Article 30.7(2) CETA. According to Article 1.1 CETA, "the Parties" includes the European Union and its Member States. Accordingly, in case of the non-ratification of CETA by one or several of the EU Member State(s), CETA cannot enter into force.[352] The possibility of an "incomplete" mixed agreement is not given.[353] However, non-ratification of a mixed agreement only has legal consequences when it is notified to the EU by the respective Member State.[354]

In the case of the non-ratification of CETA, the Council of the EU has stated that the provisional application of CETA "must be and will be terminated" following EU procedures.[355] Article 30.7.3 lit. c CETA prescribes that the provisional application may be terminated by written notice of one party to the other party and shall take effect on the first day of the second month following such notification.

5.3.3 *The Contents of CETA*

5.3.3.1 General Framework

The general framework of CETA is to a large part influenced by the WTO framework. CETA incorporates several central WTO provisions concerning trade in goods and services, such as the national treatment principle. Also, the rights and obligations laid down in the SPS and TBT Agreements are incorporated in CETA and further developed. This is a common regulatory approach for free trade agreements.[356] Rules for areas that are not yet covered by WTO law are added.[357]

CETA in Chapter 2–7 deals with trade in goods which is also addressed in other chapters.[358] Furthermore, it addresses amongst others investment (Chapter 8), trade in services (Chapters 9, 13 and 14), telecommunications and electronic commerce (Chapters 15 and 16), government procurement, state enterprises and monopolies (Chapters 18 and 19), environmental, labour and sustainability aspects in relation to trade (Chapters 22–24) as well as (regulatory) cooperation and dispute settlement (Chapters 21, 25 and 29).

[352] *Cf.* van der Loo and Wessel (2017), pp. 742–743.

[353] Except for situations after the accession of new EU Member States, see van der Loo and Wessel (2017), pp. 747–748; for the consequences of the scenario of non-ratification by one or more Member State(s), see van der Loo and Wessel (2017), pp. 742–746; see also Kleimann and Kübek (2016), pp. 23–24; van der Loo (2016), p. 5.

[354] See Articles 65(1) and 67(2) VCLT; *cf.* van der Loo and Wessel (2017), p. 743.

[355] Council of the European Union (2016b), p. 10.

[356] Stoll et al. (2016), p. 12.

[357] *Cf.* Vranes (2017), p. 49.

[358] Vranes (2017), p. 49.

5.3.3.2 Basic Principles

CETA in its Article 2.3.1 lays down the national treatment principle by incorporating Article III GATT. This principle is adapted to specifics of Union law in Article 2.3.2 CETA.[359] Article 2.11 CETA also incorporates the prohibition of quantitative trade restrictions laid down in Article XI GATT. The *Note ad Article III*[360] to the GATT, dealing with the relationship between Articles III and XI GATT,[361] is incorporated into CETA by Article 1.6 lit. a. According to this Note, a national measure that is applied upon importation of a product on the border is to be scrutinised under the national treatment principle.[362] Therefore, Chapter 2 of CETA related to trade of goods can, like the GATT, be considered a non-discrimination regime.[363]

Furthermore, and according to Article 2.4, CETA aims at the reduction and elimination of customs duties in accordance with the mechanism laid down in Annex 2-A.

5.3.3.3 Sanitary and Phytosanitary Measures

Chapter 5 of CETA deals with sanitary and phytosanitary measures. It thereby aims at protecting human, animal and plant life or health, but also at ensuring that the parties' SPS measures do not create unjustified obstacles to trade.[364] The chapter is oriented towards the SPS Agreement's provisions, but it also adds to it.[365] And, it particularly aims at harmonisation and cooperation in the context of SPS measures.

To adapt to regional conditions with respect to plants and plant products, the importing party when establishing or maintaining phytosanitary measures

> shall take into account, among other things, the pest status of an area, such as a pest-free area, pest-free place of production, pest-free production site, an area of low pest prevalence and a protected zone that the exporting Party has established.[366]

Also, the parties shall include principles and guidelines to recognise regional conditions in Annex 5-C which they have not done yet.[367]

---

[359] See also Vranes (2017), p. 50.

[360] The note reads: "Any internal tax or other internal charge, or any law, regulation or requirement of the kind referred to in paragraph 1 which applies to an imported product and to the like domestic product and is collected or enforced in the case of the imported product at the time or point of importation, is nevertheless to be regarded as an internal tax or other internal charge, or a law, regulation or requirement of the kind referred to in paragraph 1, and is accordingly subject to the provisions of Article III.", see Annex I to GATT 1947, footnote 7.

[361] And accordingly, the relationship between Articles 2.3 and 2.11 CETA.

[362] *Cf.* also Vranes (2017), p. 51.

[363] *Cf.* Vranes (2017), p. 51.

[364] See Article 5.2 CETA.

[365] *Cf.* Vranes (2017), p. 53.

[366] See Article 5.5.2(a) CETA; see also Vranes (2017), p. 53.

[367] See Article 5.5.2(b) CETA.

Furthermore, CETA adds to the rights and obligations under the SPS Agreement by requiring the importing party to recognise an SPS measure of the other party as equivalent to its own if the other party can objectively demonstrate that its measure achieves the same appropriate level of SPS protection.[368] The burden of proof for equivalence lies upon the party requesting the recognition. Principles and guidelines for the determination, recognition and maintenance of equivalence are specified in Annex 5-D to CETA.[369] Where equivalence has been recognised once, an SPS measure can only be adopted, amended or repealed in accordance with Annex 5-D to CETA. To date, the parties have not yet agreed on principles and guidelines to determine and recognise equivalence.

CETA opens up the possibility to identify priority commodities for which special SPS import requirements apply to facilitate trade with regard to these commodities.[370]

Article 5.10.1 CETA in conjunction with Annex 5-J sets out principles and guidelines for import checks and fees. Annex 5-J does not mention any requirements concerning GMOs.

Article 5.11 CETA entails certain notification and information exchange obligations regarding a party's SPS measures. Furthermore, one party can request technical consultations when it

> has a significant concern with respect to food safety, plant health, or animal health, or a SPS measure that the other party has proposed or implemented.[371]

The other party is obliged to respond to such a request without undue delay and a mutually acceptable solution should be reached.

Where emergency SPS measures are implemented, the other party must be notified within 24 h of the decision to implement.[372]

To monitor the implementation of CETA's SPS chapter to address matters related to SPS measures and to assist the parties on such matters, CETA establishes a Joint Management Committee for Sanitary and Phytosanitary Measures in Article 26.2.1(d). Its functions are laid down in Articles 5.14.2 and 5.14.3 CETA. So far, this Committee has not dealt with issues in the context of biotechnology.[373]

---

368 See Article 5.6.1 CETA.

369 See Article 5.6.2 CETA.

370 See Article 5.7 CETA.

371 See Article 5.12 CETA.

372 See Article 5.13 CETA.

373 See Sanitary and Phytosanitary Measures Joint Management Committee (2018, 2019, 2020, 2021).

5.3.3.4 Technical Barriers to Trade

CETA Chapter 4 on technical barriers to trade also incorporates the central WTO provisions on technical barriers to trade as laid down in the TBT Agreement.[374] In this regard, it is important to note that the dispute settlement provisions laid down in Chapter 28 of CETA do not encompass Article 4.2.1 lit. a. This provision incorporates Article 2 TBT Agreement, the Agreement's central provision enshrining the national treatment principle. The TBT chapter of CETA applies to technical regulations, standards and conformity assessment procedures that may affect trade in goods and thereby establishes a broad scope of application.[375] Like the TBT Agreement, Chapter 4 of CETA does not apply to SPS measures as defined in Annex A of the SPS Agreement.[376] Furthermore, CETA also envisages regulatory cooperation with regard to technical regulations and standards and lays down a procedure for the recognition of equivalence of technical regulations issued by the other party.[377] Similar to the SPS chapter, the burden of proof that a technical regulation is equivalent to one of the other party's regulations lies upon the party requesting the recognition of equivalence.[378] The WTO provisions on conformity assessment procedures as incorporated into CETA by Article 4.2.1 lit. d to g are further developed within the framework of CETA.[379]

5.3.3.5 Regulatory Cooperation

Chapter 21 on regulatory cooperation replaces the *Framework on Regulatory Co-operation and Transparency*[380] agreed upon by Canada and the European Commission in 2004.[381] Regulatory cooperation is one of the central means of CETA to reach its main objective, the removal of non-tariff barriers to trade.[382] This includes the pursuit of regulatory compatibility, recognition of equivalence and convergence as stated in Article 21.2.4 lit. a CETA. Exchanging information on existing and future regulations, their objectives and their methodology shall contribute to more harmonisation.[383] One chapter of CETA is especially dedicated to regulatory

---

374 See Article 4.2 CETA; for details on the TBT Agreement see above Sects. 5.2.5.

375 *Cf.* Vranes (2017), p. 52.

376 See Article 4.1.2 lit. a CETA.

377 See Articles 4.3 and 4.4 CETA.

378 See Article 4.3.2 CETA; *cf.* Vranes (2017), p. 53.

379 See Article 4.5 CETA and the *Protocol on the mutual acceptance of the results of conformity assessment* (as part of CETA), OJ EU 2017, L11/567.

380 See Government of Canada (2004).

381 See Article 21.2.5 CETA.

382 *Cf.* Vranes (2017), p. 67 who notes the importance of the envisaged regulatory cooperation in CETA because "the WTO has not proved to be an effective forum for negotiating regulatory issues"; see also Stoll (2017), p. 7.

383 *Cf.* Stoll et al. (2016), p. 13.

cooperation and generally applies to trade in goods and services.[384] But, regulatory cooperation is also mentioned in several other chapters, such as those on TBT measures,[385] SPS measures,[386] and trade and the environment.[387] Bilateral cooperation is also envisaged in the context of biotechnology, science, technology, research and innovation issues.[388] However, regulatory cooperation activities within the CETA framework are only voluntary according to Article 21.2.6 CETA. The party refusing regulatory cooperation must explain its reasons for refusal.[389] This raises the question of the future reach and effects of regulatory cooperation between Canada and the EU which seem to be largely dependent on political leadership and stakeholder involvement.[390]

Objectives and activities of regulatory cooperation are specified in detail in Articles 21.3 and 21.4 CETA. Such activities also include future regulatory projects of one of the parties.[391] Future technical or sanitary and phytosanitary regulations that may have an impact on trade with the other Party shall be shared at the earliest stage possible.[392] Thereby, it shall be guaranteed that comments and proposals for amendments by the other party may be taken into account. Furthermore, regulatory cooperation shall be used in the research context to establish a common scientific basis and to minimise unnecessary differences in new regulatory proposals.[393]

It is stated that "the language used in the chapters on regulatory cooperation roots in modern regulatory methodology and culture of the USA and Canada".[394] Thereby, it requires causation of risk to take preventive measures. This is in contrast to the European approach where scientific but also other regulatory criteria play a role when taking preventive measures.[395] Here, the voluntary nature of regulatory cooperation should be kept in mind.[396] Nevertheless, there is the fear that precautionary considerations will not play a role in bilateral regulatory cooperation because the EU's precautionary approach is not mentioned in the context of CETA's regulatory cooperation provisions.[397]

---

384 See chapter 21 and Article 21.1 CETA.

385 See Article 4.3 CETA.

386 See Article 5.14 CETA.

387 Article 24.12 CETA.

388 See Articles 25.1.1, 25.2 and 25.5 CETA; for details on cooperation with regard to biotechnology issues, see below.

389 See Article 21.2.6 CETA.

390 *Cf.* Vranes (2017), pp. 68–69.

391 See Article 21.7.1 CETA.

392 See Article 21.4 lit. d CETA.

393 See Article 21.4 lit. n.iv. and lit. n.vi CETA.

394 Stoll et al. (2016), p. 13.

395 *Cf.* Stoll et al. (2016), p. 13.

396 See also Stoll et al. (2016), p. 13.

397 See Stoll et al. (2016), p. 14; for the role of the precautionary principle in CETA, see below.

Regulatory cooperation shall be conducted in the *Regulatory Cooperation Forum* ('RCF').[398] To date, the RCF has *inter alia* dealt with questions concerning Consumer Product Safety, "Cosmetic-Like" Drug Products, Animal Welfare, Cybersecurity and Pediatric Medicines.[399] Most activity in this forum is concerned with exchange of experiences, views and results. At least in one case, this exchange has already led to the removal of certain requirements for the marketing of "cosmetic-like" products from the EU.[400]

5.3.3.6 Regulation of Biotechnology

The regulation of biotechnology is dealt with in Article 25.2 CETA. It incorporates the *bilateral dialogue on agricultural biotech market access issues of mutual interest* which was established following the *EC – Biotech* WTO dispute.[401] The dialogue covers all issues in the context of trade in biotechnological products. This also comprises new legislation in the field of biotechnology. Also, the EU and Canada state as their shared objectives the promotion of efficient science-based approval processes for biotechnology products and the cooperation on any new legislation in the field of biotechnology.[402] An explanation of a mutual understanding of "science-based" is not given.[403]

Furthermore, the precautionary principle which is guiding EU regulation in the field of biotechnology is not mentioned in this context.[404] On the other hand, Article 24.8.2 CETA incorporates the precautionary principle in the environmental context and Article 24.3 recognises the parties' right

> to set its environmental priorities, to establish its levels of environmental protection, and to adopt or modify its laws and policies accordingly and in a manner consistent with the multilateral environmental agreements to which it is party and with this Agreement.[405]

Furthermore, Articles 24.5.1 and 24.5.2 explicitly state that environmental standards shall not be disregarded to encourage trade and investment. Furthermore, the right to regulate in the public interest has been named as a basic underlying principle of CETA by the European Commission and the Canadian Government.[406] These

---

[398] This Regulatory Cooperation Forum is established by Article 21.6 CETA.

[399] See European Commission (2018, 2020, 2021, 2022, 2023).

[400] See European Commission (2022), p. 3.

[401] For details on the *EC – Biotech* dispute see above, p. 123; for an overview of the current work of the Dialogue see below Chap. 6, p. 244.

[402] See Articles 25.2.1 lit. e and 25.2.2 lit. b CETA.

[403] For an overview of the regulation of GMOs in Canada, see Smyth (2019); a comparison of the Canadian and the EU approach to GMO regulation is given by *Hamburger*, see Hamburger (2019), pp. 330–332.

[404] *Cf.* Stoll et al. (2016), p. 16.

[405] See Art. 24.3 CETA.

[406] *Cf.* European Commission (2016a), pp. 1, 19.

provisions may also have effects on the handling of biotechnological issues and their environmental aspects in the context of CETA.

5.3.3.7 General Exceptions

Chapter 28 deals with general exceptions to the obligations laid down in CETA. With regard to Chapter 2 on trade in goods, Chapter 5 on sanitary and phytosanitary measures and Chapter 6 on customs and trade facilitation, CETA incorporates the exception rule of Article XX GATT.[407] In this regard, it explicitly mentions Articles XX(b) and (g) GATT and clarifies the parties' understanding of what is comprised by these exceptions. Accordingly, Article XX lit. b GATT explicitly covers environmental measures which are necessary to protect human, animal or plant life or health. And Article XX lit. g GATT does not only cover non-living but also living exhaustible resources.[408]

The general exceptions do not apply to Chapter 4, incorporating the provisions of the TBT Agreement.

5.3.3.8 The Precautionary Principle in the Context of CETA

The precautionary principle, a central provision of EU regulation laid down in Article 191 TFEU,[409] has not been explicitly included in CETA. Additionally, by incorporating the provisions of the SPS Agreement, the TBT Agreement, and the GATT without mentioning the precautionary principle and its role within these agreements, it seems as if CETA takes over the existing uncertainties concerning the applicability of the principle in the context of the WTO Agreements.[410] This is of relevance since the precautionary principle is "differently conceptualised"[411] in the Canadian legal system. There, regulations are subjected to a simple cost-benefit analysis where also economic considerations may prevail.[412]

Also, the envisaged regulatory cooperation might bring up these different understandings in the handling of risk.[413] Here, it is questionable whether the EU can rely

---

[407] See Article 28.3.1 CETA; for detail on Article XX GATT, see above Sect. 5.2.3.3.

[408] Thereby, the parties clarify their understanding of "exhaustible natural resources" which has been contentious under GATT, for an overview of the dispute see Wolfrum (2011), paras 15–21.

[409] For details on the precautionary principle in EU law, see also Commission of the European Communities (2000).

[410] *Cf.* Stoll et al. (2016), pp. 5, 13.

[411] Stoll et al. (2016), p. 10.

[412] *Cf.* Stoll et al. (2016), p. 10; on the different regulatory approaches of the EU and Canada, see also Stoll et al. (2016), p. 13; Bognar (2016), pp. 186–189.

[413] *Cf.* Stoll et al. (2016), p. 13.

on the precautionary principle since it is not explicitly mentioned in the context of regulatory cooperation either.[414]

From this point of view, it seems that the EU is at a loss as far as the application of the precautionary principle in the context of Canadian-EU trade relations is concerned.[415]

But, some provisions may also guarantee the precautionary principle's application by the EU. First of all, precautionary considerations are explicitly recognized in the chapters on trade and labour and trade and the environment where Principle 15 of the *Rio Declaration on Environment and Development*[416] ('Rio Declaration') is anchored.[417] In the context of trade and the environment, CETA also contains provisions that guarantee that the level of environmental protection is not lowered.[418] Also, it lays down a right to regulate ensuring each party's right to set its own environmental laws and policies and establish its own levels of environmental protection.[419] This could have a protective effect on the status of the precautionary principle in EU environmental law. Also with regard to regulatory cooperation, it must be noted that such cooperation is only voluntary and does not limit "the ability of each Party to carry out its regulatory, legislative and policy activities".[420]

However, it remains questionable whether these provisions can guarantee an adequate recognition and application of the precautionary principle in Canadian-EU trade relations, especially for areas where CETA does not explicitly mention the precautionary principle.[421] This is for example the case in the context of biotechnology regulation. Here, CETA does neither mention the precautionary principle nor the EU's commitment to the Cartagena Protocol which aims at a regulation of biotechnology in accordance with a precautionary approach.[422]

5.3.4 Institutional Framework Under CETA

Chapter 26, dealing with the institutional and administrative framework under CETA, establishes the CETA Joint Committee as the principal treaty body which "*is responsible for all questions concerning trade and investment between the Parties*

[414] See also Stoll et al. (2016), p. 13.

[415] *Cf.* also Stoll et al. (2016), p. 14.

[416] *Rio Declaration on Environment and Development* (1992).

[417] See Articles 23.3.3 and 24.8.2 CETA.

[418] See Articles 24.5 and 24.3 CETA.

[419] See Article 24.3 CETA.

[420] See Articles 21.2.4 and 21.2.6 CETA; also *Stoll et al.* note that "this provision could [...] warrant [the] use [of the precautionary principle] in regulatory practice", see Stoll et al. (2016), p. 13.

[421] *Cf.* Stoll et al. (2016), pp. 14, 17.

[422] *Cf.* Stoll et al. (2016), p. 16.

and the implementation and application of [CETA]".[423] It has the power to take decisions binding on all parties when CETA provides for it. This can be amendments, interpretative decisions or other matters.[424] However, the bindingness of the Joint Committee's decisions is subject to the completion of any necessary internal requirements and procedures.[425] This shall guarantee democratic legitimation of the Joint Committee's decisions for example on amendments as provided for in Article 26.1.5 lit. c CETA.[426]

Additional specialised committees are established by Article 26.2 CETA. These include the Committee on Trade in Goods, the Joint Management Committee for Sanitary and Phytosanitary Measures and the Regulatory Cooperation Forum.

5.3.5 Dispute Settlement Under CETA

CETA also lays down provisions governing the settlement of disputes that might arise between the parties about the interpretation or application of the Agreement's provisions.[427] However, it is also emphasised that the parties shall seek to find solutions through cooperation and consultations first.[428]

Since various obligations under CETA are equivalent to the parties' obligations under the WTO Agreement which also provides for a dispute settlement mechanism,[429] CETA emphasises that a party can only seek redress for the violation of such an obligation in one forum.[430] This applies from the date on which proceedings have been initiated under Article 29.3.3 CETA.

5.3.6 Summary and Conclusions

Both, the WTO regime and CETA, are characterised by their objective to support free trade and remove trade barriers. To this objective, the agreements restrict the States' sovereignty to adopt internal and external measures that fall within the agreements' scopes. With its multilateral agreements, the WTO system is far-reaching and regulates a wide variety of areas, especially in our globalised world

[423] See Article 26.1 CETA.

[424] See Articles 26.1 and 26.3 CETA; another, more "broad" reading of Article 26.3.1 CETA is mentioned by Vranes (2017), p. 66.

[425] See Article 26.3.2 CETA.

[426] *Cf.* Vranes (2017), p. 66.

[427] See Article 29.2 CETA and chapter 29.

[428] See Article 29.1 CETA.

[429] See above Sect. 5.2.2.1.1.

[430] See Articles 29.3.1 and 29.3.2; see also Schill (2017), pp. 118–122 on how CETA aims at minimising potential interferences between the CETA dispute settlement provisions and the WTO DSB.

where almost every regulatory measure is in some way trade-related. The same applies to CETA with its 30 chapters and numerous attachments.

The WTO is based on the WTO Agreement. The agreements listed in Annexes 1, 2 and 3 of the WTO Agreement are binding for all WTO member states. These include the GATT, the SPS Agreement and the TBT Agreement as well as the DSU, establishing the Dispute Settlement Body of the WTO.

The underlying principles of the GATT are the principle of non-discrimination and the principle of liberalisation. The principle of non-discrimination of like products is expressed in the most-favoured-nation principle and the principle of national treatment.

The SPS Agreement establishes a framework that allows Member States to apply measures to protect human, animal or plant life or health. The SPS Agreement emphasises the scientific justification of SPS measures, which can only be dispensed with in exceptional cases and only temporarily.

The TBT Agreement applies to technical regulations and standards relating to product characteristics and production processes and methods, such as packaging, marking or labelling requirements. While such regulations and standards help to improve the efficiency of production and facilitate international trade in such products, the purpose of the TBT Agreement is to ensure that such regulations do not lead to unnecessary barriers to trade. The central principle of the TBT Agreement is also the principle of equal treatment of nationals.

The substantive provisions of these agreements can also be found partly in CETA.

The WTO agreements do not explicitly regulate the release and commercialisation of GMOs. However, the applicability of the WTO agreements to GMO regulations has repeatedly played a role, not least in connection with the Cartagena Protocol and due to a dispute brought before the WTO Dispute Settlement Body by the USA, Canada and Argentina in the early 2000s.

CETA, on the other hand, has established a dialogue on biotech market access issues, which has so far mainly served to facilitate exchanges between the EU and Canada on GMO-related topics.

While it is generally assumed that the WTO regime and CETA with their regulatory approach stand in stark contrast to the EU's regulatory approach and especially to the EU's application of the precautionary principle, such stark contrast of opposing regulatory approaches could not be identified. It is correct that the WTO system, especially with its SPS Agreement, emphasises the need for measures to be based on science. And, it does not explicitly mention the concept of precaution as a regulatory approach. However, also the WTO's SPS Agreements somehow incorporates precautionary considerations as can be seen for example from the findings of the WTO Panel Report in *EC – Biotech* and as is further analysed above.[431] And also CETA is not completely silent on precautionary considerations even if it is sometimes presented that way.

[431] See Chap. 6, p. 192.

However, at a time when we are also seeing the negative sides of a globalised world with its dependence on imports, it remains to be seen to what extent the WTO system and CETA can hinder the EU's (also possibly protectionists) efforts to become more independent.

While the regulation of biotechnological risks and the EU GMO law have already been analysed in light of the WTO's provisions to some extent, a comprehensive assessment, especially with regard to genome edited plants and in the context of CETA is still missing.

References

Literature

Anderson K, Jackson LA (2012) GMOs: trade and welfare impacts of current policies and prospects for reform. In: McMahon JA, Desta MG (eds) Research handbook on the WTO agriculture agreement: new and emerging issues in international agricultural trade law. Edward Elgar, Cheltenham, pp 157–178

Arcuri A, Violi F, Tienhaara K, Schneiderman D, Ankersmit L, Schepel H (2020) Expropriating democracy: on the right and legitimacy of not ratifying CETA. EJIL:Talk!

Biber-Klemm S, Burkard M, Cottier T, Jusoh S, Temmerman M (2011) Challenges of biotechnology in international trade regulation. In: Cottier T, Delimatsis P (eds) The prospects of international trade regulation. Cambridge University Press, Cambridge, pp 284–320. https://doi.org/10.1017/CBO9780511792496.009

Böckenförde M (2004) Grüne Gentechnik und Welthandel: Das Biosafety-Protokoll und seine Auswirkungen auf das Regime der WTO. Beiträge zum ausländischen öffentlichen Recht und Völkerrecht, vol 171. Springer, Heidelberg

Bognar J (2016) Explaining the diverging regulatory approaches to risk regulation between Canada and the EU. In: Hübner K (ed) Europe, Canada and the Comprehensive Economic and Trade Agreement, pp 180–200

Boisson de Chazournes L, Mbengue MM (2004) GMOs and trade: issues at stake in the EC Biotech dispute. Rev Eur Comp Int Environ Law 13:289–305

Burchardi J-E (2007) Die Vereinbarkeit der europäischen Vorschriften zur Kennzeichnung gentechnisch veränderter Lebensmittel mit dem Welthandelsrecht. Rechtsfragen der Globalisierung. Duncker & Humblot, Berlin

Cheyne I (2008) Life after the biotech products dispute. Environ Law Rev 10:52–71

Commission of the European Communities (2000) Communication from the Commission on the precautionary principle. COM(2000) 1 final, Brussels

Commission of the European Communities (2006) Global Europe: competing in the world: a contribution to the EU's growth and jobs strategy. Communication from the Commission to the Council, the European Parliament, the European Economic and Social Committee and the Committee of the Regions, COM(2006) 567 final

Conrad CR (2007) The EC-Biotech dispute and applicability of the SPS agreement: are the panel's findings built on shaky ground. World Trade Rev 6:233–247

Cottier T, Baumann J (2017) I.24 The shift to non-tariff barriers and product regulation. In: Cottier T, Nadakavukaren Schefer K (eds) Elgar encyclopedia of international economic law. Edward Elgar, Cheltenham, pp 56–58

Council of the European Union (2013) EU-Canada CETA = State of play: note from the Presidency to Permanent Representatives Committee / Foreign Affairs Council (Trade). ST 10288/13. https://data.consilium.europa.eu/doc/document/ST-10288-2013-INIT/en/pdf
Council of the European Union (2016a) Comprehensive Economic and Trade Agreement (CETA) between Canada, of the one part, and the European Union and its Member States, of the other part: ratification details. https://www.consilium.europa.eu/en/documents-publications/treaties-agreements/agreement/?id=2016017
Council of the European Union (2016b) Comprehensive Economic and Trade Agreement (CETA) between Canada, of the one part, and the European Union and its Member States, of the other part - Statement to the Council minutes. 13463/16 Annex. https://data.consilium.europa.eu/doc/document/ST-13463-2016-INIT/en/pdf
Council of the European Union (2016c) EU-Canada trade agreement: Council adopts decision to sign CETA. Press release 623/16, Brussels
Craig P, de Búrca G (2020) EU law: text, cases, and materials, 7th edn
Croisant G (2019) The CJEU confirms that CETA's Investment Court System is compatible with EU law. http://arbitrationblog.kluwerarbitration.com/2019/04/30/opinion-117-the-cjeu-confirms-that-cetas-investment-court-system-is-compatible-with-eu-law/
Davey WJ (2005) Institutional Framework. Chapter 4. In: Macrory PFJ, Appleton AE, Plummer MG (eds) The World Trade Organization: legal, economic and political analysis, vol I. Springer Science+Business Media Inc, Boston, pp 51–87
Davies GT (2007) Morality clauses and decision making in situations of scientific uncertainty: the case of GMOs. World Trade Rev 6:248–263
European Commission (2016a) CETA – summary of the final negotiating results. https://trade.ec.europa.eu/doclib/docs/2014/december/tradoc_152982.pdf
European Commission (2016b) European Commission proposes signature and conclusion of EU-Canada trade deal. Press release, Strasbourg
European Commission (2016c) Proposal for a Council Decision on the signing on behalf of the European Union of the Comprehensive Economic Trade Agreement between Canada of the one part, and the European Union and its Member States, of the other part. COM(2016) 444 final. https://eur-lex.europa.eu/resource.html?uri=cellar:e2e0caa3-4356-11e6-9c64-01aa75ed71a1.0001.02/DOC_1&format=PDF
European Commission (2018) 1st Meeting of the CETA Regulatory Cooperation Forum: Report
European Commission (2020) 2nd Meeting of the CETA Regulatory Cooperation Forum: Joint Report
European Commission (2021) 3rd Meeting of the CETA Regulatory Cooperation Forum: Joint Report
European Commission (2022) 4th Meeting of the CETA Regulatory Cooperation Forum: Joint Report
European Commission (2023) 5th Meeting of the Regulatory Cooperation Forum: Joint Report
European Commission (n.d.) The EU and the WTO. https://ec.europa.eu/trade/policy/eu-and-wto/
European Parliament (2017a) CETA: MEPs back EU-Canada trade agreement. Press release
European Parliament (2017b) European Parliament legislative resolution of 15 February 2017 on the draft Council decision on the conclusion of the Comprehensive Economic and Trade Agreement (CETA) between Canada, of the one part, and the European Union and its Member States, of the other part (10975/2016 – C8-0438/2016 – 2016/0205(NLE)) (P8_TA(2017)0030). https://www.europarl.europa.eu/doceo/document/TA-8-2017-0030_EN.pdf
European Parliament (2021) The European Union and the World Trade Organization. Fact Sheets on the European Union. https://www.europarl.europa.eu/ftu/pdf/en/FTU_5.2.2.pdf
European Parliamentary Research Service (2017) CETA ratification process: latest developments: at a glance. www.europarl.europa.eu/RegData/etudes/ATAG/2017/608726/EPRS_ATA(2017)608726_EN.pdf
European Union External Action (n.d.) EU-Canada Strategic Partnership Agreement. Factsheet. https://www.eeas.europa.eu/node/13529_en

Fahey E (2017) CETA and global governance law: what kind of model agreement is it really in law? Eur Papers 2:293–302. https://doi.org/10.15166/2499-8249/119
Federal Ministry for Economic Affairs and Energy (n.d.) CETA - The European-Canadian Economic and Trade Agreement. https://www.bmwi.de/Redaktion/EN/Dossier/ceta.html
Federale Overheidsdienst, Kingdom of Belgium (2017) CETA - Belgian request for an opinion from the European Court of Justice. https://diplomatie.belgium.be/sites/default/files/downloads/ceta_summary.pdf
Footer ME (2007) Post-normal science in the multilateral trading system: social science expertise and the EC-Biotech Panel. World Trade Rev 6:281–297
General Council (1999) Proposal for the Establishment of a Working Party on Biotechnology in WTO (Communication from Canada): preparations for the 1999 Ministerial Conference. WT/GC/W/359
Government of Canada (2004) Cooperative Framework to Boost Business between Canada and EU. News Release
Government of Canada (2018) Chronology of events and key milestones. https://www.international.gc.ca/trade-commerce/trade-agreements-accords-commerciaux/agr-acc/ceta-aecg/chronology-chronologie.aspx?lang=eng
Government of Canada, European Commission (n.d.) Assessing the costs and benefits of a closer EU-Canada economic partnership: a joint study by the European Commission and the Government of Canada. https://www.international.gc.ca/trade-agreements-accords-commerciaux/agr-acc/eu-ue/study-etude.aspx?lang=eng#intro
Government of the United Kingdom (n.d.) UK-Canada Trade Continuity Agreement (TCA). Guidance. https://www.gov.uk/guidance/uk-canada-trade-continuity-agreement-tca
Griller S, Obwexer W, Vranes E (2017a) Mega-regional trade agreements: new orientations for EU external relations? In: Griller S, Obwexer W, Vranes E (eds) Mega-regional trade agreements: CETA, TTIP, and TiSA: new orientations for EU external economic relations. Oxford University Press, Oxford, pp 3–16
Griller S, Obwexer W, Vranes E (2017b), Preface. In: Griller S, Obwexer W, Vranes E (eds) Mega-regional trade agreements: CETA, TTIP, and TiSA: new orientations for EU external economic relations. Oxford University Press, Oxford, pp vii–viii
Gruber M (2004) Inside or outside? The role of the WTO in the settlement of the transatlantic trade dispute on GMOs. Interecon Rev Eur Econ Policy 39:36–45
Gruszczynski LA (2018) The SPS agreement within the framework of WTO law: the rough guide to the agreement's applicability. https://doi.org/10.2139/ssrn.1152749
Hahn M (2008) Food security and agricultural production with genetically modified organisms: a comment. In: Wüger D, Cottier T (eds) Genetic engineering and the World Trade System. Cambridge University Press, pp 193–202
Hamburger D (2019) Comparative analysis: the regulation of plants derived from genome editing in Argentina, Australia, Canada, the European Union, Japan and the United States. In: Dederer H-G, Hamburger D (eds) Regulation of genome editing in plant biotechnology: a comparative analysis of regulatory frameworks of selected countries and the EU. Springer, Cham, pp 313–363
Heidfeld C (2012) Die dezentrale Durchsetzung des WTO-Rechts in der Europäischen Union. Schriftenreihe Europäisches Recht, Politik und Wirtschaft, vol 365. Nomos Verlagsgesellschaft mbH & Co. KG, Baden-Baden. https://doi.org/10.5771/9783845235844
Henckels C (2006) GMOs in the WTO: a critique of the panel's legal reasoning in the EC-Biotech. Melbourne J Int Law 7:278–305
Herdegen M (2016) Principles of international economic law, 2nd edn. Oxford University Press, Oxford
Herdegen M (2020) International economic law. Max Planck Encyclopedias of International Law (MPEPIL)

Hummer W (2018) Article 207 TFEU. In: Vedder C, Heintschel von Heinegg W, Eisenhut D, Epiney A, Epping V, Folz H-P (eds) Europäisches Unionsrecht: EUV, AEUV, GRCh, EAGV: Handkommentar, 2nd edn. Baden-Baden
Kerr WA (2014) The trade system and biotechnology. In: Smyth SJ, Phillips PWB, Castle D (eds) Handbook on agriculture, biotechnology and development. Edward Elgar, Cheltenham, pp 217–229
Kleimann D, Kübek G (2016) The signing, provisional application, and conclusion of trade and investment agreements in the EU: the case of CETA and Opinion 2/15. RSCAS 2016/58. EUI working papers
Kogan LA (2007) World Trade Organization Biotech decision clarifies central role of science in evaluating health and environmental risks for regulation purposes. Global Trade Customs J 2:149–155
Landwehr O (2007) Article 3 SPS. In: WTO - technical barriers and SPS measures. Martinus Nijhoff, Boston, pp 412–428
Lehne J (2019) Crisis at the WTO: is the blocking of appointments to the WTO Appellate Body by the United States legally justified? Carl Grossmann Verlag
Levidow L (2007) The transatlantic Agbiotech conflict as a problem and opportunity for EU regulatory policies. In: Falkner R (ed) The international politics of genetically modified food: diplomacy, trade, and law. Palgrave Macmillan, Basingstoke, pp 118–137
Levidow L, Bonneuil C (2013) The 2003–2006 WTO GMO dispute: implications for the SPS Agreement. In: Thompson PB, Kaplan DM (eds) Encyclopedia of food and agricultural ethics. Springer, Dordrecht, pp 1–8. https://doi.org/10.1007/978-94-007-6167-4_360-3
Lowenfeld A (2008) International economic law, 2nd edn
Mögele R (2018) Art. 216 AEUV. In: Streinz R (ed) EUV/AEUV: Vertrag über die Europäische Union, Vertrag über die Arbeitsweise der Europäischen Union, 3rd edn. Charta der Grundrechte der Europäischen Union
Motaal DA (2004) The "Multilateral Scientific Consensus" and the World Trade Organization. J World Trade 38:855–876
N.N (1970) Report by the working party on border tax adjustments. L/3464
N.N (1992) Rio Declaration on environment and development. In: United Nations Conference on Environment and Development (ed) Annex I. UN Doc. A/CONF.151/26 (Vol I)
N.N (2016a) Belgium Walloons block key EU Ceta trade deal with Canada. BBC News
Nettesheim M (2016) Das CETA-Urteil des BVerfG: Eine verpasste Chance? Neue Juristische Woche 69:3567–3570
Nettesheim M (2017) Umfassende Freihandelsabkommen und Grundgesetz: Verfassungsrechtliche Grundlagen der Zustimmung zu CETA. In: Tübinger Schriften zum internationalen und europäischen Recht, vol 103. Duncker & Humblot, Berlin
Office of the United States Trade Representative (2020a) Report on the Appellate Body of the World Trade Organization. https://ustr.gov/sites/default/files/Report_on_the_Appellate_Body_of_the_World_Trade_Organization.pdf
Office of the United States Trade Representative (2020b) USTR issues report on the WTO Appellate Body. Press release, Washington, D.C.
Office P (2017) Notice concerning the provisional application of the Comprehensive Economic and Trade Agreement (CETA) between Canada, of the one part, and the European Union and its Member States, of the other part
Peel J (2006) A GMO by any other name . . . might be an SPS risk!: implications of expanding the scope of the WTO Sanitary and Phytosanitary Measures Agreement. Eur J Int Law 17:1009–1031. https://doi.org/10.1093/ejil/chl033
Perez O (2007) Anomalies at the precautionary Kingdom: reflections on the GMO Panel's decision. World Trade Rev 6:264–279
Petersmann E-U (2017a) CETA, TTIP, and TiSA: new trends in international economic law. In: Griller S, Obwexer W, Vranes E (eds) Mega-regional trade agreements: CETA, TTIP, and

TiSA: new orientations for EU external economic relations. Oxford University Press, Oxford, pp 17–43
Petersmann E-U (2017b) Democratic legitimacy of the CETA and TTIP agreements? In: Rensmann T (ed) Mega-regional trade agreements. Springer, Cham, pp 37–59
Prévost D (2007) Opening Pandora's Box: the panel's finding in the EC-Biotech products dispute. Leg Issues Econ Integr 34:67–101
Prévost D, van den Bossche P (2005) The agreement on the application of sanitary and phytosanitary measures. Chapter 7. In: Macrory PFJ, Appleton AE, Plummer MG (eds) The World Trade Organization: legal, economic and political analysis, vol I. Springer Science+Business Media Inc, Boston, pp 231–370
Qureshi AH (2000) The Cartagena Protocol on biosafety and the WTO: co-existence or incoherence. Int Comp Law Q 49:835–855
Rankin J (2016) EU trade deal with Canada on brink of collapse after Belgian disarray. The Guardian
Riffel C (2018) Biotech case. Max Planck Encyclopedias of International Law (MPEPIL)
Rosas A (1998) Mixed Union - mixed agreements. In: Koskenniemi M (ed) International law aspects of the European Union. Kluwer Law International, The Hague, pp 125–148
Sander GG, Sasdi A (2006) Welthandelsrecht und "grüne" Gentechnik: Eine transatlantische Auseinandersetzung vor den Streitbeilegungsorganen der WTO. Europäische Zeitschrift für Wirtschaftsrecht:140–144
Sanitary and Phytosanitary Measures Joint Management Committee (2018) Report: 1st meeting. https://circabc.europa.eu/rest/download/e919447a-c7a1-498e-966d-d5fd378738b1?ticket=
Sanitary and Phytosanitary Measures Joint Management Committee (2019) Report: 2nd meeting. https://circabc.europa.eu/rest/download/b6a367ef-0601-4228-b762-cd2c27664ec6?ticket=
Sanitary and Phytosanitary Measures Joint Management Committee (2020) Report: 3rd meeting. https://circabc.europa.eu/rest/download/3a6fcdf4-6449-4605-b9bf-da83fef04d89?ticket=
Sanitary and Phytosanitary Measures Joint Management Committee (2021) Report: 4th meeting. https://circabc.europa.eu/rest/download/96f18dd7-d57a-4c77-9a87-6e31b0a1070c?ticket=
Schill SW (2017) Authority, legitimacy, and fragmentation in the (envisaged) dispute settlement disciplines in mega-regionals. In: Griller S, Obwexer W, Vranes E (eds) Mega-regional trade agreements: CETA, TTIP, and TiSA: new orientations for EU external economic relations. Oxford University Press, Oxford, pp 111–150
Schoenbaum TJ (2000) International trade in living modified organisms: the new regimes. Int Comp Law Q 49:856–866
Schütze R (2018) European Union law, 2nd edn. Cambridge University Press, Cambridge
Scott J (2009) The WTO Agreement on sanitary and phytosanitary measures: a commentary. Oxford commentaries on the Gatt/WTO Agreements. Oxford University Press, Oxford
Secretariat of the Convention on Biological Diversity (2022) Cartagena Protocol on Biosafety: ratification list. https://www.cbd.int/doc/lists/cpb-ratifications.pdf
Seibert-Fohr A (2007) Article 2 SPS. In: WTO - technical barriers and SPS measures. Martinus Nijhoff, Boston, pp 392–411
Sheldon I, Josling T (2002) Biotechnology regulations and the WTO: working paper 02-2
Smyth SJ (2019) Regulation of genome editing in plant biotechnology: Canada. Chapter 4. In: Dederer H-G, Hamburger D (eds) Regulation of genome editing in plant biotechnology: a comparative analysis of regulatory frameworks of selected countries and the EU. Springer, Cham, pp 111–135
Stoll P-T (2014) World Trade Organization, dispute settlement. Max Planck Encyclopedias of International Law (MPEPIL)
Stoll P-T (2017) Mega-regionals: challenges, opportunities and research questions. In: Rensmann T (ed) Mega-regional trade agreements. Springer, Cham, pp 3–24
Stoll P-T, Douma WT, Sadeleer N de, Abel P (2016) CETA, TTIP and the EU precautionary principle: legal analysis of selected parts of the draft CETA agreement and the EU TTIP proposals. Study commissioned by foodwatch

Streinz R, Ohler C, Herrmann C (2008) Der Vertrag von Lissabon zur Reform der EU: Einführung mit Synopse, Aktuelles Recht für die Praxis, 2nd edn. Beck, München
van den Bossche P, Zdouc W (2022) The law and policy of the World Trade Organization: text, cases and materials, 5th edn. Cambridge University Press, Cambridge
van der Loo G (2016) CETA's signature: 38 statements, a joint interpretative instrument and an uncertain future. CEPS Commentary. https://www.ceps.eu/ceps-publications/cetas-signature-38-statements-joint-interpretative-instrument-and-uncertain-future/
van der Loo G, Wessel RA (2017) The non-ratification of mixed agreements: legal consequences and solutions. Common Mark Law Rev 54:735–770
Vienna Convention on the Law of Treaties (n.d.) Overview provided for by the United Nations Treaty Collection. https://treaties.un.org/pages/ViewDetailsIII.aspx?src=TREATY&mtdsg_no=XXII I-1&chapter=23&Temp=mtdsg3&clang=_en
Vincenti D (2016) EU leaders on collision course with Commission over CETA. EURACTIV.com
Vöneky S, Beylage-Haarmann B (2020) Art. 216 AEUV. In: Grabitz E, Hilf M, Nettesheim M (eds) EUV/AEUV, 71st edn, vol 60
Vranes E (2017) The contents of CETA, TTIP, and TiSA: the (envisaged) trade disciplines. In: Griller S, Obwexer W, Vranes E (eds) Mega-regional trade agreements: CETA, TTIP, and TiSA: new orientations for EU external economic relations. Oxford University Press, Oxford, pp 47–86
Wahl N, Prete L (2016) Blowin' against the wind: the future of EU trade policy. https://doi.org/10.17176/20161129-174353
Wolfrum R (2011) Article XX lit. g GATT. In: WTO-trade in goods. Martinus Nijhoff, Leiden
World Trade Organization (2019) Members urge continued engagement on resolving Appellate Body issues. Press release
World Trade Organization (2020a) Minutes of the General Council Meeting on 9-10 December 2019. WT/GC/M/181
World Trade Organization (2020b) Minutes of the General Council Meeting on 3 March 2020. WT/GC/M/182
World Trade Organization (2020c) Statement on a mechanism for developing, documenting and sharing practices and procedures in the conduct of WTO disputes: Addendum. JOB/DSB/1/Add.12
World Trade Organization (2020d) Appellate Body Appointments: Proposal by Afghanistan; Angola; Argentina; Australia; Bangladesh; Benin; Plurinational State of Bolivia; Botswana; Brazil; Burkina Faso; Burundi; Cabo Verde; Cameroon; Canada; Central African Republic; Chad; Chile; China; Colombia; Congo; Costa Rica; Côte d'Ivoire; Cuba; Democratic Republic of Congo; Djibouti; Dominican Republic; Ecuador; Egypt; El Salvador; Eswatini; The European Union; Gabon; The Gambia; Ghana; Guatemala; Guinea; Guinea-Bissau; Honduras; Hong Kong, China; Iceland; India; Indonesia; Israel; Kazakhstan; Kenya; Republic of Korea; Lesotho; Liechtenstein; Madagascar; Malawi; Malaysia; Maldives; Mali; Mauritania; Mauritius; Mexico, Republic of Moldova; Morocco; Mozambique; Namibia; Nepal; New Zealand; Nicaragua; Niger; Nigeria; North Macedonia; Norway; Pakistan; Panama; Paraguay; Peru; Qatar; Russian Federation; Rwanda; Senegal; Seychelles; Sierra Leone; Singapore; South Africa; Switzerland; The Separate Customs Territory of Taiwan, Penghu, Kinmen and Matsu; Tanzania; Thailand; Togo; Tunisia; Turkey; Uganda; Ukraine; United Kingdom; Uruguay; The Bolivarian Republic of Venezuela; Viet Nam; Zambia and Zimbabwe. WT/DSB/W/609/Rev. 18
World Trade Organization (2022) MC12 Outcome Document. WT/MIN(22)/24; WT/L/1135
World Trade Organization (n.d.-a) Members and observers. https://www.wto.org/english/thewto_e/whatis_e/tif_e/org6_e.htm
World Trade Organization (n.d.-b) Sanitary and phytosanitary measures. Overview. https://www.wto.org/english/tratop_e/sps_e/sps_e.htm
World Trade Organization (n.d.-c) Technical barriers to trade. Overview. https://www.wto.org/english/tratop_e/tbt_e/tbt_e.htm

World Trade Organization (n.d.-d) The GATT years: from Havana to Marrakesh. Understanding the WTO. https://www.wto.org/english/thewto_e/whatis_e/tif_e/fact4_e.htm
WTO Appellate Body (2010) Working procedures for Appellate Review. WT/AB/WP/6*
WTO Dispute Settlement Body (2003a) European Communities - measures affecting the approval and marketing of biotech products: request for Consultations by Canada. WT/DS/292/1, G/L/628, G/SPS/GEN/398, G/AG/GEN/61, G/TBT/D/29
WTO Dispute Settlement Body (2003b) European Communities - measures affecting the approval and marketing of biotech products: request for consultations by the United States. WT/DS291/1, G/L/627, G/SPS/GEN/397, G/AG/GEN/60, G/TBT/D/28
WTO Dispute Settlement Body (2003c) European Communities - measures affecting the approval and marketing of biotech products: request for consultations by Argentina. WT/DS293/1, G/L/629, G/SPS/GEN/399, G/AG/GEN/62, G/TBT/D/30
WTO Dispute Settlement Body (2003d) European Communities - measures affecting the approval and marketing of biotech products: communication from the European Communities. WT/DS291/13, WT/DS292/10
WTO Dispute Settlement Body (2003e) European Communities - measures affecting the approval and marketing of biotech products: acceptance by the European Communities of the requests to join consultations. WT/DS292/16
WTO Dispute Settlement Body (2003f) European Communities - measures affecting the approval and marketing of biotech products: acceptance by the European Communities of the requests to join consultations. WT/DS291/22
WTO Dispute Settlement Body (2003g) European Communities - measures affecting the approval and marketing of biotech products: request for the establishment of a Panel by Argentina. WT/DS293/17
WTO Dispute Settlement Body (2003h) European Communities - measures affecting the approval and marketing of biotech products: request for the establishment of a Panel by the United States. WT/DS291/23
WTO Dispute Settlement Body (2003i) European Communities - measures affecting the approval and marketing of biotech products: request for the establishment of a Panel by Canada. WT/DS292/17
WTO Dispute Settlement Body (2003j) Minutes of the DSB Meeting of 29 August 2003. WT/DSB/M/155
WTO Dispute Settlement Body (2004a) European Communities - measures affecting the approval and marketing of biotech products: Constitution of the Panel established at the requests of the United States, Canada and Argentina (Note by the Secretariat). WT/DS291/24, WT/DS292/18, WT/DS293/18
WTO Dispute Settlement Body (2004b) European Communities - measures affecting the approval and marketing of biotech products: communication from the Chairman of the Panel. WT/DS291/25, WT/DS292/19, WT/DS293/19
WTO Dispute Settlement Body (2004c) European Communities - measures affecting the approval and marketing of biotech products: communication from the Chairman of the Panel. WT/DS291/26, WT/DS92/20, WT/DS293/20
WTO Dispute Settlement Body (2004d) European Communities - measures affecting the approval and marketing of biotech products: communication from the Chairman of the Panel. WT/DS291/27, WT/DS292/21, WT/DS293/21
WTO Dispute Settlement Body (2005a) European Communities - measures affecting the approval and marketing of biotech products: communication from the Chairman of the Panel. WT/DS291/28, WT/DS292/22, WT/DS293/22
WTO Dispute Settlement Body (2005b) European Communities - measures affecting the approval and marketing of biotech products: communication from the Chairman of the Panel. WT/DS291/29, WT/DS292/23, WT/DS293/23

WTO Dispute Settlement Body (2005c) European Communities - measures affecting the approval and marketing of biotech products: communication from the Chairman of the Panel. WT/DS291/30, WT/DS292/24, WT/DS293/24

WTO Dispute Settlement Body (2006a) European Communities - measures affecting the approval and marketing of biotech products: communication from the Chairman of the Panel. WT/DS291/31, WT/DS292/25, WT/DS293/25

WTO Dispute Settlement Body (2006b) European Communities - measures affecting the approval and marketing of biotech products: communication from the Chairman of the Panel. WT/DS291/32, WT/DS292/26, WT/DS293/26

WTO Dispute Settlement Body (2006c) Annual Report (2006). WT/DSB/42

WTO Dispute Settlement Body (2017) Minutes of the DSB Meeting of 31 August 2017. WT/DSB/M/400

Jurisprudence: Court of Justice of the European Union (former European Court of Justice)

CJEU (2019) Opinion 1/17 - EU-Canada CET Agreement. https://eur-lex.europa.eu/legal-content/EN/TXT/PDF/?uri=CELEX:62017CV0001(02)

Jurisprudence: WTO Appellate Body

WTO Appellate Body (1996a) United States - standards for reformulated and conventional gasoline

WTO Appellate Body (1996b) Japan - taxes on alcoholic beverages

WTO Appellate Body (1997) Canada - certain measures concerning periodicals

WTO Appellate Body (1998a) EC measures concerning meat and meat products (hormones)

WTO Appellate Body (1998b) United States - import prohibition of certain shrimp and shrimp products

WTO Appellate Body (2001) European Communities - measures affecting asbestos and asbestos-containing products

WTO Appellate Body (2003) United States - sunset review of anti-dumping duties on corrosion-resistant steel flat products from Japan

WTO Appellate Body (2005) European Communities - customs classification of frozen boneless chicken cuts

WTO Appellate Body (2009) China - measures affecting trading rights and distribution services for certain publications and audiovisual entertainment products

WTO Appellate Body (2011) European Communities and certain Member States - measures affecting trade in large civil aircraft

WTO Appellate Body (2012a) China - measures related to the exportation of various raw materials

WTO Appellate Body (2012b) United States - measures affecting the production and sale of clove cigarettes

WTO Appellate Body (2012c) United States - measures concerning the importation, marketing and sale of Tuna and Tuna products

Jurisprudence: WTO Panel

WTO Panel (1999) United States - Sections 301-310 of the Trade Act of 1974

WTO Panel (2005) Mexico - tax measures on soft drinks and other beverages

WTO Panel (2006) European Communities - measures affecting the approval and marketing of biotech products

WTO Panel (2011) United States - measures concerning the importation, marketing and sale of Tuna and Tuna products

Chapter 6
EU Regulations on Genome Edited Plants Under WTO Law and CETA

Abstract This chapter analyses the compatibility of the regulation of genetically modified organisms ('GMOs') in the European Union ('EU') with WTO law and CETA, particularly with regard to genome editing techniques like targeted mutagenesis. The analysis reveals that while the EU's GMO framework could have been legitimate under WTO and CETA for conventional genetic modification techniques, it no longer holds for all new genome editing techniques. This is due to the EU Commission's decision to treat the risks associated with genome editing techniques such as targeted mutagenesis and cisgenesis as similar to conventional breeding methods.

The analysis concludes that regulating GMOs under WTO and CETA frameworks is challenging, and the EU may need to adapt its laws to meet international trade requirements. The Cartagena Protocol, though more suited for GMO trade, lacks global support, especially from major biotech trade countries. Thus, the EU must navigate these complex regulations, potentially facing disputes over its GMO laws in international trade forums.

6.1 Introduction

The question of whether the European Union's ('EU') regulations on genetically modified ('GM') plants are compatible with the rules of the World Trade Organization ('WTO') is not a new one[1] and was again raised by the decision of the Court of Justice of the European Union ('CJEU') on targeted mutagenesis techniques.[2]

---

[1] See e.g. Dederer (2010); Burchardi (2007); Fricke (2004); Morgan and Goh (2004); Stökl (2003a); Stökl (2003b); Wolf (2002); Robertson (2001), pp. 207, 212; Burchardi (2001); Howse and Mavroidis (2000); Spranger (2000).

[2] *Cf.* Nationale Akademie der Wissenschaften Leopoldina et al. (2019), pp. 68–69; Dederer (2019), p. 245; Carreno and Dolle (2019), pp. 98–101; Eriksson et al. (2019); Spranger (2019); Benevides Demasi (2019).

E. A. L. Andersen, *Regulation of Biotechnological Risks in a Multi-Level System*, European Yearbook of International Economic Law 46,
https://doi.org/10.1007/978-3-032-02409-1_6

While the Dispute Settlement Body of the WTO ('DSB') was already concerned with this question in the *EC – Biotech* Case,[3] it did not deal with it conclusively.[4] Furthermore, the Panel report raises the question whether the WTO regime and CETA deliver adequate provisions to deal with GMO regulation. A question that arises even more in view of the development of genetically modified plants that do not show physical differences to conventionally bred plants and have been qualified as equivalent to these conventionally bred plants in terms of their risk potential.

The present chapter, therefore, analyses whether the EU authorisation procedures for GM plants, the labelling of GM plants and opt-out measures that may be taken by EU Member States are compatible with WTO law and the *Comprehensive Economic and Trade Agreement*[5] ('CETA'). Particular attention is given to GM plants altered by targeted mutagenesis and their particularities in comparison to conventionally bred plants.

6.2 EU Authorisation Procedures and WTO Law

This part assesses whether the legal framework for the authorisation of GM plants in the EU complies with WTO law, in particular with the *Agreement on the Application of Sanitary and Phytosanitary Measures*[6] ('SPS Agreement' or 'SPS') (1.),

---

[3] WTO Panel, *European Communities - Measures Affecting the Approval and Marketing of Biotech Products* (29 September 2006), WT/DS291/R, WT/DS292/R, WT/DS293/R; for a detailed presentation and analysis of the *EC – Biotech* Case, see above Chap. 5, p. 115.

[4] The Panel in the *EC – Biotech* case only dealth with questions within the scope of *Directive 2001/18/EC of the European Parliament and the Council of 12 March 2001 on the deliberate release into the environment of genetically modified organisms and repealing Council Directive 90/220/EC* (consolidated version from 27 March 2021) ('Directive 2001/18/EC'), Official Journal of the European Communities (OJ EC) 2001, L106/1 and did not examine *Regulation (EC) No 1829/2003 of the European Parliament and of the Council of 22 September 2003 on genetically modified food and feed* (consolidated version from 27 March 2021) ('Regulation 1829/2003'), Official Journal of the European Union ('OJ EU') 2003, L268/1 and *Regulation (EC) No 1830/2003 of the European Parliament and of the Council of 22 September 2003 concerning the traceability and labelling of genetically modified organisms and the traceability of food and feed products produced from genetically modified organisms* (consolidated version from 26 July 2019) ('Regulation 1830/2003'), OJ EU 2003, L 268/24. Also, the Panel did not analyse the EU approval procedures as such but only dealt with the legality of a *de facto* moratorium on authorisations and the compatibility of product-specific approval procedures. Furthermore, it did not rule on EU labelling provisions and the provisions that allow EU Member States to opt-out from the cultivation of GM plants. For a detailed analysis of the Panel report, see Chap. 5, p. 115.

[5] *Comprehensive Economic and Trade Agreement (CETA) between Canada, of the one part, and the European Union and its Member States, of the other part*, OJ EU 2017, L 11/23.

[6] *Agreement on the Application of Sanitary and Phytosanitary Measures* ('SPS Agreement' or 'SPS'), Annex 1 to the *Marrakesh Agreement establishing the World Trade Organization* ('WTO Agreement') (concluded 15 April 1994; entered into force 1 January 1995) 1867 UNTS 3.

the *Agreement on Technical Barriers to Trade*[7] ('TBT Agreement' or 'TBT') (2.), and the *General Agreement on Tariffs and Trade 1994*[8] ('GATT') (3.). It analyses the authorisation procedure for the placing on the market of GM plants as or in products as laid down in Part C of *Directive 2001/18/EC of the European Parliament and the Council of 12 March 2001 on the deliberate release into the environment of genetically modified organisms*[9] ('Directive 2001/18/EC' or 'Deliberate Release Directive') and in the *Regulation (EC) No 1829/2003 of the European Parliament and of the Council of 22 September 2003 on genetically modified food and feed*[10] ('Regulation 1829/2003' or 'GM Food and Feed Regulation').

6.2.1 SPS Agreement

6.2.1.1 Applicability

The SPS Agreement is applicable to all measures that fulfil two requirements: first, they constitute a sanitary or phytosanitary measure ('SPS measures') (i.). And second, they have a direct or indirect effect on international trade (ii.).[11]

6.2.1.1.1 Sanitary or Phytosanitary Measure

The definition for *sanitary or phytosanitary measure* is laid down in Annex A(1) to the SPS Agreement. This definition contains two elements: first, a measure's purpose and second, a measure's legal form and nature.[12] The purpose element is

---

[7] *Agreement on Technical Barriers to Trade* ('TBT Agreement' or 'TBT'), Annex 1 to the WTO Agreement, see footnote 6.

[8] *General Agreement on Tariffs and Trade 1994*, Annex 1 to the WTO Agreement, see footnote 6.

[9] See footnote 4.

[10] See footnote 4.

[11] See Article 1.1 SPS; *cf.* Charnovitz (2007), para 1 with reference to WTO Panel, *EC Measures Concerning Meat and Meat Products (Hormones) (Complaint by the United States)* (18 August 1997), WT/DS26/R/USA, para 8.36.

[12] While the Panel in *EC – Biotech* had differentiated between a measure's legal form and its nature, *cf.* WTO Panel, *European Communities - Measures Affecting the Approval and Marketing of Biotech Products* (29 September 2006), WT/DS291/R, WT/DS292/R, WT/DS293/R, para 7.149, the Panels in *Australia – Apples* and *US – Poultry (China)* did not explicitly differentiated between form and nature and only found two elements to be contained in the definition, *cf.* WTO Panel, *Australia - Measures Affecting the Importation of Apples from New Zealand* (9 August 2010), WT/DS367/R, paras 7.144–7.145; WTO Panel, *United States - Certain Measures Affecting Imports of Poultry from China* (29 September 2010), WT/DS392/R, paras 7.98–7.101; this view was implicitly confirmed by the Appellate Body in *Australia – Apples*, *cf.* WTO Appellate Body, *Japan - Measures Affecting the Importation of Apples* (26 November 2003), WT/DS245/AB/R, paras 170–176.

reflected in subparagraphs (a)-(d) and covers all measures which are *applied* to obtain the objectives laid down therein.[13] These are namely all measures

1. *to protect animal or plant life or health within the territory of the Member from risks arising from the entry, establishment or spread of pests, diseases, disease-carrying organisms or disease-causing organisms;*
2. *to protect human or animal life or health within the territory of the Member from risks arising from additives, contaminants, toxins or disease-causing organisms in foods, beverages or feedstuffs;*
3. *to protect human life or health within the territory of the Member from risks arising from diseases carried by animals, plants or products thereof, or from the entry, establishment or spread of pests; or*
4. *to prevent or limit other damage within the territory of the Member from the entry, establishment or spread of pests.*

There has to be a link between the measure and the protected interest.[14] Whether this is the case has "to be ascertained on the basis of objective considerations", meaning the objective must be apparent from the measure itself or from circumstances related to its application.[15] These include a measure's design and application as well as its regulatory context.[16]

The second sentence of Annex A(1) lists different types of legal instruments that can constitute SPS measures, including laws, decrees, regulations and different procedures. This list is not exclusive but rather indicative and reflects the necessary connection between the two elements that are required for an SPS measure.[17]

6.2.1.1.2 EU Authorisation Procedures as SPS Measures

6.2.1.1.2.1 Authorisation Procedures Laid Down in Directive 2001/18/EC as SPS Measures in Terms of Their Purpose

The authorisation procedures laid down in Directive 2001/18/EC qualify as SPS measures in case they are applied for one of the purposes listed in Annex A(1) (a)-(d) SPS.

---

[13] *Cf.* WTO Appellate Body, *Australia - Measures Affecting the Importation of Apples from New Zealand* (29 November 2010), WT/DS367/AB/R, para 172, emphasis added.

[14] *Cf.* WTO Appellate Body, *Australia - Measures Affecting the Importation of Apples from New Zealand* (29 November 2010), WT/DS367/AB/R, para 172.

[15] WTO Appellate Body, *Australia - Measures Affecting the Importation of Apples from New Zealand* (29 November 2010), WT/DS367/AB/R, para 172.

[16] WTO Appellate Body, *Australia - Measures Affecting the Importation of Apples from New Zealand* (29 November 2010), WT/DS367/AB/R, para 173; *cf.* also Scott (2009), 17 with reference to WTO Panel, *Australia - Measures Affecting Importation of Salmon* (12 June 1998), WT/DS18/R, paras 8.31–8.37.

[17] *Cf.* WTO Appellate Body, *Australia - Measures Affecting the Importation of Apples from New Zealand* (29 November 2010), WT/DS367/AB/R, 175–176.

Purposes Pursued by Directive 2001/18/EC in Light of Annex A(1) of the SPS Agreement

In the following, it will be analysed whether the adverse effects that the Deliberate Release Directive is designed to protect against by requiring authorisation procedures, fall within the ambit of one of the alternatives of Annex A(1) of the SPS Agreement.[18] The above elaboration on the objectives pursued by the Deliberate Release Directive constitutes the basis for the following analysis.[19]

Annex A(1)(a) of the SPS Agreement Annex A(1)(a) covers all measures that are applied "to protect animal or plant life or health within the territory from risks arising from the entry, establishment or spread of pests, diseases, disease-carrying organisms or disease-causing organisms".

EU Authorisation Procedures as Measures to Protect Animal or Plant Life or Health from Risks Arising from the Entry, Establishment or Spread of Pests The EU authorisation procedures for GM plants can be qualified as measures applied to protect plants from the entry, establishment or spread of pests in three ways.

First, to the extent that the procedures are applied to protect animal or plant health from adverse effects associated with the altered susceptibility to pathogens facilitating the dissemination of infectious diseases or creating new reservoirs or vectors. The term *pest* includes pathogenic agents or the potential of a *living modified organism*[20] ('LMO') to act as a vector for the introduction of a gene presenting a potential phytosanitary risk.

This meaning of pests can be derived from an interpretation in accordance with the customary rules of treaty interpretation laid down in Article 31 *Vienna Convention on the Law of Treaties*[21] ('VCLT'),[22] especially from the context of Annex A(1)(a).

[18] As has also been examined by the Panel in *EC – Biotech*, see WTO Panel, *European Communities - Measures Affecting the Approval and Marketing of Biotech Products* (29 September 2006), WT/DS291/R, WT/DS292/R, WT/DS293/R, para 7.278; see also above Chap. 5, p. 115.

[19] For a detailed analysis of the objectives pursued by Directive 2001/18/EC as the basis for the present analysis of the applicability of the SPS Agreement, see above Chap. 4, p. 60.

[20] The term *living modified organism* is further defined in Article 3 lit. g of the *Cartagena Protocol on Biosafety to the Convention on Biological Diversity* ('Cartagena Protocol') (adopted 29 January 2000, entered into force 11 September 2003) 2226 UNTS 208.

[21] *Vienna Convention on the Law of Treaties* ('VCLT') (adopted 22 May 1969, entered into force 27 January 1980) 1155 UNTS 331.

[22] As provided for by Article 3.2 of the *Understanding on Rules and Procedures Governing the Settlement of Disputes* ('DSU' or 'Dispute Settlement Understanding'), Annex 2 to the WTO Agreement, see footnote 6; see also WTO Appellate Body, *Japan - Taxes on Alcoholic Beverages* (4 October 1996), WT/DS8/AB/R, WT/DS10/AB/R, WT/DS11/AB/R, 10.

The context of the SPS Agreement comprises the *International Plant Protection Convention*[23] ('IPPC') and its *International Standards for Phytosanitary Measures* ('ISPM').[24] The IPPC defines a pest as "any species, strain or biotype of plant, animal or pathogenic agent injurious to plants or plant products".[25] ISPM No. 11 on pest risk analysis for quarantine pests explicitly mentions the possibility of LMOs to be qualified as pests.[26] Also, it sets out criteria to determine the potential for LMOs to be a pest in its Annex 3. In this regard, it states that LMOs "in cases of phytosanitary risks related to gene flow, [...] [are] acting more as a potential vector or pathway for introduction of a genetic construct of phytosanitary concern rather than as a pest in and of itself. Therefore, the term pest should be understood to include the potential of an LMO to act as a vector or pathway for introduction of a gene presenting a potential phytosanitary risk."[27]

In accordance with this meaning of the term pests, the authorisation procedures laid down in the Deliberate Release Directive fall within Annex A(1)(a) to the extent they are applied to protect animal or plant health from adverse effects associated with the altered susceptibility to pathogens facilitating the dissemination of infectious diseases or creating new reservoirs or vectors.

Second, the authorisation procedures fall within Annex A(1)(a) to the extent they are applied to protect plant health from adverse effects associated with the persistence and invasiveness of GM plants, including plant-to-plant gene transfer. In this respect, the *Guidance on the environmental risk assessment of genetically modified plants*[28] ('ERA guidance') by the *European Food Safety Authority*[29] ('EFSA') mentions weed problems as one adverse effect that authorisation procedures should protect from.[30] Furthermore, it mentions that "flow to wild relative may decrease the fitness of hybrid offspring".[31] In this respect, Annex III B I.B.3. of Directive 2001/18/EC also requires applicants to submit information on "[a]ny change to the persistence or invasiveness of the GMHP, and its ability to transfer genetic material to sexually compatible relatives and the adverse environmental effects thereof". Since

---

[23] *International Plant Protection Convention* ('IPPC') (entered into force 3 April 1952), 150 UNTS 67.

[24] See above Chap. 5, p. 109; this has been seen differently by the WTO Panel in *EC – Biotech*, see WTO Panel, *European Communities - Measures Affecting the Approval and Marketing of Biotech Products* (29 September 2006), WT/DS291/R, WT/DS292/R, WT/DS293/R, para 7.300; however, the Panel has also acknowledged that "the term 'pest' in the IPPC may in some respects be informative to, and hence aid, an interpreter of the SPS Agreement", WTO Panel, *European Communities - Measures Affecting the Approval and Marketing of Biotech Products* (29 September 2006), WT/DS291/R, WT/DS292/R, WT/DS293/R, para 7.241; for an extensive analysis of the Panel report, see also Chap. 5, p. 115.

[25] See Article 2(1) IPPC; see also Secretariat of the International Plant Protection Convention (2007).

[26] Secretariat of the International Plant Protection Convention (2019a), p. 9.

[27] Secretariat of the International Plant Protection Convention (2019a), p. 30.

[28] EFSA Panel on Genetically Modified Organisms (2010a).

[29] See Official website of the European Food Safety Authority, https://www.efsa.europa.eu/en.

[30] See EFSA Panel on Genetically Modified Organisms (2010a), p. 40.

[31] EFSA Panel on Genetically Modified Organisms (2010a), p. 40.

weeds are considered pests in the sense of Annex A(1)(a)[32] and since the term pests includes the potential of LMOs to present a phytosanitary risk in the case of gene flow,[33] the authorisation procedures to this extent fall within Annex A(1)(a) of the SPS Agreement.

Third, the authorisation procedures can be considered as measures protecting from risks against pests to the extent, they are applied to protect from risks arising out of plant to micro-organisms gene transfer. Although plant to micro-organism gene transfer is considered a rare event by EFSA, it can have potential consequences for animal health or the environment.[34] And, especially in the phytosanitary context, pathogenic agents which are micro-organisms that cause diseases[35] are qualified as pests. Therefore, by protecting against plant to micro-organism gene transfer, the authorisation procedures laid down in the Deliberate Release Directive are applied to protect plants from risks arising out of pests in the sense of Annex A(1)(a) of the SPS Agreement.

Accordingly, the authorisation procedure's purposes as mentioned above serve the protection of plants from the entry, establishment or spread of *pests* as laid down in Annex A(1)(a) of the SPS Agreement.

EU Authorisation Procedures as Measures to Protect Animal or Plant Life or Health from Risks Arising from the Entry, Establishment or Spread of Diseases, Disease-Carrying Organisms or Disease-Causing Organisms As laid down in Annex C.3.1.b of Directive 2001/18/EC, authorisation procedures are applied to protect animals and plants from diseases "including toxic, and, in the case of animals, allergenic reactions".

Furthermore, the Deliberate Release Directive aims at the protection of animals or plants from risks arising from the entry, establishment or spread of disease-carrying or disease-causing organisms. This has already been analysed by the Panel in *EC – Biotech* under reference to definitions of the World Health Organisation ('WHO'). According to the WHO's definitions, a disease-causing organism is a pathogen and a disease-carrying organism is a vector.[36] Insofar as the Directive protects from adverse effects caused by the "altered susceptibility [of humans, animals or plants] to pathogens (= disease-causing organisms) facilitating the dissemination of infectious diseases or creating new reservoirs or vectors (= disease carrying organisms)",[37] it falls within the scope of Annex A(1)(a) of the SPS Agreement.

---

[32] This is explicitly stated in the footnote to Annex A. Also *The Oxford English Dictionary* defines a pest as "a plant that is an invasive weed", see 'pest' in *The Oxford English Dictionary (OED)*, https://www.oed.com/.

[33] See Secretariat of the International Plant Protection Convention (2019a), p. 9.

[34] EFSA Panel on Genetically Modified Organisms (2010a), p. 50.

[35] See 'pathogen' in Stevenson (2010).

[36] See WTO Panel, *European Communities - Measures Affecting the Approval and Marketing of Biotech Products* (29 September 2006), WT/DS291/R, WT/DS292/R, WT/DS293/R, para 7.277 and footnote 434; for an analysis of the Panel report, see also Chap. 5, .p 115.

[37] See Annex C.2.1 of Directive 2001/18/EC.

Annex A(1)(b) of the SPS Agreement According to Annex A(1)(b) of the SPS Agreement, measures that are applied to protect human or animal life or health from risks arising from additives, contaminants, toxins or disease-causing organisms in foods, beverages or feedstuffs fall within the SPS Agreement.

In this context, one has to keep in mind that the authorisation procedures for GM food and GM feed are laid down in Regulation 1829/2003. *Food* in the sense of Regulation 1829/2003 includes "any substance or product, whether processed, partially processed or unprocessed, intended to be, or reasonably expected to be ingested by humans" except for feed and plants before harvesting.[38] *Feed* is "any substance or product, including additives, whether processed, partially processed or unprocessed, intended to be used for oral feeding to animals".[39] As such they are not subject to Directive 2001/18/EC.[40]

Therefore, the question arises whether plants not intended for food or feed use are also comprised by Annex A(1)(b) of the SPS Agreement. Then, the approval procedures laid down in the Deliberate Release Directive could also be considered to fall within this alternative of Annex A(1).

In *EC – Biotech*, the Panel only considered "GM crop[s] grown for the explicit purpose of providing food to animals, and in particular to farmed animals" as *feedstuff* in the sense of Annex A(1)(b). Accordingly, GM plants not intended for feed use are not comprised by this term.

In *EC – Biotech*, the Panel qualified plants not intended for feed use, but nevertheless eaten by animals as *food* for animals in the sense of Annex A(1)(b). According to its view, this would include pollen of GM crops consumed by insects, GM plants consumed by wild fauna or GM seeds eaten by birds.[41] However, it is questionable whether such a broad interpretation of Annex A(1)(b) is legitimate.

While food is defined as "any nutritious substance that people or animals eat or drink to maintain life and growth",[42] this is different in the context of sanitary measures. Food is concerned with the consumption by humans whereas feed is any nutritious substance for animal consumption. This differentiation is for example made by the Codex Alimentarius Commission[43] which establishes standards

---

[38] See Article 2(1) Regulation 1829/2003 and Article 2 *Regulation (EC) No 178/2002 of the European Parliament and of the Council of 28 January 2002 laying down the general principles and requirements of food law, establishing the European Food Safety Authority and laying down procedures in matters of food safety* (consolidated version from 26 May 2021) ('Regulation 178/2002'), OJ EC 2002, L 31/1.

[39] See Article 2(1) of Regulation 1829/2003 and Article 3(4) of Regulation 178/2002.

[40] See Article 12 Directive 2001/18/EC.

[41] *Cf.* WTO Panel, *European Communities - Measures Affecting the Approval and Marketing of Biotech Products* (29 September 2006), WT/DS291/R, WT/DS292/R, WT/DS293/R, paras 7.291–7.292; for an analysis of the Panel report, see also Chap. 5, p. 115.

[42] 'food' in *The Oxford English Dictionary (OED)*, https://www.oed.com/; see also *cf.* 'food' in Stevenson (2010).

[43] See http://www.fao.org/fao-who-codexalimentarius/thematic-areas/animal-feed/en/#c437068.

relevant to the SPS Agreement and can be taken into account as context in the sense of Article 31(1) VCLT.[44]

Furthermore, this interpretation is supported by the French and Spanish versions of the SPS Agreement which can be taken into account according to Article 33 VCLT.[45] The *Agreement establishing the World Trade Organization*[46] ('WTO Agreement') mentions the English, French and Spanish versions as the authoritative ones. The French version of the SPS Agreement speaks of "produits alimentaires" and "aliments pour animaux" in Annex A(1)(b), the Spanish version of "los productos alimenticios" and "los piensos". The terms "produits alimentaires" and "los productos alimenticios" both mean products for human consumption and do not encompass products or feed for animals. Instead, feed for animals is comprised by the terms "aliments pour animaux" and "los piensos". In cases of differences between the authoritative languages, "the meaning which best reconciles the texts [...] shall be adopted" according to Article 33(4) VCLT. To reconcile the meaning of all three versions, the English version of Annex A(1)(b) has to be interpreted accordingly. Thus, "food" only encompasses products/substances for human consumption and does not comprise plants not intended for feed use, but nevertheless eaten by animals.

Accordingly, the authorisation procedures laid down in the Deliberate Release Directive do not fall within the ambit of Annex A(1)(b) of the SPS Agreement.

Annex A(1)(c) of the SPS Agreement To the extent that the authorisation procedures laid down in the Deliberate Release Directive are applied to protect from "diseases affecting humans, including allergenic or toxic reactions",[47] they fall within the ambit of Annex A(1)(c) of the SPS Agreement.[48]

Annex A(1)(d) of the SPS Agreement According to Annex A(1)(d) of the SPS Agreement, all measures applied to prevent or limit other damage from the entry, establishment or spread of pests fall within the SPS Agreement's scope. To assess whether the authorisation procedures laid down in the Deliberate Release Directive fall within the scope of Annex A(1)(d) of the SPS Agreement, the meaning of *other damage* needs to be assessed. However, it is important to note that only measures

---

[44] See above Chap. 5, p. 109.

[45] The applicability of Article 33 VCLT to the WTO Agreements has been confirmed by the Appellate Body, see e.g. WTO Appellate Body, *United States - Final Countervailing Duty Determination with respect to certain Softwood Lumber from Canada* (19 January 2004), WT/DS257/AB/R, para 59.

[46] *Marrakesh Agreement establishing the World Trade Organization* ('WTO Agreement') (concluded 15 April 1994; entered into force 1 January 1995) 1867 UNTS 3.

[47] See Annex II.C.3.1(b) of Directive 2001/18/EC; see also EFSA Panel on Genetically Modified Organisms (2009), 21–26.

[48] See also WTO Panel, *European Communities - Measures Affecting the Approval and Marketing of Biotech Products* (29 September 2006), WT/DS291/R, WT/DS292/R, WT/DS293/R, paras 7.345–7.362; for an analysis of the Panel report, see also Chap. 5, p. 115.

protecting such other damage from risks *related to pests* are comprised of Annex A(1)(d).

As has been elaborated on above,[49] the term *pests* can comprise the potential of a genetically modified organism ('GMO') to act as a vector or pathway for the introduction of a gene presenting a potential phytosanitary risk. Furthermore, a pest is any species, strain or biotype of plant, animal or pathogenic agent injurious to plants or plant products. Also, a plant that is an invasive weed can be considered as a pest.

Also, risks arising from pests that directly concern animals, plants and humans are already listed in Annex A(1)(a) and (c). Therefore, the term *other damage* must be different from animals, plants and humans.[50]

While measures to protect plants and animals as such fall within Annex A(1)(a)-(b) of the SPS Agreement, it is questionable whether measures to protect biodiversity also fall within these alternatives. The Panel in *EC – Biotech* has answered this question in the affirmative. According to its findings, damage to biodiversity implies damage to living organisms which is not comprised by the term "other damage" in the sense of Annex A(1)(d). Instead, damage to biodiversity as such is comprised by the alternatives of Annex A(1)(a) and (b).[51]

However, this implicit finding that biodiversity consists of plant and animal health and life falls too short. The *Convention on Biological Diversity*[52] ('CBD') defines biological diversity as *the variability among living organisms from all sources including, inter alia, terrestrial, marine and other aquatic ecosystems and the ecological complexes of which they are part; this includes diversity within species, between species and of ecosystems.*[53]

According to this definition biological diversity has an "independent value beyond the life and health of single plants and animals".[54] It goes further by protecting "the total amount of genetic information of all living organisms including wild

[49] See above p. 166.

[50] See also WTO Panel, *European Communities - Measures Affecting the Approval and Marketing of Biotech Products* (29 September 2006), WT/DS291/R, WT/DS292/R, WT/DS293/R, para 7.369; for an analysis of the Panel report, see also Chap. 5, p. 115.

[51] *Cf.* WTO Panel, *European Communities - Measures Affecting the Approval and Marketing of Biotech Products* (29 September 2006), WT/DS291/R, WT/DS292/R, WT/DS293/R, para 7.372; for an analysis of the Panel report, see also Chap. 5, p. 115.

[52] *Convention on Biological Diversity* ('CBD') (adopted 5 June 1992, entered into force 29 December 1993) 1760 UNTS 79.

[53] See Article 2 CBD.

[54] Conrad (2007), p. 242; see also Matz-Lück (2008), paras 22–24; this can also be derived from Annex II of Directive 2001/18/EC which mentions biological diversity independently from flora and fauna: "'Cumulative long-term effects' refers to the accumulated effects of consents on human health and the environment, including inter alia flora and fauna, soil fertility, soil degradation of organic material, the feed/food chain, biological diversity, animal health and resistance problems in relation to antibiotics".

as well as cultivated species".[55] This includes genetic diversity, species diversity and ecosystem diversity.[56] Therefore, measures to protect biological diversity cannot fall solely within Annex A(1)(a) and (b) of the SPS Agreement.

While measures falling within Annex A(1)(a) and (b) might qualify as measures protecting biological diversity, it is rather questionable whether measures to protect biological diversity as such are comprised by the SPS Agreement.[57]

The SPS Agreement arose as an outgrowth of Article XX(b) GATT,[58] which shows a close relationship between the Agreement and Article XX(b) GATT.[59] This exception encompasses measures to protect human, animal or plant life or health. And it is questioned whether and how Article XX(b) GATT covers measures for biodiversity and environmental protection.[60] While this might also be reasoned by the fact that environmental protection at the time when the GATT was drafted did not have the importance it has nowadays, this does not apply for the time in which the SPS Agreement was drafted. And nevertheless, there were no explicit references to environmental or biodiversity protection included in the SPS Agreement.[61] Measures aiming at the conservation of species and the protection of biological resources rather seem to be covered by Article XX(g) GATT, comprising measures relating to the conservation of exhaustible natural resources.[62]

Furthermore, the question arises whether the SPS Agreement, the scope of which is limited to the territory of a Member State, can adequately cover the global value that is inherent in biological diversity.[63],[64] And, Annex A(1)(d) only covers measures protecting against risks from pests which would not meet the objective of adequate biodiversity protection.

Also, the international context with the *Cartagena Protocol on Biosafety to the CBD*[65] ('Cartagena Protocol') which is specifically designed to protect biodiversity against risks arising from trade in GMOs, supports the foregoing argumentation.[66]

Therefore, it is argued that negative effects on biological diversity are not comprised by the term of *other damage*.

---

[55] Matz Lück (2008), paras 1, 2.

[56] *Cf.* Matz-Lück (2008), para 1.

[57] Arguing for an application of the SPS Agreement to measures protecting biological diversity: Barton (1996), p. 101; *cf.* also Bernasconi-Osterwalder (2008), pp. 658–659.

[58] See Preamble, para. 7 and Article 2.4 of the SPS Agreement; see also Scott (2009), p. 9; *cf.* Seibert-Fohr (2007), para 5.

[59] *Cf.* Stoll and Strack (2011), paras 9, 65.

[60] *Cf.* Stoll and Strack (2011), para 25.

[61] *Cf.* Stoll and Strack (2011), para 25.

[62] *Cf.* Stoll and Strack (2011), para 60; Conrad (2007), p. 244.

[63] See Preamble, para. 3 of the CBD; *cf.* also Feichtner (2007), para 19.

[64] *Cf.* also Conrad (2007), p. 244.

[65] See footnote 20.

[66] However, with regard to this argument it needs to be pointed out that WTO law would precede the Cartagena Protocol in case of a dispute before the WTO DSB, see above Chap. 5, p. 131.

Conclusion

As can be seen from the foregoing considerations on how the authorisation procedures fit within the alternatives of Annex A(1) to the SPS Agreement, the SPS Agreement's scope is not perfectly designed to cover measures addressing potential risks arising out of placing on the market of GM plants.

This has also been noticed by scholarship.[67] *Conrad* even asks whether the SPS Agreement "has the capacity to adequately deal with measures that address unusually diffuse risks for undefined objects."[68] Since the SPS Agreement was negotiated in the context of the *Agreement on Agriculture,*[69] it is said to primarily cover "traditional 'sanitary and phytosanitary' concern[s], such as quarantine risks associated with the entry and spread of pests and diseases via traded agricultural products, or risks posed by toxins, additives or contaminants in imported human foods or animal feed".[70]

Nevertheless, the Panel in *EC-Biotech* qualified all measures under the Deliberate Release Directive to fall within the SPS Agreement. This extensive interpretation of the SPS Agreement's scope has been criticised by scholarship for being too broad.[71] Such a broad scope stands in contrast to the very specific definitions listed in Annex A(1).[72] At the heart of the criticism is the question of how far environmental measures and regulations are comprised by the SPS Agreement or, whether the Agreement is not rather only addressing quarantine and food safety measures.[73]

The foregoing analysis shows that the authorisation procedures laid down in the Deliberate Release Directive serve SPS as well as non-SPS purposes. Therefore, the

---

[67] See Stökl (2003b), p. 77; Stökl (2003a), pp. 135–137; Conrad (2007), pp. 240–241; Peel (2006), pp. 1016, 1019–1020; *cf.* also Biber-Klemm et al. (2011), p. 285, 304 and Robertson (2001), p. 207, 214 who states that "none of the Uruguay Round agreements deal[s] specifically with biotechnology" and that "GM products would not be generally covered by the SPS Agreement [since] GM modifications are not normally regarded as additives, contaminants, toxic, disease carrying or pests"; also *Wolf* acknowledges that the SPS Agreement's wording does not allow its applicability to GMOs, but argues in favour of the Agreement's applicability to GMOs in the context of measures aimed at protecting health by virtue of the Agreement's object and purpose, *cf.* Wolf (2002), p. 14.

[68] Conrad (2007), p. 241.

[69] *Agreement on Agriculture*, Annex 1 to the WTO Agreement, see footnote 46.

[70] Peel (2006), p. 1014; see also Peel (2006), pp. 1016, 1018, 1026–1027 and *cf.* Conrad (2007), pp. 240–241; see also Zarrilli (2006), p. 253 who states that the WTO framework "is not specific to biotechnology and was actually developed at a time when biotechnology was not an issue".

[71] *Cf.* Franken and Burchardi (2007), pp. 87–90 with further references; Conrad (2007), pp. 240–241; Gruszczynski (2018); Peel (2006), p. 1009; Gruszczynski (2018); on the contrary, *Stökl* argues that measures related to genetically modified food can be qualified as SPS measures due to the SPS Agreement's general purpose to scientifically justify sanitary measures, see Stökl (2003a), pp. 136–137.

[72] *Cf.* Conrad (2007), pp. 238–239; see also Scott (2003), p. 228.

[73] *Cf.* Peel (2006), p. 1016; see also Biber-Klemm et al. (2011), p. 304 stating that the SPS Agreement "is ill-suited to deal effectively with increasing scientific requirements in assessing risks deriving from the application of new technologies in food production and agriculture, e.g. biotechnology"; *cf.* also Commission of the European Communities (2000), p. 11.

authorisation procedures only fall within the SPS Agreement's scope to the extent they are applied to serve SPS purposes. This does not cover the authorisation procedures to the extent that they protect biodiversity as such. It will be further analysed whether the authorisation procedures fall within the TBT Agreement or the GATT to the extent they are applied to serve non-SPS purposes.[74]

6.2.1.1.2.2 Authorisation Procedures Laid Down in Regulation 1829/2003 as SPS Measures in Terms of Their Purpose

The authorisation procedures under the GM Food and Feed Regulation are required for GMOs for food and feed use, for food and feed containing or consisting of GMOs and for food produced from or containing ingredients produced from GMOs as well as feed produced from GMOs.[75]

The Regulation was not scrutinised in the *EC – Biotech* Case since it had not yet been adopted when the WTO Panel was established. The Panel instead dealt with *Regulation (EC) No 258/97 of the European Parliament and of the Council of 27 January 1997 concerning novel foods and novel food ingredients*[76] which was the predecessor of Regulation 1829/2003 with regard to the authorisation of GM food.[77]

Annex A(1)(a), (c) and (d) of the SPS Agreement

Concerning the question of whether the authorisation procedures for GM plants that qualify as food or feed laid down in the GM Food and Feed Regulation fall within the alternatives of Annex A(1)(a), (c) and (d) of the SPS Agreement, the same considerations apply as for the authorisation procedures laid down in the Deliberate Release Directive.[78]

Annex A(1)(b) of the SPS Agreement

In contrast to the Deliberate Release Directive, Regulation 1829/2003 lays down specific authorisation procedures for genetically modified food and feed. Whether GM food and feed can be considered additives or contaminants is disputed.[79] But,

---

[74] It has been stated that the provisions of the TBT Agreement and GATT better capture measures aiming at environmental protection in the context of GMO regulation, *Cf.* Peel (2006), p. 1019 and Conrad (2007), p. 236; see also Gruszczynski (2010), p. 3.

[75] See Articles 3(1) and 15(1) Regulation 1829/2003.

[76] *Regulation (EC) No 258/97 of the European Parliament and of the Council of 27 January 1997 concerning novel foods and novel food ingredients* (latest consolidated version from 07 August 2009) ('Regulation 258/97'), OJ EC 1997, L 43/1 (no longer in force).

[77] See recitals 5 and 6 of Regulation 1829/2003; *cf.* Delewski et al. (2016), pp. 2–3; van Calster and Reins (2018), p. 304; an overview of both regulations is provided for by Fricke (2004), pp. 57–97.

[78] See above pp. 166–173.

[79] *Cf.* Burchardi (2007), p. 245; Böckenförde (2004), pp. 322–323; Kerr (1999), p. 250; Stökl (2003b), p. 77; Wolf (2002), p. 14.

the Regulation aims at the protection of human and animal health and life from diseases caused by allergenic[80] or toxic effects which may arise as adverse effects of GM food and feed.[81] Accordingly, to this extent, the authorisation procedures can be considered to fall within Annex A(1)(b) of the SPS Agreement.

The Protection of Consumer Interests in Relation to Genetically Modified Food and Feed

As laid down in Article 1(a) of Regulation 1829/2003, the Regulation is designed to protect consumer interests in relation to genetically modified food and feed. Articles 4(1) and 16(1) further specify consumer interests in the way that genetically modified food and feed must not mislead the consumer and that genetically modified feed must not harm or mislead the consumer by impairing the distinctive features of the animal products. Since consumer interests as such are not mentioned in one of the alternatives of Annex A(1) of the SPS Agreement, the Regulation's authorisation procedures, to the extent that they aim at the protection of consumer interests, do not fall within the Annex's ambit.[82]

Conclusion

Concluding, the authorisation procedures laid down in the GM Food and Feed Regulation can be qualified as SPS measures in terms of their purpose to the extent they are applied to protect against the risks listed in Annex A(1)(a)-(d) of the SPS Agreement.

6.2.1.1.2.3 Legal Form and Nature

Annex A(1), second sentence lists the different forms that SPS measures may take. This list is only indicative.[83] Approval procedures are explicitly mentioned as one possible form that SPS measures may take.

---

[80] "Allergy is a pathological deviation of the immune response to a particular substance which affects only some individuals where a combined effect of variations in the environment and genetic predisposition has resulted in allergic sensitisation.", EFSA Panel on Genetically Modified Organisms (2010b), p. 10.

[81] *Cf.* Articles 5(5)(a), 6(4), 17(5)(a) and 18(4) of Regulation 1829/2003 in conjunction with Annex II.C.3.b of Directive 2001/18/EC; *cf.* also EFSA Panel on Genetically Modified Organisms (2010b), p. 10.

[82] *Cf.* also Scott (2003), p. 228.

[83] *Cf.* van den Bossche and Zdouc (2022), pp. 1024–1025 with reference to WTO Appellate Body, *Australia - Measures Affecting the Importation of Apples from New Zealand* (29 November 2010), WT/DS367/AB/R, paras 175–176.

6.2.1.1.2.4 Conclusion

The authorisation procedures laid down in the Deliberate Release Directive and the GM Food and Feed Regulation can be considered as falling within Annex A(1) of the SPS Agreement to the extent that they are applied for the protection of human and animal life and health. To the extent that these authorisation procedures are applied for the protection of biodiversity and the environment in a way not comprised by the alternatives of Annex A(1), as well as for the protection of consumer interests, they do not fall within Annex A(1) of the SPS Agreement and thus fall outside the Agreement's scope.

6.2.1.1.3 Direct or Indirect Affect on International Trade

The term *affect* in Article 1.1 of the SPS Agreement is to be interpreted broadly and does not require showing a quantifiable impact on trade.[84] Such a broad interpretation is supported by the term *may* in Article 1.1 as well as by the inclusion of indirect trade impacts.[85] This has also been confirmed by the Panel in *EC – Biotech* which did not find a necessity to show that a measure has an actual effect on trade.[86] Since the authorisation procedures laid down in Deliberate Release Directive and the GM Food and Feed Regulation are a necessary condition for placing GM plants on the market in the European Union, these procedures directly or indirectly affect trade.

6.2.1.1.4 Conclusion

As can be seen from the foregoing analysis and the difficulties to qualify EU GMO regulations as falling within or outside of the Agreement's scope, the SPS Agreement is not adequately designed to cover the risks associated with GMOs. This displays the general difficulty to design comprehensive regulations for scenarios that are characterised by uncertainty. Also, it shows the complexity of comprehensively regulating GMOs with its multi-facetted risk profile, with possible effects on people, animals and the environment in all its dimensions. Regardless of these difficulties, authorisation procedures laid down in the Deliberate Release Directive and the GM Food and Feed Regulation to the extent they pursue the aims laid down in Annex A(1)(a)-(d) of the SPS Agreement constitute SPS measures.

---

[84] Charnovitz (2007), para 1.

[85] *Cf.* Gruszczynski (2018), p. 5.

[86] WTO Panel, *European Communities - Measures Affecting the Approval and Marketing of Biotech Products* (29 September 2006), WT/DS291/R, WT/DS292/R, WT/DS293/R, para 7.435; for an analysis of the Panel report, see also Chap. 5, p. 115.

6.2.1.2 Compatibility

The compatibility of the EU authorisation procedures with the SPS Agreement is reviewed in two ways.[87] On the one hand, the general requirement for an authorisation for GM plants and its compliance with the SPS Agreement is assessed.[88] On the other hand, the compatibility of the authorisation procedures' concrete design as set out in the Deliberate Release Directive and the GM Food and Feed Regulation in conjunction with the associated decision of approval or disapproval is analysed.[89]

6.2.1.2.1 International Harmonisation: Article 3

Article 3.1 encourages the Member States to base their sanitary and phytosanitary measures on international standards, guidelines or recommendations, where they exist.[90] But, Member States may also choose a higher level of sanitary and phytosanitary protection in accordance with the requirements laid down in Article 3.3 or where otherwise provided for in the SPS Agreement. The international standards SPS measures shall be based on are further specified in Annex A(3) of the SPS Agreement.

In the case that a Member State's authorisation procedure conforms to international standards, guidelines or recommendations, meaning the Member State's measure completely embodies the international standard,[91] the measure's consistency with the SPS Agreement and the GATT is presumed according to Article 3.2.

6.2.1.2.1.1 Presumption of Conformity with the SPS Agreement: Article 3.2

The EU authorisation procedures as such and their existence, in general, would be presumed to comply with the SPS Agreement and GATT in case they conform to international standards, guidelines and recommendations. This means that they have to completely embody the international standard and be identical to it concerning structure and the desired level of protection, converting it into national law.[92]

The relevant international standards are laid down in Annex A(3) of the SPS Agreement.

---

[87] *Cf.* concerning a similar approach assessing the Cartagena Protocol, Böckenförde (2004), pp. 361–363.

[88] *Cf.* also Fricke (2004), pp. 187–198.

[89] *Cf.* also Dederer (2010), pp. 216–217; Stökl (2003a), pp. 142–204.

[90] Prévost and van den Bossche (2005), p. 266 which stresses that the SPS Agreement "does not oblige Members to use harmonized SPS measures".

[91] *Cf.* WTO Appellate Body, *EC Measures Concerning Meat and Meat Products (Hormones)* (16 January 1998), WT/DS26/AB/R, WT/DS48/AB/R, para 170.

[92] *Cf.* Prévost and van den Bossche (2005), p. 276; see also WTO Appellate Body, *EC Measures Concerning Meat and Meat Products (Hormones)* (16 January 1998), WT/DS26/AB/R, WT/DS48/AB/R, para 170.

For food safety considerations, the "standards, guidelines and recommendations established by the *Codex Alimentarius Commission* ('CAC') relating to food additives, veterinary drug and pesticide residues, contaminants, methods of analysis and sampling, and codes and guidelines of hygienic practice"[93] apply. Standards and guidelines relevant for the authorisation procedure of genetically modified plants used as food that have been issued by the CAC are: the *Principles for the Risk Analysis of Foods Derived from Modern Biotechnology,*[94] the *Guideline for the Conduct of Food Safety Assessment of Foods Derived from Recombinant-DNA Plants,*[95] the *Guidelines on Performance Criteria and Validation of Methods for Detection, Identification and Quantification of Specific DNA Sequences and Specific Proteins in Foods*[96] and a *Compilation of Codex texts relevant to the labelling of foods derived from modern biotechnology.*[97] However, it is questionable whether these standards fall within the ambit of Annex A(3)(a) which is confined to very specific standards.[98]

Furthermore, "the international standards, guidelines and recommendations developed under the auspices of the Secretariat of the International Plant Protection Convention in cooperation with regional organizations operating within the framework of the International Plant Protection Convention"[99] apply in the context of plant health. The Secretariat of the IPPC has published an *Overview on International Standards for Phytosanitary Measures (ISPMs) and their application to living modified organisms (LMOs)*[100] indicating the existing ISPMs that provide guidance for the plant pest risk analysis of GMOs. These standards are, inter alia, *ISPM 1: Phytosanitary principles for the protection of plants and the application of phytosanitary measures in international trade,*[101] *ISPM 2: Framework for pest risk analysis,*[102] *ISPM 11: Pest risk analysis for plants as quarantine pests,*[103] *ISPM 6: Guidelines for surveillance*[104] and *ISPM 9: Guidelines for pest eradication programmes*[105] as well as Annexes 1 to 3 to ISPM 11. Relevant for the authorisation procedures of genetically modified plants are especially ISPMs 1, 2 and 11.

Lastly, Annex A(3)(d) of the SPS Agreement together with Articles 3.5 and 12.4 SPS Agreement offers the possibility for the SPS Committee to identify further

---

[93] See Annex A(3)(a) of the SPS Agreement.

[94] Ad Hoc Intergovernmental Task Force on Food Derived from Biotechnology (2011).

[95] Ad Hoc Intergovernmental Task Force on Food Derived from Biotechnology (2008).

[96] Codex Committee on Methods of Analysis and Sampling (2010).

[97] Codex Committee on Food Labelling (2011).

[98] *Cf.* also Böckenförde (2004), p. 334.

[99] See Annex A(3)(c) of the SPS Agreement.

[100] Secretariat of the International Plant Protection Convention (2016).

[101] Secretariat of the International Plant Protection Convention (2015a).

[102] Secretariat of the International Plant Protection Convention (2019b).

[103] Secretariat of the International Plant Protection Convention (2019a).

[104] Secretariat of the International Plant Protection Convention (2018).

[105] Secretariat of the International Plant Protection Convention (2015b).

standards, guidelines and recommendations for matters not covered by the aforementioned organisations.[106] The SPS Committee has adopted a procedure to monitor the process of international harmonization[107] which is, however, focused on standards by the organisations mentioned in Annex A(3).[108] While one can think of the Cartagena Protocol as a standard in the sense of Annex A(3)(d) of the SPS Agreement,[109] the Protocol has not yet been considered as such by the SPS Committee and also, this seems rather unlikely.[110] For now, the WTO only considers "the three sisters", the *Codex Alimentarius Commission*, the *World Organization for Animal Health* and the *International Plant Protection Convention*, as relevant standard-setting bodies.[111]

6.2.1.2.1.2 Applicability of Article 3.2 to the EU Authorisation Procedures

General Pre-Marketing Authorisation Requirement

The first question to assess in this context is whether the general requirement of authorisation procedures conforms to international standards, guidelines and recommendations. While there are documents laying down specific criteria for risk analyses of genetically modified plants, there is no document explicitly requiring authorisation procedures. Nevertheless, from the fact that the CAC and the IPPC have issued explicit guidelines for the risk analysis of genetically modified plants, one can assume that the existence of authorisation procedures, in general, is in conformance with these standards. However, the present analysis will be based on the assumption that there are no standards, guidelines or recommendations addressing this question. Instead, the compatibility of a general requirement of authorisation procedures for genetically modified plants with the SPS Agreement will be reviewed in detail.

The Authorisation Procedures's Design Conforming to International Standards?

Addressing the second question on whether the authorisation procedures' concrete design conforms to international standards, it is not only uncertain which of the above-mentioned standards are comprised by Annex A(3).[112] But also, whether

[106] *Cf.* also Böckenförde (2004), p. 336 who does not identify an explicit competence of the SPS Committee in these provisions but rather finds that the SPS Committee has decided to exercise this competence by adopting the „Procedure to Monitor the Process of International Harmonization".

[107] See Committee on Sanitary and Phytosanitary Measures (2004) and Committee on Sanitary and Phytosanitary Measures (2006).

[108] *Cf.* Böckenförde (2004), p. 336.

[109] See Böckenförde (2004), pp. 333–336 with further references.

[110] Böckenförde (2004), p. 336.

[111] See World Trade Organization, https://www.wto.org/english/tratop_e/sps_e/sps_e.htm.

[112] See above and footnote 98.

compliance of the EU authorisation procedures for genetically modified plants with these standards would render the procedures as a whole compatible with the SPS Agreement. The relevant standards address risk analyses concerning specific types of genetically modified plants,[113] single parts of the authorisation procedure[114] or specific types of risks.[115] The present analysis, however, does not assess the authorisation procedure in regard to specific products, but the authorisation procedure as a whole on an abstract level. Therefore, the conformity of the authorisation procedure with some of the above-mentioned standards would only partly lead to the presumption provided for in Article 3.2. With regard to products, risks or parts not covered by the relevant standards, a detailed analysis would be necessary. In light of this, it is not possible to sufficiently answer the question on whether the authorisation procedures' design conforms to international standards. Instead, their compatibility with the SPS Agreement shall be reviewed in detail.

6.2.1.2.1.3 Role of Article 3.1 for the Further Analysis

Article 3.1 encourages Member States to base their SPS measures on international standards, guidelines or recommendations. The standard required by "based on" in Article 3.1 is less strict than that laid down by "conform to" in Article 3.2.[116] Therefore, the non-compliance of SPS measures with this provision has no direct legal consequence.[117] The SPS measures simply have to comply with the other SPS Agreement's provisions, similar to Article 3.3.[118] Therefore, a determination of whether the EU authorisation procedures are based on international standards or pursue a higher level of protection than laid down in relevant standards is not necessary at the present stage. But, that SPS measures are based on international standards, guidelines or recommendations, could be an indicator for their conformity with the SPS Agreement. This should be taken into account when assessing the authorisation procedure's compliance with the SPS Agreement's provisions.

6.2.1.2.1.4 Conclusion

The presumption of conformity laid down in Article 3.2 SPS does neither apply to the general authorisation requirement nor to the authorisation procedures' concrete design since both do not conform (entirely) to international standards, guidelines or recommendations. However, where the EU authorisation procedures are based on international standards issued in the context of the CAC and IPPC this should be taken into account in the further assessment. Since the conformity of the EU

[113] See Ad Hoc Intergovernmental Task Force on Food Derived from Biotechnology (2008).

[114] See Codex Committee on Methods of Analysis and Sampling (2010).

[115] Secretariat of the International Plant Protection Convention (2019a).

[116] World Trade Organization, paras 7–8.

[117] *Cf.* Landwehr (2007), p. 23, 26.

[118] *Cf.* Landwehr (2007), para 24.

authorisation procedures with the SPS Agreement cannot be presumed, its compatibility with the SPS provisions has to be assessed provision by provision.

6.2.1.2.2 EU Authorisation Procedures Based on Science?

The SPS Agreement obliges Member States to base their sanitary and phytosanitary measures on a scientific basis.[119]

First, the relevant science-based obligations that exist under the SPS Agreement are outlined (1.). Second, the compatibility of the EU authorisation procedures with these science-based obligations is discussed (2.).

6.2.1.2.2.1 The Science-Based Obligations Under the SPS Agreement: An Overview

Article 2.2

Article 2.2 obliges Member States to apply SPS measures only to the extent necessary to protect human, animal or plant life or health and requires SPS measures to be based on scientific principles and not to be maintained without sufficient scientific evidence, except for cases falling within the scope of Article 5.7. All three elements have to be met cumulative.[120] The obligation laid down in Article 2.2 applies to the adoption, maintenance, and application of SPS measures.[121] And, it requires a continuous review of SPS measures.[122] In cases where scientific evidence is insufficient, Member States may resort to Article 5.7 SPS to adopt provisional SPS measures on the basis of available pertinent information.[123]

While the concept of "sufficient scientific evidence" has been analysed in multiple cases before the WTO DSB, the other two requirements have not yet been discussed in detail in the DSB's jurisprudence.[124]

The burden of proof for a violation of Article 2.2 SPS lies with the complaining party, but a request under Article 5.8 SPS may be possible.[125]

Article 5

Article 5 SPS lays down requirements that Member States must observe when enacting sanitary or phytosanitary measures. Article 5.1 SPS requires Member States to base their SPS measures on a risk assessment. This obligation is only

---

[119] According to Articles 2.2 and 5 SPS Agreement.

[120] Scott (2009), p. 85.

[121] Seibert-Fohr (2007), para 15.

[122] Seibert-Fohr (2007), para 15.

[123] For details see below pp. 189–190.

[124] *Cf.* Scott (2009), p. 85; for a more recent analysis, see World Trade Organization.

[125] According to Seibert-Fohr (2007), para 29.

modified in cases of insufficient scientific evidence in accordance with Article 5.7 SPS. Furthermore, Articles 5.3, 5.4, 5.5 and 5.6 SPS inform the determination of the appropriate level of sanitary or phytosanitary protection.

In general, the process of decision-making in the field of risk regulation is divided into the part of risk assessment and risk management (as well as risk communication).[126] The risk assessment is the scientific process of identifying risk, evaluating the consequences of taking that risk and determining the likelihood of its occurrence according to the SPS measures applied.[127] The risk assessment is explicitly regulated in Article 5 SPS.

Risk management is the process of evaluating the given policy options to choose the appropriate prevention and control options. The risk management process takes account of the risk assessment, citizens' interests, and other factors, such as economic considerations or the health protection of consumers.[128] The risk management stage is not explicitly mentioned in the SPS Agreement. This was also emphasised by the Appellate Body which made clear that the term *risk management* is nowhere to be found in the SPS Agreement.[129] Nevertheless, the SPS Agreement contains parts that are usually considered as part of the risk management stage, although not expressly labelled as such. These are the provisions that give Member States the right to choose their own appropriate level of protection and to choose an SPS measure to reach this level of protection.[130] And, also the requirement of "based on" in Article 5.1 SPS informs the risk management stage to some extent.[131]

Article 5.1 According to Article 5.1 SPS, sanitary and phytosanitary measures must be based on a risk assessment, assessing the risks to human, animal or plant life or health.

Risk Assessment The risk assessment required by Article 5.1 SPS is "'a scientific process aimed at establishing the scientific basis for the sanitary measure a Member intends to take'".[132] It is "characterized by systematic, disciplined and objective enquiry and analysis, that is, a mode of studying and sorting out facts and

---

[126] *Cf.* Biber-Klemm et al. (2011), p. 303 with further references; see also Stökl (2003a), pp. 161–162 with further references; see also Bognar (2016), p. 187; Codex Alimentarius Commission (2007), p. 44.

[127] *Cf.* van den Bossche and Zdouc (2022), p. 1040; Prévost and van den Bossche (2005), p. 291; Bognar (2016), p. 187 with reference to Caswell (2000).

[128] *Cf.* Prévost and van den Bossche (2005), p. 291; Codex Alimentarius Commission (2007), p. 44.

[129] WTO Appellate Body, *EC Measures Concerning Meat and Meat Products (Hormones)* (16 January 1998), WT/DS26/AB/R, WT/DS48/AB/R, para 181; see also Biber-Klemm et al. (2011), p. 304 noting that "the SPS Agreement does not distinguish between the two" and laying down possible consequences.

[130] See on this issue also Prévost and van den Bossche (2005), p. 292 and Walker (1998), pp. 255–256, 268; *cf.* also Biber-Klemm et al. (2011), p. 307.

[131] See below; *cf.* also Prévost and van den Bossche (2005), p. 292.

[132] WTO Appellate Body, *EC Measures Concerning Meat and Meat Products (Hormones)* (16 January 1998), WT/DS26/AB/R, WT/DS48/AB/R, para 187.

opinions".[133] When carrying out a risk assessment, Member States shall consider risk assessment techniques developed by the relevant international organisations.[134] But, a risk assessment must not only evaluate the respective risks under laboratory conditions, it should also evaluate the risks under real-world conditions, meaning "the actual potential for adverse effects on human health in the real world where people live and work and die".[135]

Also, a risk assessment in the sense of Article 5.1 SPS does not necessarily have to be carried out by a Member State itself, but a Member State can also base its SPS measures on a risk assessment carried out by another Member State or by an international organisation.[136]

There are two types of risk assessment: The first type concerns risks associated with the establishment or spread of a post or disease in the importing States' territory. The second type concerns adverse effects on human or animal health arising from the presence of additives, contaminants, toxins or disease-causing organisms in food, beverages or feedstuffs.[137]

Under the first type of risk assessment, two types of risks have to be evaluated: first, risks of the entry, establishment or spread of a pest or disease and second, associated potential biological and economic consequences.[138] This type of risk assessment entails three steps:[139]

---

[133] WTO Appellate Body, *EC Measures Concerning Meat and Meat Products (Hormones)* (16 January 1998), WT/DS26/AB/R, WT/DS48/AB/R, para 187.

[134] See Article 5.1 SPS; however, this "does not mean that a risk assessment must be based on or conform to such techniques, nor does it mean that compliance with such techniques alone suffices to show that the risk assessment is consistent with the requirements under the SPS Agreement", van den Bossche and Zdouc (2022), p. 1043; the relevant international organisations can be assumed to be the Codex Alimentarius Commission, the World Organisation for Animal Health and the International Plant Protection Convention as the most relevant organisations for SPS matters, see Prévost and van den Bossche (2005), p. 290.

[135] WTO Appellate Body, *EC Measures Concerning Meat and Meat Products (Hormones)* (16 January 1998), WT/DS26/AB/R, WT/DS48/AB/R, para 187; see also Prévost and van den Bossche (2005), p. 281.

[136] *Cf.* WTO Appellate Body, *EC Measures Concerning Meat and Meat Products (Hormones)* (16 January 1998), WT/DS26/AB/R, WT/DS48/AB/R, para 190; the Appellate Body repeated this statement in its Report WTO Appellate Body, *Australia - Measures Affecting Importation of Salmon* (20 October 1998), WT/DS18/AB/R, Fn. 68; see also Scott (2009), p. 91. The possibility to „borrow" a risk assessment is very important for developing countries, *cf.* Prévost and van den Bossche (2005), p. 290.

[137] See Annex A(4) of the SPS Agreement.

[138] *Cf.* also Prévost and van den Bossche (2005), p. 281; Scott (2009), pp. 91–92.

[139] These criteria were mentioned for the first time by the Appellate Body, see WTO Appellate Body, *Australia - Measures Affecting Importation of Salmon* (20 October 1998), WT/DS18/AB/R, para 121; they were repeated by the Panel in *EC – Biotech*, see WTO Panel, *European Communities - Measures Affecting the Approval and Marketing of Biotech Products* (29 September 2006), WT/DS291/R, WT/DS292/R, WT/DS293/R, para 7.3040; *cf.* Prévost and van den Bossche (2005), pp. 281–282 and Scott (2009), p. 92.

(1) *Identification of the diseases or pests* whose entry, establishment or spread a Member wants to prevent on its territory and, *identification of the potential biological and economic consequences* associated with the entry, establishment or spread of these diseases
(2) *Evaluation of the likelihood of entry, establishment or spread* of these diseases or pests and, *evaluation of the likelihood of the associated potential biological and economic consequences*
(3) *Evaluation of the likelihood* of entry, establishment or spread of these diseases or pests *in light of the SPS measures which might be applied*

The assessment of likelihood under the second and third criteria requires an evaluation of the *probability of risk occurrence* as such and according to the SPS measure which might be applied. The mere assessment of the possibility of risk occurrence does not suffice.[140] But, it is not required that "a risk assessment establishes a certain magnitude or threshold level of degree of risk".[141] Thus, already a small probability of risk occurrence is sufficient to satisfy the second criterion.[142]

This requirement of "likelihood" is different to the requirement of "potential" in the second type of risk assessment under Annex A(4).[143] However, doubts are raised with regard to the usefulness of the probability criterion since States may nevertheless institute a "zero-risk" policy.[144] According to *Prévost* and *van den Bossche*, "the more stringent criterion ("probability" as opposed to "potential") [...] only serves to make it harder to satisfy the risk assessment requirement without serving any real purpose."[145]

The requirements for the second type of risk assessment are less clearly established than for the first type.[146] The Panel in *EC – Hormones* established a two-fold approach:[147]

---

[140] *Cf.* Prévost and van den Bossche (2005), pp. 282–283 with reference to WTO Appellate Body, *Australia - Measures Affecting Importation of Salmon* (20 October 1998), WT/DS18/AB/R, para 123; see also Scott (2009), p. 93.

[141] WTO Appellate Body, *Australia - Measures Affecting Importation of Salmon* (20 October 1998), WT/DS18/AB/R, para 124 with reference to WTO Appellate Body, *EC Measures Concerning Meat and Meat Products (Hormones)* (16 January 1998), WT/DS26/AB/R, WT/DS48/AB/R, para 186; *Prévost* and *van den Bossche* point out that it "is not clear what kind of qualitative determination of probability would satisfy" the requirement of likelihood, *cf.* Prévost and van den Bossche (2005), p. 284.

[142] Prévost and van den Bossche (2005), p. 284.

[143] Prévost and van den Bossche (2005), p. 282; see also Scott (2009), p. 93.

[144] *Cf.* Prévost and van den Bossche (2005), p. 284; see also Scott (2009), p. 94.

[145] Prévost and van den Bossche (2005), p. 284.

[146] *Cf.* Scott (2009), p. 92.

[147] WTO Panel, *EC Measures Concerning Meat and Meat Products (Hormones) (Complaint by the United States)* (18 August 1997), WT/DS26/R/USA, para 8.98; WTO Panel, *EC Measures Concerning Meat and Meat Products (Hormones) (Complaint by Canada)* (18 August 1997), WT/DS48/R/CAN, para 8.101; the bracketed part of the approach was rejected by the Appellate Body, *cf.* WTO Appellate Body, *EC Measures Concerning Meat and Meat Products (Hormones)* (16 January 1998), WT/DS26/AB/R, WT/DS48/AB/R, para 184.

(1) *Identification* of the adverse effects on human or animal health
(2) *Evaluation* of the potential [or probability] of occurrence of these effects

This approach was modified by the Appellate Body.[148] It made clear that "probability" must not be used as an alternative for "potential". While potential is related to possibility, probability implies a higher threshold and introduces a quantitative dimension to the notion of risk which finds no basis in the SPS Agreement.[149] Related to that, the Appellate Body made clear that there is no requirement to establish a minimum level of risk when conducting a risk assessment. The requirement to identify a risk is meant to exclude theoretical uncertainty which always remains in science. Instead, a risk must be ascertainable.[150]

Furthermore, it is important to note that an equivalent to the third criterion of the first type of risk assessment, to consider alternatives, is missing for the second type of risk assessment under Annex A(4) of the SPS Agreement.[151]

Both types of risk assessment require a high degree of specificity. Accordingly, Member States have to make sure that their scientific findings are sufficiently specific to the issue at hand regardless of the methodological approach they are using.[152] Risks, therefore, have to be evaluated on a disease- or product-specific basis.[153] This means that a risk assessment has to "address the particular kind of risk at stake from the product at issue".[154],[155]

Articles 5.2 and 5.3 SPS determine further factors that Member States "shall take into account" when assessing risks to life or health.[156] The obligation "to take into account" is different from an obligation "to base on" in that not each and every factor has to be respected, but it is rather a requirement to consider certain factors in the process of risk assessment.[157]

The factors enlisted in Article 5.3 are of an economic nature showing that also external factors can be considered when assessing risks to animal and plant life or health.[158] Important to note in this regard: economic factors are not to be taken into

---

148 *Cf. WTO Appellate Body, EC Measures Concerning Meat and Meat Products (Hormones) (16 January 1998), WT/DS26/AB/R, WT/DS48/AB/R, para 183.*

149 WTO Appellate Body, *EC Measures Concerning Meat and Meat Products (Hormones)* (16 January 1998), WT/DS26/AB/R, WT/DS48/AB/R, paras 184–186; see also Scott (2009), p. 93.

150 *Cf.* WTO Panel, *EC Measures Concerning Meat and Meat Products (Hormones) (Complaint by the United States)* (18 August 1997), WT/DS26/R/USA, para 186; see also Prévost and van den Bossche (2005), p. 281.

151 *Cf.* also Scott (2009), pp. 95–96.

152 Scott (2009), p. 94.

153 *Cf.* Scott (2009), p. 95.

154 Prévost and van den Bossche (2005), p. 287.

155 For the requirement of specificity, see also WTO Appellate Body, *Japan - Measures Affecting the Importation of Apples* (26 November 2003), WT/DS245/AB/R, para 202.

156 See Scott (2009), pp. 98–99.

157 See also Scott (2009), p. 99.

158 *Cf.* Prévost and van den Bossche (2005), p. 294.

account when it comes to risks for human health or life.[159] Furthermore, the factors listed in Article 5.3 SPS are not only relevant in the risk assessment phase, but may also be taken into account at the risk management stage when determining the applicable SPS measure.[160]

Based On Article 5.1 SPS does not only oblige Member States to carry out a risk assessment, but also to base their SPS measures on such risk assessment. This requires a "certain objective relationship" between an SPS measure and the risk assessment.[161] Such an "objective relationship" exists where the risk assessment "sufficiently warrants", i.e. "reasonably supports" the SPS measure at stake.[162] As such, it corresponds to the requirement of a rational relationship between scientific evidence and the SPS measure as required by Article 2.2 SPS.[163]

As is the case for Article 2.2 SPS, the objective relationship between a risk assessment and an SPS measure can also be established on the basis of minority scientific opinions coming from qualified and respected sources.[164] This is, even more, the case "where the risk involved is life-threatening in character and is perceived to constitute a clear and imminent threat to public health and safety", but always depends on the specific circumstances of the case.[165] Still, the question remains of how many or what kind of minority opinions are necessary to rationally ground an SPS measure.[166]

But, an objective relationship is not given where an SPS measure is based on theoretical uncertainty with regard to SPS risks.[167] Also, "an unequivocally positive risk assessment will in general not be able to serve as a rational basis for a

[159] *Cf.* Prévost and van den Bossche (2005), p. 294; on inconsistencies in the relationship between Article 5.3 SPS and the first risk assessment under Annex A(4) of the SPS Agreement, see Scott (2009), pp. 102–104.

[160] See also above for the introductory remarks to Article 5, p. 182.

[161] WTO Appellate Body, *EC Measures Concerning Meat and Meat Products (Hormones)* (16 January 1998), WT/DS26/AB/R, WT/DS48/AB/R, para 189.

[162] WTO Appellate Body, *EC Measures Concerning Meat and Meat Products (Hormones)* (16 January 1998), WT/DS26/AB/R, WT/DS48/AB/R, para 193.

[163] *Cf.* WTO Appellate Body, *EC Measures Concerning Meat and Meat Products (Hormones)* (16 January 1998), WT/DS26/AB/R, WT/DS48/AB/R, para 193; note that the criterion of rational relationship in Article 2.2 SPS has been informed by Article 5.1 SPS, *cf.* Scott (2009), p. 110.

[164] WTO Appellate Body, *EC Measures Concerning Meat and Meat Products (Hormones)* (16 January 1998), WT/DS26/AB/R, WT/DS48/AB/R, para 194; for an overview of the rational relationship concept in Article 2.2, see Seibert-Fohr (2007), paras 23–28 with further references.

[165] WTO Appellate Body, *EC Measures Concerning Meat and Meat Products (Hormones)* (16 January 1998), WT/DS26/AB/R, WT/DS48/AB/R, para 194; *Scott* points out that this statement by the Appellate Body could be read as implying a balancing of risks and protected interests, similar to the proportionality test in Article 2.2., see Scott (2009), pp. 109–110; see also Prévost and van den Bossche (2005), pp. 295–296.

[166] *Cf.* Prévost and van den Bossche (2005), pp. 295–296.

[167] *Cf.* Scott (2009), pp. 105–106.

categorical prohibition on the substance or product in question."[168] Such a finding has also been made by the WTO Panel in *EC – Biotech* with regard to Member States' safeguard measures.[169] It held that an SPS measure cannot be said to be based on a risk assessment when the SPS measure reflects a divergent opinion that is not expressed in the risk assessment.[170]

This also shows the differences between risk assessment on the one hand, risk management on the other hand, and the criterion of "based on" in between these two stages of decision-making.[171] While the Member States are free to choose their appropriate level of protection and may even pursue a "zero-risk" policy,[172] the requirement "based on" does however seem to limit the Member States' level of discretion to some extent.

Article 5.7 Article 5.7 SPS gives Member States the right to provisionally enact SPS measures on the basis of available pertinent information.[173] It does, however, not allow Member States to bypass the requirement for a risk assessment as laid down in Article 5.1 SPS.[174] It rather enables Member States to temporarily overcome the lack of sufficient information that is necessary for the assessment of risks.[175]

To invoke Article 5.7 SPS, four requirements have to be met cumulatively:[176]

1. A situation of insufficiency of relevant scientific evidence
2. Adoption of the measure on the basis of available pertinent information
3. the Member State seeks to obtain the additional information necessary for a more objective assessment of risk
4. review of the measure within a reasonable period of time

[168] Scott (2009), p. 107.

[169] For an overview of the *EC – Biotech* case and the WTO Panel's findings, see above Chap. 5, p. 115.

[170] *Cf.* WTO Panel, *European Communities - Measures Affecting the Approval and Marketing of Biotech Products* (29 September 2006), WT/DS291/R, WT/DS292/R, WT/DS293/R, para 7.3060.

[171] See also Scott (2009), p. 104: "For an SPS measure to be 'based on' a risk assessment, there must be an adequate risk assessment, but there must also be something more".

[172] *Cf.* Scott (2009), p. 106.

[173] The legal nature of Article 5.7 SPS is not entirely clear. While the Appellate Body characterises Article 5.7 SPS as a qualified exemption, the Panel in *EC – Biotech* qualified Article 5.7 SPS as an autonomous right, see WTO Appellate Body, *Korea - Import Bans, and Testing and Certification Requirements for Radionuclides* (11 April 2019), WT/DS495/AB/R, 5.106 referring to WTO Appellate Body, *Japan - Measures Affecting Agricultural Products* (22 February 1999), WT/DS76/AB/R, para 80; WTO Panel, *European Communities - Measures Affecting the Approval and Marketing of Biotech Products* (29 September 2006), WT/DS291/R, WT/DS292/R, WT/DS293/R, para 7.2969; see also Seibert-Fohr (2007), pp. 34–35.

[174] Kogan (2007), p. 152.

[175] *Cf.* Böckenförde (2004), p. 376.

[176] WTO Appellate Body, *Japan - Measures Affecting Agricultural Products* (22 February 1999), WT/DS76/AB/R, para 89.

Insufficiency of Relevant Scientific Evidence The first criterion of Article 5.7 SPS requires such a lack of scientific evidence that the performance of a risk assessment as required by Article 5.1 SPS is not possible.[177] Insufficiency can also occur in cases where the evidence is inconclusive or unreliable and therefore does not allow for the performance of a risk assessment.[178] It is, however, important to note that scientific insufficiency must not be equated with scientific uncertainty and that only the former triggers the application of Article 5.7 SPS.[179]

Measure Adopted on the Basis of Available Pertinent Information The second criterion requires that the existing information must reasonably support the measure at issue. It must indicate that the risk the measure is adopted to protect against is at least theoretically plausible.[180]

Seek to Obtain the Additional Information Necessary for a More Objective Assessment of Risk The Member State relying on Article 5.7 SPS must obtain the information that is necessary to conduct a risk assessment under Article 5.1 SPS.[181] This is an obligation of conduct.[182]

Review Within a Reasonable Period of Time Furthermore, the SPS measure based on Article 5.7 SPS must be reviewed within a reasonable period of time. The amount of time that is considered reasonable depends on the specific case and its circumstances.[183] Here, the difficulty of obtaining additional information to carry out a risk assessment and the characteristics of the SPS measure adopted can play a role.[184] According to the European Commission, a reasonable period of time includes the time needed to carry out a risk assessment and the time needed to perform a risk evaluation based on the conclusions of the risk assessment.[185] Thus, according to the EU, the time needed for risk management is also comprised by a reasonable review time.

---

[177] *Cf.* Prévost and van den Bossche (2005), pp. 303–304 with reference to WTO Appellate Body, *Japan - Measures Affecting the Importation of Apples* (26 November 2003), WT/DS245/AB/R, para 179; see also WTO Appellate Body, *Korea - Import Bans, and Testing and Certification Requirements for Radionuclides* (11 April 2019), WT/DS495/AB/R, para 5.106.

[178] Prévost and van den Bossche (2005), p. 304.

[179] WTO Appellate Body, *Japan - Measures Affecting the Importation of Apples* (26 November 2003), WT/DS245/AB/R, para 184.

[180] *Cf.* Prévost and van den Bossche (2005), p. 304.

[181] *Cf.* Prévost and van den Bossche (2005), p. 305; WTO Appellate Body, *Japan - Measures Affecting the Importation of Apples* (26 November 2003), WT/DS245/AB/R, para 179.

[182] *Cf.* Prévost and van den Bossche (2005), p. 306.

[183] WTO Appellate Body, *Japan - Measures Affecting Agricultural Products* (22 February 1999), WT/DS76/AB/R, para 93.

[184] Prévost and van den Bossche (2005), 307; see also WTO Appellate Body, *Japan - Measures Affecting Agricultural Products* (22 February 1999), WT/DS76/AB/R, para 93.

[185] Commission of the European Communities (2000), p. 20.

The SPS Agreement and the Precautionary Principle as Understood in EU Law

While the precautionary principle is not explicitly laid down in the SPS Agreement, it finds reflection in Article 5.7 SPS as stated by the Appellate Body in *EC – Hormones* and again repeated in *US/Canada – Continued Suspension.*[186] Also, it is reflected in the Member States' right to determine their own level of SPS protection granted by Article 3.3 SPS and paragraph six of its preamble.[187]

However, it is stated that due to a lack of legal anchoring in the WTO agreements, the precautionary principle cannot on its own form a legal basis for Member States to relieve them from obligations under the WTO agreements.[188] Also, it is questionable to what extent the precautionary principle can influence the interpretation of Article 2.2 SPS since "[a]n overly broad and flexible interpretation of that obligation would render Article 5.7 meaningless"[189] according to the Appellate Body in *Japan – Agricultural Products II.*[190]

This part does not concern the question of whether the precautionary principle in international law is reflected in the SPS Agreement's provisions, but concerns the precautionary principle as understood and applied in EU law and its reflection in the SPS Agreement's provisions.

The European Commission in its *Communication on the precautionary principle*[191] states that the precautionary principle as applied in EU law complies with WTO law since "each Member of the WTO has the independent right to determine

[186] WTO Appellate Body, *EC Measures Concerning Meat and Meat Products (Hormones)* (16 January 1998), WT/DS26/AB/R, WT/DS48/AB/R, para 124; WTO Appellate Body, *Canada - Continued Suspension of Obligations in the EC - Hormones Dispute* (16 October 2008), WT/DS321/AB/R, para 680; also *Prévost* and *van den Bossche* state that Article 5.7 "could be said to reflect a particular formulation of the precautionary principle", Prévost and van den Bossche (2005), pp. 297–298; however, they also mention that the need to strengthen the precautionary principle was raised before the Seattle Ministerial Conference since Article 5.7 SPS was said to not go far enough, see Prévost and van den Bossche (2005), p. 259.

[187] *Cf.* WTO Appellate Body, *EC Measures Concerning Meat and Meat Products (Hormones)* (16 January 1998), WT/DS26/AB/R, WT/DS48/AB/R, para 124; see also Commission of the European Communities (2000), 2.

[188] See Eggers (2001), p. 237 referring to Articles 3.2, 7.2 and 11 DSU; *cf.* Prévost and van den Bossche (2005), p. 262; see also WTO Appellate Body, *EC Measures Concerning Meat and Meat Products (Hormones)* (16 January 1998), WT/DS26/AB/R, WT/DS48/AB/R, para 125.

[189] WTO Appellate Body, *Japan - Measures Affecting Agricultural Products* (22 February 1999), WT/DS76/AB/R, para 80.

[190] This is questioned by *Prévost* and *van den Bossche* who suggest an application of the precautionary principle to the risk assessment stage in the way that it lowers the threshold for the requirement of sufficient scientific evidence, see Prévost and van den Bossche (2005), p. 262, 308 referring to the Appellate Body's statement in *EC – Biotech* that "a panel charged with determining [...] whether 'sufficient scientific evidence' exists [...] may, of course, and should, bear in mind that responsible, representative governments commonly act from perspectives of prudence and precaution where risks of irreversible, e.g. life-terminating, damage to human health are concerned", WTO Appellate Body, *EC Measures Concerning Meat and Meat Products (Hormones)* (16 January 1998), WT/DS26/AB/R, WT/DS48/AB/R, para 124.

[191] Commission of the European Communities (2000).

the level of environmental or health protection they consider appropriate."[192] It classifies the precautionary principle as belonging to the stage of risk management.[193] With regard to Article 5.7 SPS, it observes that this provision allows for a precautionary approach in situations of inadequate scientific data and stresses that it does not determine any time limits although provisional in nature.[194] Furthermore, the European Commission refers to the concept of risk assessment under the SPS Agreement as a flexible one and thereby seems to state that it also enables the application of a precautionary approach in situations not comprised by Article 5.7 SPS.[195] Accordingly, the European Commission seems to argue that the precautionary approach enacted by the EU can either be based on Article 5.1 SPS in accordance with the Member States' right to determine their own appropriate level of protection or on Article 5.7 SPS.[196]

However, the decisive question is whether Articles 5.1 and 5.7 provide an adequate basis for all situations in which the precautionary principle can be applied according to EU law.

In EU law, the precautionary principle is applicable at the risk management stage in situations where potentially negative effects resulting from a phenomenon, product or procedure have been identified and, where it is impossible to determine, in a scientific evaluation, the risk in question with sufficient certainty because of the insufficiency of the data, their inconclusive or imprecise nature.[197] Thus, scientific uncertainty from an EU perspective correlates with the appearance of insufficiency, inconclusiveness, or impreciseness of scientific evidence. To apply precautionary measures in cases of scientific uncertainty is thus compatible with Article 5.7 SPS which does not only cover situations of insufficiency of scientific evidence, but also cases where "the available evidence is more than minimal in quantity, but has not led to reliable or conclusive results"[198] as stated by the Appellate Body in *Japan – Apples*. In these situations, Article 5.7 SPS allows enacting SPS measures in accordance with a Member States appropriate level of protection which comprises precautionary measures.

The precautionary approach under EU law also conforms to the review requirement laid down in Article 5.7 SPS. According to this requirement, Member States shall seek to obtain the additional information necessary for a more objective

---

[192] Commission of the European Communities (2000), p. 8, 10; see also *Gruszczynski* finding that "the [Commission's] Communication was clearly influenced by the language of the SPS Agreement", see Gruszczynski (2010), p. 175.

[193] *Cf.* Commission of the European Communities (2000), p. 7, 8, 10, 12.

[194] Commission of the European Communities (2000), p. 11.

[195] *Cf.* Commission of the European Communities (2000), p. 11.

[196] This possibility has also been mentioned by the Panel in *EC – Biotech*, see WTO Panel, *European Communities - Measures Affecting the Approval and Marketing of Biotech Products* (29 September 2006), WT/DS291/R, WT/DS292/R, WT/DS293/R, para 7.3065.

[197] Commission of the European Communities (2000), p. 3, 14.

[198] WTO Appellate Body, *Japan - Measures Affecting the Importation of Apples* (26 November 2003), WT/DS245/AB/R, para 185.

assessment of risk in order to achieve scientific certainty and accordingly, they have to review the sanitary or phytosanitary measure within a reasonable period of time. The precautionary approach as applied in the EU also complies with this review requirement.[199] As laid down in the Commission's Communication on the precautionary principle, the measure applied "should be subjected to regular scientific monitoring" to gain "a more advanced or more complete scientific [risk] assessment".[200] As long as this scientific monitoring does not lead to more adequate, precise or conclusive scientific data, but scientific uncertainty remains, precautionary measures may be upheld under EU law.[201]

Accordingly, the understanding of the precautionary principle in EU law as articulated by the European Commission finds reflection in Article 5.7 SPS.

Relationship Between Articles 2.2 and 5 SPS

Article 5.1 SPS is a specification of Article 2.2 SPS (especially its second and third criterion[202])[203] which in turn is the more general obligation.[204] Accordingly, a violation of Article 5.1 SPS implies a violation of Article 2.2 SPS.[205] In such a case, the burden of proof with regard to a violation of Article 2.2 is reversed.[206] But, Article 2.2 can also be violated in cases where an SPS measure complies with Article 5.1.[207] Both provisions should "constantly be read together"[208]

Article 5.7 SPS applies to cases where a risk assessment under Article 5.1 SPS cannot be conducted due to insufficient scientific evidence. It operates as a qualified

199 See Commission of the European Communities (2000), pp. 19–20; this review element has also been discussed by *Böckenförde* with regard to the Cartagena Protocol's precautionary approach, see Böckenförde (2004), pp. 376–379.

200 Commission of the European Communities (2000), p. 19.

201 Commission of the European Communities (2000), p. 19.

202 WTO Panel, *European Communities - Measures Affecting the Approval and Marketing of Biotech Products* (29 September 2006), WT/DS291/R, WT/DS292/R, WT/DS293/R, 7.1439.

203 Prévost and van den Bossche (2005), p. 256; Seibert-Fohr (2007), para 21.

204 *Cf. WTO Appellate Body, Japan - Measures Affecting Agricultural Products (22 February 1999), WT/DS76/AB/R, para 82*; WTO Appellate Body, *EC Measures Concerning Meat and Meat Products (Hormones)* (16 January 1998), WT/DS26/AB/R, WT/DS48/AB/R, para 180; Prévost and van den Bossche (2005), p. 256; Seibert-Fohr (2007), para 21.

205 *Cf.* Prévost and van den Bossche (2005), p. 263; Seibert-Fohr (2007), para 21; this question was not decided by the Appellate Body in *EC – Hormones*, but in *Australia – Salmon*, see Scott (2009), p. 83 with reference to WTO Appellate Body, *Australia - Measures Affecting Importation of Salmon* (20 October 1998), WT/DS18/AB/R, para 138; this is criticised by Scott (2009), pp. 83–84 who points out that a measure not based on a risk assessment or not having a rational relationship to a risk assessment may nevertheless be scientifically founded.

206 *Cf.* Scott (2009), p. 83.

207 Seibert-Fohr (2007), para 21; Prévost and van den Bossche (2005), pp. 263–264; Scott (2009), p. 84; see also Stökl (2003a), p. 164 who expresses doubt that there might be a measure in compliance with Article 5.1 and in violation of Article 2.2 at the same time.

208 WTO Appellate Body, *EC Measures Concerning Meat and Meat Products (Hormones)* (16 January 1998), WT/DS26/AB/R, WT/DS48/AB/R, para 180.

exemption to Article 2.2 SPS,[209] especially for the third obligation laid down in Article 2.2.[210]

Discretion of Member States Under These Science-Based Obligations

The science-based obligations under the SPS Agreement are of a procedural nature as their focus lies on the Member States' process of decision-making and methodology when enacting sanitary or phytosanitary measures.[211] Accordingly, a panel must not conduct a risk assessment on its own.[212] However, DSB panels in their jurisprudence often tend to look at the available science that Member States have found to reason their measures.[213] This approach has explicitly been incorporated by the Appellate Body in *Japan – Apples* stating that "total deference to the findings of the national authorities would not ensure an objective assessment as required by Article 11 of the DSU".[214] Yet, the Appellate Body is said to give greater leeway to national choices.[215]

This DSB practice has been criticised since it enables panels to analyse a Member States risk assessment by privileging its view on scientific evidence.[216] Also, Member States' influence on evidence in the dispute is extremely reduced.[217]

6.2.1.2.2.2 Compatibility of the EU Authorisation Procedures for GM Plants with the SPS Agreement's Science-Based Obligations

While the question of whether EU authorisation procedures for GMOs comply with the SPS Agreement's science-based obligations has already been discussed to some extent in scholarship,[218] this contribution assesses the currently applicable framework. It discusses in detail the compatibility of a general authorisation requirement

[209] WTO Appellate Body, *Korea - Import Bans, and Testing and Certification Requirements for Radionuclides* (11 April 2019), WT/DS495/AB/R, 5.106; WTO Appellate Body, *Japan - Measures Affecting Agricultural Products* (22 February 1999), WT/DS76/AB/R, para 80.

[210] While this question has been left open according to *Seibert-Fohr* (see Seibert-Fohr (2007), para 32), this conclusion seems plausible since the application of Article 5.7 SPS is triggered by the requirement of insufficiency of scientific evidence.

[211] *Cf.* Scott (2009), p. 78, 84.

[212] Seibert-Fohr (2007), paras 30–31.

[213] *Cf.* Scott (2009), p. 84.

[214] WTO Appellate Body, *Japan - Measures Affecting the Importation of Apples* (26 November 2003), WT/DS245/AB/R, para 165 referring to WTO Appellate Body, *EC Measures Concerning Meat and Meat Products (Hormones)* (16 January 1998), WT/DS26/AB/R, WT/DS48/AB/R, para 117.

[215] *Cf.* Prévost and van den Bossche (2005), p. 260.

[216] *Cf.* Burchardi (2007), pp. 261–262.

[217] Burchardi (2007), p. 262.

[218] See Howse and Mavroidis (2000); with regard to the authorisation procedure laid down in Regulation 258/97, *cf.* Stökl (2003a), pp. 142–203; *cf.* Spranger (2000) and *cf.* Wolf (2002), pp. 15–19; with regard to the incorporation of socio-economic factors in the authorisation proce-

and the specificities that arise out of the similarities between plants obtained by targeted mutagenesis and those obtained by conventional mutagenesis, respectively and the decision by the CJEU from 2018 on targeted mutagenesis techniques.[219]

General Authorisation Requirement Based on Science?

First, there is the question of whether the general requirement of a pre-marketing authorisation procedure for all plants that have been genetically modified and fall within the ambit of the Deliberate Release Directive and the GM Food and Feed Regulation complies with the SPS Agreement.

Existence of a Risk Assessment as Required by Article 5.1? Since any violation of Article 5.1 SPS also includes a violation of Article 2.2 SPS, the compatibility with the former will be assessed first. To comply with Article 5.1 SPS, an obligatory authorisation procedure has to be based on a risk assessment.[220] However, such a risk assessment does not exist for the general requirement of an authorisation procedure. For the time that the authorisation procedure takes place, there is a *de facto* temporary ban on the deliberate release or placing on the markets of genetically modified plants.[221] And this is without a prior risk assessment. The risk assessment is carried out during the authorisation procedure.

However, if this missing risk assessment automatically led to an incompatibility with the SPS Agreement, this would be a contradiction in terms. The EU carries out the authorisation procedure precisely to be able to base its authorisation decision on a risk assessment.[222] Can the risk assessment that is carried out during the authorisation process serve as a basis for the general requirement of an authorisation procedure? This is answered in the affirmative by *Böckenförde* referring to a statement by the Appellate Body that the relevant risk assessment does not necessarily need to precede the respective SPS measure.[223] However, this view seems to support contradicting results in cases where a GM plant is under a pre-marketing ban for the time of the authorisation procedure and afterwards authorised for placing on the market. Then, the risk assessment must warrant a *de facto* pre-marketing ban and a marketing authorisation at the same time. To base a pre-marketing ban on an overly positive

dure, see Dederer (2010), pp. 216–223; see also with regard to the Advanced Informed Agreement Procedure laid down in the Cartagena Protocol, *cf.* Böckenförde (2004), pp. 361–363.

[219] The consequences of the CJEU's decision on the EU law's compatibility with WTO law are also addressed by *Spranger*, see Spranger (2019).

[220] In the sense of Annex A(4) to the SPS Agreement.

[221] *Cf.* also WTO Panel, *European Communities - Measures Affecting the Approval and Marketing of Biotech Products* (29 September 2006), WT/DS291/R, WT/DS292/R, WT/DS293/R, para 7.1359.

[222] See below pp. 201–204.

[223] Böckenförde (2004), p. 363; see also WTO Panel, *European Communities - Measures Affecting the Approval and Marketing of Biotech Products* (29 September 2006), WT/DS291/R, WT/DS292/R, WT/DS293/R, para 7.3030.

risk assessment recommending the release or marketing of a GM plant would constitute a violation of Article 5.1 SPS.[224]

Stökl simply refers to the general risk that is associated with GMOs. He does not further elaborate on how the specific requirements for a risk assessment as laid down in Annex A(4) and as required by Article 5.1 SPS are fulfilled for the EU's general authorisation requirement. According to his view, the general risks associated with GMOs suffice for the institution of a general authorisation procedure.[225]

However, it is questionable whether the general possibility that GMOs cause risks to human health or the environment suffice to fulfil the specific requirements of a risk assessment that justifies the temporary ban that comes along with the authorisation procedure. It is especially questionable for plants modified by genome editing techniques, in particular targeted mutagenesis techniques, since the assumption that those plants carry specific risks is heavily disputed.[226]

Provisional Measure in Accordance with Article 5.7? Instead, it seems more coherent to base the EU's requirement for the general authorisation of GM plants on Article 5.7 SPS.[227] This provision explicitly captures the case where it is not possible to carry out a risk assessment as required by Article 5.1 SPS.

Insufficient Evidence Concerning the Risks of GM Plants? For Article 5.7 SPS to apply there must be either a lack of scientific evidence or inconclusive or unreliable evidence.

The existence of risks associated with genetically modified plants is still disputed. While some consider them safe, others raise concerns about their implications for human health and the environment.[228] This scientific status can be considered as inconclusive evidence or even as a lack of scientific evidence since it is not possible to carry out a risk assessment in the sense of Article 5.1.

In this case, there is information that supports the occurrence of risks caused by the release or cultivation of genetically modified plants and thus reasonably supports the general requirement of an authorisation procedure. Furthermore, the EU by conducting an authorisation procedure to assess the risks of every single genetically modified plant complies with its obligation to seek to obtain the additional information necessary for a more objective risk assessment that suffices the requirements of Article 5.1 SPS. There are clear requirements on the information that applicants must submit to obtain an approval for their product.

Insufficient Evidence Concerning the Risks of Plants Altered by Targeted Mutagenesis Techniques? However, this analysis does no longer apply to plants modified by targeted mutagenesis techniques and cisgenesis. As stated by EFSA

[224] See above for the requirement of "based on" under Article 5.1 SPS, p 187.

[225] Stökl (2003a), pp. 172–173.

[226] See above Chap. 3, p. 36.

[227] Recourse to Article 5.7 SPS is denied by Böckenförde (2004), p. 362.

[228] For a brief overview, *cf.* Beck (2022), pp. 73–75; see also above Chap. 2, p. 15.

and as reiterated by the European Commission in its study on the status of new genomic techniques,[229] "EFSA did not identify new hazards specifically linked to the genomic modification produced via SDN-1, SDN-2 or ODM, compared with conventional breeding".[230] Furthermore, "EFSA noted that recently published experimental evidence confirmed that the off-target mutations potentially induced by SDNs are of the same type as, and fewer than, mutations in conventional breeding, including spontaneous mutations and those produced by physical and chemical mutagenesis".[231] With regard to conventional breeding, there is a long safety record according to the CJEU.[232]

In its proposal for a new regulation on plants obtained by new genomic techniques, the EU Commission has explicitly stated that "there are no specific hazards linked to targeted mutagenesis or cisgenesis [with regard to risks for human and animal health and the environment]."[233] An assumption that is reflected throughout the whole proposal.

Thus, a lack of scientific evidence or inconclusive evidence can no longer be generally assumed with regard to risks of plants modified by targeted mutagenesis and cisgenesis techniques. Accordingly, the general requirement for an authorisation procedure for GM plants modified by those techniques cannot be based on Article 5.7 SPS. This results in a violation of Article 5.1 SPS and accordingly in a violation of Article 2.2 SPS.

Review Within a Reasonable Period of Time? Lastly and in case scientific evidence is insufficient, the question arises whether the SPS measure, i.e. the *de facto* pre-marketing ban caused by the general authorisation procedure, is reviewed within a reasonable period of time. The period for the authorisation of GM plants is precisely regulated in the Deliberate Release Directive and the GM Food and Feed Regulation. It can be divided into the part of risk assessment and the part of risk management.

The risk assessment for Part C notifications under Directive 2001/18/EC must not take longer than 90 days.[234] The risk assessment for genetically modified food and feed shall be carried out within 6 months.[235] All these time periods may be extended where the authority carrying out the risk assessment seeks further information from the applicant.[236]

---

[229] European Commission (2021a).

[230] European Commission (2021a), p. 29 referring to European Food Safety Authority (2021).

[231] European Commission (2021a), p. 30.

[232] See CJEU, *Case C-528/16 - Confédération paysanne et al.* (25 July 2018), ECLI:EU:C:2018:583, para 51.

[233] European Commission (2023), p. 1–2.

[234] See Article 14(2), (4) Directive 2001/18/EC.

[235] See Articles 6(1), (2) and 18(1), (2) Regulation 1829/2003.

[236] See also above Chap. 4, p. 67.

Since the time period is adapted to the specific case, there is no indication that the risk assessment takes longer than is reasonably required. Also, the extension of review time by the time required by applicants to submit further information cannot render the time period needed for the risk assessment unreasonable.[237]

For Part C notifications under Directive 2001/18/EC the risk management phase may take at least 135 days. This time can be extended when objections raised by the European Commission or other Member States are maintained.[238]

For authorisations under the GM Food and Feed Regulation, the European Commission shall submit a draft decision to be taken in respect of an application to the *Standing Committee on Plants, Animals, Food and Feed* ('SCoPAFF') within three months from receiving the scientific opinion from EFSA.[239] In case, a decision on the draft decision is not taken by the SCoPAFF, the draft is submitted to the Appeal Committee within one months for a decision.[240] Once the Appeal Committee has taken a decision, there is no time indicated for the European Commission to render its decision.[241] However, as we can see from the tables in Chap. 4 above,[242] the European Commission does neither strictly adhere to the three months period for forwarding its draft decision nor to the one-month period for calling the Appeal Committee. Instead, the risk management phase, meaning the phase from publication of EFSA's opinion to the issuance of the implementing decision, takes on average one year.

While the time periods that are indicated in Directive 2001/18/EC for Part C notifications and in Regulation 1829/2003 may generally be considered reasonably to review the authorisation of GM plants, it is questionable whether the time taken by the current voting behaviour of the Member States in the comitology procedure can still be considered reasonable. The voting behaviour in both Committees is the same since the Deliberate Release Directive and the GM Food and Feed Regulation

---

[237] *Cf.* the assessment of the WTO Panel in *EC – Biotech* with regard to Annex C(1)(a) of the SPS Agreement stating that "delays attributable to action, or inaction, of an applicant must not be held against a Member when a determination is made regarding whether that Member has undertaken or completed approval procedures 'without undue delay'", see WTO Panel, *European Communities - Measures Affecting the Approval and Marketing of Biotech Products* (29 September 2006), WT/DS291/R, WT/DS292/R, WT/DS293/R, para 7.1497.

[238] The shortest period would be 30 days for the circulation of the assessment report to the competent authorities of other Member States by the Commission plus 60 days for possible comments and objections and additional 45 days for discussing comments and objections, see Articles 14(2), 15(1) Directive 2001/18/EC. To this period could be added 120 days in case that objections raised are maintained and it is necessary to carry out the comitology procedure as provided for by Article 18(1) and Article 30(2) Directive 2001/18/EC. However, these 120 days do not include the time that the Standing Committee and the Appeal Committee need to take their decisions, see Article 18(1) Directive 2001/18/EC.

[239] See Articles 7(1) and 19(1) Regulation 1829/2003.

[240] See Article 5(4) Regulation 182/2001.

[241] See also above Chap. 4., p 69.

[242] See above Chap. 4, p 78.

came into force.[243] There is no decision on the draft decisions forwarded by the European Commission. In the end, it is always the European Commission that must take a decision without endorsement by the Member States. Therefore, one could question whether this procedure has any added value or could not simply be left out, the European Commission directly taking its decision based on the opinion issued by EFSA.[244]

The European Commission interprets *reasonable period of time* to include the "time needed for [the] performance of a risk evaluation based on the conclusions [of the risk assessment]"[245] which in the EU's case comprises the time needed for democratic decision-making procedures due to its supranational character. Also, there is no indication that the time needed for democratic decision-making processes is considered as unreasonable under Article 5.7 SPS in general when these processes are needed for the review of SPS measures. However, the decision-making process for the authorisation of GM plants seems more like an empty shell. It seems that a serious engagement with the risk assessment and an evaluation of its results to apply a suitable SPS measure does not take place. Accordingly, the time currently required at the risk management stage appears to be *unreasonable* in the sense of Article 5.7 SPS.

This assessment is also supported by the findings of the WTO Panel in *EC – Biotech* with regard to the requirement of *undue delay* in Annex C(1)(a) of the SPS Agreement.[246] There, the Panel stated that "Members applying such [approval] procedures must in principle be allowed to take the time that is reasonably needed to determine with adequate confidence whether their relevant SPS requirements are fulfilled".[247]

In case, this review procedure is seen as unreasonable in terms of time, the EU cannot base its general authorisation procedure on Article 5.7 SPS which would directly result in a violation of Article 5.1 SPS and accordingly in a violation of Article 2.2 SPS. However, it must be kept in mind that the Directive 2001/18/EC for Part C notifications as well as Regulation 1829/2003 leave room for decisions that can be considered as reasonable in the sense of Article 5.7 SPS. For Part C notifications there is the possibility to completely skip the comitology procedure when there are no maintained objections. And for authorisations of GM food and feed plants, there is the possibility that the SCoPAFF takes a decision.

Conclusion The general authorisation requirement for GM plants in the EU cannot be based on Article 5.1 SPS due to the lack of a risk assessment.

---

[243] See above Chap. 4, pp 70, 78.

[244] On the voting pattern by the EU Member States during the comitology procedure see also Eriksson et al. (2020), p. 350.

[245] Commission of the European Communities (2000), p. 20.

[246] Annex C(1)(a) can be considered as context to Article 5.7 SPS in the sense of Article 31(1) VCLT.

[247] WTO Panel, *European Communities - Measures Affecting the Approval and Marketing of Biotech Products* (29 September 2006), WT/DS291/R, WT/DS292/R, WT/DS293/R, para 7.1498.

With regard to plants modified by targeted mutagenesis techniques it can neither be based on Article 5.7 SPS. The EU Commission has explicitly stated that plants modified by these techniques do not carry specific hazards. This statement leaves no room for the assumption of missing, insufficient or inconclusive scientific evidence. Accordingly, the general authorisation requirement for these plants violates Articles 5.1 and 2.2 SPS.[248]

With regard to all other GM plants, the question of whether the general requirement of a pre-marketing authorisation can be based on Article 5.7 SPS depends on two points: First, there needs to be insufficient evidence on the risk of GM plants. And second, the pre-marketing ban must be reviewed within a reasonable period of time. At the moment, this is rather not the case. The review time taken for the approval decision is unreasonably extended by the Member States' voting behaviour in the comitology procedure. Accordingly, the authorisation procedure even in cases where a lack of scientific evidence is found cannot be based on Article 5.7 SPS. This also leads to a violation of Articles 5.1 and 2.2 SPS.

Authorisation Procedure as Such Based on Science?

Whether the design of the authorisation procedure as such and the decisions arising out of this procedure are compatible with the science-based obligations under the SPS Agreement is assessed from an abstract perspective and not with regard to a specific product.[249] Thus, the analysis focuses on whether the legislative frameworks of the Deliberate Release Directive and the GM Food and Feed Regulation allow for an SPS-compatible decision.

The authorisation procedure for genetically modified plants in the EU is divided into two stages, risk assessment and risk management. The risk assessment for the placing on the market of genetically modified plants under the Deliberate Release Directive is conducted by the competent authorities in the Member States, and in some cases also by the European Food Safety Authority.[250] For the placing on the market of genetically modified plants used as or in food and feed, the risk assessment is carried out by the European Food Safety Authority together with the relevant national authorities of the Member States.[251]

Risk Assessment in Accordance with Article 5.1 SPS The risk assessment procedures laid down in the Deliberate Release Directive and the GM Food and Feed Regulation can fall within both types of risk assessment under Annex A(4) of the

[248] The applicability of the general authorisation procedure to these types of plants directly arises from the decision of the Court of Justice of the European Union in the case *Confédération paysanne et al.*, see Chap. 3, p 31.

[249] See also the analysis by Dederer (2010), pp. 216–217.

[250] See Articles 13(1), 14 Directive 2001/18/EC; EFSA Panel on Genetically Modified Organisms (2009), 2.2. and Figure 1.

[251] See Articles 6, 18 Regulation 1829/2003; see also EFSA Panel on Genetically Modified Organisms (2009), 2.3. and Figure 1.

SPS Agreement. Under both legislative frameworks, the potential diseases, pests and adverse health effects for humans and animals are identified and the likelihood and probability of their occurrence are assessed. Also, the potential biological consequences are evaluated.[252]

Furthermore, the risk assessment process comprises the evaluation of risk occurrence in comparison to different risk management strategies.[253] Thereby, the requirement "to evaluate the likelihood of entry, establishment or spread of these diseases [or pests] according to the SPS measures which might be applied" under the first type of risk assessment listed in Annex A(4) of the SPS Agreement is fulfilled.

Additionally, the risk assessment in the EU is carried out on a case-by-case basis.[254] Accordingly, the risks and adverse effects identified are evaluated individually. Hence, the requirement of specificity is also complied with.

In addition to the requirements laid down in Annex A(4) of the SPS Agreement and Article 5.1 SPS, a risk assessment shall take into account the factors provided for in Articles 5.2 and 5.3 SPS. This is not a mandatory obligation. The EU risk assessment process considers some of the factors listed in Article 5.2 SPS.[255] The economic factors as listed in Article 5.3 SPS do not play a role during the risk assessment process. However, these factors might also be considered during the risk management phase.[256]

Authorisation Decision *based on* the Risk Assessment The concrete authorisation decision must be *based on* the risk assessment.

For applications under Part C of Directive 2001/18/EC concerning the placing on the market of genetically modified plants, the competent authority shall indicate in its assessment report whether the respective GMO should be placed on the market or not.[257] The decision to reject an application shall state the reasons.[258] Accordingly, the authorisation decision for Part C applications under Directive 2001/18/EC, in general, is based on a risk assessment.[259]

---

[252] See Annex II of Directive 2001/18/EC and the different guidance documents on risk assessments prepared by EFSA: EFSA Panel on Genetically Modified Organisms (2011), 2.2.; EFSA Panel on Genetically Modified Organisms (2010a), 2.2.; EFSA Panel on Genetically Modified Organisms (2009), 3.2. (the requirements for risk assessment laid down in Directive 2001/18/EC are also applicable to authorisation procedures under Regulation 1829/2003, see Articles 6(4), 18(4) Regulation 1829/2003).

[253] See Annex II.C.3.5 of Directive 2001/18/EC.

[254] See Article 4(3) and Annex II B of Directive 2001/18/EC; see also Schulte and Schröder (2011), p. 519 and Palme (1997), para 135.

[255] See Annex II of Directive 2001/18/EC taking account *inter alia* of already available scientific data, of the receiving environment and environmental conditions, relevant testing methods.

[256] See above for the factors laid down in Article 5(2) and (3) SPS Agreement, p. 187.

[257] See Article 14(3) of Directive 2001/18/EC.

[258] See Article 15(2) of Directive 2001/18/EC.

[259] For the discretion that Member States can exercise when authorising or rejecting GMO applications, see also Palme (1997), paras 26–28, 33–34.

However, the authorisation decision is not taken by the competent authority of the Member State where the application was submitted when other Member States or the Commission raise and maintain objections with regard to the circulated assessment report. In these cases, the comitology procedure applies.[260] This procedure is also the standard decision-making procedure for the authorisation of the placing on the market of genetically modified food and feed under Regulation 1829/2003.[261]

Under this procedure, there can be a situation where neither the SCoPAFF nor the Appeal Committee[262] delivers an opinion on whether to authorise the placing on the market of genetically modified plants or not. In this case, the Commission *may* adopt the draft implementing act.[263] Here, the question arises whether the Commission is bound to adopt a positive decision in case of a positive risk assessment in order to comply with the EU's obligations under the SPS Agreement. So far, there is no case known where the EU Commission denied an authorisation although there had been a risk assessment in favour of an authorisation.[264]

Furthermore, the comitology procedure offers the possibility that the Commission is bound to deny an authorisation although the risk assessment has been in favour of an authorisation.[265] This is the case where Member States in the SCoPAFF or in the Appeal Committee decide to vote for non-authorisation. The rejection of an application on the basis of an overly positive risk assessment would constitute a violation of Article 5.1 SPS since such decision would not be based on the risk assessment.[266]

Conclusion The risk assessment carried out in accordance with the Deliberate Release Directive, the GM Food and Feed Regulation and the guidances issued by EFSA complies with the requirements laid down in Article 5.1 and Annex A(4) of the SPS Agreement. Problematic is that the EU GMO law is generating its overall authorisation decision in the comitology procedure. Thereby, it provides for the possibility to reject an application although the risk assessment has been overly positive. Such a decision could not be considered to be *based on* the respective risk assessment, thereby violating Article 5.1 SPS. This case shows the political dimension of the GMO authorisation procedure in EU law.

---

[260] See Article 18 of Directive 2001/18/EC.

[261] See Articles 7(3), 19(3), 35(2) Regulation 1829/2003 and Articles 13 (1)(c) and (e), 5, 10 and 11 of *Regulation (EC) No 182/2011 of the European Parliament and of the Council of 16 February 2011 laying down rules and general principles concerning mechanisms for control by Member States of the Commission's exercise of implementing powers*, OJ EU 2011, L 55/13 ('Regulation 182/2011').

[262] See Article 6 Regulation 182/2011.

[263] See Article 6(3) subpara. 2 Regulation 182/2011.

[264] For further details on the concrete decisions, see table 1 and 2 in Annex Chap. 3, p 78.

[265] See Article 6(3) subpara. 3 Regulation 182/2011.

[266] See above for the criterion of *based on* as laid down in Article 5.1 SPS, p. 187.

6.2.1.2.3 Obligations of Non-Discrimination Under the SPS Agreement

In addition to its science-based obligations, the SPS Agreement also entails obligations of non-discrimination, laid down in Articles 2.3 and 5.5 SPS.

Since plants modified by targeted mutagenesis need a pre-marketing authorisation while plants altered by conventional mutagenesis techniques do not, the question arises whether the difference in regulatory oversight for these plants constitutes a discrimination under Articles 2.3 and 5.5 SPS.[267] The changes introduced by both techniques can be identical and the plants obtained by both techniques are said to carry the same risks.[268]

6.2.1.2.3.1 Prohibition of Arbitrary or Unjustifiable Discrimination Between Member States: Article 2.3

Article 2.3 SPS lays down a non-discrimination rule which reflects the national treatment principle laid down in Article III GATT and the most-favoured-nation principle laid down in Article I GATT.[269] For a violation of Article 2.3 SPS, three requirements have to be fulfilled: (1) a discrimination between Members, (2) which is arbitrary or unjustifiable and, (3) in a situation where identical or similar conditions prevail.[270]

Furthermore, "sanitary and phytosanitary measures shall not be applied in a manner which would constitute a disguised restriction on international trade" according to Article 2.3, sentence 2.

---

[267] With regard to a possible violation of Article 5.5 SPS because of the differentiation between organisms obtained by targeted mutagenesis and those obtained by conventional breeding techniques, see also Spranger (2019), pp. 10–12.

[268] See above Chap. 2, p. 15.

[269] See also Seibert-Fohr (2007), para 36.

[270] *Cf.* Seibert-Fohr (2007), pp. 36, 37; Prévost and van den Bossche (2005), pp. 264–265 with reference to WTO Art. 21(5) DSU Panel, *Australia - Measures Affecting Importation of Salmon - Recourse to Article 21.5 by Canada* (18 February 2000), WT/DS18/RW, paras 7.111–7.112.

6.2.1.2.3.2 *Prohibition of Arbitrary or Unjustifiable Distinctions in the Appropriate Levels of Protection: Article 5.5*

The obligation laid down in Article 5.5 SPS pursues the long-term goal of achieving consistency in the application of the appropriate level of sanitary or phytosanitary protection.[271] The SPS Committee has published *guidelines to further the practical implementation of Article 5.5*[272] to achieve this goal.[273]

For a violation of Article 5.5, a Member State first has to set different levels of protection in different, but comparable situations.[274] Second, the difference in levels of protection has to be arbitrary or unjustifiable in their treatment of different situations. And third, these arbitrary or unjustifiable differences must lead to a discrimination or a disguised restriction on trade.[275] These three requirements have to be met cumulatively.[276]

Determining a Member State's Appropriate Level of Protection

The appropriate level of protection ('ALOP') has to be set "in a sufficiently clear manner"[277] and can be contained in government policy statements or other government documents and statements.[278] Also, the appropriate level of protection applied can be deduced from a measure that is actually applied.[279] This is also the case where a Member State has expressly stated its level of protection.[280] Otherwise, Member States by relying on generically stated levels of protection could circumvent their obligation under Article 5.5 SPS.[281]

[271] *Cf.* Prévost and van den Bossche (2005), p. 310; see also WTO Appellate Body, *EC Measures Concerning Meat and Meat Products (Hormones)* (16 January 1998), WT/DS26/AB/R, WT/DS48/AB/R, para 213.

[272] Committee on Sanitary and Phytosanitary Measures (2000).

[273] WTO Appellate Body, *EC Measures Concerning Meat and Meat Products (Hormones)* (16 January 1998), WT/DS26/AB/R, WT/DS48/AB/R, para 213.

[274] WTO Panel, *Australia - Measures Affecting the Importation of Apples from New Zealand* (9 August 2010), WT/DS367/R, 7.937; WTO Art. 21(5) DSU Panel, *Australia - Measures Affecting Importation of Salmon - Recourse to Article 21.5 by Canada* (18 February 2000), WT/DS18/RW, 7.89–7.93.

[275] WTO Appellate Body, *Australia - Measures Affecting Importation of Salmon* (20 October 1998), WT/DS18/AB/R, para 140 referring to WTO Appellate Body, *EC Measures Concerning Meat and Meat Products (Hormones)* (16 January 1998), WT/DS26/AB/R, WT/DS48/AB/R, para 214.

[276] See Prévost and van den Bossche (2005), p. 311.

[277] Committee on Sanitary and Phytosanitary Measures (2000), A.1.

[278] Committee on Sanitary and Phytosanitary Measures (2000), A.1.

[279] WTO Panel, *United States - Certain Measures Affecting Imports of Poultry from China* (29 September 2010), WT/DS392/R, para 7.244 with reference to WTO Appellate Body, *Australia - Measures Affecting Importation of Salmon* (20 October 1998), WT/DS18/AB/R, para 207.

[280] *Cf.* WTO Panel, *United States - Certain Measures Affecting Imports of Poultry from China* (29 September 2010), WT/DS392/R, para 7.244.

[281] *Cf.* WTO Panel, *United States - Certain Measures Affecting Imports of Poultry from China* (29 September 2010), WT/DS392/R, para 7.244.

Different, But Comparable Levels of Protection

For the comparison of different levels of protection, the situations dealt with must be comparable.[282] This is the case where the situations present some common elements.[283] The Appellate Body in its *EC – Hormones* report and in its *Australia – Salmon* report dealt with the question of when different situations are comparable under Article 5.5 SPS. Accordingly, "situations can be compared under Article 5.5 if these situations involve either a risk of entry, establishment or spread of the same or a similar disease, or a risk of the same or similar 'associated potential biological and economic consequences'".[284] Furthermore, "for situations to be comparable under Article 5.5, it is sufficient for these situations to have in common a risk of entry, establishment or spread of *one* disease of concern. There is no need for these situations to have in common a risk of entry, establishment or spread of *all* diseases of concern".[285]

Arbitrary or Unjustifiable Difference in the Levels of Protection

In general, the existence of an arbitrary or unjustifiable difference is to be determined on a case-by-case basis, but the difference in levels of protection may serve as an indicator.[286] In *Australia – Salmon* the WTO Panel found a violation of this requirement since Australia had imposed more lenient sanitary measures for two categories of non-salmonid fish than for ocean-caught Pacific salmon although the risk presented by the two categories of non-salmonids could be presumed to be as high or even higher than the risk presented by ocean-caught Pacific salmon.[287] This finding was confirmed by the Appellate Body.[288]

---

[282] Prévost and van den Bossche (2005), p. 311.

[283] WTO Appellate Body, *EC Measures Concerning Meat and Meat Products (Hormones)* (16 January 1998), WT/DS26/AB/R, WT/DS48/AB/R, para 217; see also Committee on Sanitary and Phytosanitary Measures (2000), A.2.

[284] WTO Appellate Body, *Australia - Measures Affecting Importation of Salmon* (20 October 1998), WT/DS18/AB/R, para 146; see also Committee on Sanitary and Phytosanitary Measures (2000), A.2. and A.4.

[285] WTO Appellate Body, *Australia - Measures Affecting Importation of Salmon* (20 October 1998), WT/DS18/AB/R, para 152.

[286] *Cf.* Committee on Sanitary and Phytosanitary Measures (2000), A.2.

[287] *Cf.* WTO Panel, *Australia - Measures Affecting Importation of Salmon* (12 June 1998), WT/DS18/R, paras 8.134, 8.141.

[288] WTO Appellate Body, *Australia - Measures Affecting Importation of Salmon* (20 October 1998), WT/DS18/AB/R, para 158.

Discrimination or a Disguised Restriction on Trade

Whether there is a discrimination or a disguised restriction on trade under Article 5.5, can be determined on the basis of certain warning signals and additional factors.[289] Relevant warning signals are the arbitrary or unjustifiable character of differences in levels of protection, a substantial degree of difference in the levels of protection of the compared situations and the inconsistency of the relevant SPS measure with Articles 5.1 and 2.2 SPS.[290] This third criterion is the most important of Article 5.5 SPS according to the Appellate Body in *EC – Hormones* and must also be read in the context of Article 2.3 SPS.[291] However, one has to bear in mind as can be seen from the Appellate Body's decision in *EC – Hormones* "that the mere incorporation of various non-scientific considerations in the decision to impose a certain health measure is not sufficient to invalidate the measure by rendering it a 'disguised restriction on trade'."[292]

6.2.1.2.3.3 Relationship Between Article 2.3 and 5.5 SPS

As found by the Appellate Body in *Australia – Salmon*, a violation of Article 5.5 SPS which entails a discrimination or disguised restriction on trade implies a violation of Article 2.3 SPS.[293] But, the scope of Article 2.3 SPS is broader and the provision may be violated by conduct that does not constitute a violation of Article 5.5 SPS.[294]

---

[289] WTO Appellate Body, *Australia - Measures Affecting Importation of Salmon* (20 October 1998), WT/DS18/AB/R, paras 159, 177.

[290] WTO Appellate Body, *Australia - Measures Affecting Importation of Salmon* (20 October 1998), WT/DS18/AB/R, paras 161–166; see also WTO Appellate Body, *EC Measures Concerning Meat and Meat Products (Hormones)* (16 January 1998), WT/DS26/AB/R, WT/DS48/AB/R, para 240 and Committee on Sanitary and Phytosanitary Measures (2000), A.2.

[291] *Cf.* WTO Appellate Body, *EC Measures Concerning Meat and Meat Products (Hormones)* (16 January 1998), WT/DS26/AB/R, WT/DS48/AB/R, paras 238, 240.

[292] Prévost and van den Bossche (2005), p. 318 referring to WTO Appellate Body, *EC Measures Concerning Meat and Meat Products (Hormones)* (16 January 1998), WT/DS26/AB/R, WT/DS48/AB/R, paras 240–246.

[293] See WTO Panel, *Australia - Measures Affecting Importation of Salmon* (12 June 1998), WT/DS18/R, para 8.109 (as upheld by WTO Appellate Body, *Australia - Measures Affecting Importation of Salmon* (20 October 1998), WT/DS18/AB/R, para 178); see also WTO Appellate Body, *Australia - Measures Affecting Importation of Salmon* (20 October 1998), WT/DS18/AB/R, para 252; WTO Panel, *United States - Certain Measures Affecting Imports of Poultry from China* (29 September 2010), WT/DS392/R, para 7.318.

[294] See Prévost and van den Bossche (2005), pp. 256–266, 319.

6.2.1.2.3.4 Discriminatory Difference in Levels of Protection Applied to Plants Bred by Conventional Breeding and Those Modified by Targeted Mutagenesis Techniques?

A violation of Article 5.5 SPS which implies a violation of Article 2.3 SPS needs to be assessed first.

For such a violation, the EU must have set different levels of protection with regard to plants modified by targeted mutagenesis techniques and plants that have been bred by conventional methods. Such a difference in the level of protection could be taken from the fact that only plants modified by the former techniques require authorisation to be marketed in the EU. Plants obtained by conventional mutagenesis breeding are exempt from the scope of the Deliberate Release Directive and the GM Food and Feed Regulation[295] This exemption is justified by the long safety record of organisms altered by conventional mutagenesis.[296] But, does this exemption indicate a difference in the level of protection for both types of plants?

On the one hand, one could argue that the protection level set by the EU is the same for both types of plants. Plants obtained by conventional mutagenesis are also considered as genetically modified organisms in the sense of Article 2(2) Directive 2001/18/EC in the first place and only exempt in a second step. Accordingly, the EU's objective to protect human and animal health and the environment from adverse effects as well as consumer interests also applies to this type of plants. The EU simply considers them as safe enough to comply with their appropriate level set and does not consider it necessary to subject those plants to authorisation procedures in order to reach their chosen level of protection.

On the other hand, one could take the different handling of both types of plants as an indicator for a difference in the level of protection. This can be especially the case where a generic ALOP is stated, but the concrete measures applied lead to a *de facto* difference in levels of protection.[297] The measure applied though different from the ALOP can be indicative for the level of protection chosen.[298]

The level of protection set by the EU with regard to genetically modified plants can be considered as being rather generic. But, with regard to the different techniques, the EU considers plants obtained by conventional mutagenesis breeding as safe due to their long period of application and associated long safety record.[299] This is why these plants do not need authorisation under the EU GMO law. The level of protection is that of safety which is established by their long safe use. In contrast,

---

[295] See Article 3(1) of Directive 2001/18/EC and Article 2(2) of Regulation 1829/2003, both in conjunction with Annex I B of Directive 2001/18/EC.

[296] See Recital 17 of Directive 2001/18/EC and CJEU, *Case C-528/16 - Confédération paysanne et al.* (25 July 2018), ECLI:EU:C:2018:583, para 51.

[297] *Cf.* WTO Panel, *Australia - Measures Affecting the Importation of Apples from New Zealand* (9 August 2010), WT/DS367/R, para 7.973.

[298] WTO Panel, *Australia - Measures Affecting Importation of Salmon* (12 June 1998), WT/DS18/R, para 7.974-7.975 with reference to further WTO jurisprudence.

[299] *Cf.* CJEU, *Case C-528/16 - Confédération paysanne et al.* (25 July 2018), ECLI:EU:C:2018:583, paras 43–51.

plants obtained by genome editing techniques do need authorisation in order to assess their adverse effects on human and animal health and the environment. The level of protection is that of safety as evidenced in a risk assessment. Accordingly, the different measures applied to both types of technique indicate a (*de facto*) difference in the level of protection.

Also, the differentiation in levels of protection is arbitrary or unjustifiable. The situation under EU law with regard to plants obtained by targeted mutagenesis techniques is comparable to the situation in *Australia – Salmon*. EFSA as well as the European Commission have stated that targeted mutagenesis techniques "carry the same level of risk as conventional breeding techniques".[300] Nevertheless, the regulation of plants obtained by conventional, random mutagenesis techniques is less stringent than the regulation of plants obtained by targeted mutagenesis.

This arbitrary or unjustifiable difference can serve as one indicator that the differentiation also qualifies as a discrimination or disguised restriction on trade. Furthermore, the high burden that is associated with authorisation procedures for genome edited plants which is in stark contrast to the non-requirement of approval for plants obtained by conventional mutagenesis techniques although both plants carry the same risks is a strong indicator of existing discrimination.

6.2.1.2.3.5 Conclusion

Accordingly, the fact that plants modified by targeted mutagenesis need to be authorised although they carry the same risks as conventionally bred plants which do not need a comparable authorisation constitutes a discrimination, thereby violating Article 5.5 SPS. This also implies a violation of Article 2.3 SPS.

6.2.1.2.4 The Appropriate Level of Protection

Furthermore, the SPS Agreement also regulates the determination of Member States' appropriate level of protection.

6.2.1.2.4.1 Application of the Least Trade Restrictive Measures

In this regard Article 5.6 SPS obliges Member States to apply the least trade restrictive measures to achieve the chosen level of protection when taking SPS measures, provided that it is technically and economically feasible. A least trade restrictive measure in the sense of Article 5.6 is any measure that is reasonably available,

[300] European Commission (2021a), p. 3; see also European Commission (2021a), pp. 29–30 referring to European Food Safety Authority (2021); see further European Commission (2023), pp. 1–2; a different assessment was taken by Spranger in his analysis, *cf.* Spranger (2019), p. 12.

achieves the Member State's appropriate level of protection and is significantly less trade restrictive.[301]

Whether an alternative measure is technically and economically feasible is determined in accordance with the Member States' capacities.[302]

For an alternative measure to be significantly less trade restrictive minor differences do not suffice. Instead, market access must be substantially improved under the alternative measure compared to the measure applied.[303]

6.2.1.2.4.2 Obligation to Exempt Plants Obtained by Targeted Mutagenesis from the Authorisation Requirement?

The EU has enacted its GMO law to protect human health and the environment from risks potentially arising when marketing genetically modified plants.[304] The EU's appropriate level of protection is that of safety which is given for plants that have conventionally been used in a number of applications and have a long safety record.[305] Also, the safety assessment of GMOs includes a comparison to their non-GM counterpart.[306]

Since conventionally bred plants have a long safety record, they are exempt from regulatory oversight. On the contrary, organisms obtained by targeted mutagenesis are not exempt from regulatory oversight and need to be authorised before being marketed in the EU. In light of EFSA's statement that plants modified by targeted mutagenesis carry the same risks or even fewer risks than conventionally bred plants which has been adopted by the EU Commission,[307] Article 5.6 SPS requires the EU to also exempt such plants from its GMO regulations. The envisaged level of protection can also be achieved without an authorisation procedure. Such an exemption substantially improves market access for these genetically modified plants and therefore can be considered a least trade restrictive measure in the sense of Article 5.6 SPS.

---

[301] As has been laid down in the footnote to Article 5.6 SPS; these three elements have also been acknowledged by the Appellate Body in *Australia – Salmon*, see WTO Appellate Body, *Australia - Measures Affecting Importation of Salmon* (20 October 1998), WT/DS18/AB/R, para 194.

[302] Prévost and van den Bossche (2005), p. 320.

[303] *Cf.* Prévost and van den Bossche (2005), p. 323.

[304] See above Chap. 4, p. 60.

[305] See recital 17 of Directive 2001/18/EC and *cf.* CJEU, *Case C-528/16 - Confédération paysanne et al.* (25 July 2018), ECLI:EU:C:2018:583, paras 44–45.

[306] See Annex II B of Directive 2001/18/EC.

[307] See European Commission (2021a), pp. 29–30 referring to European Food Safety Authority (2021); see also European Commission (2023), pp. 1–2.

6.2.1.2.5 Conclusions on the Analysis of EU Authorisation Procedures Under the SPS Agreement

Based on the foregoing analysis of the compatibility of the EU authorisation procedures for the placing on the market of GM plants the following conclusions can be taken:

(1) The EU authorisation procedures do not conform to international standards, guidelines or recommendations in the sense of Article 3.2 SPS. Accordingly, conformity of the procedures with the SPS Agreement cannot automatically be presumed.
(2) The general authorisation requirement for GM plants is not based on a risk assessment as required by Article 5.1 SPS. Also, the requirements for Article 5.7 SPS are not fulfilled. First, there is no insufficiency of scientific evidence for the risks associated with targeted mutagenesis techniques. Accordingly, an authorisation requirement for plants modified by targeted mutagenesis techniques cannot be based on Article 5.7 SPS. And second, the time period for the review of scientific evidence in the authorisation procedure is unreasonably extended by the voting behaviour of the EU Member States during the risk management phase. Therefore, the general authorisation procedure for plants modified by targeted mutagenesis techniques and for GM plants, in general, violates Article 5.1 SPS.
(3) The design of the authorisation procedures in the Deliberate Release Directive and the GM Food and Feed Regulation offers the possibility to reject an application for the marketing of GM plants although the risk assessment has been overly positive and in favour of authorisation. Such a decision would not conform to the requirement of *based on* as laid down in Article 5.1 SPS.
(4) Article 5.5 SPS is violated to the extent that plants modified by targeted mutagenesis techniques carrying the same risks as plants modified by conventional mutagenesis are subject to the EU authorisation procedures. This differentiation of appropriate levels of protection is unjustifiable and amounts to a disguised restriction on trade.
(5) Article 5.6 SPS requires to exempt plants modified by targeted mutagenesis techniques that carry the same risks as conventionally bred plants from the EU authorisation requirement.

Beyond these conclusions, the foregoing analysis shows that the EU's precautionary approach which it has apparently adapted to the SPS Agreement's requirements is comprised by Article 5.7 SPS. However, this is not necessarily the case for all possible forms of precautionary action. It is questionable whether the precautionary approach as allowed under the Cartagena Protocol is comprised by the SPS Agreement's provisions.

But, contrary to the general assumption, the SPS Agreement does not force societies to take risks that they do not want to take. Where there is information or evidence on risks, protection measures may be taken at least provisionally. What is not possible is to base policy action on hypothetical risks. Accordingly, it is up to the

Member State to decide which information or evidence it wants to base its policy action on. The EU's GMO rules concerning authorisation could be legitimate under the SPS Agreement if the EU provided information or evidence on these risks which could also be minority opinions, but from qualified and respected sources. Instead, the EU Commission deliberately decided to adopt EFSA's statement on the equivalent risk profiles of targeted mutagenesis techniques and conventional breeding and to make this the basis of its political actions. It is bound by this decision and must align its policy actions accordingly to comply with the SPS Agreement's obligations.

Consequences that arise out of this adoption by the EU Commission can also be analysed in regard to the SPS Agreement's non-discrimination rules. These rules constitute a challenge for the EU authorisation procedure and its applicability to targeted mutagenesis techniques. Since the European Commission has stated that it considers plants modified by targeted mutagenesis to be not riskier than conventionally bred plants, it seems difficult to justify the different level of protection that is installed with regard to these plants. Accordingly, a harmonisation of the rules applicable to both types of plants is necessary.

6.2.2 TBT Agreement

The EU authorisation procedures do not fall under the TBT Agreement since they do neither qualify as technical regulations or standards nor as conformity assessment procedures.

6.2.3 GATT

The Panel in *EC – Biotech*, did not decide on the consistency of several safeguard measures with Articles III:4 and X:1 GATT since it had already found the safeguard measure's inconsistency with the SPS Agreement.[308] This argument could also be raised here to the extent that the authorisation procedures are covered by the SPS Agreement and an incompatibility with the SPS Agreement has already been found.

However, there are important questions that arise in an analysis of the compatibility of the authorisation procedures with the GATT: Are GM and non-GM plants *like products* and does a different treatment of both lead to a violation of GATT provisions although there might not be a *de jure* discrimination on the basis of a

[308] See WTO Panel, *European Communities - Measures Affecting the Approval and Marketing of Biotech Products* (29 September 2006), WT/DS291/R, WT/DS292/R, WT/DS293/R, paras 7.3415–7.3430; for a comprehensive overview of the Panel decision in *EC – Biotech*, see also above Chap. 5, p. 115.

product's origin? And in case there is a violation of GATT, is such different treatment justified under Article XX GATT?[309]

6.2.3.1 Applicability

The GATT applies to EU approval procedures to the extent that they are not in compliance with the SPS Agreement or not comprised by the SPS Agreement at all.[310] Also, the applicability of the TBT Agreement does not exclude the GATT's applicability.[311]

6.2.3.2 Compatibility

6.2.3.2.1 Article III:4: National Treatment

Article III:4 GATT lays down the national treatment obligation for internal laws, regulations, and requirements.[312]

The Note *Ad* Article III states that

> Any internal tax or other internal charge, or any law, regulation or requirement of the kind referred to in paragraph 1 which applies to an imported product and to the like domestic product and is collected or enforced in the case of the imported product at the time or point of importation, is nevertheless to be regarded as an internal tax or other internal charge, or a law, regulation or requirement of the kind referred to in paragraph 1, and is accordingly subject to the provisions of Article III.[313]

This is the case for EU authorisation procedures which accordingly fall within the ambit of Article III:4 GATT.

For a violation of Article III:4 GATT, the relevant imported and domestic products must be considered *like products* (1), the relevant measure must qualify as a law, regulation or requirement covered by Article III:4 (2) and, accord less favourable treatment to the imported products than to the domestic products (3).[314]

---

[309] See also Conrad (2007), p. 234 and Scott (2003), pp. 230–231.

[310] See Article 2.4 SPS Agreement which states "Sanitary or phytosanitary measures which conform to the relevant provisions of this Agreement shall be presumed to be in accordance with the obligations of the Members under the provisions of GATT 1994 which relate to the use of sanitary or phytosanitary measures, in particular the provisions of Article XX(b)".

[311] For further details, see van den Bossche and Zdouc (2022), pp. 977–978.

[312] van den Bossche and Zdouc (2022), p. 415.

[313] See Annex I to the *General Agreement on Tariffs and Trade 1947* (concluded 30 October 1947) 55 UNTS 187.

[314] See WTO Appellate Body, *Korea - Measures Affecting Imports of Fresh, Chilled and Frozen Beef* (11 December 2000), WT/DS161/AB/R, WT/DS169/AB/R, para 133; see also van den Bossche and Zdouc (2022), p. 415.

Since the EU does not differentiate between imported and domestic GM products at first sight, but between GM and conventionally bred plants regardless of their origin, the question of less favourable treatment of imported products will be addressed first.

6.2.3.2.1.1 Less Favourable Treatment of Imported Products

For a measure to violate Article III:4 GATT, it must distinguish between imported and like domestic products.[315] The conditions of competition accorded to the group of imported products by a measure have to be less favourable in comparison to conditions accorded to the group of like domestic products.[316] A less favourable treatment is given where opportunities are effectively unequal.[317] It is important that the conditions of competition are affected. Formal discrimination between imported and domestic products must not necessarily imply a violation of Article III:4 GATT.[318]

With regard to GM plants, the EU is not differentiating between imported and domestic products. And while the EU is differentiating between GM and non-GM plants this is not because of their origin but because of their different characteristics. Accordingly, *de jure* there is no differentiation between GM and non-GM products because of their origin.[319]

However, it is possible to think about a situation of *de facto* differentiation between GM and non-GM plants caused by their origin. Such a *de facto* differentiation can occur where the majority of imported products are genetically modified and the majority of domestic products are not genetically modified.

This could be the case for soybeans and soybean products. On average 90% of EU soybean and soybean products are imported from the US, Canada, Argentina and Brazil.[320] The soybeans grown in these countries are to 90 to 100% genetically modified.[321] Therefore, most soybeans and soybean products imported to the EU are genetically modified. In contrast, domestic soybeans and soybean products are not genetically modified since GM soybeans are not approved for cultivation in the EU.[322]

---

[315] van den Bossche and Zdouc (2022), p. 428.

[316] *Cf.* van den Bossche and Zdouc (2022), pp. 390–391 with reference to WTO Appellate Body, *Korea - Measures Affecting Imports of Fresh, Chilled and Frozen Beef* (11 December 2000), WT/DS161/AB/R, WT/DS169/AB/R, paras 135–137.

[317] *Cf.* van den Bossche and Zdouc (2022), p. 390 with further references.

[318] See van den Bossche and Zdouc (2022), pp. 391–392 with further references.

[319] *Cf.* also Howse and Mavroidis (2000), p. 324–325.

[320] See European Commission, table 'Trade by main MS & Partners'; Kuepper and Stravens (2022), para 2.2 and table 5; see also Foreign Agricultural Service (2021), p. 20.

[321] *Cf.* International Service for the Acquisition of Agri-biotech Applications (2019); International Service for the Acquisition of Agri-biotech Applications.

[322] See European Commission, https://webgate.ec.europa.eu/fip/GMO_Registers/GMO_Part_C.php; European Commission, https://ec.europa.eu/food/plants/genetically-modified-organisms/gmo-register_en.

Under these circumstances, it is possible to argue that the general requirement of authorisation for GM soybeans and soybean products modifies the conditions of competition to the detriment of imported soybean plants and their products. Accordingly, these plants and plant products are accorded less favourable treatment in the sense of Article III:4 GATT.

6.2.3.2.1.2 GM Plants and Their Conventional Counterparts as Like Products?

This question has already been addressed by scholarship.[323] However, these analyses do not take account of the special case of targeted mutagenesis techniques in comparison to conventionally bred plants but only address transgenic GM plants.

Accordingly, the following part analyses the likeness of plants obtained by targeted mutagenesis and plants bred by conventional mutagenesis. The *like products* analysis is only carried out for soybean plants and their products since the requirement of *less favourable treatment* is fulfilled for these plants. However, one could also analyse other plants where the majority of imports to the EU are genetically modified.

Like Products Under the GATT as Analysed by the DSB

To determine the likeness of products under the GATT, the following criteria should be taken into account:

(1) the properties, nature, and quality of the products
(2) the extent to which the products are capable of serving the same or similar end uses
(3) the extent to which consumers perceive and treat the products as alternative means of performing particular functions in order to satisfy a particular want or demand
(4) the tariff classification of the products.[324]

These criteria were provided for by the Appellate Body in *EC – Asbestos* as tools to assist in the determination of the likeness of two products.[325] They were established

[323] See Wong (2005); Böckenförde (2004), pp. 391–404; for this question in the context of the TBT-Agreement, see also Burchardi (2007), pp. 331–347; Morgan and Goh (2004), pp. 315–318 and Stökl (2003a), p. 210–221.

[324] See WTO Appellate Body, *European Communities - Measures Affecting Asbestos and Asbestos-Containing Products* (12 March 2001), WT/DS135/AB/R, para 101.

[325] WTO Appellate Body, *European Communities - Measures Affecting Asbestos and Asbestos-Containing Products* (12 March 2001), WT/DS135/AB/R, paras 101–102 as referred to by WTO Panel, *European Communities - Measures Prohibiting the Importation and Marketing of Seal Products* (25 November 2013), WT/DS400/R, WT/DS401/R, para 7.136; see also Tamiotti (2007), para 11.

by the *Report of the Working Party on Border Tax Adjustments*[326] from 1970 and further developed by the Appellate Body's Report in *Japan – Alcoholic Beverages II*.[327] They do not qualify as absolute criteria for "likeness" as stated by the Appellate Body in *Japan – Alcoholic Beverages II*.[328] Rather, "[t]he concept of 'likeness' is a relative one that evokes the image of an accordion. The accordion of 'likeness' stretches and squeezes in different places as different provisions of the WTO Agreement are applied. The width of the accordion in any one of those places must be determined by the particular provision in which the term 'like' is encountered as well as by the context and the circumstances that prevail in any given case to which that provision may apply."[329] Therefore, the likeness of products has to be determined on a case-by-case basis by taking into account the criteria provided for by the Appellate Body in *EC – Asbestos*.[330] In this regard, the Appellate Body also emphasised that it is important to take account of the competitive relationship between products in the marketplace when determining their likeness.[331]

Physical Properties

A comparison of the physical properties of two products must be made on a case-by-case basis. For transgenic GM plants, the insertion of foreign DNA (standing for deoxyribonucleic acid) leads to a clear differentiation from conventionally bred plants.[332] This is different with regard to plants obtained by targeted mutagenesis. The mutations induced are of the same characteristics as mutations that have been induced by conventional mutagenesis or occurred naturally.[333] This supports the *likeness* of both types of plants.

But, one could argue that the difference in modification techniques used is relevant in the case of GM plants because of the risks that come along with a genetic modification. In *EC – Asbestos*, the Appellate Body acknowledged that the molecular structure and chemical composition of chrysotile asbestos fibres are important for the determination of a competitive relationship with other fibres because of their

326 *Report by the Working Party on Border Tax Adjustments* (1970), para 18.

327 Holzer (2017), p. 186.

328 WTO Appellate Body, *Japan - Taxes on Alcoholic Beverages* (4 October 1996), WT/DS8/AB/R, WT/DS10/AB/R, WT/DS11/AB/R, 21.

329 WTO Appellate Body, *Japan - Taxes on Alcoholic Beverages* (4 October 1996), WT/DS8/AB/R, WT/DS10/AB/R, WT/DS11/AB/R, 21.

330 *Cf.* Morgan and Goh (2004), p. 315; Holzer (2017), p. 186; see also WTO Appellate Body, *European Communities - Measures Affecting Asbestos and Asbestos-Containing Products* (12 March 2001), WT/DS135/AB/R, para 102; see also *Appleton* who pleads for a case-by-case assessment and states that "likeness 'cannot be reduced to definable criteria'", Appleton (2014), p. 99.

331 WTO Appellate Body, *European Communities - Measures Affecting Asbestos and Asbestos-Containing Products* (12 March 2001), WT/DS135/AB/R, para 103; see also Appleton (2014), p. 93.

332 *Cf.* Burchardi (2007), pp. 342–344; see also Hestermeyer (2011), p. 75; for a different view see Morgan and Goh (2004), pp. 316–317 and Baumüller (2004), p. 41.

333 See above Chap. 2, p. 15.

carcinogenic impact on humans.[334] This carcinogenicity had been acknowledged by international bodies and confirmed by the experts consulted by the Panel in its analysis.[335] However, risks that come along with the genetic modification of plants are not recognised internationally to the same extent as the carcinogenicity of asbestos fibres. The impact of GM plants on the environment and its biodiversity is disputed and also depends on the specific modification introduced.[336] Furthermore, with regard to plants obtained by targeted mutagenesis, even EFSA has acknowledged that those plants do not carry more risks than their conventional counterparts.[337] Therefore, differentiation between these products due to their risks is rather unlikely.

This could be different when the public perception of risk is decisive for a differentiation of products as argued by *Burchardi*. He reasons his argument by the formulation "evidence relating to the health risks *associated* with chrysotile asbestos" used by the Appellate Body in *EC – Asbestos*.[338] Also, the Appellate Body in *EC – Asbestos* stated that "panels must examine those physical properties of products that are likely to influence the competitive relationship between products in the marketplace"[339] which supports the view by *Burchardi*. In case public perception is decisive, a comparison of plants obtained by targeted mutagenesis and their conventional counterparts would probably come to a difference in both types of plants in the food sector. However, in the feed sector, such a differentiation is not made.[340] Since imported soybean plants and their products are mainly used in the EU feed sector,[341] the differentiation proposed by *Burchardi* is not relevant for the analysed case.

---

[334] See WTO Appellate Body, *European Communities - Measures Affecting Asbestos and Asbestos-Containing Products* (12 March 2001), WT/DS135/AB/R, para 114; a similar finding was made by the Appellate Body in *US – Clove Cigarettes* where it stated that „regulatory concerns underlying a measure, such as the health risks associated with a given product, may be relevant to an analysis of the 'likeness' criteria under Article III:4 of the GATT 1994, as well as under Article 2.1 of the TBT Agreement, to the extent they have an impact on the competitive relationship between and among the products concerned", see WTO Appellate Body, *United States - Measures Affecting the Production and Sale of Clove Cigarettes* (4 April 2012), WT/DS406/AB/R, para 119.

[335] See WTO Appellate Body, *European Communities - Measures Affecting Asbestos and Asbestos-Containing Products* (12 March 2001), WT/DS135/AB/R, para 114 with reference to WTO Panel, *European Communities - Measures Affecting Asbestos and Asbestos Containing Products* (18 September 2000), WT/DS135/R, para 8.188.

[336] See above Chap. 2, p. 15.

[337] European Commission (2021a), p. 29 referring to European Food Safety Authority (2021).

[338] Burchardi (2007), pp. 343–344.

[339] WTO Appellate Body, *European Communities - Measures Affecting Asbestos and Asbestos-Containing Products* (12 March 2001), WT/DS135/AB/R, para 114.

[340] See below p 219.

[341] European Commission (2018b), p. 5; see also transparenz Gentechnik, https://www.transgen.de/lebensmittel/1049.futtermittelimporte-europa-sojabohnen-gentechnik.html; *cf.* also Bundesinformationszentrum Landwirtschaft, https://www.landwirtschaft.de/diskussion-und-dialog/tierhaltung/gentechnik-in-futtermitteln; Centre for the Promotion of Imports from developing countries, https://www.cbi.eu/market-information/grains-pulses-oilseeds/trade-statistics; European Commission (2019a).

Accordingly, imported genetically modified soybean plants and their products and domestic conventionally bred soybean plants and their products could be considered as like with regard to their physical properties.

End Uses

While a lot of plants are modified to adapt them to changing environmental conditions (herbicide, pesticide, or drought resistance), their end uses are still the same. A different end-use can be assumed in cases where the genetic modification leads to a difference in the nutritional content of food or feed.[342] But, also in these cases, the GM product and the conventional product are still in a competitive relationship which is the decisive criterion for the determination of likeness.[343]

Consumers' Tastes and Habits

Under this criterion, the tastes and habits of the consumers in the relevant market, being the EU market in the present case, are assessed.

Food Sector A study commissioned by EFSA and the EU Commission found that EU consumers mention food safety concerns with regard to genetically modified ingredients.[344] However, there are substantially fewer concerns with regard to genome editing techniques since these techniques are less of an issue in the context of food safety.[345] Also, there might be a decline in the number of consumers that mention food safety concerns with regard to genetically modified ingredients since 2010.[346] Another survey conducted in Germany in 2017 found that most respondents are against the use of genetically modified organisms in food production.[347] However, only one-third is taking into account that products are GM-free when grocery shopping. Most of the respondents take that fact only sometimes into account.[348] Another German study conducted in 2014 found that half of the respondents would under no circumstances buy GM food.[349]

---

[342] *Cf.* Burchardi (2007), p. 344.

[343] See above for the requirement of *likeness* under the GATT, p 215.

[344] See European Food Safety Authority and European Commission (2019), pp. 39–43; see also Ipsos (2018) where more than half of the respondents from EU countries considered in the study stated that they would never eat a genetically modified food.

[345] European Food Safety Authority and European Commission (2019), pp. 39–43, 30; but see also a study analysing the Austrian market which showed that while new genomic techniques were unknown to most of the respondents, most of them stated that they would rather not buy food produced by new genomic techniques, see Marketagent (2019), p. 17, 19.

[346] European Food Safety Authority and European Commission (2019), p. 39; this has been differently analysed in a study commissioned by the *Gesellschaft für Konsumforschung*, see Gesellschaft für Konsumforschung (2014), p. 8.

[347] Statista (2017a).

[348] Statista (2017b).

[349] Gesellschaft für Konsumforschung (2014), p. 7.

In sum, it seems as if EU consumers still make a difference between GM and non-GM food, but this could change especially with regard to food produced by genome editing techniques.[350]

Feed Sector The analysis of consumer perceptions is different with regard to feed products as can be seen from the example of soybean plants. The EU imports 80 to 95% of soybean products,[351] which are used mainly for feed.[352] On average 90% of EU soybean and soybean products are imported from the US, Canada, Argentina and Brazil.[353] The soybeans grown in these countries are to 90 to 100% genetically modified.[354] Therefore, most soybean feed products used in conventional agriculture in the EU are genetically modified. Accordingly, conventional farmers as consumers of soybean feed products do not distinguish between GM soybean and non-GM soybean products. Only farmers in the organic sector and farmers that want their products to be labelled as GM-free ask for non-GM feed products.[355] However, this makes up a minor part of the demand for soybean products in the EU.

This analysis shows that consumer tastes and habits vary with regard to the different end uses of a product. With regard to the analysed example of soybean plants used as feed in conventional agriculture, consumer perceptions and habits do not differentiate between GM and non-GM plants.

Influence of EU GMO Regulations on Consumer Perceptions? Another question that can be raised in this regard is whether the EU by imposing strict regulations is influencing consumer habits and tastes to the detriment of GM products.[356] However, this is denied by *Burchardi* who states that the legislative history of the EU GMO framework shows that GM products have already been rejected before. Also, he points to the fact that the marketing of GM products failed already before

[350] A similar conclusion is reached by Böckenförde (2004), pp. 400–401.

[351] European Commission (2018b), p. 5; *cf.* Brüggemann (2020); EST GmbH, https://www.soja-toaster.com/hintergrundinfos/sojaanbau-globale-mengenverteilung-und-mengenstroeme/.

[352] European Commission (2018b), p. 5; see also transparenz Gentechnik, https://www.transgen.de/lebensmittel/1049.futtermittelimporte-europa-sojabohnen-gentechnik.html; Kuepper and Stravens (2022), pp. 15–17 which estimate that "the production of animal products accounted for around 90% of the total EU27+UK use of soy products"; *cf.* also Bundesinformationszentrum Landwirtschaft, https://www.landwirtschaft.de/diskussion-und-dialog/tierhaltung/gentechnik-in-futtermitteln; Centre for the Promotion of Imports from developing countries, https://www.cbi.eu/market-information/grains-pulses-oilseeds/trade-statistics; European Commission (2019a); Bund für Umwelt und Naturschutz e.V. and Friends of the Earth Germany (2019), pp. 7–9.

[353] See European Commission, table 'Trade by main MS & Partners'; Kuepper and Stravens (2022), para 2.2 and table 5; see also Foreign Agricultural Service (2021), p. 20.

[354] *Cf.* International Service for the Acquisition of Agri-biotech Applications (2019); International Service for the Acquisition of Agri-biotech Applications.

[355] Under EU law, the use of GMOs is not allowed in organic farming, see Articles 5(f)(iii) and 11 of the *Regulation (EU) 2018/848 of the European Parliament and of the Council of 30 May 2018 on organic production and labelling of organic products* ('Regulation 2018/848'), OJ EU 2018, L 150/1; for an overview of GM-free labels in the EU, see Smith et al. (2015).

[356] *Cf.* Wong (2005), p. 13; Hestermeyer (2011), para 70.

the current GMO law was enacted. Furthermore, a comparison to the markets of other countries does not lead to another conclusion either since the population's rejection of GM food products is also growing in other countries.[357]

Conclusion The analysis of consumers' tastes and habits shows that consumers still differentiate between plants or products that have been modified by using genetic modification techniques and plants or plant products that have been produced by conventional breeding methods. However, such a differentiation is not made in the feed sector for conventional agriculture where GM feed is used as an equivalent to non-GM feed products. Accordingly, the analysed example of soybean plants used in conventional agriculture can be considered as like with regard to consumer perceptions.

Tariff Classification

The tariff classification in the EU[358] is based on the integrated tariff of the European Union ('TARIC') which is legally based on *Council Regulation (EEC) No 2658/87 of 23 July 1987 on the tariff and statistical nomenclature and on the Common Customs Tariff.*[359] This integrated tariff does not differentiate between conventional plants and genetically modified plants as can be seen from the example of maize or soybeans.[360] Accordingly, conventional and genetically modified plants can be considered as like according to their tariff classification.[361]

Processes and Production Methods

Also, there is a discussion on whether processes and production methods ('PPMs') can influence the likeness of products.[362] The term PPMs refers to the manufacturing or production processes of products.[363] These methods are divided into product-related and non-product-related PPMs. "Product-related PPMs are based on the

---

[357] See Burchardi (2007), p. 345.

[358] For an overview of the tariff classification system in the EU, see European Commission, https://taxation-customs.ec.europa.eu/business/calculation-customs-duties/customs-tariff/classification-goods_en, last.

[359] *Council Regulation (EEC) No 2658/87 of 23 July 1987 on the tariff and statistical nomenclature and on the Common Customs Tariff* (consolidated version from 22 June 2022), OJ EC 1987, 1.

[360] See TARIC Consultation, Section II Vegetable Products, Chapter 10 for maize or Chapter 12 for soybeans, European Commission, https://ec.europa.eu/taxation_customs/dds2/taric/taric_consultation.jsp?Lang=en&Expand=true&SimDate=20220411; see also Morgan and Goh (2004), p. 316.

[361] *Cf.* Strack (2014), p. 832.

[362] See van den Bossche and Zdouc (2022), pp. 426–427; for an overview of the PPM debate under GATT see Conrad (2011), pp. 20–31.

[363] Koebele (2007), para 30; for ambiguities regarding the term PPMs, see Conrad (2011), pp. 27–28.

physical characteristics of the end product",[364] non-product-related PPMs exclusively concern the production process and are not reflected in the end product's characteristics.[365]

In *US-Tuna*, the GATT Panel found that non-product-related PPMs do not influence the determination of likeness.[366] However, it is noted that this view could have changed for example due to consumers that distinguish between different production methods although these different methods are not reflected in the end product.[367] In light of the importance of a competitive relationship between products for establishing their likeness, it is persuasive to also take into account non-product-related PPMs that have an impact on the competitive relationship.

Therefore, the differences in consumer perception are determinative for the likeness of GM and non-GM plants rather than the PPM differences.[368]

Relevance of Regulatory Intention

While Article 2.1 TBT Agreement allows for legitimate regulatory distinctions between like products,[369] the regulatory intention does not have an impact on the determination of likeness under GATT anymore.[370] Therefore, it is irrelevant that the EU does not aim at protecting domestic production when differentiating the regulation of GM and non-GM plants.

Conclusion of the Like Products Analysis

Concluding the foregoing analysis, there is the possibility that two products, one containing a genetic modification and one not containing a genetic modification, are considered *like products* in the sense of Article III:4 GATT. This can be the case where the genetic modification is induced by a technique that is similar to conventional breeding methods, the end-uses are the same and where consumers do not differentiate between the GM and the non-GM product.

While the likeness of products can only be determined with regard to concrete products and on a case-by-case basis, it seems rather unlikely that GM plants used as food are considered like due to the different consumer perceptions of GM and non-GM food. However, a different analysis has been made in the context of GM soybean plants used as feed in conventional agriculture. Here, imported soybean

---

[364] Koebele (2007), para 30.

[365] Koebele (2007), para 30; see also Conrad (2011), pp. 28–29.

[366] *Cf.* van den Bossche and Zdouc (2022), pp. 426–427 with reference to GATT Panel, *United States - Restrictions on Imports of Tuna* (3 September 1991), DS21/R - 39S/155.

[367] See van den Bossche and Zdouc (2022), p. 427.

[368] *Cf.* also Conrad (2011), pp. 204–206; for the different consumer perceptions see above 218–220.

[369] See WTO Appellate Body, *United States - Measures Affecting the Production and Sale of Clove Cigarettes* (4 April 2012), WT/DS406/AB/R, para 182.

[370] See van den Bossche and Zdouc (2022), p. 426.

plants modified by targeted mutagenesis techniques could be qualified as like their domestic non-GM counterpart.

6.2.3.2.1.3 Conclusion

Whether the EU GMO authorisation procedures violate Article III:4 GATT cannot be determined in general term. An actual violation depends heavily on the circumstances of the individual case. Two criteria are likely to be decisive: first, whether a de facto differentiation between imported and domestic products can be assumed. This is only likely to be the case if imports consist of almost 100% GM products and domestic products consist of almost 100 % non-GM products. The second criterion being, how consumers behave with regard to the specific GM product in comparison to the non-GM product.

In the specific case of GM soybean plants used as feed in conventional agriculture which has been taken as an example, the general authorisation requirement for GM plants modified by targeted mutagenesis can constitute a violation of Article III:4 GATT.

6.2.3.2.2 Article XI:1

While the authorisation procedures as internal regulations are primarily governed by Article III GATT, it is questionable whether Article XI:1 GATT could also apply to the authorisation procedures. "Other measures are virtually any requirement or regulation designed to restrict or resulting in the restriction of imports or exports whether intended or not."[371] While the intention of a measure is irrelevant, the effect is relevant. Article XI:1 GATT also covers prohibitions or restrictions of a de facto nature.[372] Accordingly, the authorisation procedures, in general, could be qualified as "other measures" in the sense of Article XI:1 GATT.

However, the question is whether Article XI:1 GATT only applies to border measures and whether its applicability to internal measures is barred by Article III. On the one hand, it is argued that Article III is a special application of the more general obligation laid down in Article XI GATT.[373] On the other hand, the Note *Ad* Article III is seen as a clarification that the application of internal restrictions to imported products even though enforced at the time or point of importation is solely governed by Article III and not by Article XI.[374] Where a measure falls within Article III, it no

---

[371] Wolfrum (2011a), para 14.

[372] Wolfrum (2011a), para 11; in contrast, *Herdegen* states that „Article XI:1 of the GATT establishes a general prohibition on quantitative and other restrictions to trade which are *directly linked* to the import or export of goods", see Herdegen (2016), p. 233 (emphasis added).

[373] *Cf.* Zedalis (2004), p. 655.

[374] Herdegen (2016), pp. 233–234; see also van den Bossche and Zdouc (2022), pp. 382–383 with reference to GATT Panel, *Canada - Administration of the Foreign Investment Review Act (FIRA)* (7 February 1984), L/5504 - 30S/140, para 5.14.

longer falls within the scope of Article XI:1.[375] This is only different with regard to non-product related PPMs which exclusively fall within Article XI GATT.[376]

In view of the explicit wording of the Note *Ad* Article III, the latter view seems favourable. Accordingly, the authorisation procedures which at best qualify as product-related PPMs fall within Article III:4 GATT and are not governed by Article XI:1 GATT.

6.2.3.2.3 Article XX

Article XX GATT provides for exceptions that Member States can invoke to protect certain policy areas as laid down in Article XX lit. a to j.[377] The application of Article XX follows a two-tiered approach: first, a measure must fall within one of the categories laid down in lit. a to j. And second, the measure must comply with the requirements laid down in the *Chapeau* of Article XX.[378] The standard set by the *Chapeau* can vary in relation to the type of justification a Member State bases its measure on.[379]

The exceptions that are relevant for the EU authorisation procedures are those laid down in Article XX lit. b, lit. g and lit. a.

6.2.3.2.3.1 Article XX lit. b: The Protection of Human, Animal or Plant Life or Health

Article XX lit. b allows for Member States' measures that are necessary to protect human, animal or plant life or health. Since the SPS Agreement is based on this exception, the authorisation measures falling within this exception are already covered by the SPS Agreement and therefore are not comprised by GATT. Accordingly, the exception provided for in Article XX lit. b is not relevant here.

6.2.3.2.3.2 Article XX lit. g: The Conservation of Exhaustible Natural Resources

Under Article XX lit. g, Member States may take measures relating to the conservation of exhaustible resources if such measures are made effective in conjunction with restrictions on domestic production or consumption.

---

[375] Wolfrum (2011a), p. 25.

[376] Herdegen (2016), p. 221 with reference to GATT Panel, *United States - Restrictions on Imports of Tuna* (3 September 1991), DS21/R - 39S/155, paras 5.11–5.14.

[377] Wolfrum (2011b), para 1.

[378] Wolfrum (2011b), p. 8 with reference to WTO jurisprudence; van den Bossche and Zdouc (2022), p. 602.

[379] Wolfrum (2011b), para 9.

Requirements lit. g

As has been clarified by the jurisprudence of the DSB, the exception laid down in Article XX lit. g GATT applies to non-living as well as living exhaustible resources that are capable of reproduction.[380] Thus, it may in principle also comprise the protection of biological diversity and the protection of animals and plants.[381] However, these resources are only comprised when they are threatened with extinction.[382]

Also, the measure sought to be justified by invoking Article XX lit. g must be *reasonably related* to the conservation of an exhaustible natural resource.[383] This means that the measure must not be disproportionately wide in its scope and reach in relation to the policy objective sought, i.e. the protection and conservation of an exhaustible resource.[384]

According to this requirement, it would be difficult to justify the general authorisation requirement for GM plants in the EU. While this general authorisation aims at protecting biological diversity, this protection goal is very general in scope and reach and not limited to a specific endangered animal or plant. Thus, it is not reasonably related to the conservation of a specific endangered species.

This could be different for a concrete decision refusing the approval of the deliberate release or placing on the market of a GM plant due to its potential to threaten the existence of an endangered plant or animal species. In such a case, the refusal would be related to the conservation of a specific species that is otherwise threatened. However, whether the requirements for the invocation of Article XX lit. g would be fulfilled can only be determined for each specific case.

Conclusion

Concluding, the EU's general requirement for approval for imported soybean plants modified by targeted mutagenesis and used as feed in conventional agriculture does not fall within the exception laid down in Article XX lit. g GATT.

380 *Cf.* Wolfrum (2011c), paras 4, 16–21; see also van den Bossche and Zdouc (2022), pp. 625–626 with reference to WTO Appellate Body, *United States - Import Prohibition of Certain Shrimp and Shrimp Products* (12 October 1998), WT/DS58/AB/R, paras 128–131; this understanding has also been clarified by the European Union and Canada in the *Comprehensive Economic Trade Agreement* (CETA), see Article 28.3.1 CETA and above Chap. 5, p. 146.

381 *Cf.* Kluttig (2003), pp. 18–19.

382 *Cf.* Kluttig (2003), p. 19.

383 *Cf.* WTO Appellate Body, *United States - Import Prohibition of Certain Shrimp and Shrimp Products* (12 October 1998), WT/DS58/AB/R, para 141.

384 van den Bossche and Zdouc (2022), p. 626; WTO Appellate Body, *United States - Import Prohibition of Certain Shrimp and Shrimp Products* (12 October 1998), WT/DS58/AB/R, para 141.

6.2.3.2.3.3 Article XX lit. a: The Protection of Public Morals

While the alternative laid down in Article XX lit. a GATT does not seem relevant at first sight, it has been proposed as an adequate way to justify GMO regulation by *Davies*.[385] He argues that the taking of unnecessary risks coming along with the presence of GMOs in the public sphere is contrary to public morals in the EU.[386] While such an argumentation could have worked in the past, it does no longer work for plants obtained by targeted mutagenesis techniques in the EU since the European Commission does not consider these plants to be riskier than plants obtained by conventional breeding.[387] Accordingly, it will not base a general authorisation requirement for plants obtained by targeted mutagenesis on public perception of unnecessary risk coming along with plants obtained by targeted mutagenesis techniques.

6.2.3.2.4 Conclusion on the GATT's Analysis

Summarising the analysis of the EU authorisation procedure for GM plants under GATT, there are certain circumstances under which a violation of Article III:4 GATT is possible. Namely, the general authorisation requirement for imported soybean plants genetically modified by targeted mutagenesis and used as feed in conventional agriculture can be in violation of Article III:4 GATT. Also, in this case, a justification by invoking Article XX GATT is not possible.

6.2.4 *Conclusion: EU Authorisation Procedures Violate WTO Law*

The analysis of whether the EU authorisation procedures and its applicability to targeted mutagenesis techniques are compatible with the obligations under WTO law has shown that there are certain situations and scenarios in which the EU framework would not be compatible with the obligations under the SPS Agreement and GATT.[388]

---

[385] See Davies (2007).

[386] Davies (2007), pp. 257–258.

[387] See above, Chap. 2, p. 16.

[388] For the specific provisions violated see above the conclusions on the SPS Agreement's analysis, p 210 and the conclusions on the GATT's analysis, p 225.

6.3 EU Labelling Requirements and WTO Law

The compatibility of the EU's labelling requirements for GMOs has already been assessed, but especially with regard to GMO legislation that has become obsolete.[389] Also, no analysis was concerned with the new genome editing techniques. Accordingly, the present analysis focuses on the particularities of the applicable EU GMO framework, especially the GM Food and Feed Regulation as well as on the particularities of genome editing techniques, especially of targeted mutagenesis techniques.

Due to the primacy of the SPS Agreement in relation to the TBT Agreement and the GATT, the compatibility of the EU labelling provisions with the SPS Agreement is assessed first (1.), followed by an analysis of the compatibility with the TBT Agreement (2.) and the GATT (3.).

6.3.1 SPS Agreement

6.3.1.1 Applicability

The SPS Agreement is applicable to the EU labelling provisions to the extent that the purposes of the EU labelling requirements fall within one of the four alternatives of Annex A(1) of the SPS Agreement. Furthermore, the labelling requirements must be directly related to food safety to fall within the SPS Agreement's scope.[390] While reference is made to the non-exhaustive nature of the list in Annex A(1), second sentence, the explicit limitation laid down with regard to labelling requirements speaks against the SPS Agreement's applicability to other labelling requirements.[391]

---

[389] See Burchardi who provides an in-depth analysis of the compatibility of EU labelling requirements for genetically modified food laid down in Regulation 258/97, Directive 2001/18/EC and *Council Regulation (EC) No 1139/98 of 26 May 1998 concerning the compulsory indication of the labelling of certain foodstuffs produced from genetically modified organisms of particulars other than those provided for in Directive 79/112/EEC* (latest consolidated version from 10 April 2000), OJ EC 1998, L 159/4 (no longer in force); *Commission Regulation (EC) No 49/2000 of 10 January 2000 amending Council Regulation (EC) No 1139/98 concerning the compulsory indication on the labelling of certain foodstuffs produced from genetically modified organisms of particulars other than those provided for in Directive 79/112/EEC*, OJ EC 2000, L 6/13 (no longer in force); *Commission Regulation (EC) No 50/2000 of 10 January 2000 on the labelling of foodstuffs and food ingredients containing additives and flavourings that have been genetically modified or have been produced from genetically modified organisms* (latest consolidated version from 10 April 2000), OJ EC 2000, L 6/15 (no longer in force); see also Sheldon and Josling (2002); Morgan and Goh (2004); Appleton (2000).

[390] *Cf.* Burchardi (2007), pp. 246–247.

[391] *Cf.* Burchardi (2007), p. 247 referring to Zedalis (2001), p. 344; Charnovitz (2000), p. 296.

Therefore, labelling requirements that are not directly related to food safety do not fall within the SPS Agreement's scope.[392]

The only labelling requirement that is directly related to food safety is laid down in Article 13(2)(a)(iv) Regulation 1829/2003. Another labelling requirement that could also be linked to food safety is the one laid down in Article 13(2)(a)(i) Regulation 1829/2003.[393]

All other labelling requirements serve the purpose of consumer information and therefore do not fall within the SPS Agreement's scope.[394]

6.3.1.2 Compatibility with Articles 2.2 and 5.1 of the SPS Agreement: Labelling Requirements Based on Scientific Evidence and Risk Assessment?

The labelling of genetically modified products because of their implications for the health of certain sections of the population is specified in the authorisation.[395] This indicates that such specific labelling is only required where health implications have been identified during the risk assessment as part of the authorisation procedure. Accordingly, labelling requirements related to food safety, falling within the SPS Agreement's scope, are based on a risk assessment in the sense of Article 5.1 SPS and on scientific evidence as required by Article 2.2 SPS.[396]

For labelling requirements serving the purpose of consumer information, it is questionable whether they comply with Articles 2.2 and 5.1 SPS.[397] However, these labelling requirements fall outside of the SPS Agreement's scope but within the TBT Agreement's scope.[398]

6.3.2 TBT Agreement

6.3.2.1 Applicability

The TBT Agreement comprises all products including industrial and agricultural products[399] and lays down rules for technical barriers to trade such as technical regulations, standards and conformity assessment procedures as defined in Annex 1.

---

[392] See also Burchardi (2007), p. 247.

[393] See above Chap. 4, p. 72.

[394] See above Chap. 4, p. 72.

[395] See Article 13(2) of Regulation 1829/2003.

[396] For a more detailed analysis, see Burchardi (2007), pp. 262–263.

[397] *Cf.* Burchardi (2007), pp. 263–269.

[398] See below for the analysis of the EU labelling requirements and the TBT Agreement.

[399] See Article 1.4 TBT Agreement.

6.3.2.1.1 EU Labelling Requirements as Technical Regulations

A technical regulation is a "document which lays down product characteristics or their related processes and production methods [...] with which compliance is mandatory".[400] To qualify as a technical regulation, a document must fulfil three criteria. "*First*, the document must apply to an identifiable product or group of products. The *identifiable* product or groups of products need not, however, be expressly *identified* in the document. *Second*, the document must lay down one or more characteristics of the products. These product characteristics may be intrinsic, or they may be related to the product. They may be prescribed or imposed in either a positive or a negative form. *Third*, compliance with the product characteristics must be mandatory."[401]

Articles 13(2)(f) and 21 in conjunction with Annex IV.A.8 and Annex IV.B.9 of Directive 2001/18/EC lay down mandatory labelling requirements for the placing on the market of GM plants. The same requirements apply to GM plants intended for deliberate release.[402] The presence of GMOs must be indicated by the statement "This product contains genetically modified organisms". Accordingly, the mandatory labelling requirements apply to an identifiable group of products and lay down product characteristics. The same applies to the labelling requirements laid down in Articles 13 and 25 Regulation 1829/2003 and laid down in Article 4(6) of *Regulation (EC) No 1830/2003 of the European Parliament and of the Council of 22 September 2003 concerning the traceability and labelling of genetically modified organisms and the traceability of food and feed products produced from genetically modified organisms*[403] ('Regulation 1830/2003').

As such, the labelling requirements qualify as technical regulation in the sense of Annex 1.1 to the TBT Agreement.[404] However, this is only to the extent that labelling requirements do not fall within the SPS Agreement's scope. This is the case for the labelling requirements directly related to food safety as laid down in Article 13(2)(a)(iv) and Article 13(2)(a)(i).

Accordingly, labelling requirements that serve consumer interests and information fall within the TBT Agreement's scope.[405]

[400] See Annex 1.1 to the TBT Agreement.

[401] WTO Appellate Body, *European Communities - Trade Description of Sardines* (26 September 2002), WT/DS231/AB/R, para 176.

[402] See Articles 26(1) and 2(4) of Directive 2001/18/EC.

[403] See footnote 4.

[404] *Cf.* also Burchardi (2007), pp. 327–328.

[405] Burchardi (2007), pp. 322–328.

6.3.2.1.2 Processes and Production Methods Covered by the TBT Agreement?

While the term of technical regulation in Annex 1.1 to the TBT Agreement covers products or their related processes and production methods ('PPMs'), it is disputed in literature which types of methods are comprised by processes and production methods.[406] The term "refers to the ways in which and techniques by which a product is manufactured or produced".[407] These methods are divided into product-related and non-product-related PPMs. "Product-related PPMs are based on the physical characteristics of the end product",[408] non-product-related PPMs exclusively concern the production process and are not reflected in the end product's characteristics.[409]

While it is widely acknowledged that product-related processes and production methods are covered by the TBT Agreement,[410] the coverage of non-product-related PPMs is disputed.[411] The negotiation history of the TBT Agreement seems to support the exclusion of non-product-related PPMs from the Agreement's scope.[412]

Since the applicability of Directive 2001/18/EC and Regulation 1829/2003 and its provisions on safety and labelling requirements is dependent on the process of genetic modification,[413] these provisions constitute PPMs. However, these PPMs can be qualified as product-related when the genetic modification is reflected in the end product as is the case for conventional GMOs.[414] Questionable is whether the provisions also qualify as product-related PPMs to the extent that they regulate GM plants modified by targeted mutagenesis. While the modification induced by targeted mutagenesis techniques seems to be detectable in the end product, it is difficult to identify whether such modification has been induced by targeted mutagenesis, conventional mutagenesis or natural mutation.[415] But, since the modification as such is detectable and physically impacts the end product, it seems more plausible to qualify requirements linked to the modification by targeted mutagenesis techniques as product-related PPMs. This is also in light of typical non-product-related PPMs such as environmental-friendly fishing techniques or social standards that have to be

[406] *Cf.* Charnovitz (2002), pp. 65–66.

[407] Koebele (2007), para 30.

[408] Koebele (2007), para 30.

[409] Koebele (2007), para 30; for an overview of the PPM debate under GATT see Conrad (2011), pp. 20–31.

[410] Koebele (2007), para 31; Burchardi (2007), pp. 323–326 with further references; *cf.* Marceau and Trachtmann (2002), p. 861.

[411] Koebele (2007), para 31; Appleton (2003), 2.2.2; Dederer (2010), p. 230.

[412] *Cf.* Koebele (2007), para 33; Burchardi (2007), pp. 323–326; see also Maggio (2017), p. 176.

[413] See Article 2(2) Directive 2001/18/EC.

[414] See also Burchardi (2007), p. 328.

[415] *Cf.* European Network of GMO Laboratories (2019), 1, 9.

fulfilled during the production process[416] but do not have any physical impact on the end product.

Furthermore, it is even suggested to apply the TBT Agreement to provisions regulating GMOs where the genetic modification is no longer detectable in the end product and which qualify as non-product-related.[417]

6.3.2.1.3 Conclusion

The labelling requirements laid down in Directive 2001/18/EC and Regulations 1829/2003 and 1830/2003 to the extent that they serve consumer interests and information fall within the TBT Agreement's scope. This is also the case for the application of labelling requirements to plants modified by targeted mutagenesis since these labelling requirements can be qualified as product-related PPMs.

6.3.2.2 Compatibility

6.3.2.2.1 Article 2.1 TBT

Article 2.1 TBT lays down the most-favoured nation treatment and the national treatment obligations with regard to technical regulations.[418] For a violation of Article 2.1 TBT, three requirements have to be fulfilled: first, the measure at issue qualifies as a technical regulation in the sense of Annex 1.1. Second, imported and domestic product are considered like. And third, the treatment accorded to the imported product is less favourable than that accorded to the like domestic product.[419]

The first requirement is fulfilled since the labelling requirements for GM plants for the purpose of consumer information under the Deliberate Release Directive, the GM Food and Feed Regulation and Regulation 1830/2003 qualify as technical regulations in the sense of Annex 1.1.[420]

---

[416] *Cf.* Charnovitz (2002), p. 65; van den Bossche and Zdouc (2022), p. 427.

[417] *Cf.* Dederer (2010), pp. 230–231.

[418] World Trade Organization, para 1; see also WTO Appellate Body, *United States - Certain Country of Origin Labelling (COOL) Requirements* (29 June 2012), WT/DS384/AB/R, WT/DS386/AB/R, para 267.

[419] See WTO Appellate Body, *United States - Measures concerning the Imporatation, Marketing and Sale of Tuna and Tuna Products* (16 May 2012), WT/DS381/AB/R, para 202 with reference to WTO Appellate Body, *United States - Measures Affecting the Production and Sale of Clove Cigarettes* (4 April 2012), WT/DS406/AB/R, para 87; these criteria had already been spelled out by the WTO Panel in *EC – Trademarks*, see WTO Panel, *European Communities - Protection of Trademarks and Geographical Indications for Agricultural Products and Foodstuffs, Complaint by Australia* (15 March 2005), WT/DS290/R, para 7.444.

[420] See above for the EU labelling requirements qualifying as technical regulations, p 227.

For the second requirement, it needs to be determined whether plants obtained by genetic modification and their conventional counterparts are considered like products.

Third, it needs to be analysed whether less favourable treatment is accorded to the imported GM plants in comparison to their conventional counterpart, in case both are considered like products.

6.3.2.2.1.1 GM Plants and Their Conventional Counterparts as "Like Products" Under Article 2.1 TBT

The question of whether GM plants and their conventional counterpart can be considered *like products* has already been analysed for authorisation requirements under Article III:4 GATT.[421] While the analysis of like products under Article 2.1 TBT is informed by Article III:4 GATT and jurisprudence on this provision, the immediate context of the TBT Agreement should also be taken into account, as stated by the Panel in *US – Clove Cigarettes*.[422] This context of like products under the TBT Agreement has already been addressed by scholarship in the context of biotechnology.[423] However, this was before the first reports by the DSB considering this question explicitly under the TBT Agreement were issued.[424]

"Like Products" Under the TBT Agreement as Analysed by the DSB

In *US – Clove Cigarettes*, the Panel took account of the TBT Agreement as immediate context.[425] Therefore, it considered the public health objective pursued by the relevant technical regulation as more decisive for the determination of likeness than the competitive relationship between the products.[426] While the Appellate Body confirmed the approach that an interpretation of Article 2.1 TBT "should start with the text of that provision in light of the context provided by Article 2.1 itself, by other provisions of the *TBT Agreement*, and by the *TBT Agreement* as a whole",[427] it rejected the Panel's statement that a determination of "likeness" under the TBT Agreement should rather focus on the technical regulation's objectives than taking

---

[421] See above for the analysis of likeness under Article III:4 GATT, p 214.

[422] WTO Panel, *United States - Measures Affecting the Production and Sale of Clove Cigarettes* (2 September 2011), WT/DS406/R, para 7.117.

[423] See Burchardi (2007), pp. 331–347; Morgan and Goh (2004), pp. 315–318; see also Wong (2005) who analyses this question under Article III:4 GATT.

[424] See Burchardi (2007), p. 332 and WTO Panel, *United States - Measures Affecting the Production and Sale of Clove Cigarettes* (2 September 2011), WT/DS406/R, paras 7.80–7.81.

[425] WTO Panel, *United States - Measures Affecting the Production and Sale of Clove Cigarettes* (2 September 2011), WT/DS406/R, para 7.117.

[426] WTO Panel, *United States - Measures Affecting the Production and Sale of Clove Cigarettes* (2 September 2011), WT/DS406/R, para 7.119.

[427] WTO Appellate Body, *United States - Measures Affecting the Production and Sale of Clove Cigarettes* (4 April 2012), WT/DS406/AB/R, para 108.

into account the competitive relationship of two products.[428] Instead, it emphasised that the term "no less favourable treatment" "informs the determination of likeness, suggesting that likeness is about the 'nature and extent of a competitive relationship between and among products'".[429] Also, it did not object to the Panel's findings that the interpretation of Article 2.1 TBT is informed by the jurisprudence to Article III:4 GATT.[430]

In *US – Tuna II*, the Panel's approach, although issued before, was more in line with the Appellate Body's findings in *US – Clove Cigarettes*. It acknowledged the importance that has to be given to the particular context of the TBT Agreement and stated that the interpretation of Article 2.1 TBT can be informed by the jurisprudence of Article III:4 GATT.[431] Also, it emphasised that the determination of "likeness" under the TBT Agreement is informed by the competitive relationship of two products as can be derived from the Agreement's context.[432] Furthermore, it relied on the criteria developed in the jurisprudence of Article III:4 GATT in order to determine the likeness of the two products at stake.[433] These findings were not appealed by the parties and therefore not considered by the Appellate Body in this specific case. However, the Appellate Body Report in *US – Clove Cigarettes* which was issued after the Panel Report in *US – Tuna II* confirmed the Panel's findings.

The Panel in *US – COOL* only shortly addressed the question of how to determine "likeness" but came to the conclusion that Article III:4 GATT "provides relevant context for interpreting Article 2.1 of the TBT Agreement".[434] It did not mention any particularities that arise out of the TBT Agreement in comparison to the GATT. Also, the findings were not appealed.

The Panel in *EC – Seal Products* determined "likeness" by having recourse to the criteria established by the *Report of the Working Party on Border Tax Adjustments*[435] from 1970 and the Appellate Body's Report in *Japan – Alcoholic Beverages II*.[436],[437]

---

[428] WTO Appellate Body, *United States - Measures Affecting the Production and Sale of Clove Cigarettes* (4 April 2012), WT/DS406/AB/R, paras 108–112.

[429] WTO Appellate Body, *United States - Measures Affecting the Production and Sale of Clove Cigarettes* (4 April 2012), WT/DS406/AB/R, para 111.

[430] *Cf.* also World Trade Organization, para 5.

[431] WTO Panel, *United States - Measures concerning the Importation, Marketing and Sale of Tuna and Tuna Products* (15 September 2011), WT/D381/R, paras 7.222–7.223.

[432] WTO Panel, *United States - Measures concerning the Importation, Marketing and Sale of Tuna and Tuna Products* (15 September 2011), WT/D381/R, paras 7.224–7.225.

[433] WTO Panel, *United States - Measures concerning the Importation, Marketing and Sale of Tuna and Tuna Products* (15 September 2011), WT/D381/R, para 7.240.

[434] WTO Panel, *United States - Certain Country of Origin Labellling (COOL) Requirements* (18 November 2011), WT/DS384/R, WT/DS386/R, para 7.234.

[435] *Report by the Working Party on Border Tax Adjustments* (1970), para 18.

[436] Holzer (2017), p. 186.

[437] WTO Panel, *European Communities - Measures Prohibiting the Importation and Marketing of Seal Products* (25 November 2013), WT/DS400/R, WT/DS401/R, para 7.136; the reference by the Panel to the four criteria can serve as an indication, although the Panel's findings under Article 2.1 TBT were declared moot by the Appellate Body due to its finding that the EC seal regime did not

The Appellate Body in *EC – Asbestos* also emphasised that it is important to take account of the competitive relationship between products in the marketplace when determining their "likeness".[438] But, especially by scholarship, it is suggested that also policy objectives as acknowledged by the TBT Agreement should be taken into account.[439]

GM Plants as Like Products Under Article 2.1 TBT

As has already been analysed for authorisation procedures under Article III:4 GATT, GM plants and their conventional counterparts are not considered "like" in most cases due to different consumer perceptions. However, this can be different for GM soybean plants used as feed in conventional agriculture.[440] Also, it is important to note that the likeness of products in the end can only be determined for each specific case and not on an abstract level.

6.3.2.2.1.2 Less Favourable Treatment of Imported GM Plants in Comparison to Their Domestic Conventional Counterpart

The simple differentiation of a technical regulation between imported and like domestic products does not suffice to fulfil the requirement of "less favourable treatment" as laid down in Article 2.1 TBT.[441] Rather, "a panel examining a claim of violation under Article 2.1 should seek to ascertain whether the technical regulation at issue modifies the conditions of competition in the market of the regulating Member to the detriment of the group of imported products vis-à-vis the group of like domestic products."[442] Accordingly, Article 2.1 TBT prohibits both *de jure* and *de facto* discrimination against imported products that are like domestic products.[443] However, in the case of *de facto* discrimination, a detrimental impact that exclusively stems from a legitimate regulatory distinction does not lead to inconsistency with Article 2.1 TBT.[444]

qualify as a technical regulation, see WTO Appellate Body, *European Communities - Measures Prohibiting the Importation and Marketing of Seal Products* (22 May 2014), WT/DS400/AB/R, WT/DS401/AB/R, para 5.70.

438 WTO Appellate Body, *European Communities - Measures Affecting Asbestos and Asbestos-Containing Products* (12 March 2001), WT/DS135/AB/R, para 103; see also Appleton (2014), p. 93.

439 *Cf.* Appleton (2014), p. 94.

440 See above for the analysis of *likeness* under Article III:4 GATT and the criterion of consumers' tastes and habits, p 218.

441 van den Bossche and Zdouc (2022), p. 982.

442 WTO Appellate Body, *United States - Measures Affecting the Production and Sale of Clove Cigarettes* (4 April 2012), WT/DS406/AB/R, para 180.

443 WTO Appellate Body, *United States - Measures Affecting the Production and Sale of Clove Cigarettes* (4 April 2012), WT/DS406/AB/R, para 181; *cf.* van den Bossche and Zdouc (2022), p. 982.

444 WTO Appellate Body, *United States - Measures Affecting the Production and Sale of Clove Cigarettes* (4 April 2012), WT/DS406/AB/R, paras 181–182.

But, before analysing the "less favourable treatment" requirement, the question arises whether imported GM plants and their domestic conventional counterparts are sufficiently comparable.

Comparability

The comparability of imported GM plants and their like conventional domestic counterparts could be questioned due to the fact that imported GM plants are treated like domestic GM plants. A similar question was raised in the appeal of the Panel Report in *Clove – Cigarettes*.[445] Here, the Panel had compared clove cigarettes, as the product imported from the territory of any Member, with domestic menthol cigarettes, but not with other domestic flavoured cigarettes.[446] However, the Appellate Body made clear that "for the purposes of the less favourable treatment analysis, treatment accorded to products imported from the complaining Member is to be compared with that accorded to like domestic products and like products of any other origin."[447] While the products suggested for by the complainant are the starting point of a Panel's analysis, a Panel is nevertheless required to assess "the universe of domestic products [on the market of the regulating Member State] that are like the products imported from the complaining Member."[448] In the analysis of "less favourable treatment", the group of imported products identified is to be compared with the group of like domestic products identified.[449] Accordingly, not the comparison between each imported product and the like domestic product is decisive, but the comparison of the whole group of imported products with the whole group of like domestic products.[450]

The Appellate Body has expressly stated that "[t]he "treatment no less favourable" standard of Article 2.1 does not prohibit regulatory distinctions between products found to be like, provided that the group of like products imported from the complaining Member is treated no less favourably than the group of domestic like products."[451]

---

445 See WTO Appellate Body, *United States - Measures Affecting the Production and Sale of Clove Cigarettes* (4 April 2012), WT/DS406/AB/R, 183–189.

446 See WTO Appellate Body, *United States - Measures Affecting the Production and Sale of Clove Cigarettes* (4 April 2012), WT/DS406/AB/R, paras 184–185 referring to WTO Panel, *United States - Measures Affecting the Production and Sale of Clove Cigarettes* (2 September 2011), WT/DS406/R, para 7.277.

447 WTO Appellate Body, *United States - Measures Affecting the Production and Sale of Clove Cigarettes* (4 April 2012), WT/DS406/AB/R, para 190.

448 WTO Appellate Body, *United States - Measures Affecting the Production and Sale of Clove Cigarettes* (4 April 2012), WT/DS406/AB/R, 192, 194.

449 WTO Appellate Body, *United States - Measures Affecting the Production and Sale of Clove Cigarettes* (4 April 2012), WT/DS406/AB/R, 193, 194.

450 WTO Appellate Body, *United States - Measures Affecting the Production and Sale of Clove Cigarettes* (4 April 2012), WT/DS406/AB/R, para 193.

451 WTO Appellate Body, *United States - Measures Affecting the Production and Sale of Clove Cigarettes* (4 April 2012), WT/DS406/AB/R, para 193.

Since it is rather unlikely that GM and non-GM food plants will generally be considered *like products*, the present analysis is based on the example of soybean plants and products used as feed. Here, 90 to 100 % of imported plants and products consists of GM soybean and only a small amount is GM-free. In contrast, all domestic products of soybean are not genetically modified.[452]

Detrimental Impact of Labelling Requirements on Imported Products

Since the majority of imported soybean plants and products used for feed in conventional agriculture are genetically modified and therefore fall within the EU law on GMOs, the group of imported products is treated differently from the group of domestic soybean products used as feed for conventional agriculture which does not comprise GMOs.

The question is whether this different labelling of GM soybean plants is to the detriment of these products since consumers of soybean plants used for feed in conventional agriculture do not differentiate between GM and non-GM soybeans.[453] Also, the end consumer buying meat from animals fed with GM soybeans does not know about it since labelling for this meat is not required.[454]

However, there is still a general aversion against GM products in the EU which could also have a possible impact on the competition between GM and GM-free soybean products used for feed. Furthermore, the general differentiation between GM and GM-free soybeans in the EU requires a separation of both products during the entire production process which negatively impacts the conditions of competition for GM soybean products.

Therefore, imported soybean plants are treated less favourable in comparison to domestic soybean feed products which do not fall under the EU regulations on GMOs.

Since imported GM soybean products are treated in the same way as domestic GM soybean products, we do not have a *de jure* discrimination in the present case. But, due to the fact that the majority of imported products are genetically modified in contrast to the majority of domestic products, there is a *de facto* discrimination, as was also found by the Appellate Body in *Japan – Alcoholic Beverages II* concerning a similar situation.[455]

---

[452] See above for the requirement of less favourable treatment under Article III:4 GATT, p 213.

[453] See above for consumer perceptions in the feed sector, p 219.

[454] This is different for organic meat or meat carrying a gm-free label. In this cases, farmers are not allowed to feed their animals with feed containing GM products, see for organic meat Article 11 of Regulation 2018/848; for an overview of GM-free labels in the EU, see Smith et al. (2015).

[455] WTO Appellate Body, *Japan - Taxes on Alcoholic Beverages* (4 October 1996), WT/DS8/AB/R, WT/DS10/AB/R, WT/DS11/AB/R.

Legitimate Regulatory Distinction

However, the TBT Agreement in cases of *de facto* discrimination allows for the different treatment of a group of imported products in case that the detrimental impact "stems exclusively from a legitimate regulatory distinction rather than reflecting discrimination against the group of imported products."[456] According to the Appellate Body, this can be derived from the TBT Agreement's object and purpose and its context, especially Annex 1.1 to the TBT Agreement and Article 2.2. Also, the TBT Agreement does not contain an exception clause comparable to Article XX GATT. Instead, its Preamble recognizes the Member States' rights to pursue policy objectives such as the protection of human health and the environment or the prevention of deceptive practices, at the levels it considers appropriate.[457] To determine whether the detrimental impact stems from a legitimate regulatory distinction, a panel must "carefully scrutinize the particular circumstances of the case, that is, the design, architecture, revealing structure, operation, and application of the technical regulation at issue, and, in particular, whether that technical regulation is even-handed, in order to determine whether it discriminates against the group of imported products."[458]

Labelling requirements in the EU are only mandatory for GM plants and do not apply to conventionally bred plants. This is the case for imported as well as for domestic products. The different labelling of GM and non-GM plants is reasoned by the objective of consumer information.[459] This objective of consumer information can be considered either as being comprised by the legitimate objective to prevent deceptive practices which is expressly listed in Article 2.2 TBT and the TBT Agreement's preamble.[460] Also, the Appellate Body considered the objective of consumer information on product origin as being related to the prevention of deceptive practices and therefore as a legitimate objective in the sense of Article 2.2 TBT.[461]

---

[456] WTO Appellate Body, *United States - Measures Affecting the Production and Sale of Clove Cigarettes* (4 April 2012), WT/DS406/AB/R, para 182.

[457] See Preamble, para. 6 to the TBT Agreement; *cf.* also van den Bossche and Zdouc (2022), p. 984 with reference to WTO Appellate Body, *United States - Measures Affecting the Production and Sale of Clove Cigarettes* (4 April 2012), WT/DS406/AB/R, paras 169–173.

[458] WTO Appellate Body, *United States - Measures Affecting the Production and Sale of Clove Cigarettes* (4 April 2012), WT/DS406/AB/R, para 182.

[459] See above Chap. 4, p 72.

[460] *Cf.* Burchardi (2007), pp. 352–353 with further references who analyses whether the objective of consumer information is legitimate in the sense of Article 2.2 TBT Agreement.

[461] See WTO Appellate Body, *United States - Certain Country of Origin Labelling (COOL) Requirements* (29 June 2012), WT/DS384/AB/R, WT/DS386/AB/R, para 445; the objective of consumer information has also been indirectly accepted as legitimate by the Appellate Body in *US – Tuna II*, *cf.* Matsushita et al. (2017), p. 452 referring to WTO Appellate Body, *United States - Measures concerning the Imporatation, Marketing and Sale of Tuna and Tuna Products* (16 May 2012), WT/DS381/AB/R, para 337 and WTO Panel, *United States - Measures concerning the Importation, Marketing and Sale of Tuna and Tuna Products* (15 September 2011), WT/D381/R, paras 7.437 et seq.

Accordingly, it seems appropriate to consider the objective of consumer information as legitimate to distinguish in the regulation of like products.

This differentiation must be even-handed. The same treatment of imported and domestic GM plants and imported and domestic GM-free plants speaks for an even-handed regulation. However, this can be different with regard to plants modified by targeted mutagenesis. Plants modified by this technique are not considered riskier than plants conventionally bred which do not require to be labelled. Due to the similarities with conventionally bred plants, one can question the even-handedness of the different labelling for plants modified by targeted mutagenesis. Again, a concrete result can only be found on a case-by-case basis, considering the particularities of the specific case.

6.3.2.2.1.3 Conclusion

There are certain circumstances where the EU labelling requirements could violate Article 2.1 TBT. This could be the case where the majority of imported products is genetically modified while the like domestic products are not genetically modified. Furthermore, the detrimental effect must not be justified by a legitimate regulatory purpose. This could be the case where the genetic modification does not carry any risks and where the GM plant is perfectly comparable to the non-GM plant, as can be the case for plants modified by targeted mutagenesis in comparison to conventionally bred plants.

6.3.2.2.2 Article 2.2 TBT

According to Article 2.2 TBT, technical regulations must not be "prepared, adopted or applied with a view to or with the effect of creating unnecessary obstacles to international trade". When assessing a violation of Article 2.2 TBT, the following requirements should be analysed:

(1) whether the technical regulation at issue is trade-restrictive
(2) whether the technical regulation at issue fulfils a legitimate objective
(3) whether the technical regulation at issue is not more trade-restrictive than necessary to fulfil a legitimate objective, taking account of the risks non-fulfilment would create.[462]

[462] *Cf.* van den Bossche and Zdouc (2022), p. 993.

6.3.2.2.2.1 Consumer Information as Legitimate Objective

Article 2.2 TBT lists certain legitimate objectives, such as *national security requirements, the prevention of deceptive practices, protection of human health or safety, animal or plant life or health*, or *the environment*. This list is not exhaustive.[463] However, the listed objectives serve as an indication of which other objectives may be considered legitimate.[464] Furthermore, the objectives listed in the sixth and seventh recital of the TBT Agreement's preamble as well as objectives laid down in provisions of other covered agreements can inform the determination of what is considered legitimate.[465]

The EU labelling requirements for GM plants aim at informing the consumer about the presence of a genetic modification.[466] This aim of consumer information can be considered either as being comprised by the legitimate objective to prevent deceptive practices or as another legitimate objective not expressly listed in Article 2.2 TBT.[467] Also, the Appellate Body considered the objective of consumer information on product origin as being related to the prevention of deceptive practices and therefore as a legitimate objective in the sense of Article 2.2 TBT.[468]

6.3.2.2.2.2 Labelling Requirements Fulfilling the Legitimate Objective of Consumer Information?

To fulfil a legitimate objective under Article 2.2 TBT, the measure must not completely achieve the objective but must be suitable or objectively capable to contribute to the objective.[469] "No minimum level of success or satisfaction is needed."[470]

---

[463] As can be seen by the addendum "inter alia", see Article 2.2 TBT; see also WTO Appellate Body, *United States - Measures concerning the Imporatation, Marketing and Sale of Tuna and Tuna Products* (16 May 2012), WT/DS381/AB/R, para 313.

[464] See WTO Appellate Body, *United States - Measures concerning the Imporatation, Marketing and Sale of Tuna and Tuna Products* (16 May 2012), WT/DS381/AB/R, para 313.

[465] *Cf.* WTO Appellate Body, *United States - Measures concerning the Imporatation, Marketing and Sale of Tuna and Tuna Products* (16 May 2012), WT/DS381/AB/R, para 313.

[466] See above Chap. 4, p. 72.

[467] Burchardi (2007), pp. 352–353 with further references.

[468] See WTO Appellate Body, *United States - Certain Country of Origin Labelling (COOL) Requirements* (29 June 2012), WT/DS384/AB/R, WT/DS386/AB/R, para 445; the objective of consumer information has also been indirectly accepted as legitimate by the Appellate Body in *US – Tuna II*, *cf.* Matsushita et al. (2017), p. 452 referring to WTO Appellate Body, *United States - Measures concerning the Imporatation, Marketing and Sale of Tuna and Tuna Products* (16 May 2012), WT/DS381/AB/R, para 337 and WTO Panel, *United States - Measures concerning the Importation, Marketing and Sale of Tuna and Tuna Products* (15 September 2011), WT/D381/R, paras 7.437 et seq.

[469] Matsushita et al. (2017), pp. 454–455 with reference to WTO Appellate Body, *United States - Measures concerning the Imporatation, Marketing and Sale of Tuna and Tuna Products* (16 May 2012), WT/DS381/AB/R, para 315.

[470] Matsushita et al. (2017), p. 455 referring to WTO Appellate Body, *United States - Certain Country of Origin Labelling (COOL) Requirements* (29 June 2012), WT/DS384/AB/R, WT/

The labelling of GM products that they are genetically modified, contain genetically modified ingredients or are produced from genetically modified ingredients is suitable to contribute to the objective of consumer information.[471] Accordingly, labelling requirements can be considered as fulfilling a legitimate objective in the sense of Article 2.2 TBT.

6.3.2.2.2.3 *Labelling Requirements Not More Trade-Restrictive Than Necessary?*

The analysis of whether a measure is not more trade-restrictive than necessary includes the following elements according to the Appellate Body in *US – Tuna II*[472]:

(1) degree of contribution made by the measure to the legitimate objective at issue
(2) the trade-restrictiveness of the measure
(3) the nature of the risks at issue and the gravity of consequences that would arise from non-fulfilment of the objective(s) pursued by the Member through the measure

Also, possible alternatives to the challenged measure should be analysed and whether these are reasonably available, less trade restrictive and whether these constitute an equivalent to the challenged measures to achieve the legitimate objective pursued.[473]

Possible alternatives to the system of mandatory labelling requirements are voluntary labelling (in a positive "genetically modified/containing genetically modified ingredients" or negative "GM-free" way) or the information that a product "may contain" genetically modified ingredients.[474] When compared to the positive labelling requirements mandatory in the EU, these alternatives do not equally contribute to the legitimate objective of consumer information pursued by the EU's labelling requirements.[475]

However, the question arises whether the high costs caused by the necessary segregation of GM and non-GM plants could outweigh the consequences that come along with less strict labelling requirements. In this context, it needs to be noticed that segregation systems do currently exist and seem to be economically feasible.[476] Furthermore, the WTO supports the labelling of products as can be seen from

DS386/AB/R, para 468.

[471] See also Burchardi (2007), pp. 353–354.

[472] WTO Appellate Body, *United States - Measures concerning the Imporatation, Marketing and Sale of Tuna and Tuna Products* (16 May 2012), WT/DS381/AB/R, para 322.

[473] *Cf.* WTO Appellate Body, *United States - Measures concerning the Imporatation, Marketing and Sale of Tuna and Tuna Products* (16 May 2012), WT/DS381/AB/R, para 323; see also Matsushita et al. (2017), pp. 455–456 and van den Bossche and Zdouc (2022), pp. 998–999.

[474] See Burchardi (2007), p. 355.

[475] Burchardi (2007), pp. 355–357.

[476] Burchardi (2007), p. 357 with further references.

Article IX GATT.[477] These two aspects argue against the high costs of separation systems outweighing the benefits of consumer information in the trade-offs.[478] However, with regard to plants modified by targeted mutagenesis, there is another aspect that should be considered. Plants modified by these techniques are not considered riskier than plants conventionally bred which do not require labelling. Therefore, it is questionable whether plants modified by targeted mutagenesis still require labelling for consumer information considering the high costs that are caused by labelling requirements. In this situation, the interest of consumer information could also be outweighed by the high costs caused by labelling requirements. Accordingly, the labelling requirements could be considered more trade-restrictive than necessary under Article 2.2 TBT.

6.3.2.2.2.4 Conclusion

In summary, it can be stated that the EU labelling requirements serving the purpose of consumer information fulfil a legitimate objective in the sense of Article 2.2 TBT. However, with regard to plants modified by targeted mutagenesis, it is questionable whether labelling requirements stand up to a cost-benefit analysis. Since these plants are not considered riskier than plants conventionally bred which do not require to be labelled, it is questionable whether the aim of consumer information can still outweigh the high costs that are caused by labelling requirements. Due to these reasons, labelling requirements for plants modified by targeted mutagenesis could also be considered more trade-restrictive than necessary thereby violating Article 2.2 TBT.

6.3.2.2.3 Conclusion on the TBT Agreement's Analysis

The TBT Agreement in particular calls into question the applicability of the EU labelling requirements to plants modified by targeted mutagenesis techniques. These plants are comparable and not considered riskier than conventionally bred plants. Accordingly, labelling requirements for these plants could be considered more trade-restrictive than necessary thereby violating Article 2.2 TBT. A violation of Article 2.1 TBT Agreement is also possible, but it depends heavily on the individual circumstances of the case.

---

[477] *Cf.* Burchardi (2007), p. 357.

[478] *Cf.* also Burchardi (2007), pp. 357–358.

6.3.3 *GATT*

Since the TBT Agreement takes precedence over the GATT in the event of a conflict between provisions of the two agreements,[479] it has to be assessed whether there is such a conflict in the case at hand.

In the present case, an analysis of the labelling requirements' compatibility with Article III:4 GATT would come to the same results as the analysis under Article 2.1 TBT Agreement.[480] However, the possibility to legitimately differentiate in the regulation of like products under Article 2.1 TBT opens up a wider scope for justification than the exceptions laid down in Article XX GATT. Therefore, the TBT Agreement would take precedence over the GATT. Accordingly, the compatibility of the labelling requirements with GATT does not need to be analysed.[481]

6.4 The EU Opt-Out Procedure and WTO Law

6.4.1 *Standard of Review*

According to Article 26b Directive 2001/18/EC, EU Member States have the possibility to restrict the geographical scope of a GMO authorisation for cultivation. Thereby, they may prohibit the cultivation of GM plants for all or part of their territory. However, this is only possible where the applicant agrees with this prohibition or where a Member State brings forward one of the grounds listed in Article 26b(3)(a)-(f) Directive 2001/18/EC.

Since none of these grounds can be considered to fall within one of the purposes laid down in Annex A(1)(a)-(d) of the SPS Agreement, opt-out measures do not constitute SPS measures. Therefore, the SPS Agreement is not applicable.[482]

Also, opt-out measures do not fall within the TBT Agreement's scope since they neither qualify as technical regulations or standards nor as conformity assessment procedures.[483]

Accordingly, opt-out measures adopted in accordance with Article 26b Directive 2001/18/EC can only be scrutinised under GATT.

---

[479] See above Chap. 5, p. 113.

[480] For the comparability of the analysis under both provisions, see above p. 231.

[481] *Cf.* also Burchardi (2007), p. 239 who came to the same conclusion when analysing the EU labelling requirements' compatibility with WTO law.

[482] See also Mögele and Möhler (2022), p. 129; Legal Service of the Council of the European Union (2010), para 37; this is assessed differently by *Monien* who at the same time criticises the broad scope of the SPS Agreement, see Monien (2016), pp. 110–111; *Strack* also briefly assesses the opt-out rule's compatibility with the SPS Agreement's provisions, see Strack (2014), p. 831.

[483] *Cf.* also Legal Service of the Council of the European Union (2010), para 37.

6.4.2 GATT

As has already been stated by the Legal Service of the Council of the EU, the opt-out procedure under Article 26(b) Directive 2001/18/EC, including a cultivation ban for the whole or part of a Member State's territory, would constitute a less favourable treatment in the sense of Article III:4 GATT.[484] However, Article III:4 GATT is only violated when GM and non-GM products are considered *like products*.[485]

Nevertheless, a cultivation ban for GMOs might be justified in accordance with Article XX GATT. The grounds which can be brought forward for a cultivation ban listed in Article 26b(3) could be comprised by the exceptions relating to public morals, human, animal or plant life or health, or the conservation of exhaustible natural resources laid down in Article XX(a), (b) or (g) GATT.[486] Since it is difficult to analyse a justification under Article XX GATT on an abstract level, actual examples could be assessed. But, the opt-out mechanism laid down in Article 26(b) Directive 2001/18/EC has not yet been applied by the EU Member States.[487] Instead, the Member States have only relied on transitional measures as provided for by Article 26(c) Directive 2001/18/EC to restrict the geographical scope of GMO cultivation. Therefore, Article 26(b) and the grounds laid down in its paragraph three do not have any practical relevance so far.

6.5 The EU Regulation of Genome Edited Plants and CETA

6.5.1 CETA Chapter Five on SPS Measures

Chapter 5 comprises the EU authorisation procedures and labelling requirements to the same extent as the SPS Agreement. According to Article 5.3 CETA, it applies to SPS measures that may, directly or indirectly, affect trade between the Parties. SPS measures are defined by reference to the definitions laid down in Annex A of the SPS Agreement.[488] Accordingly, the above-made considerations with regard to the

[484] *Cf.* Legal Service of the Council of the European Union (2010), para 40; Legal Service of the Council of the European Union (2011), para 26.

[485] See above for the like products analysis under Article III:4 GATT, p 214; see also the considerations by the Legal Service of the Council of the European Union, Legal Service of the Council of the European Union (2010), paras 38–39 and Legal Service of the Council of the European Union (2011), paras 20–24.

[486] See also Legal Service of the Council of the European Union (2011), paras 26–31 and Strack (2014), pp. 831–833.

[487] See European Commission, https://food.ec.europa.eu/plants/genetically-modified-organisms/gmo-authorisation/gmo-authorisations-cultivation/restrictions-geographical-scope-gmo-applicationsauthorisations-eu-countries-demands-and-outcomes_en.

[488] See Article 5.1.1 lit.a CETA.

SPS Agreement's applicability equally apply to the application of CETA's Chap. 5 to the EU authorisation procedures and labelling requirements to the extent that they affect trade between Canada and the EU.

However, the considerations regarding the compatibility of the EU provisions with the SPS Agreement cannot simply be taken over, since the SPS Agreement's provisions are not incorporated into CETA.

What could become relevant in the context of authorisation procedures, labelling requirements or other EU provisions on genome edited plants falling within the SPS Agreement's scope is the obligation laid down in Article 5.6 CETA to accept the exporting party's SPS measure as equivalent if the measure achieves the importing party's appropriate level of SPS protection. However, the principles and guidelines for the determination, recognition and maintenance of equivalence have not yet been adopted. Therefore, no detailed analysis of this obligation is possible.

6.5.2 The Principle of National Treatment as Laid Down in Article 2.3 CETA

Since Article III GATT is incorporated into CETA by Article 2.3, the considerations with regard to Article III:4 GATT[489] equally apply to the compatibility of the EU authorisation procedures, labelling requirements and opt-out procedure with CETA. Also, Article 28.3.1 CETA gives the opportunity to invoke the exceptions laid down in Article XX GATT. However, in case, the EU authorisation procedures violate Article III:4 GATT, such a violation could not be justified by Article XX GATT. Thus, the circumstances leading to a violation of Article III:4 GATT would also lead to a violation of CETA. The same applies to the EU opt-out procedure.

6.5.3 CETA Chapter Four on TBT Measures

As Articles 2.1 and 2.2 TBT are incorporated into CETA, the same considerations as for the analysis of the TBT Agreement's compatibility apply here. Therefore, in case the EU labelling requirements would violate Articles 2.1 and 2.2 TBT, this would also constitute a violation of CETA.

---

[489] See above for the analysis of authorisation procedures, labelling requirements and opt-out mechanism under GATT, pp. 212, 241, 242.

6.5.4 The Dialogue on Biotech Market Access Issues

So far,[490] the Dialogue between Canada and the EU on Biotech Market Access Issues as established by Article 25.2 CETA has *inter alia* dealt with the EU's risk assessment and management procedures, the status of specific applications in the EU and in Canada, possible legislative amendments in the EU concerning the comitology procedure and the possibility for Member States to restrict or prohibit the use of GM food and feed in their territory, the EU's plans under the European Green Deal and the Farm to Fork strategy, as well as international activities in the context of biotechnology.[491] Also, Canada informed the EU about its support of the *International Statement on Agricultural Applications of Precision Biotechnology*[492] submitted by WTO members to the SPS Committee in November 2018.[493]

Canada subsequently expressed concerns about the length of the EU's risk assessment procedure. It enquired pre-submission meetings between applicants and EFSA to speed up the risk assessment period.[494] Also, Canada stressed the importance of timely approval decisions once the EFSA opinion has been issued and explicitly addressed delays in the approval procedure due to the insufficient frequency of SCOPAFF meetings.[495] Also, Canada criticised the EU's re-authorisation requirement which does not exist in Canada and raised concerns regarding the EU's risk assessment of stacked events.[496]

Furthermore, Canada asked the Commission about plans for new legislation on products obtained from new plant breeding techniques following the CJEU's decision on targeted mutagenesis since in this context many other countries apply an approach different from the EU.[497] The EU constantly informed Canada of the process leading to the proposal of a new regulation on plants produced by certain new

---

[490] Only Joint Reports up to the 15th meeting of the Bilateral Biotech Market Access Issues in October 2023 have been considered as the Joint Report of the 16th meeting in November 2024 was not yet available in January 2025.

[491] See European Commission (2018a); European Commission (2019b); European Commission (2020); European Commission (2021b).

[492] Committee on Sanitary and Phytosanitary Measures (2018).

[493] European Commission (2019b), p. 4.

[494] See European Commission (2018a), p. 1; European Commission (2019b), p. 1; European Commission (2020), pp. 1–2; European Commission (2021b), pp. 1–2.

[495] See European Commission (2019b), p. 2; European Commission (2020), p. 3; European Commission (2021b), p. 3; however in the fourteenth meeting of the Dialogue, the Government of Canada also acknowledged "that timelines for GM approvals and renewals by the EU [had] improved over the past two years", see Government of Canada (2022); see also Government of Canada (2023).

[496] European Commission (2020), p. 2; European Commission (2021b), p. 2; see also Government of Canada (2022).

[497] European Commission (2019b), pp. 2–3.

genomic techniques.[498] This process was welcomed by Canada encouraging the EU Commission to ensure an innovative, trade-facilitative, science-based and risk-proportionate policy approach towards new breeding techniques facilitating their use in the agricultural sector.[499] Also, Canada stressed that in its view a regulatory approach towards new genomic techniques should incorporate a product-based approach, focusing on a product's safety for humans, animals, and the environment. While sustainability factors are important they should in Canada's view not be considered in a marketing authorisation procedure.[500]

So far, the Dialogue has an informational character, but it also becomes clear that Canada has very specific interests when it comes to the regulation of biotechnology in the EU. It does not hesitate to name these interests again and again to put (slight) pressure on the EU. However, the EU Commission stands up to this pressure and clearly sets out the EU's regulatory requirements to which it adheres.

6.6 Conclusions

The foregoing analysis of the EU GMO law and its applicability to targeted mutagenesis techniques in light of WTO law and CETA shows a complicated interlocking of different levels. The analysis at the interface of EU law and international trade law is complemented by scientific questions concerning genetic engineering techniques that are highly relevant to the analysis' outcome.

The analysis shows that the EU regulatory framework for GMOs might have been legitimate under WTO law and CETA with regard to conventional genetic engineering methods. But this assessment does no longer apply with regard to new genome editing techniques, especially with regard to targeted mutagenesis techniques. However, the reasons for this different assessment are not to be found in the WTO rules and CETA, but in the decision of the EU Commission to categorise the risks of targeted mutagenesis techniques as equivalent to the risks of conventional plant breeding techniques. While the EU legislator must act now, it is also responsible for this itself.

Due to this assessment, it is also likely that potential disputes on the EU regulation of plants modified by targeted mutagenesis techniques or genome editing are brought before the WTO dispute settlement body. Whether these rules of international trade law are the adequate standard of review for GMO regulations remains questionable.

Especially the SPS Agreement is not adequately designed to cover the multi-facetted risks associated with GMOs. Additionally, it heavily focusses on the

[498] See European Commission (2020), p. 4; European Commission (2021b), p. 4; Government of Canada (2022); Government of Canada (2023).

[499] *Cf.* European Commission (2020), p. 4; Government of Canada (2022); Government of Canada (2023).

[500] *Cf.* Government of Canada (2022).

scientific basis of measures and unfortunately leaves little leeway for society or government decisions based on other grounds than science, such as ethical or sustainability concerns. It thereby fails to keep with the times.

Also with regard to the TBT Agreement and the GATT, there are difficulties to categorise the EU GMO regulations under these agreements. This is exemplified by the difficulties to adequately categorise measures taken in light of GMO risks under the exception clause laid down in Article XX GATT.

The GATT and the TBT Agreement do not focus on the scientific basis of a measure but instead on non-discrimination and on the competitive relationship of products. Thereby, both agreement leave more room for societies' perceptions and concerns which is different in comparison to the SPS Agreement. Where the public decides to treat two products differently, leading to them not being in a competitive relationship, this different treatment is legitimate under GATT and TBT. Accordingly, GM plants and non-GM plants may be treated differently where the public differentiates between those plants. In the EU, this is currently still the case for food products. However, with regard to plants used as feed in conventional agriculture, such differentiation does not seem to exist. Accordingly, a different regulatory treatment is more difficult to justify in this sector.

A measure's objectives, such as environmental or health protection, do not play a role when scrutinising a measure under the national treatment principle. Such reasons can only be considered if they qualify as legitimate regulatory purposes under the TBT Agreement or are laid down in Article XX GATT. National governments can rely on these reasons to treat like products differently. However, it is difficult to classify GMOs and associated risks and consumer perceptions in the existing categories. The reasons for justification laid down in Article XX GATT are very specific and while measures for health protection or the conservation of exhaustible resources might be comprised, the provisions leave little room for differentiated regulatory decisions incorporating several factors and views. This again shows the inadequacy of WTO law to adequately deal with GMOs.

In conclusion, the analysis has shown that it is not impossible, but difficult to adequately deal with GMO regulation under WTO law and CETA. While the Cartagena Protocol is often referred to as the more appropriate international agreement for trade in biotechnology, it does not enjoy worldwide recognition and is especially not accepted by the States most involved in biotechnological trade, such as Argentina, Canada and the US. And in light of the different perceptions towards biotechnology regulation worldwide, it seems difficult to agree on international rules. This leaves the EU legislator with no choice but to adapt the EU regulations to the requirements of the WTO regime and CETA. A task that the EU Commission has now taken on with its new legislative proposal for a regulation on plants obtained by new genomic techniques.

References

Literature

Ad Hoc Intergovernmental Task Force on Food Derived from Biotechnology (2008) Guideline for the Conduct of Food Safety Assessment of Foods Derived from Recombinant-DNA Plants. CAC/GL 45-2003

Ad Hoc Intergovernmental Task Force on Food Derived from Biotechnology (2011) Principles for the Risk Analysis of Foods Derived from Modern Biotechnology. CAC/GL 44-2003

Appleton AE (2000) The labelling of GMO products pursuant to international trade rules. New York Univ Environ Law J 8:566–578

Appleton AE (2003) 3.10 Technical Barriers to Trade. In: United Nations Conference on Trade and Development (ed) Dispute Settlement: World Trade Organization, New York, Genf

Appleton AE (2014) National treatment under the TBT Agreement. Chapter 4. In: Kamperman Sanders A (ed) The principle of national treatment in international economic law: trade, investment and intellectual property. Edward Elgar Publishing, Cheltenham, pp 92–124

Barton JH (1996) Biotechnology, the environment, and international agricultural trade. Georgetown Int Environ Law Rev 9:95–118

Baumüller H (2004) Domestic import regulations for genetically modified organisms and their compatibility with WTO rules. Asian Biotechnol Dev Rev 6:33–42

Beck F (2022), Self-Spreading Biotechnology and International Law: Prevention, Responsibility, and Liability in a Transboundary Context. Beiträge zum ausländischen öffentlichen Recht und Völkerrecht, vol 316

Benevides Demasi JO (2019) The precautionary principle, the labelling of gene-edited products, and the WTO case law. In: Dürnberger C, Pfeilmeier S, Schleissing S (eds) Genome editing in agriculture: between precaution and responsibility. Nomos, Baden-Baden, pp 153–178

Bernasconi-Osterwalder N (2008) The Cartagena protocol on biosafety: a multilateral approach to regulation GMOs. Chapter 21. In: Weiss EB, Jackson JH, Bernasconi-Osterwalder N (eds) Reconciling environment and trade, 2nd edn. Martinus Nijhoff Publishers, Leiden, pp 645–677

Biber-Klemm S, Burkard M, Cottier T, Jusoh S, Temmerman M (2011) Challenges of biotechnology in international trade regulation. In: Cottier T, Delimatsis P (eds) The prospects of international trade regulation. Cambridge University Press, Cambridge, pp 284–320. https://doi.org/10.1017/CBO9780511792496.009

Böckenförde M (2004) Grüne Gentechnik und Welthandel: Das Biosafety-Protokoll und seine Auswirkungen auf das Regime der WTO. Beiträge zum ausländischen öffentlichen Recht und Völkerrecht, vol 171. Springer, Heidelberg

Bognar J (2016), Explaining the diverging regulatory approaches to risk regulation between Canada and the EU. In: Hübner K (ed) Europe, Canada and the Comprehensive Economic and Trade Agreement, pp 180–200

Brüggemann C (2020), EU importiert mehr Sojabohnen. top agrar ONLINE

Bund für Umwelt und Naturschutz e.V., Friends of the Earth Germany (2019) Soja-Report: Wie kann die Eiweißpflanzenproduktion der EU auf nachhaltige und agrarökologische Weise angekurbelt werden?, Berlin, https://www.bund.net/fileadmin/user_upload_bund/publikationen/landwirtschaft/landwirtschaft_sojareport.pdf

Bundesinformationszentrum Landwirtschaft (2021) Gentechnik in Futtermittel. https://www.landwirtschaft.de/diskussion-und-dialog/tierhaltung/gentechnik-in-futtermitteln

Burchardi J-E (2001) Labelling of genetically modified organisms: a possible conflict with the WTO? Zeitschrift für das gesamte Lebensmittelrecht:83–103

Burchardi J-E (2007) Die Vereinbarkeit der europäischen Vorschriften zur Kennzeichnung gentechnisch veränderter Lebensmittel mit dem Welthandelsrecht. Rechtsfragen der Globalisierung. Duncker & Humblot, Berlin

Carreno I, Dolle T (2019) The Court of Justice of the European Union's Judgment on mutagenesis and international trade: a case of GMO, Mutagenesis and International Trade. Global Trade Cust J 14:91–101

Caswell JA (2000), An evaluation of risk analysis as applied to agricultural biotechnology (with a case study of GMO labeling). In: Transitions in Agbiotech: Economics of Strategy and Policy, Chapter 36, pp 665–674

Centre for the Promotion of Imports from Developing Countries (2021) What is the demand for grains, pulses and oilseeds on the European market?, https://www.cbi.eu/market-information/grains-pulses-oilseeds/trade-statistics

Charnovitz S (2000) The supervision of health and biosafety regulation by world trade rules. Tulane Environ Law J 13:271–302

Charnovitz S (2002) The law of environmental "PPMs" in the WTO: debunking the myth of illegality. Yale J Int Law 37:59–110. https://doi.org/10.1142/9789814513258_0012

Charnovitz S (2007) Article 1 and Annex A SPS. In: WTO - technical barriers and SPS measures. Martinus Nijhoff Publishers, Boston, pp 375–391

Codex Alimentarius Commission (2007) Procedural manual, 17th edn.

Codex Committee on Food Labelling (2011) Compilation of Codex texts relevant to the labelling of foods derived from modern biotechnology. CAC/GL 76-2011

Codex Committee on Methods of Analysis and Sampling (2010) Guidelines on Performance of Criteria and Validation of Methods for Detection, Identification and Quantification of Specific DNA Sequences and Specific Proteins in Food. CAC/GL 74-2010

Commission of the European Communities (2000) Communication from the Commission on the precautionary principle. COM(2000) 1 final, Brussels

Committee on Sanitary and Phytosanitary Measures (2000) Guidelines to further the practical implementation of Article 5.5. G/SPS/15

Committee on Sanitary and Phytosanitary Measures (2004) Revision of the Procedure to Monitor the Process of International Harmonization: Decision of the Committee. G/SPS/11/Rev.1

Committee on Sanitary and Phytosanitary Measures (2006) Decision to Modify and Extend the Provisional Procedure to Monitor the Process of International Harmonization. G/SPS/40

Committee on Sanitary and Phytosanitary Measures (2018) International Statement on agricultural applications of precision biotechnology: Communication from Argentina, Australia, Brazil, Canada, The Dominican Republic, Guatemale, Honduras, Paraguay, The United States of America and Uruguay. G/SPS/GEN/1658/Rev.3

Conrad CR (2007) The EC-biotech dispute and applicability of the SPS Agreement: are the Panel's findings built on shaky ground. World Trade Rev 6:233–247

Conrad CR (2011) Processes and production methods (PPMs) in WTO law: interfacing trade and social goals, 1st edn. Cambridge international trade and economic law. Cambridge University Press, Cambridge, https://doi.org/10.1017/CBO9780511807398

Davies GT (2007) Morality clauses and decision making in situations of scientific uncertainty: The Case of GMOs. World Trade Rev 6:248–263

Dederer H-G (2010) Weiterentwicklung des Gentechnikrechts - GVO-freie Zonen und sozioökonomische Kriterien für die GVO-Zulassung: Eine Untersuchung der Regelungsspielräume und ihrer europa- und welthandelsrechtlichen Grenzen. Recht der Lebenswissenschaften, vol 2. LIT, Münster

Dederer H-G (2019) Genomeditierung ist Gentechnik. Europäische Zeitschrift für Umwelt- und Planungsrecht:236–245

Delewski M, Grube M, Karsten J (2016) Novel-Food-Verordnung, 1st edn. Behr's Verlag, Hamburg

EFSA Panel on Genetically Modified Organisms (2009) Scientific Opinion on Guidance for the risk assessment of genetically modified plants used for non-food or non-feed purposes. Scientific Opinion

EFSA Panel on Genetically Modified Organisms (2010a) Guidance on the environmental risk assessment of genetically modified plants. Scientific Opinion, Parma, Italy. https://doi.org/10.2903/j.efsa.2010.1879

EFSA Panel on Genetically Modified Organisms (2010b) Scientific Opinion on the assessment of allergenicity of GM plants and microorganisms and derived food and feed. Scientific Opinion. https://doi.org/10.2903/j.efsa.2010.1700

EFSA Panel on Genetically Modified Organisms (2011) Guidance for risk assessment of food and feed from genetically modified plants. Scientific Opinion. https://doi.org/10.2903/j.efsa.2011.2150

Eggers B (2001), The precautionary principle in WTO law, Hamburg, http://ediss.sub.uni-hamburg.de/volltexte/2001/451/

Eriksson D, Kershen D, Nepomuceno A, Pogson BJ, Prieto H, Purnhagen K, Smyth S, Wesseler J, Whelan A (2019) A comparison of the EU regulatory approach to directed mutagenesis with that of other jurisdictions, consequences for international trade and potential steps forward. New Phytol 222:1673–1684

Eriksson D, Custers R, Edvardsson Björnberg K, Hansson SO, Purnhagen K, Qaim M, Romeis J, Schiemann J, Schleissing S, Tosun J, Visser RG (2020) Options to reform the European Union legislation on GMOs: risk governance. Trends Biotechnol 38:349–351. https://doi.org/10.1016/j.tibtech.2019.12.016

EST GmbH, Soja - Globale Mengenverteilung und Mengenströme, https://www.sojatoaster.com/hintergrundinfos/sojaanbau-globale-mengenverteilung-und-mengenstroeme/

European Commission (2018a) Meeting of The Dialogue on Biotech Market Access Issues, 26 April 2018. Report. https://circabc.europa.eu/rest/download/3be63631-a1d8-4b56-9012-6effe0074635?ticket=

European Commission (2018b) Development of plant proteins in the European Union. https://www.martin-haeusling.eu/images/Boger_DG_AGRI__COM_EU_protein_plan_presentation_9_October.pdf

European Commission (2019a) United States is Europe's main soya beans supplier with imports up by 112%. Press release, Brussels

European Commission (2019b) The Eleventh Meeting of the Bilateral Dialogue on Biotech Market Access Issues, 4 March 2019. Joint Report, https://circabc.europa.eu/rest/download/ea175654-7d7e-4b9b-a9d3-fd51c3c94df8?ticket=

European Commission (2020) Meeting of the Canada-EU Dialogue on Biotech Market Access Issues, 21 October 2020. Joint Report, https://circabc.europa.eu/rest/download/c557e189-a2e5-44b7-a156-724ac35ea9c7?ticket=

European Commission (2021a) Study on the status of new genomic techniques under Union law and in light of the Court of Justice ruling in Case C-528/16: Commission Staff Working Document. SWD(2021) 92 final, Brussels

European Commission (2021b) Meeting of the Canada-EU Dialogue on Biotech Market Access Issues, 3 December 2021. Joint Report, https://circabc.europa.eu/rest/download/c05b997a-31ce-4c7c-bf98-de981746dd4b?ticket=

European Commission (2023) Proposal for a Regulation of the European Parliament and of the Council on plants obtained by certain new genomic techniques and their food and feed, and amending Regulation (EU) 2017/625. COM(2023) 411 final, Brussels

European Commission, Community register of GM food and feed, https://ec.europa.eu/food/plants/genetically-modified-organisms/gmo-register_en

European Commission, Deliberate Release and Placing on the EU Market of GMOs: GMO Register Notifications authorized under Directive 2001/18/EC - GMO Part C, https://webgate.ec.europa.eu/fip/GMO_Registers/GMO_Part_C.php

European Commission, EU trade for oilseeds and protein crops, https://circabc.europa.eu/sd/a/4d9aeffa-bca9-49a3-b3d3-28ca1a4e7520/oilseeds-monthly_trade-eurostat_en.xlsx

European Commission, Restrictions of geographical scope of GMO applications/authorisations: EU countries demands and outcomes. Overview, https://food.ec.europa.eu/plants/genetically-modified-organisms/gmo-authorisation/gmo-authorisations-cultivation/restrictions-geographical-scope-gmo-applicationsauthorisations-eu-countries-demands-and-outcomes_en

European Commission, Taxation and Customs Union: TARIC Consultation, https://ec.europa.eu/taxation_customs/dds2/taric/taric_consultation.jsp?Lang=en&Expand=true&SimDate=20220411

European Commission, Taxation and Customs Union: Classification of goods. Overview, https://taxation-customs.ec.europa.eu/business/calculation-customs-duties/customs-tariff/classification-goods_en

European Food Safety Authority (2021) Overview of EFSA and European national authorities' scientific opinions on the risk assessment of plants developed through New Genomic Techniques. https://doi.org/10.2903/j.efsa.2021.6314

European Food Safety Authority, European Commission (2019) Special Eurobarometer Wave EB91.3: Food Safety in the EU. Report

European Network of GMO Laboratories (2019) Detection of food and feed plant products obtained by new mutagenesis techniques. JRC116289

Feichtner I (2007) Community Interest. Max Planck Encyclopedias of International Law (MPEPIL)

Foreign Agricultural Service (2021) Oilseeds: World Markets and Trade. Global Market Analysis. https://downloads.usda.library.cornell.edu/usda-esmis/files/tx31qh68h/b5645q33m/h128pd28h/oilseeds.pdf

Franken L, Burchardi J-E (2007) Beyond biosafety - an analysis of the EC-biotech panel report. Aussenwirtschaft 62:77–106

Fricke M (2004) Genetisch veränderte Lebensmittel im Welthandelsrecht: Die welthandelsrechtliche Konformität der divergierenden Regulierungsansätze in den USA und der EU. Europäisches und internationales Integrationsrecht, vol 5. LIT, Münster

Gesellschaft für Konsumforschung (2014) Umfrage der Gesellschaft für Konsumforschung zu gentechnisch veränderten Lebensmitteln

Government of Canada (2022) The fourteenth Canada-EU biotech market access issues dialogue, September 23, 2022. Joint Report, https://www.international.gc.ca/trade-commerce/trade-agreements-accords-commerciaux/agr-acc/ceta-aecg/2022-09-23-summary-rapport.aspx?lang=eng

Government of Canada (2023) The Fifteenth Canada-EU Biotech Market Access Issues Dialogue, October 11, 2023. Joint Report. https://www.international.gc.ca/trade-commerce/trade-agreements-accords-commerciaux/agr-acc/ceta-aecg/2023-10-11-summary-rapport.aspx?lang=eng

Gruszczynski L (2010) Regulating health and environmental risks under WTO law: a critical analysis of the SPS agreement. International economic law series. Oxford University Press, Oxford

Gruszczynski LA (2018) The SPS Agreement Within the Framework of WTO Law: The Rough Guide to the Agreement's Applicability. https://doi.org/10.2139/ssrn.1152749

Herdegen M (2016) Principles of international economic law, 2nd edn. Oxford University Press, Oxford

Hestermeyer H (2011) Article III GATT. In: WTO-trade in goods. Martinus Nijhoff Publishers, Leiden Netherlands, Boston, pp 116–165

Holzer K (2017) II.11 comparability in international economic law: goods. In: Cottier T, Nadakavukaren Schefer K (eds) Elgar encyclopedia of international economic law. Edward Elgar Publishing, Cheltenham, pp 185–187

Howse R, Mavroidis P (2000) Europe's evolving regulatory strategy for GMOs: the issue of consistency with WTO law: of Kine and Brine. Fordham Int Law J 24:317–370

International Service for the Acquisition of Agri-biotech Applications (2019) Brief 55: Global Status of Commercialized Biotech/GM Crops: 2019. Executive Summary, https://www.isaaa.org/resources/publications/briefs/55/executivesummary/default.asp

International Service for the Acquisition of Agri-biotech Applications, Biotech Country: Facts & Trends - Brazil, https://www.isaaa.org/resources/publications/biotech_country_facts_and_trends/download/Facts%20and%20Trends%20-%20Brazil.pdf

Ipsos (2018) Global Views on Food - 2018: What are the world's food habits?, https://www.ipsos.com/sites/default/files/ct/news/documents/2018-12/ipsos_global_advisor_views_on_food_2018.pdf
Kerr WA (1999) International trade in transgenic food products: a new focus for agricultural trade disputes. World Econ 22:245–259
Kluttig B (2003) Welthandelsrecht und Umweltschutz: Kohärenz statt Konkurrenz. Arbeitspapiere aus dem Institut für Wirtschaftsrecht, Halle (Saale)
Koebele M (2007) Article 1 and Annex I TBT. In: WTO - technical barriers and SPS measures. Martinus Nijhoff Publishers, Boston, pp 178–209
Kogan LA (2007) World Trade Organization biotech decision clarifies central role of science in evaluating health and environmental risks for regulation purposes. Global Trade Cust J 2:149–155
Kuepper B, Stravens M (2022) Mapping the European Soy Supply Chain: Embedded Soy in Animal Products Consumed in the EU27+UK
Landwehr O (2007) Article 3 SPS. In: WTO - technical barriers and SPS measures. Martinus Nijhoff Publishers, Boston, pp 412–428
Legal Service of the Council of the European Union (2010) Opinion of the Legal Service on a Proposal for a Regulation of the European Parliament and of the Council amending Directive 2001/18/EC as regards the possibility for the Member States to restrict or prohibit the cultivation of GMOs in their territory. 15696/10, Brussels
Legal Service of the Council of the European Union (2011) Opinion of the Legal Service on a Proposal for a Regulation of the European Parliament and of the Council amending Directive 2001/18/EC as regards the possibility for the Member States to restrict or prohibit the cultivation of GMOs in their territory. 8994/11, Brussels
Maggio AR (2017), Environmental policy, non-product related process and production methods and the law of the world trade organization. EYIEL Monographs - Studies in European and International Economic Law, vol 1. Springer International Publishing, Cham. https://doi.org/10.1007/978-3-319-61155-6
Marceau G, Trachtmann JP (2002) The technical barriers to trade agreement, the sanitary and phytosanitary measures agreement, and the general agreement on tariffs and trade: a map of the World Trade Organization law of domestic regulation of goods. J World Trade 36:811–881
Marketagent (2019) Einkaufsverhalten und Einstellung zu Gentechnik. study commissioned by ARGE Gentechnik-frei. https://de.statista.com/statistik/studie/id/67611/dokument/marktforschungsstudie-zum-thema-einkaufsverhalten-und-einstellung-zu-gentechnik-in-oesterreich-2019/
Matsushita M, Schoenbaum TJ, Mavroidis PC, Hahn M (2017) The World Trade Organization: law, practice, and policy, 3rd edn. The Oxford international law library. Oxford University Press, Oxford, United Kingdom, New York, NY
Matz-Lück N (2008) Biological diversity, International Protection. Max Planck Encyclopedias of International Law (MPEPIL). https://doi.org/10.1093/law:epil/9780199231690/e1562
Mögele R, Möhler (2022) 4. Das Übereinkommen über die Anwendung gesundheitspolizeilicher und pflanzenschutzrechtlicher Maßnahmen (SPSÜ). In: Krenzler HG, Herrmann C, Niestedt M (eds) EU-Außenwirtschafts- und Zollrecht, 19th edn
Monien J (2016) § 8 The new opt-out rule - new challenges in the legal multi-level system of the usage of GMOs. In: Härtel I, Budzinowski R (eds) Food security, food safety, food quality: current developments and challenges in European Union Law, 1st edn. Nomos Verlagsgesellschaft mbH & Co, KG, Baden-Baden, pp 103–113
Morgan D, Goh G (2004) Genetically modified food labelling and the WTO Agreements. Rev Euro Comp Int Environ Law 13:306–319
N.N (1970) Report by the Working Party on Border Tax Adjustments. L/3464
Nationale Akademie der Wissenschaften Leopoldina, Union der Deutschen Akademien der Wissenschaften, Deutsche Forschungsgemeinschaft (2019) Towards a scientifically justified, differentiated regulation of genome edited plants in the EU. Statement, Halle (Saale),

Bonn, Mainz, https://www.leopoldina.org/uploads/tx_leopublication/2019_Stellungnahme_Genomeditierte_Pflanzen_web.pdf
Palme C (1997) EG-Richtlinie "Freisetzung" Einleitung. In: Eberbach WH, Lange P, Ronellenfitsch M (eds) Recht der Gentechnik und Biomedizin: GenTR/BioMedR, vol 3, 114th edn. C.F. Müller, Heidelberg
Peel J (2006) A GMO by Any Other Name . . . Might Be an SPS Risk!: implications of expanding the scope of the WTO sanitary and phytosanitary measures agreement. Eur J Int Law 17:1009–1031. https://doi.org/10.1093/ejil/chl033
Prévost D, van den Bossche P (2005) The agreement on the application of sanitary and phytosanitary measures. Chapter 7. In: Macrory PFJ, Appleton AE, Plummer MG (eds) The World Trade Organization: legal, economic and political analysis, vol I(1). Springer Science+Business Media Inc, Boston, MA, pp 231–370
Robertson D (2001) GM foods and global trade. In: Robertson D, Kellow A (eds) . Edward Elgar Publishing, Globalization and the environment: risk assessment and the WTO, pp 206–226
Schulte M, Schröder R (2011) Handbuch des Technikrechts. Springer, Berlin, Heidelberg. https://doi.org/10.1007/978-3-642-11884-5
Scott J (2003) European regulation of GMOs and the WTO. Columb J Eur Law 9:213–240
Scott J (2009) The WTO agreement on sanitary and phytosanitary measures: a commentary. Oxford commentaries on the Gatt/WTO Agreements. Oxford University Press, Oxford
Secretariat of the International Plant Protection Convention (2007) ISPM 5: Glossary of Phytosanitary Terms. International Standard for Phytosanitary Measures, https://www.ippc.int/largefiles/adopted_ISPMs_previousversions/en/ISPM_05_2007_En_2007-07-26.pdf
Secretariat of the International Plant Protection Convention (2015a) ISPM 1: Phytosanitary principles for the protection of plants and the application of phytosanitary measures in international trade. International Standard for Phytosanitary Measures
Secretariat of the International Plant Protection Convention (2015b) ISPM 9: Guidelines for pest eradication programmes. International Standard for Phytosanitary Measures
Secretariat of the International Plant Protection Convention (2016) Overview on International Standards for Phytosanitary Measures (ISPMs) and their application to living modified organisms (LMOs). https://www.ippc.int/static/media/uploads/ippc_ispmsforlmos_2016-02-24.pdf
Secretariat of the International Plant Protection Convention (2018) ISPM 6: Surveillance. International Standard for Phytosanitary Measures
Secretariat of the International Plant Protection Convention (2019a) ISPM 11: Pest risk analysis for quarantine pests. International Standard for Phytosanitary Measures. https://assets.ippc.int/static/media/files/publication/en/2019/05/ISPM_11_2013_En_PRA_QPs_2019-04-30_PostCPM14_InkAm.pdf
Secretariat of the International Plant Protection Convention (2019b) ISPM 2: Framework for pest risk analysis. International Standard for Phytosanitary Measures
Seibert-Fohr A (2007) Article 2 SPS. In: WTO - technical barriers and SPS measures. Martinus Nijhoff Publishers, Boston, pp 392–411
Sheldon I, Josling T (2002) Biotechnology Regulations and the WTO: Working Paper 02-2
Smith E, Jarvis A, Conway M (2015) State of play in the EU on GM-free food labelling schemes and assesment of the need for possible harmonisation: Final report. Document prepared for the European Commission. https://food.ec.europa.eu/system/files/2016-10/gmo-traceability-gm-final_report_en.pdf
Spranger TM (2000) WTO-rechtliche Probleme der Genehmigungspflicht für neuartige Lebensmittel im Hinblick auf das SPS-Übereinkommen. Zeitschrift für das gesamte Lebensmittelrecht:111–117
Spranger TM (2019) Memorandum on the international trade law implications of the judgment of the European Court of Justice in case C-528/16. Commissioned by the Federal Agency for Nature Conservation (BfN), Bonn

Statista (2017a) Sind Sie für oder gegen die Verarbeitung von genetisch modifizierten Oganismen in der Lebensmittelherstellung? Statista survey, https://de.statista.com/statistik/daten/studie/722780/umfrage/meinung-zum-thema-gen-food-in-deutschland/
Statista (2017b) Wie häufig achten Sie bei der Auswahl von Lebensmittel darauf, dass auf Gentechnik verzichtet wurde? Statista survey. https://de.statista.com/statistik/daten/studie/6847/umfrage/einstellung-zum-kauf-von-gen-food/
Stevenson A (2010) The Oxford dictionary of English, 3rd edn. Oxford University Press, Oxford
Stökl L (2003a) Der welthandelsrechtliche Gentechnikkonflikt: Die europarechtlichen Handelsbeschränkungen für gentechnisch veränderte Lebensmittel und ihre Vereinbarkeit mit Welthandelsrecht. In: Tübinger Schriften zum internationalen und europäischen Recht, vol 65, 1st edn. Duncker & Humblot GmbH, Berlin. https://doi.org/10.3790/978-3-428-51084-9
Stökl L (2003b) WTO und Gentechnik: Die Anforderungen des WTO-Rechts für Beschränkungen des Handels mit gentechnisch veränderten Organismen und Lebensmitteln. In: Nettesheim M, Sander GG (eds) WTO-Recht und Globalisierung. Duncker & Humblot, Berlin, pp 73–101
Stoll P-T, Strack A (2011) Article XX lit. b GATT. In: WTO-trade in goods. Martinus Nijhoff Publishers, Leiden Netherlands, Boston
Strack A (2014) Der lange Weg zum Opt-out von der Gentechnik: Zur neuen Freiheit der EU-Mitgliedsstaaten, den Anbau von gentechnisch veränderten Organismen zu beschränken. Natur und Recht 36:829–835. https://doi.org/10.1007/s10357-014-2740-2
Tamiotti L (2007) Article 2 TBT. In: WTO - technical barriers and SPS measures. Martinus Nijhoff Publishers, Boston, pp 210–234
The Oxford English Dictionary (OED), https://www.oed.com/
Transparenz Gentechnik (2021) Futtermittel: Ohne Sojaimporte geht es nicht. https://www.transgen.de/lebensmittel/1049.futtermittelimporte-europa-sojabohnen-gentechnik.html
van Calster G, Reins L (2018) EU environmental law. Elgar European law. Edward Elgar Publishing, Cheltenham. https://doi.org/Geert
van den Bossche P, Zdouc W (2022) The law and policy of the World Trade Organization: text, cases and materials, 5th edn. Cambridge University Press, Cambridge
Walker VR (1998) Keeping the WTO from Becoming the "World Trans-science Organization": Scientific Uncertainty, Science Policy, and Factfinding in the Growth Hormones Dispute. Cornell Int Law J 31:251–320
Wolf S (2002) Regulative Maßnahmen zum Schutz vor gentechnisch veränderten Organismen und Welthandelsrecht. Arbeitspapiere aus dem Institut für Wirtschaftsrecht, Halle (Saale)
Wolfrum R (2011a) Article XI GATT. In: WTO-trade in goods. Martinus Nijhoff Publishers, Leiden Netherlands, Boston, pp 281–295
Wolfrum R (2011b) Article XX GATT (Introduction). In: WTO-trade in goods. Martinus Nijhoff Publishers, Leiden Netherlands, Boston, pp 455–463
Wolfrum R (2011c) Article XX lit. g GATT. In: WTO-trade in goods. Martinus Nijhoff Publishers, Leiden Netherland Measures Affecting Imports of Fresh s, Boston
Wong J (2005) Are Biotech Crops and Conventional Crops Like Products? An Analysis Under GATT
World Trade Organization, Sanitary and Phytosanitary Measures. Overview, https://www.wto.org/english/tratop_e/sps_e/sps_e.htm
World Trade Organization, SPS Agreement - Article 2 (Jurisprudence). In: World Trade Organization (ed) WTO Analytical Index
World Trade Organization, SPS Agreement - Article 3 (Jurisprudence). In: World Trade Organization (ed) WTO Analytical Index
World Trade Organization, TBT Agreement - Article 2 (Jurisprudence). In: World Trade Organization (ed) WTO Analytical Index
Zarrilli S (2006) International Trade in GMOs - Legal frameworks and developing country concerns, 2006. In: Francioni F, Scovazzi T (eds) Biotechnology and international law. Hart Publishing, Oxford, pp 231–254

Zedalis RJ (2001) Labelling of genetically modified foods: the limits of GATT rules. J World Trade 35:301–347

Zedalis RJ (2004) The United States/European Communities biotech products case: opportunity for World Trade Organization consideration of whether internally applied non-tax measures fall within the scope of the general agreement on tariffs and Trade Article XI(1)'s reference to "Other Measures". J World Trade 38:647–659

Jurisprudence – Court of Justice of the European Union (Former European Court of Justice)

CJEU (2018) Case C-528/16 - Confédération paysanne et al.

Jurisprudence – WTO Appellate Body

WTO Appellate Body (1996), *Japan - Taxes on Alcoholic Beverages*

WTO Appellate Body (1998a), *EC Measures Concerning Meat and Meat Products (Hormones)*

WTO Appellate Body (1998b), *United States - Import Prohibition of Certain Shrimp and Shrimp Products*

WTO Appellate Body (1998c), *Australia - Measures Affecting Importation of Salmon*

WTO Appellate Body (1999), *Japan - Measures Affecting Agricultural Products*

WTO Appellate Body (2000) *Korea - Measures Affecting Imports of Fresh. Beef, Chilled and Frozen*

WTO Appellate Body (2001), *European Communities - Measures Affecting Asbestos and Asbestos-Containing Products*

WTO Appellate Body (2002), *European Communities - Trade Description of Sardines*

WTO Appellate Body (2003), *Japan - Measures Affecting the Importation of Apples*

WTO Appellate Body (2004), *United States - Final Countervailing Duty Determination with respect to certain Softwood Lumber from Canada*

WTO Appellate Body (2008), *Canada - Continued Suspension of Obligations in the EC - Hormones Dispute*

WTO Appellate Body (2010), *Australia - Measures Affecting the Importation of Apples from New Zealand*

WTO Appellate Body (2012a), *United States - Measures Affecting the Production and Sale of Clove Cigarettes*

WTO Appellate Body (2012b) *United States - Measures concerning the Imporatation. Products, Marketing and Sale of Tuna and Tuna*

WTO Appellate Body (2012c), *United States - Certain Country of Origin Labelling (COOL) Requirements*

WTO Appellate Body (2014), *European Communities - Measures Prohibiting the Importation and Marketing of Seal Products*

WTO Appellate Body (2019), *Korea - Import Bans, and Testing and Certification Requirements for Radionuclides*

Jurisprudence – WTO Panel

WTO Art. 21(5) DSU Panel (2000), *Australia - Measures Affecting Importation of Salmon - Recourse to Article 21.5 by Canada*
WTO Panel (1997a), *EC Measures Concerning Meat and Meat Products (Hormones) (Complaint by Canada)*
WTO Panel (1997b), *EC Measures Concerning Meat and Meat Products (Hormones) (Complaint by the United States)*
WTO Panel (1998), *Australia - Measures Affecting Importation of Salmon*
WTO Panel (2000), *European Communities - Measures Affecting Asbestos and Asbestos-Containing Products*
WTO Panel (2005) *European Communities - Protection of Trademarks and Geographical Indications for Agricultural Products and Foodstuffs. Complaint by Australia*
WTO Panel (2006), *European Communities - Measures Affecting the Approval and Marketing of Biotech Products*
WTO Panel (2010a), *Australia - Measures Affecting the Importation of Apples from New Zealand*
WTO Panel (2010b), *United States - Certain Measures Affecting Imports of Poultry from China*
WTO Panel (2011a), *United States - Measures Affecting the Production and Sale of Clove Cigarettes*
WTO Panel (2011b) *United States - Measures concerning the Importation. Products, Marketing and Sale of Tuna and Tuna*
WTO Panel (2011c), *United States - Certain Country of Origin Labellling (COOL) Requirements*
WTO Panel (2013), *European Communities - Measures Prohibiting the Importation and Marketing of Seal Products*

Jurisprudence – GATT Panel

GATT Panel (1984), *Canada - Administration of the Foreign Investment Review Act (FIRA)*
GATT Panel (1991), *United States - Restrictions on Imports of Tuna*

Chapter 7
The Future of Genome Edited Plants in the EU

Abstract While the legal debate on whether genome edited organisms fall under the European Union ('EU') law regulating genetically modified organisms ('GMOs') has been settled by the Court of Justice of the European Union ('CJEU'), the discussion on whether the current legislation adequately regulates genome edited organisms continues. Since the CJEU's judgement, calls for a less stringent EU regulation of genome edited organisms have increased, with stakeholders emphasising especially their potential for a more sustainable and climate-friendly agriculture. In July 2023, the EU Commission responded to these calls and published a proposal for a new regulation on plants obtained by certain new genomic techniques ('NGTs').

This chapter outlines the process leading to the Commission's proposal and compares the proposal to other reform suggestions that have been published so far. Furthermore, it analyses the Commission's proposal in light of the findings of Chap. 6 and provides further recommendations.

7.1 Introduction

Since the first genome editing techniques have been developed and applied, there is a debate on how to best regulate these techniques and plants derived thereof. In the academic debate it has been extensively stated that the current European Union ('EU') framework governing the deliberate release and placing on the market of genetically modified organisms ('GMOs') is inadequate to govern genome editing techniques. The previous chapter also emphasised this inadequacy in light of the EU's obligations under the law of the World Trade Organisation ('WTO') and the *Comprehensive Economic and Trade Agreement*[1] ('CETA').

[1] *Comprehensive Economic and Trade Agreement (CETA) between Canada, of the one part, and the European Union and its Member States, of the other part* ('CETA'), Official Journal of the European Union ('OJ EU') 2017, L 11/23.

E. A. L. Andersen, *Regulation of Biotechnological Risks in a Multi-Level System*, European Yearbook of International Economic Law 46,
https://doi.org/10.1007/978-3-032-02409-1_7

While the legal discussion on whether genome edited organisms are comprised by the EU GMO law or not has been settled by the decision of the Court of Justice of the European Union ('CJEU'), the debate on the adequate regulation of genome edited organisms has not stopped. Calls for a more lenient regulation of genome edited plants in the EU have even become louder since the CJEU's ruling. Proposals have been submitted by a variety of stakeholders and are often reasoned by the need of genome edited plants for a more sustainable, climate-friendly and resilient agriculture and the need for a stable food production.[2] Finally, the EU Commission, following a study requested by the Council of the EU, has submitted a proposal on the regulation of plants derived by new genomic techniques in 2023.

The chapter briefly summarises the problems that arise at the interface of EU GMO law and international trade law as analysed in Chap. 6 which serve as a standard to analyse the reform proposals brought forward so far (Sect. 7.1). It then presents the current developments regarding a reform of the EU GMO law, including the proposal of the EU Commission on a regulation for plants obtained by new genomic techniques (Sect. 7.3). Furthermore, it outlines other proposals for the regulation of genome edited organisms brought forward by academia and industry and places the Commission's proposal in the context of these proposals (Sect. 7.4). Subsequently, it analyses the different proposals in light of the conclusions drawn from the analysis in Chap. 6 (Sect. 7.5). Finally, it gives recommendations on future regulations and provides an overview of the next steps at the EU level (Sect. 7.6).

7.2 Problems a New Framework Should Tackle

The analysis in Chap. 6 has shown that the current EU regulation of GMOs and in particular its applicability to targeted mutagenesis techniques leads to a violation of WTO law and CETA.[3]

Most problematic is the requirement of an authorisation procedure. While the general requirement for an authorisation is legitimate where information on the risks of GM plants is available or where scientific data on the risk is insufficient, inconclusive or inadequate, such scientific uncertainty can no longer be assumed for plants modified by targeted mutagenesis techniques and cisgenesis. Due to the

[2] See *inter alia* Association Francaise des Biotechnologies Végétales and Wissenschaftlerkreis Grüne Gentechnik e.V. (2020), p. 1 (Explanatory note); Hjort et al. (2021), pp. 2–3; Huang et al. (2016), p. 109, 111; Seitz (2018), p. 764; this view is critically commented by *Oehen* who also emphasises the role of agricultural practices for a sustainable agriculture adapted to changing climatic conditions, see Oehen (2020); critic on these "old and new overblown promises" is also mentioned by Gelinsky and Hilbeck (2018), pp. 56–57; see also Gelinsky (2021) and Wember (2021); an analysis of expectations attached to genome editing and of current developments of genome editing in crop plant research is provided by Hüdig et al. (2022).

[3] Such incompatibility was already mentioned in academia after the judgment of the Court of Justice of the European Union on targeted mutagenesis techniques in 2018, see above, Chap. 3, p. 43.

European Commission's assumption that plants modified by targeted mutagenesis techniques carry the same risks as conventionally bred plants, the different regulatory approaches for both types of plants are difficult to justify. The EU might even be under an obligation to abandon the authorisation procedure for plants modified by targeted mutagenesis techniques and cisgenesis. Furthermore, the EU is obliged to review its pre-market ban for GMOs coming along with the authorisation requirement within a reasonable period of time. In this regard, it is difficult to argue that the duration of the comitology procedure which is caused by the Member States' inconclusive voting behaviour in the *Standing Committee on Plants, Animals, Food and Feed* ('SCoPAFF') and the corresponding Appeal Committee is still reasonable.

A violation of Article III:4 of the *General Agreement on Tariffs and Trade*[4] ('GATT') by the EU authorisation procedure is only possible in very specific cases.[5] The same considerations apply to a possible violation of Article 2.1 of the *Agreement on Technical Barriers to Trade*[6] ('TBT Agreement' or 'TBT') by the labelling requirements. The labelling requirements for plants modified by targeted mutagenesis only violate WTO law in cases where these plants are considered like conventionally bred plants and the different labelling cannot be considered even-handed. However, labelling requirements for plants modified by targeted mutagenesis techniques can be considered more trade-restrictive than necessary. For these cases, a new legal framework has to omit labelling requirements for plants modified by targeted mutagenesis techniques to comply with WTO law.

The EU opt-out mechanism is also problematic in light of WTO law. Where plants modified by targeted mutagenesis and conventionally bred plants are considered like products, a complete ban on cultivation could violate Article III:4 GATT. Whether such a violation is justified under Article XX GATT is questionable. Accordingly, the mechanism would have to be reconsidered for a new framework.

Since the relevant obligations have been incorporated in CETA except for the SPS Agreement's obligations, the same problems arise for the EU's obligations under CETA.

Another reason that was brought forward with respect to a reform of the EU GMO law is the missing harmonisation with the legislation of major trade partners possibly leading to trade disruptions. However, this is not a problem that arises at the interface of EU law and WTO law as analysed in Chap. 6. And, also at the interface of EU law and CETA, a missing harmonisation seems to be less problematic than expected. Nevertheless, CETA's impact on a future EU GMO regulation will be analysed.

---

[4] *General Agreement on Tariffs and Trade 1994* ('GATT'), Annex 1 to the *Marrakesh Agreement establishing the World Trade Organization* (concluded 15 April 1994, entered into force 1 January 1995) 1867 UNTS 3.

[5] For more details, see Chap. 6, p. 213.

[6] *Agreement on Technical Barriers to Trade*, Annex 1 to the *Marrakesh Agreement establishing the World Trade Organization*, see footnote 4.

7.3 The Proposal for a New Regulation by the EU Commission

First, the debate on a new regulatory framework for genome edited plants was merely academic. As of 2019, this is no longer the case. The Council of the EU took the CJEU's judgement on targeted mutagenesis as a reason to request a study from the EU Commission on the status of new genomic techniques under EU law in 2019. In its study, the European Commission found that regulatory steps are necessary and accordingly submitted a proposal on the regulation of new genomic techniques in 2023.

7.3.1 EU Action Leading to the EU Commission's Proposal

7.3.1.1 Council Request Under Article 241 of the Treaty on the Functioning of the European Union

In 2019, the Council of the EU requested the Commission "to submit a study in light of the CJEU's judgment in Case C-528/16 regarding the status of novel genomic techniques under Union law".[7] Furthermore, it asked the Commission to submit a proposal or other measures that the Commission deems necessary in light of its study. In its request, the Council referred to practical questions that were raised by the CJEU's judgment for the national authorities as well as the plant breeding and research sector in the EU, such as difficulties to distinguish products obtained by new mutagenesis techniques from those products obtained by conventional mutagenesis techniques.[8]

7.3.1.2 The EU Commission's Study on New Genomic Techniques

With its study, the European Commission aimed at providing clarity on the regulation of new genomic techniques[9] ('NGTs') including a variety of topics and perspectives.[10] The study should provide a basis to decide on any further action on the regulation of NGTs.[11]

---

[7] Council of the European Union (2019); Šefčovič (2021).

[8] Council of the European Union (2019), para 4.

[9] According to the Commission, the term "new genomic techniques" comprises all techniques "that are capable of altering the genetic material of an organism and that have emerged or have been developed since 2001, when the current legislation on genetically modified organisms was adopted", see European Commission (2021a), p. 2, 6.

[10] *Cf.* European Commission (2021a), p. 6.

[11] *Cf.* European Commission (2021a), p. 6.

The Commission's study was based on and informed by contributions that were collected via targeted consultations with Member States' competent authorities and EU-level stakeholders.[12] Additional contributions from EFSA, the Commission's *Joint Research Centre*[13] ('JRC'), the *Group of Chief Scientific Advisors,*[14] the *European Network of GMO Laboratories*[15] ('ENGL') and the *European Group on Ethics in Science and New Technologies* were taken into account.[16]

Additionally, the Commission took the *European Green Deal*[17] and the *'farm to fork' strategy*[18] into account when considering the status of new genomic techniques under EU law.[19]

7.3.1.2.1 Main Part: The Status of New Genomic Techniques Under EU Law

The study's main part concerns the status of new genomic techniques under EU law. In this part, the Commission elaborates on different aspects of the status of NGTs.[20] The Commission primarily summarises the results of its targeted consultation and presents the views and opinions expressed on different aspects by Member States' competent authorities and stakeholders as well as by expert bodies.

Concluding the main part, the findings by the Commission, including the Member States' and stakeholders' views as well as expert opinions, are discussed.[21]

In this discussion, the Commission states that there is a high interest in NGT-related research in the EU, but that the current regulatory framework already has had and will have a negative impact on such research in the EU.[22]

Furthermore, the Commission finds that several plant NGT products could contribute to "a more resilient and sustainable agri-food system" and thereby could help to achieve the objectives of the European Green Deal, more specifically the "farm to fork" and biodiversity strategy and fulfil the United Nations Sustainable Development

[12] European Commission (2021a), p. 7.

[13] See European Commission, https://joint-research-centre.ec.europa.eu/index_en.

[14] See European Commission, https://research-and-innovation.ec.europa.eu/strategy/support-policy-making/scientific-support-eu-policies/group-chief-scientific-advisors_en.

[15] See European Commission, https://gmo-crl.jrc.ec.europa.eu/.

[16] European Commission (2021a), p. 7.

[17] European Commission (2019).

[18] European Commission (2020).

[19] European Commission (2021a), p. 6.

[20] These different aspects include the state of the art on NGTs, the legal status of organisms developed through NGTs, the implementation and enforcement of EU GMO legislation with regard to NGTs, the safety of NGTs, research and innovation aspects, external views on potential NGT-related opportunities and benefits, external views on potential NGT-related challenges and concerns, views relating to SMEs and intellectual property, views on the labelling of NGT products as well as ethical aspects of NGTs, see European Commission (2021a), pp. 11–50.

[21] European Commission (2021a), pp. 51–58.

[22] *Cf.* European Commission (2021a), p. 51.

Goals.[23] It adds that "sustainability in the food system goes beyond the environment and can involve seed and food security, safety, nutrition, competitiveness and social aspects."[24] Accordingly, the assessment of NGTs' impact on the agri-food system should not only focus on the immediate effects but should have a broader perspective.[25] An upcoming legislative initiative under the "farm to fork" strategy will provide a framework for assessing the sustainability of food systems and will also include NGT products.[26]

With regard to the safety of NGT products, the Commission states that the study has shown that NGTs and NGT products vary considerably and that it is, therefore, impossible to draw general conclusions.[27] Instead, it points to the wide recognition of the case-by-case approach when it comes to the risk assessment of NGTs and their products.[28] But, it repeats and adopts EFSA's view that "SDN-1, SDN-2 and cisgenesis techniques present similar hazards to conventional breeding".[29]

Also, the Commission in its discussion lists several terms of the EU GMO legislation for which there is a lack of appropriate definition leading to regulatory uncertainty, including the term *mutagenesis* and the concept of *long safety record* or *conventionally used in a number of applications*, respectively.[30]

Furthermore, it elaborates on the problem that comes along with the lack of detection methods for NGT products and that has been raised by Member States' competent authorities, stakeholders as well as by the *European Union Reference Laboratory for Genetically Modified Food and Feed* ('EURL GMFF') and ENGL.[31] As a solution, it points to document-based traceability systems but also mentions additional costs of such systems that could negatively impact international competitiveness.[32]

The Commission also shortly summarises the regulatory approach to NGTs adapted by non-EU countries and notes that diverging regulatory approaches are of concern for Member States and stakeholders in the EU, especially for the feed sector.[33] In this respect, it also mentions the potential of trade disputes over technical barriers to trade in the WTO forum.[34]

As one of the last points, the European Commission addresses the public perception of NGTs which is rather negative although public knowledge of NGTs is scarce.

[23] European Commission (2021a), p. 52.
[24] European Commission (2021a), p. 52.
[25] *Cf.* European Commission (2021a), p. 52.
[26] European Commission (2021a), p. 52.
[27] European Commission (2021a), p. 52.
[28] *Cf.* European Commission (2021a), p. 53.
[29] *Cf.* European Commission (2021a), pp. 53–54.
[30] European Commission (2021a), p. 54.
[31] European Commission (2021a), pp. 55–56.
[32] European Commission (2021a), p. 56.
[33] European Commission (2021a), p. 56.
[34] European Commission (2021a), p. 57.

In this regard, it stresses the importance of consumers' possibility to make informed choices which includes labelling.[35]

7.3.1.2.2 Conclusions of the Study

The EU Commission concludes its study by pointing to the benefits and concerns of NGTs. "[F]urther policy action should aim to reap the benefits of innovation while addressing concerns."[36] To achieve this aim opposing views must be reconciled to find common ground.[37] According to the Commission, NGTs have the potential to contribute to a more sustainable agri-food system as envisaged by the European Green Deal and the "farm to fork" strategy.[38]

The Commission labels the GMO legislation as stringent with "rigid risk assessment guidance" which makes it difficult to adapt the legislation to scientific progress, especially in the case of NGTs.[39] This also affects the implementation stage.[40] Furthermore, it questions the legality of applying different levels of regulatory oversight to similar products with similar risks, as is the case for organisms obtained by conventional breeding and those obtained by certain genome editing techniques or *cisgenesis*.[41] Overall, there are many signs that suggest that the current legal framework is not appropriate for NGTs and their products, but instead needs to be adapted to scientific progress.[42]

Therefore, "the follow-up to this study should confirm whether adaptation is needed and, if so, what form it should take and which policy instruments should be used in order for the legislation to be resilient, future-proof and uniformly applied as well as contribute to a sustainable agri-food system."[43]

7.3.1.3 Preparatory Steps for a Proposal Taken by the EU Commission

As a follow-up to its study, the European Commission has initiated the process of proposing a legal framework for plants obtained by targeted mutagenesis and *cisgenesis* and for their food and feed products.[44] It has published an inception impact

---

[35] European Commission (2021a), pp. 57–58.

[36] European Commission (2021a), p. 59.

[37] European Commission (2021a), p. 59.

[38] European Commission (2021a), p. 59.

[39] European Commission (2021a), p. 59.

[40] European Commission (2021a), p. 59.

[41] European Commission (2021a), p. 59.

[42] European Commission (2021a), p. 59.

[43] European Commission (2021a), pp. 59–60.

[44] For an overview of the legislative process and the current status, European Commission, https://ec.europa.eu/info/law/better-regulation/have-your-say/initiatives/13119-Legislation-for-plants-produced-by-certain-new-genomic-techniques_en.

assessment as a first step of the legislative process.[45] Public consultation on a proposal of *a regulation for plants obtained by targeted mutagenesis and cisgenesis and for their food and feed products* has taken place from April to July 2022.[46]

7.3.2 The Commission's Proposal for a New Regulation on Plants Obtained by Certain New Genomic Techniques

In July 2023, the Commission has published its proposal for a new regulation on plants obtained by certain new genomic techniques and their food and feed.[47]

7.3.2.1 The Proposal's Objectives

As has already been outlined in the Commission's study on NGTs,[48] there is a high interest in the use of plants obtained by new genomic techniques, not only in the EU but globally. Plants obtained by new genomic techniques are considered helpful to tackle the impact of current challenges, such as climate change and biodiversity loss, on the agri-food system and to develop a more resilient and sustainable agriculture.[49]

Furthermore, the Commission states that the use of new genomic techniques in the agricultural sector could help to decrease the EU's dependencies on imports of plant proteins, a dependence that has been revealed by the Covid-19 pandemic and the Russian war against Ukraine.[50]

To achieve all these objectives, the Commission with its proposal aims at enabling the development and placing on the market of plants and plant products that contribute to the sustainability objectives of the European Green Deal and of the Farm to Fork and Biodiversity strategies.[51]

---

[45] European Commission (2021b); "Impact assessments examine whether there is a need for EU action and analyse the possible impacts of available solutions. These are carried out during the preparation phase, before the Commission finalises a proposal for a new law. They provide evidence to inform and support the decision-making process.", see European Commission, https://ec.europa.eu/info/law/law-making-process/planning-and-proposing-law/impact-assessments_en.

[46] See European Commission, https://ec.europa.eu/info/law/better-regulation/have-your-say/initiatives/13119-Legislation-for-plants-produced-by-certain-new-genomic-techniques_en.

[47] European Commission (2023b).

[48] See above, p. 262.

[49] See European Commission (2023b), p. 2; this connection between plants obtained by new biotechnological methods and a more sustainable agriculture has also been outlined in the Farm to Fork Strategy as part of the European Commission's Green Deal, see European Commission (2020), p. 8.

[50] See European Commission (2023b), p. 2.

[51] See European Commission (2023b), p. 4.

According to the Commission, its study has disclosed several challenges for new genomic techniques under the regulatory framework currently applicable: first, the risk assessment requirements and authorisation procedure are not adequate for the variety of plants that can be obtained by targeted mutagenesis and cisgenesis. Second, there are difficulties to enforce the current applicable GMO legislation with regard to certain plants obtained by new genomic techniques due to the lack of detection methods. And third, the current GMO legislation hinders the development of innovative products with potential benefits for breeders, farmers, food business operators, consumers and the environment.[52]

Furthermore, the Commission points to other countries which have already taken measures to adapt their regulation to the particularities of new genomic techniques. There is a risk that the EU will be left behind on this issue if it does not adapt its legislation accordingly.[53] This again, "would lead to less strategic autonomy for the Union."[54]

7.3.2.2 The Proposal's Scope

The proposal's scope comprises plants obtained by targeted mutagenesis and cisgenesis, including intragenesis, so-called new genomic techniques, as well as products containing or consisting of these plants and food and feed containing, consisting or produced from these plants.[55] The new proposal only comprises these techniques and products thereof because these techniques, in contrast to transgenesis techniques, do not introduce genetic material from non-crossable species.[56] Due to their mode of operation EFSA considers them as carrying less risks than transgenesis or conventional breeding techniques.[57] The scope is limited to plants since most research and development has been conducted with plants. And some plant applications are close to enter the market.[58]

7.3.2.3 Specific Features of the Legislative Proposal

The proposal establishes two categories of NGT plants for which different rules apply, category 1 NGT plants (Sect. 7.3.2.3.1) and category 2 NGT plants (Sect. 7.3.2.3.2).

---

[52] See European Commission (2023b), p. 3; for an analysis of the EU Commission's study on new genomic techniques, see above, p. 262.

[53] See European Commission (2023b), p. 3.

[54] See European Commission (2023b), p. 3.

[55] See European Commission (2023b), p. 1.

[56] See European Commission (2023b), p. 1.

[57] See European Commission (2023b), pp. 1–2.

[58] See European Commission (2023b), p. 1.

7.3.2.3.1 Category 1 NGT Plants

Category 1 NGT plants are completely excluded from the scope of the EU GMO law[59] and only subject to the rules laid down in the proposed regulation. NGT plants are qualified as category 1 NGT plant when they fulfil the criteria of equivalence to conventional plants laid down in Annex I or are progeny of such a category 1 NGT plant.[60] According to Annex I, a category 1 NGT plant is considered equivalent to conventional plants when it differs from the recipient or parental plant *by no more than 20 individual genetic modifications* in any DNA sequence sharing sequence similarity with the targeted site that can be predicted by bioinformatic tools. Furthermore, the modification induced must be of one of the following types:

(1) substitution or insertion of no more than 20 nucleotides
(2) deletion of any number of nucleotides
(3) on the condition that the genetic modification does not interrupt an endogenous gene:
   (a) targeted insertion of a contiguous DNA sequence existing in the breeder's gene pool
   (b) targeted substitution of an endogenous DNA sequence with a contiguous DNA sequence existing in the breeder's gene pool
(4) targeted inversion of a sequence of any number of nucleotides
(5) any other targeted modification of any size, on the condition that the resulting DNA sequences already occur (possibly with modifications as accepted under points (1) and/or (2)) in a species from the breeder's gene pool.[61]

As the Commission has explicitly clarified, these types of modification do not encompass intragenesis techniques since EFSA could not rule out the possibility of additional hazards of intragenic plants in comparison to conventionally bred plants.[62] In contrast, targeted mutagenesis and cisgenesis techniques are comprised by the types of modification listed in Annex I to the proposed regulation and plants modified by these techniques are in general considered equivalent to conventionally bred plants.[63]

The Commission's proposal also establishes a publicly available database where declarations of the category 1 status of NGT plants shall be listed.[64]

[59] Meaning the regulatory framework that is applicable to all genetically modified plants at the time when the proposal has been submitted; for details on this framework, see Chap. 4.

[60] See European Commission (2023b), Art. 3 No 7 (p 27).

[61] European Commission (2023b), Annex I.

[62] European Commission (2023a), p. 2.

[63] European Commission (2023a), p. 2.

[64] See European Commission (2023b), Art. 9 (p 32).

7.3.2.3.1.1 Verification Procedure for Category 1 NGT Plants

NGT plants to be qualified as falling within category 1 must pass a verification procedure.[65] In the case of the deliberate release of NGT plants such verification procedure is carried out by the competent authority of the Member State.[66] For the placing on the market of NGT products the verification procedure is carried out by EFSA.[67]

7.3.2.3.1.2 Deliberate Release of Category 1 NGT Plants

Within 30 days from the date of receipt of a verification request, the competent authority of a Member State shall verify whether the requested NGT plants fulfils the criteria of Annex I. The verification report shall be made available to the other Member States and the EU Commission. They can comment on the verification report within 20 days. In the absence of comments, the competent authority of the Member State shall adopt a decision on the status of the NGT plant within 10 days from the date of the deadline for comments. When comments are made, the competent authority forwards such comments to the EU Commission which consults EFSA and prepares a draft decision. This draft is delivered in accordance with the advisory procedure laid down in Article 4 of *Regulation (EU) No 182/2011 of the European Parliament and of the Council of 16 February 2011 laying down the rules and general principles concerning mechanisms for control by Member States of the Commission's exercise of implementing powers*[68] ('Regulation 182/2011'). In this advisory procedure, the *Standing Committee on Plants, Animals, Food and Feed* ('SCoPAFF') only has advisory powers and does not vote on the Commission's draft. Instead, the final decision is taken by the EU Commission.

7.3.2.3.1.3 Placing on the Market of Category 1 NGT Plants

A verification declaration for the placing on the market of category 1 NGT plants is only necessary where such declaration has not yet been submitted under Article 6 of the proposed regulation. EFSA shall deliver its statement on the fulfilment of the criteria set out in Annex I within 30 days from the receipt of the verification request and make it available to Member States and the EU Commission. Within 30 days from the receipt of EFSA's statement, the EU Commission shall deliver a draft decision on the status of the request's NGT product. The decision on this draft is also taken in accordance with the advisory procedure laid down in Article 4 of Regulation 182/2011.

---

[65] See European Commission (2023b), Arts. 6 and 7 (pp 29, 30).

[66] See European Commission (2023b), Art. 6(1) (p 29).

[67] See European Commission (2023b), Art. 7(1) (p 30).

[68] *Regulation (EU) No 182/2011 of the European Parliament and of the Council of 16 February 2011 laying down the rules and general principles concerning mechanisms for control by Member States of the Commission's exercise of implementing powers* ('Regulation 182/2011'), OJ EU 2011, L 55/13.

7.3.2.3.1.4 No Labelling and Traceability Requirements

Category 1 NGT plants are no longer subject to labelling requirements. Instead, they shall obtain an identification number and be listed in a database.[69] Only plant seeds of category 1 NGT plants shall be labelled when made available to third parties.[70] Traceability of category 1 NGT plants shall be ensured by the identification number assigned to them.[71] Also, the possibility for Member States to restrict or prohibit the cultivation of category 1 NGT plants is no longer given.[72]

7.3.2.3.2 Category 2 NGT Plants

All NGT plants and products thereof that do not fulfil the criteria of Annex I or are progeny of such plants, qualify as category 2 NGT plants.[73] Category 2 NGT plants are subject to *Directive 2001/18/EC of the European Parliament and the Council of 12 March 2001 on the deliberate release into the environment of genetically modified organisms*[74] ('Directive 2001/18/EC' or 'Deliberate Release Directive') as well as Regulations 1829/2003 and 1830/2003 in so far as the EU Commission's proposal on new genomic techniques does not derogate from these legislative acts. In principle, such NGT plants remain subject to notification and authorisation procedures which are adapted by the Commission's proposal with regard to category 2 NGT plants.[75]

7.3.2.3.2.1 Modification of the Requirements for the Environmental Risk Assessment

The requirements for the environmental risk assessment as laid down in Regulation 2001/18/EC shall no longer apply to category 2 NGT plants. Instead, the proposal sets out new criteria for the risk assessment in its Annex II.[76] The biggest change in comparison to Directive 2001/18/EC is that the risk assessment shall be adapted to the specific risk profile of the plant being assessed.[77] Dependent on this risk profile are the type and information necessary for the risk assessment which are laid down

---

[69] See European Commission (2023b), Art. 9 (p 32).

[70] See European Commission (2023b), Art. 10 (p 32).

[71] See European Commission (2023b), recital 21 (p 20).

[72] This is in contrast to Art. 26(b) Directive 2001/18/EC.

[73] See European Commission (2023b), Art. 3 No 8 (p 28).

[74] *Directive 2001/18/EC of the European Parliament and the Council of 12 March 2001 on the deliberate release into the environment of genetically modified organisms and repealing Council Directive 90/220/EC* (consolidated version from 27 March 2021) ('Directive 2001/18/EC'), Official Journal of the European Communities ('OJ EC') 2001, L 106/1.

[75] See European Commission (2023b), Arts. 13, 14, 19 (pp 33, 34, 37).

[76] See European Commission (2023b), Art. 31 (p 44).

[77] See European Commission (2023b), Annex II, Part 1.

in Annex III to Directive 2001/18/EC. The concrete risk profile is determined in consideration of the following factors: characteristics of the NGT plants and the trait(s) introduced, the function of the modified genome sequence(s), the function of any gene disrupted by the insertion of a cisgene, prior experience with the consumption of similar plants or their products, prior experience of cultivation of the same plant species or plants exhibiting similar traits, the scale and conditions of the planned release, the intended conditions of the use of the NGT plant.[78] However, the risk assessment shall always require certain information on hazard identification and characterisation, exposure assessment and risk characterisation as set out in Annex II, Part 1. The information laid down in Annex II, Parts 2 and 3 shall only be required when the specific characteristics and intended use of the category 2 NGT plant give rise to a plausible risk hypothesis in that regard.

7.3.2.3.2.2 Unlimited Validity of Authorisation After Renewal

In principle, the consent allowing for the placing of the market of category 2 NGT products shall be valid unlimitedly after it has been renewed once.[79]

7.3.2.3.2.3 Detection Methods

The submission of detection methods is still required for the notification and authorisation of category 2 NGT products.[80] However, in cases where it is not feasible to provide an analytical detection method the modalities to comply with the analytical method requirements may be adapted.[81] This must be justified by the notifier or the applicant. In case of NGT products as or in food or feed, such infeasibility of detection methods may also be concluded by the Europan Union Reference Laboratory.[82] The adaption modalities shall be specified in a EU Commission implementing act and further guidance by the *European Union Reference Laboratory for Genetically Modified Food and Feed*.[83]

7.3.2.3.2.4 Labelling Requirements

The labelling requirements set out in Directive 2001/18/EC and *Regulation (EC) No 1829/2003 of the European Parliament and of the Council of 22 September 2003 on genetically modified food and feed*[84] ('Regulation 1829/2003') and *Regulation (EC)*

---

[78] See European Commission (2023b), Annex II, Part 1.

[79] See European Commission (2023b), Arts. 17 and 21 (pp 36, 39).

[80] See European Commission (2023b), Arts. 14 and 19 (pp 34, 37).

[81] See European Commission (2023b), Arts. 14(1)(l) and 19(4) (pp 35, 38).

[82] See European Commission (2023b), Art. 19(4) (p 38).

[83] See European Commission (2023b), Arts. 27(e) and 29(2) (p 43).

[84] *Regulation (EC) No 1829/2003 of the European Parliament and of the Council of 22 September 2003 on genetically modified food and feed* (consolidated version from 27 March 2021), OJ EU 2003, L 268/1 ('Regulation 1829/2003').

No 1830/2003 of the European Parliament and of the Council of 22 September 2003 concerning the traceability and labelling of genetically modified organisms and the traceability of food and feed products produced from genetically modified organisms[85] ('Regulation 1830/2003') remain applicable to category 2 NGT plants.[86]

7.3.2.3.2.5 *Sustainability Incentives*

The EU Commission's proposal establishes a new incentive system for category 2 NGT plants and products that contain traits relevant for sustainability. Such traits are further specified in Annex III to the proposal and include *inter alia* traits that induce tolerance/resistance to biotic or abiotic stresses, support a more efficient use of resources, such as water and nutrients, induce characteristics that enhance the sustainability of storage or processing, or reduce the need for external inputs, such as plant protection products or fertilisers.[87]

For such plants, the EU Commission's proposal contains two simplifications for the authorisation procedure: the opinion by EFSA shall be delivered within 4 months instead of 6 months and SME applicants shall be exempted from paying financial contributions to the Union Reference Laboratory and to the European Network of GMO Laboratories as provided for in Article 32 of Regulation 1829/2003.[88] Furthermore, a pre-submission advice shall be provided by EFSA on plausible risk hypotheses that a notifier or applicant has identified and that needs to be addressed in an environmental risk assessment prior to notification or authorisation. In case of SMEs, EFSA is even allowed to give advice on the design of studies.[89]

7.3.2.3.2.6 *Opt-Out Not Applicable to Category 2 NGT Plants*

The possibility for Member States to prohibit or restrict the cultivation of GM plants for reasons of environmental policy objectives, town and country planning, land use, socioeconomic impacts, avoidance of GMO presence in other products, agricultural policy objectives and public policy[90] is not applicable to category 2 NGT plants.[91]

---

[85] *Regulation (EC) No 1830/2003 of the European Parliament and of the Council of 22 September 2003 concerning the traceability and labelling of genetically modified organisms and the traceability of food and feed products produced from genetically modified organisms* (consolidated version from 26 July 2019), OJ EU 2003, L 268/24 ('Regulation 1830/2003').

[86] See European Commission (2023b), Arts. 16 and 23 (pp 36, 44).

[87] This list may be adopted to scientific and technological progress and to new evidence by delegated acts by the EU Commission in accordance with Arts. 26 and 22(8) of European Commission (2023b).

[88] See European Commission (2023b), Art. 22(2) (p 39).

[89] See European Commission (2023b), Art. 22(3), (4) (p 40).

[90] As provided for by Article 26(b) Directive 2001/18/EC.

[91] See European Commission (2023b), Art. 25 (p 42).

7.3.3 European Economic and Social Committee's Opinion

The European Economic and Social Committee[92] ('EESC') during the legislative process has adopted an opinion on the EU Commission's proposal.[93] The EESC welcomes the principle of an environmental and health risk assessment tailored to the type of modification applied. However, it raises several points that need to be improved in the EU Commission's proposal to get full support from EESC. Three of them will be displayed in further detail.

First, the Committee calls on the Commission to ensure an adequate monitoring of potential systemic effects on human health and the environment that could be caused using new genomic techniques.[94] Such an approach differs from the case-by-case assessment currently envisaged.[95]

Second, the Committee sees a need for changes that help to ensure that the organic sector and the GM-free sector can continue to exist as before.[96] Since category 1 NGT plants will not be allowed in the organic sector,[97] the Committee emphasises that the missing labelling and detection possibilities will pose a threat to the organic and GM-free sector. Extensive monitoring processes will be required for the organic and GM-free sector to stay free from category 1 NGT plants or plant material which could entail high costs that could weigh heavily on the sector.[98] The Committee also calls on the Commission to further assess the long-term effects that the proposal could have on alternative agricultural models, such as organic, ecological, regenerative and traditional farming methods, also taking into account the social and cultural aspects of these farming methods.[99]

Third, the EESC mentions the challenges that patents on new genomic techniques could pose to farmers and seed SMEs which want to use plants modified with these new techniques.[100] It therefore calls on the EU Commission to consider these questions at the same time as it discusses the proposal at hand and not at a later stage as originally planned.[101]

Additionally, the EESC criticises the Commission's statement of potential equivalence between natural plants and category 1 NGT plants,[102] it addresses the issue

---

[92] The European Economic and Social Committee is composed of 329 Members (appointed for a 5-year term) that belong to one of these groups: employers, workers or civil society organisations, for more information see https://www.eesc.europa.eu/en/about.

[93] See European Economic and Social Committee (2023).

[94] See European Economic and Social Committee (2023), 1.1.

[95] See European Economic and Social Committee (2023), 3.7.

[96] See European Economic and Social Committee (2023), 1.3.

[97] See European Commission (2023b), Art. 5(2) (p. 28).

[98] See European Economic and Social Committee (2023), 3.10.

[99] See European Economic and Social Committee (2023), 3.18.

[100] See European Economic and Social Committee (2023), 1.4.

[101] See European Economic and Social Committee (2023), 3.9.

[102] See European Economic and Social Committee (2023), 4.4.1.3.

of potential irreversibility which brings with it a high responsibility,[103] and it calls on the Commission to regulate the technologies of new genomic techniques themselves, also to prevent bioterrorism.[104]

7.4 The Commission's Proposal in the Context of Other Reform Proposals

In between the CJEU's decision and the publication of the EU Commission's proposal, there have been a number of proposals from academia and industry on a new regulatory framework for genome edited plants. In particular, calls for a more lenient regulation of genome edited plants in the EU have become more prominent since the CJEU's ruling.

The following part presents these reform proposals in relation to the Commission's proposal and points out differences and similarities.

7.4.1 Using the Flexibility of the Currently Applicable Framework

While some proposals that were published in the past wanted to focus on the instruments already laid down in Directive 2001/18/EC before discussing major changes,[105] this option is rather unlikely in light of the EU Commission's proposal for a new regulation.

7.4.2 Changing the Current Legal Framework

Other stakeholders argue one step further and want to amend the current GMO law. They criticise the current regulation as being time-consuming and costly, thereby hampering innovation.[106] Also, the current regime cannot be applied to genome

---

[103] See European Economic and Social Committee (2023), 1.5.

[104] See European Economic and Social Committee (2023), 1.6, 4.3.1–4.3.2.

[105] See Wasmer (2019), pp. 1–5, 7–8; Jones (2019), p. 110; van der Meer et al. (2021), pp. 9–10, 17–18; see also Group of Chief Scientific Advisors (2018), p. 4; *cf.* Dederer (2019a), p. 245; Dederer (2019b), pp. 113–114; Eriksson et al. (2020c), p. 233; The Norwegian Biotechnology Advisory Board (2018a), p. 2; The Norwegian Biotechnology Advisory Board (2018b), pp. 32–33.

[106] Ministerie van Infrastructuur en Waterstaat (2017), p. 2-x; Sowa et al. (2021), p. 184; Group of Chief Scientific Advisors (2018), pp. 5–6; see also Purnhagen and Wesseler (2019), p. 2310.

edited organisms in a scientifically sound way.[107] Therefore, any amendment should be informed by scientific evidence.[108] Where other reasons, such as ethical, economic or social ones, inform decision-making, this should be clearly mentioned.[109]

While these proposals prefer an amendment of the current legislative framework over developing a new framework due to time constraints,[110] the decision for a totally new framework for targeted mutagenesis techniques has been made by the EU Commission with its new proposal. Nevertheless, the proposals contain elements and concepts that can also be relevant for the design of a new regulation.

7.4.2.1 Product-Based Scope

The CJEU, with its judgment in 2018, ended a decade-long controversy by implicitly opting for a primarily process-based interpretation of the GMO definition.[111] This was heavily criticised by scientists and scholars who do not want genome editing applications to be covered by the Directive's GMO definition.[112] Rather, the Directive's application should be triggered by the product itself and not the techniques of modification.[113] Such product-based regulation is justified on the grounds that it is more scientifically sound than process-based regulation.[114] It is stated that risks are related to the new trait introduced by genetic modification and not to the modification technique used.[115]

To implement such a product-based approach, it is *inter alia* suggested that the EU could follow the definition of a *living modified organism* ('LMO') laid down in the *Cartagena Protocol on Biosafety to the Convention on Biological Diversity*[116]

---

[107] The *Leopoldina* criticises Directive 2001/18 as "scientifically and technically ambiguous", see Nationale Akademie der Wissenschaften Leopoldina et al. (2019), p. 71; also *EPSO* notes a "paradoxical legal situation", see EPSO Agricultural Technology Working Group (2019), p. 2.

[108] Group of Chief Scientific Advisors (2018), p. 7.

[109] Group of Chief Scientific Advisors (2018), p. 7.

[110] Nationale Akademie der Wissenschaften Leopoldina et al. (2019), p. 73; Association Francaise des Biotechnologies Végétales and Wissenschaftlerkreis Grüne Gentechnik e.V. (2020), Explanatory note, p. 1–2; for an overview of the different options see Wasmer (2019), p. 6.

[111] CJEU, *Case C-528/16 Confédération paysanne et al.* (25 July 2018), ECLI:EU:C:2018:583, 27–38.

[112] See for an overview Andersen and Schreiber (2020), pp. 101–103.

[113] *Cf.* Group of Chief Scientific Advisors (2018), p. 4; Eriksson et al. (2020c), p. 232; Ministerie van Infrastructuur en Waterstaat (2017), pp. 3–4; Huang et al. (2016), p. 110 this has already been proposed before the CJEU's judgment, *cf.* Araki and Ishii (2015), p. 147.

[114] EPSO Agricultural Technology Working Group (2019), p. 1, 3; Nationale Akademie der Wissenschaften Leopoldina et al. (2019), p. 73; *cf.* Eriksson et al. (2020c), p. 232; Group of Chief Scientific Advisors (2018), pp. 4, 6; Kok et al. (2019), pp. 24–25 with further references; Lassoued et al. (2020), p. 1; Ricroch et al. (2016), pp. 1366–1367.

[115] Eriksson et al. (2020c), p. 232; see also Ricroch et al. (2016), p. 1366.

[116] *Cartagena Protocol on Biosafety to the Convention on Biological Diversity* ('Cartagena Protocol') (adopted 29 January 2000, entered into force 11 September 2003) 2226 UNTS 208.

('Cartagena Protocol').[117] The Protocol's definition requires a novel trait for an organism to be genetically modified[118] and is thereby linked to the product as such.

The EU Commission in its new proposal has again implemented a rather process-based approach since regulation is triggered by the use of certain techniques.[119] Nevertheless, the proposal also contains some product-based elements, e.g. regulatory simplifications for category 2 NGT plants that are related to the trait of the plants.[120]

7.4.2.2 Exempt Genome Editing from EU GMO Law

Due to detection difficulties of genome edited plants and similarities to conventionally bred plants, most stakeholders want to exempt genome edited organisms from the current GMO law in the EU.[121] It is stressed that genetically identical products derived from conventional breeding techniques on the one hand and genome editing techniques on the other should be regulated in the same way.[122] This is reasoned by the fact that the application of genome editing techniques is more precise and therefore at least as safe as conventional breeding methods.[123] Also, applicants have

---

[117] Eriksson et al. (2020c), p. 232; see also EPSO Agricultural Technology Working Group (2019), p. 4.

[118] The definition of an LMO in Art. 3 lit. g Cartagena Protocol reads as follows: "any living organism that possesses **a novel combination** of genetic material (…)" (emphasis added). The Cartagena Protocol is implemented in EU law by *Regulation (EC) No 1946/2003 of the European Parliament and of the Council of 15 July 2003 on transboundary movements of genetically modified organisms*, OJ EU 2003, L 287/1.

[119] See above, p. 267.

[120] See above, p. 272.

[121] Jorasch (2019), p. 85 who suggests to exempt those GMOs from regulatory oversight that (a) do not contain a novel combination of genetic material, (b) do only contain genetic material from sexually compatible plant species, and (c) are the result of spontaneous or induced mutagenesis; see also Bioökonomierat (2019), p. 2 which suggests to exempt techniques from the EU law that do not alter more than 20 base pairs; *cf.* Eriksson et al. (2020c), p. 232; Deutsche Industrievereinigung Biotechnologie and Verband der Chemischen Industrie e.V. (2020), p. 2; Dederer (2019b), p. 114 the exemption of GMOs with minor changes from approval procedure has already been proposed by Voß in 2006, *cf.* Voß (2006), p. 262.

[122] *Cf.* Eriksson et al. (2020c), p. 232; Eriksson (2019), p. 571; *EPSO Agricultural Technology Working Group (*2019*), 2*; Nationale Akademie der Wissenschaften Leopoldina et al. (2019), p. 73; Wasmer (2019), p. 9; Duensing et al. (2018), p. 1; Jorasch (2019), p. 85; Seitz (2018), p. 764; in this regard some scholars also mention the principle of non-discrimination which is laid down in EU law and mandates for an equivalent regulation of mutagenesis techniques, see e.g. Hjort et al. (2021), p. 2.

[123] *Cf.* EPSO Agricultural Technology Working Group (2019), p. 2; Hamburger (2018), p. 3; Deutsche Industrievereinigung Biotechnologie and Verband der Chemischen Industrie e.V. (2020), p. 2; Huang et al. (2016), p. 110; see also Group of Chief Scientific Advisors (2018), p. 3 stating that "[gene editing] products are potentially safer than the products of random mutagenesis"; already in 2017 the *High Level Group of Scientific Advisors* of the Scientific Advice Mechanism of the European Commission noted that "genetically and phenotypically similar products deriving

difficulties in complying with the requirement to provide detection and identification methods for the induced mutation(s) that is laid down in the current framework.[124] The methods of detection for genome edited organisms, especially in the case of the alteration of only one or two base pairs, are currently limited.[125] Due to these limitations, the detection of unauthorised GMOs is a practical challenge.[126]

Regarding possible changes, it is generally stated that a broad generic definition would allow for a flexible adaption to technological progress but still entail legal uncertainty for applicants. Whereas a specifically defined scope would bring legal certainty for applicants but make it more difficult for regulation to adapt to future innovation.[127]

According to the German science academy *Leopoldina*, organisms with genetic information that could only have been inserted artificially should qualify as GMOs under the Deliberate Release Directive.[128] Genome edited organisms in which a combination of genetic material is present that could also have been inserted naturally or by means of conventional breeding methods should not fall under the legal definition of the Directive.[129]

Furthermore, changes to Annex I of Directive 2001/18/EC are proposed.[130] Most proposals suggest an amendment of Annex I part A and part B.

One proposal is to add *targeted molecular techniques* to the exhaustive list of techniques that do not result in a genetic modification laid down in Annex I A, part 2.[131] Others suggest updating Annex I B to also exclude targeted mutagenesis techniques from the Directive's scope.[132] Therefore, the term "mutagenesis" should be

---

from the use of different techniques are not expected to present significantly different risks", High Level Group of Scientific Advisors (2017), p. 19.

[124] Sowa et al. (2021), pp. 184–185; see also Group of Chief Scientific Advisors (2018), p. 4.

[125] Sowa et al. (2021), p. 184; *cf.* Kok et al. (2019), p. 28; this is disputed by Engelhard et al. (2021), p. 5 and Hissting (2021).

[126] Sowa et al. (2021), p. 184; *cf.* Group of Chief Scientific Advisors (2018), p. 5; Jorasch (2019), p. 85; Kok et al. (2019), p. 28; Eriksson et al. (2020c), p. 231; this is questioned by *Habets et al.* who note that "plant breeders will want their genome edited crops to be distinguishable from other crops. They will most likely provide the genetic modification in order to obtain intellectual property rights", see Habets et al. (2019), p. 20–21; this is also questioned by Duensing et al. (2018), p. 9.

[127] Commissie Genetische Modificatie COGEM (2019), p. 25.

[128] They propose to amend the definition to: "in which the genetic material **is** altered **in the shape of insertions of genetic information into the genome** in a way that does not occur naturally, see Nationale Akademie der Wissenschaften Leopoldina et al. (2019), p. 74.

[129] Nationale Akademie der Wissenschaften Leopoldina et al. (2019), p. 74; see also Wasmer (2019), p. 9.

[130] Ministerie van Infrastructuur en Waterstaat (2017), pp. 2–3; see also Nationale Akademie der Wissenschaften Leopoldina et al. (2019), p. 74.

[131] Nationale Akademie der Wissenschaften Leopoldina et al. (2019), p. 74; EPSO Agricultural Technology Working Group (2019), p. 4; see also Wasmer (2019), p. 9; Association Francaise des Biotechnologies Végétales and Wissenschaftlerkreis Grüne Gentechnik e.V. (2020), Explanatory note, p. 2.

[132] *Cf.* Dederer (2019a), p. 245; the CJEU opted for a strict interpretation of this term deciding that it only refers to conventional random mutagenesis techniques, see CJEU, *Case C-528/16 - Confédération paysanne et al.* (25 July 2018), ECLI:EU:C:2018:583, paras 51–54.

defined to explicitly include modern mutagenesis techniques.[133] In addition to any amendment, the German science academy *Leopoldina* recommends a mandatory preliminary examination procedure conducted by a competent authority to examine on a case-by-case basis whether genome edited organisms fall within the scope of Annex I A, part 2 or Annex I B.[134]

In contrast to excluding specific techniques from the Directive's scope, the Dutch *Ministerie van Infrastructure en Waterstaat* suggests a "revised exemption mechanism"[135] with general criteria to be incorporated into Annex I B.[136] The Ministry prefers to focus on general criteria rather than listing specific techniques due to difficulties in clear distinctions.[137] Annex I B should be divided into two parts.[138] Part A should exempt conventional random mutagenesis in general from the Directive's scope.[139] Part B should exempt GMOs that fulfil the following criteria:

(1) no genetic material is introduced other than material from the same plant species or which could be exchanged through traditional breeding methods, and
(2) mutations are created by using recombinant nucleic acid molecules that are only transiently present in plant cells.[140]

The exemption mechanism should be designed in a manner "that allows any person to determine whether or not the Directive applies to the GMOs resulting from the use of any technique.“[141] According to the Dutch Ministry, such an exemption mechanism with generally formulated criteria makes it easier for the legislator to keep the Directive up to date.[142]

While all these amendments to the currently applicable Deliberate Release Directive are rather unlikely in light of the EU Commission's proposal for a new regulation, the proposal nevertheless incorporates some of these proposals. Both the proposals from the *Leopoldina* and the Dutch *Ministerie van Infrastructure en*

---

[133] EPSO Agricultural Technology Working Group (2019), p. 4.

[134] The *Leopoldina* suggests laying down this preliminary examination procedure in a new Annex I C. EFSA should be involved in the procedure by giving a binding scientific option, *cf.* Nationale Akademie der Wissenschaften Leopoldina et al. (2019), 74-x; a similar procedure is proposed by Association Francaise des Biotechnologies Végétales and Wissenschaftlerkreis Grüne Gentechnik e.V. (2020), pp. 3–4 (Explanatory note).

[135] Ministerie van Infrastructuur en Waterstaat (2017), pp. 5–6.

[136] Ministerie van Infrastructuur en Waterstaat (2017), p. 4.

[137] Ministerie van Infrastructuur en Waterstaat (2017), p. 7.

[138] Ministerie van Infrastructuur en Waterstaat (2017), p. 6.

[139] Ministerie van Infrastructuur en Waterstaat (2017), p. 6.

[140] Ministerie van Infrastructuur en Waterstaat (2017), p. 6; the main underlying assumption is that organisms fulfilling these criteria can also be obtained by traditional breeding and therefore can be considered equally safe, *cf.* Ministerie van Infrastructuur en Waterstaat (2017), p. 9; this proposal is also referred to by Eriksson et al. (2020c), p. 232.

[141] Ministerie van Infrastructuur en Waterstaat (2017), pp. 3–4.

[142] Ministerie van Infrastructuur en Waterstaat (2017), p. 3, 4.

Waterstaat incorporate the idea that genome edited organisms or plants which could also have been obtained by natural mutation or conventional breeding should not be regulated under the current EU GMO law. This idea is also included in the EU Commission's proposal which exempts category 1 NGT plants[143] from regulatory oversight.[144]

7.4.2.3 Changing Risk Assessment and Risk Management

Proposals are not only concerned with the scope of the EU GMO law but also with tailoring the current risk assessment and risk management processes to the particularities of genome edited plants. Additionally, there are proposals to also include ethical and value considerations in the assessment of genome edited organisms.[145]

7.4.2.3.1 Tailoring Risk Assessment to the Particularities of Genome Edited Plants

The overall aim of these proposals is to update the current risk assessment procedures to technological progress.[146] To achieve this aim, it is proposed to transform the Annexes of the Deliberate Release Directive as well as *Commission Implementing Regulation (EU) No 503/2013 of 3 April 2013 on applications for authorisation of genetically modified food and feed in accordance with Regulation (EC) No 1829/2003*[147] and *Commission Directive (EU) 2018/350 of 8 March 2018 amending Directive 2001/18/EC as regards the environmental risk assessment of genetically modified organisms*[148] into implementing acts that would make them amendable by comitology procedure.[149] Criticism is in particular formulated with regard to the mandatory animal feeding studies and the mandatory field trials.[150]

---

[143] "category 1 NGT plants" are defined as plants that (a) fulfil the criteria of equivalence to conventional plants, set out in Annex I of the EU Commission's proposal or (b) are progeny of the NGT plant(s) referred to in point (a), including progeny derived by crossing of such plants, on the condition that there are no further modifications that would make it subject to Directive 2001/18/EC or Regulation 1829/2003, see European Commission (2023b), Art. 3 No 7 (p 27).

[144] See European Commission (2023b), Art. 5(1) (p 28).

[145] See Bechtold (2018); Antonsen and Dassler (2021).

[146] Eriksson et al. (2020b), p. 349; Wasmer (2019), p. 9.

[147] *Commission Implementing Regulation (EU) No 503/2013 of 3 April 2013 on applications for authorisation of genetically modified food and feed in accordance with Regulation (EC) No 1829/2003 of the European Parliament and of the Council and amending Commission Regulations (EC) No 641/2004 and (EC) No 1981/2006*, OJ EU 2013, L 157/1.

[148] *Commission Directive (EU) 2018/350 of 8 March 2018 amending Directive 2001/18/EC of the European Parliament and of the Council as regards the environmental risk assessment of genetically modified organisms*, OJ EU 2018, L 67/30.

[149] Eriksson et al. (2020b), p. 349.

[150] See Wasmer (2019), p. 9; Eriksson et al. (2020b), p. 349.

While the opportunity to change the rules concerning preparation and presentation of notifications and applicants is already given under the currently applicable framework,[151] this opportunity remains under the new EU Commission's proposal for category 2 NGT plants.[152] However, even in the new proposal, this does not include the possibility of changing the annexes by implementing act. Whether animal feeding studies and mandatory field trials as requirements for an application for category 2 NGT plants will remain, is dependent on the concrete Commission implementing act to be adopted. Category 1 NGT plants will no longer be subject to an environmental risk assessment according to the EU Commission's proposal.

In addition to criticism of the risk assessment, there are suggestions on how to adapt the risk assessment framework to the particularities of products arising from new and emerging genome editing techniques.[153] These include *inter alia* shifting the focus of risk assessment from the single trait that has been modified to the whole plant and selecting test organisms on a case-by-case basis.[154] Also, the need for suitable approaches to identify off-target mutations and their effects is stressed.[155] Moreover, scholars emphasise the need to develop tangible regulatory goals for the risk assessment procedure, ensuring a high level of environmental protection.[156] In their opinion, further clarification of the terminology of environmental harm is needed.[157]

The EU Commission's proposal is amending the risk assessment for category 2 NGT plants. The biggest change is the adaption of the risk assessment to the risk profile of the individual plant.[158] This adaption especially concerns data requirements that applicants must comply with. Whether this adaption will also have effects on the methods of risk assessment remains to be seen.

7.4.2.3.2 Changing the Risk Management Strategy

Proposals to change the risk management strategy and the comitology procedure do not play a major role in the debate. One proposal in this direction is to change the regulatory strategy underlying the Deliberate Release Directive from maximum to minimum harmonization.[159] This could either be achieved by switching the risk management decision to the member state level, while keeping the risk assessment

[151] See Arts. 5(7) and 17(7) of Regulation 1829/2003.
[152] See European Commission (2023b), Art. 27 lit. d (p 43).
[153] Agapito-Tenfen et al. (2018), pp. 6–8.
[154] *Cf.* Agapito-Tenfen et al. (2018), pp. 7–8.
[155] *Cf.* Agapito-Tenfen et al. (2018), pp. 10–12; see also Araki and Ishii (2015), p. 147.
[156] Eriksson et al. (2020b), p. 349; *cf.* also Agapito-Tenfen et al. (2018), pp. 12–13.
[157] Eriksson et al. (2020b), p. 349.
[158] See European Commission (2023b), Annex II, Part 1.
[159] See Purnhagen and Wesseler (2019), p. 2310 and Eriksson et al. (2020b), p. 350.

fully harmonized at the EU level.[160] Or by a so-called *opt-in procedure*.[161] Maintaining the currently fully harmonized risk management procedure, Member States would be allowed to opt-in to the cultivation of genome edited plants whenever the committee voting procedure fails.[162]

The EU Commission's proposal does not incorporate these proposals but keeps the Union-wide authorisation of category 2 NGT plants. Also, the proposal keeps the comitology procedure for the authorisation of category 2 NGT plants which continues to allow Member States to block authorisation decisions.

7.4.2.4 Abandoning labelling and detection requirements for genome edited plants

Most stakeholders argue for an exemption of genome edited plants from GMO law.[163] This would also mean that genome edited plants would no longer have to be labelled as such.[164] In case genome edited organisms with only minor alterations that are indistinguishable from conventionally altered plants are not exempt from the EU GMO law, it is stressed that those plants must be exempt from labelling requirements.[165] Mandatory labelling requirements for those plants would lead to legal uncertainty, especially for applicants during the authorisation process, and to problems for authorities controlling compliance with EU law.[166]

Another approach to overcome detection difficulties is to include so-called DNA tags into a genome edited organism to overcome these difficulties and ensure legal certainty.[167]

Furthermore, the use of the voluntary label "GM-free" is recommended for products that were produced without the use of genetic engineering.[168]

The EU Commission's proposal partly incorporates the proposals to exempt genome edited plants from labelling requirements. Category 1 NGT plants are no longer subject to labelling and detection requirements. And, also for category 2 NGT plants there is the possibility to adapt detection requirements where it is not

---

[160] Eriksson et al. (2020b), p. 350.

[161] Eriksson et al. (2020b), p. 350.

[162] Eriksson et al. (2020b), p. 350.

[163] See above for the proposals to change the scope of Directive 2001/18/EC, p 275.

[164] Ministerie van Infrastructuur en Waterstaat (2017), p. 10; Nationale Akademie der Wissenschaften Leopoldina et al. (2019), p. 75; Eriksson et al. (2020a), p. 465.

[165] *Cf.* also European Group on Ethics in Science and New Technologies (2021), p. 92.

[166] *Cf.* Bioökonomierat (2019), p. 4.

[167] Araki and Ishii (2015), pp. 148–149.

[168] Nationale Akademie der Wissenschaften Leopoldina et al. (2019), p. 76 with reference to Bioökonomierat (2019).

feasible to provide an analytical detection method.[169] But labelling requirements still apply to all category 2 NGT plants.[170]

7.4.3 New Approaches to the Regulation of Genome Edited Plants

Finally, it is also discussed to develop a new regulatory framework for genome edited plants.[171] Proposals in this regard give general criteria that a new framework should observe rather than provide specific rules. All proposals have in common that they want to include societal, ethical or sustainability aspects to the assessment of genome edited organisms.[172]

The *Federal Agency for Nature Conservation*[173] wants to keep the current regulatory framework but also add a sustainability analysis when assessing new technologies.[174] Currently, the agency is working on the implementation of a technology assessment that takes into account societal needs as reflected in the United Nations Sustainable Development Goals ('UN SDGs') and requires proof of the benefit of GMOs to society or the environment.[175] The agency stresses the importance of the precautionary principle in the regulation of new technologies and opposes the assumption that certain types of genome editing techniques can be considered safe in general.[176] Instead, it wants to keep the case-by-case approach currently in force assessing each modified organism individually.[177] Furthermore, it suggests the establishment/introduction of an international GMO registry to improve the detection and identification of GMOs in the EU.[178]

The *European Group on Ethics in Science and New Technologies*[179] ('EGE') suggests a cost-benefit analysis with a so-called "eco(systems) approach" taking into

---

[169] See European Commission (2023b), Arts. 14(1)(l) and 19(4) (pp 35, 38).

[170] See European Commission (2023b), Art. 23 (p 41).

[171] *Cf.* also Ammann (2019), p. 22.

[172] See also Seitz (2018), p. 764; for more general considerations on the inclusion of different interests in the regulation and the assessment of genome edited organisms, see Hamburger (2018) and Myskja and Myhr (2020).

[173] The *Federal Agency for Nature Conservation* is a German higher federal authority providing professional, scientific and administrative expertise in nature conservation and landscape management, see *Federal Agency for Nature Conservation (Germany). Official website*, https://www.bfn.de/en.

[174] Engelhard et al. (2021), p. 18.

[175] Engelhard et al. (2021), p. 18.

[176] Engelhard et al. (2021), pp. 17, 18–19; see also Winter (2021), p. 41.

[177] Engelhard et al. (2021), p. 17.

[178] Engelhard et al. (2021), p. 20.

[179] The *European Group on Ethics in Science and New Technologies* (EGE) is an independent, multi-disciplinary body appointed by the President of the European Commission which advises on

account the impact of GMOs on ecosystems and agricultural and natural biodiversity, land use, the economy and food security.[180] Future regulation should be proportional to the risk associated with the specific GMO.[181] Accordingly, only light regulation should apply to organisms that could also have been obtained naturally or where the editing involves the introduction of genetic material from sexually compatible plants.[182] Where major changes are introduced to the genome, field testing should be mandatory to assess possible risks.[183] Furthermore, the EGE stresses the importance to support smaller actors in undertaking risk assessments to give them an actual opportunity to enter the market with their genome edited products.[184]

The *Rathenau Instituut*[185] from the Netherlands suggests a so-called "level-based approach" as has been provided for by the *Norwegian Biotechnology Advisory Board*.[186,187] They present this approach as a middle way to keeping the current framework on the one side or exempting genome edited organisms completely from regulation on the other side. Under this level-based approach, the authorisation procedures for GMOs shall differ in relation to the assumed risks.[188] According to the *Norwegian Biotechnology Advisory Board's* proposal, a notification to the authorities may be sufficient at the lowest level, while at higher levels, organisms would require approval before their release, but may be subject to differentiated risk assessment requirements.[189] This differentiation shall also apply to labelling requirements.[190] Also, societal and ethical aspects shall play a major role when assessing genome edited organisms.[191] Examples given by the institute which could be taken

all policies where ethical, societal and fundamental rights issues intersect with the development of science and new technologies, see European Commission, https://ec.europa.eu/info/research-and-innovation/strategy/support-policy-making/scientific-support-eu-policies/ege_en.

[180] European Group on Ethics in Science and New Technologies (2021), p. 91.

[181] European Group on Ethics in Science and New Technologies (2021), p. 91.

[182] European Group on Ethics in Science and New Technologies (2021), p. 91.

[183] European Group on Ethics in Science and New Technologies (2021), pp. 91–92.

[184] European Group on Ethics in Science and New Technologies (2021), p. 92; see also Hjort et al. (2021), pp. 4–5 and Ladeur (2018), p. 200.

[185] The *Rathenau Instituut* stimulates public and political opinion forming on social aspects of science and technology. We perform research and organise debate relating to science, innovation and new technologies. The Rathenau Instituut works on the basis of an institutional decision by the government. While it remains an independent and autonomous organization, the institute now falls under the administrative responsibility of the Royal Netherlands Academy of Arts and Sciences (KNAW), see *Rathenau Instituut (Netherlands). Official website*, https://www.rathenau.nl/en.

[186] See The Norwegian Biotechnology Advisory Board (2018b); for a summary of the Proposal, see The Norwegian Biotechnology Advisory Board (2018a).

[187] Habets et al. (2019), p. 5; another approach based on the changes introduced is presented by Ammann (2019), pp. 6–12; see also Ricroch et al. (2016), pp. 1367–1368.

[188] *Cf.* Habets et al. (2019), pp. 40–41; this is also proposed by *Dederer*, see Dederer (2019a), p. 245.

[189] See The Norwegian Biotechnology Advisory Board (2018a), p. 3.

[190] *Cf.* Habets et al. (2019), p. 41.

[191] See Habets et al. (2019), pp. 5, 42; an ethical assessment of GMOs is also proposed by Antonsen and Dassler (2021).

into account comprise the goal of a specific innovation, the contribution to societal challenges, and the desirability of GMOs as a solution to these challenges.[192] In this respect, the institute also points to the factors listed in Article 26b Directive 2001/18 that Member States may rely on when opt-out of cultivation of GMOs.[193]

The EU Commission with its proposal partly incorporates the approaches brought forward by the EGE, the *Rathenau Instituut* and the *Norwegian Biotechnology Advisory Board.* It proposes a regulatory framework that differentiates between plants dependent on their risk profile. Furthermore, the EU Commission also takes up the proposal from the EGE to support SMEs. This support is given where SMEs want to bring genome edited plants with sustainable traits on the market.[194] While the EU Commission's proposal tries to establish incentives for the development and placing on the market of plants with sustainable traits, it does not incorporate ethical or societal aspects as called for by the EGE as well as by the *Rathenau Instituut*. The lack of societal aspects is also criticised by Member States stating that the EU Commission's proposal does no longer adequately ensure the consumers' freedom of choice.[195]

7.4.4 Calls to Keep the Current Regulatory Framework and Its High Level Of Protection

In contrast to proposals aiming for a change of the EU GMO law, there are calls to keep the current regulatory framework with its mandatory risk assessment procedure and its high level of protection due to unknown risks associated with genome editing techniques.[196] They also state that there are substantial differences between conventional breeding techniques and new genome editing techniques.[197] Additionally, it is stated that the current risk assessment procedures are not adequate with respect to potential risks that could arise in the case of genome edited organisms and should be adapted.[198] Furthermore, the unregulated release of genome edited organisms into the environment is seen as a threat to organic farming.[199] The lack of detection methods for genome edited plants can be overcome with the help of databases or sequences specifically induced for detection and identification.[200]

[192] Habets et al. (2019), p. 42.

[193] *Cf.* Habets et al. (2019), p. 5.

[194] See European Commission (2023b), Art. 22(2)(b), (3)(b) (p. 40).

[195] Council of the European Union (2023b), para 2; Council of the European Union (2023d).

[196] Kawall et al. (2020), p. 26.

[197] See Kawall et al. (2020).

[198] See Bauer-Panskus et al. (2020); Bøhn et al. (2020); see also the considerations by Eckerstorfer et al. (2021) and by Eckerstorfer et al. (2020).

[199] Agra Europe (2020); see also Brockmann (2021).

[200] *Cf.* Winter (2021), p. 39.

Also, it is questioned whether the new genome editing techniques really help small and medium enterprises to develop new plants since large enterprises often have patents on the use of new breeding techniques.[201]

With its proposal, the EU Commission has made clear that it does not want to keep the currently applicable framework for plants modified by targeted mutagenesis and cisgenesis. Whether a new framework for NGT plants will come and how it will look like remains to be seen. Already some Member States have raised concerns that the EU Commission's proposal no longer provides for the opportunity of Member States to restrict or prohibit the cultivation of NGT plants on their territory.[202] This demand at least gives the impression that not all Member States are in favour of a new regulation and would prefer to keep the current EU GMO law.

7.4.5 Summary

All in all, the EU Commission's proposal takes up some of the suggestions made in the literature and by industry stakeholders, but also opts for other regulatory approaches in some cases. In general, the Commission is lowering the regulatory requirements for NGT plants what many stakeholders have called for. However, the EU Commission does not opt for a product-based approach which would have also comprised the regulation of traditional GMOs, but restricts its proposal to plants modified by targeted mutagenesis and cisgenesis. This does not fulfil the demand for a technology-neutral regulatory approach. Also, societal and ethical aspects which play a major role in GMO regulation are not included in the proposal, but the EU Commission is meeting the demand for a regulation that includes sustainability aspects.

7.4.6 Addendum: Proposals on the International Regulation of Genome Edited Plants

In addition to the proposals for a reform of EU GMO law, the need for an international regulatory regime for genome edited plants is stressed repeatedly.[203] The international regulation of biotechnology is fragmented: on the one hand, this is due

---

[201] See Vollenweider (2021), p. 19.

[202] See Council of the European Union (2023a), p. 3; see also Council of the European Union (2023b), para 1.

[203] See Jorasch (2020), p. 166; Food Standards Australia New Zealand (2019), pp. 18–19; *cf.* Araki and Ishii (2015), pp. 147–149; already in the 1990s, the Transatlantic Business Dialogue called for "a common approach across the Atlantic, and ideally a centralised approval procedure", see Levidow (2007), pp. 121–122.

to different national regulatory approaches to genome edited plants.[204] On the other hand, this is due to different international treaties that regulate biotechnology and its applications and whose relationship to each other is unclear.[205]

7.4.6.1 WTO

As has been analysed, a large part of plant biotechnology regulation falls within the scope of the *Agreement on the Application of Sanitary and Phytosanitary Measures*[206] ('SPS Agreement' or 'SPS').[207] Also, the regulation of genome edited plants under EU GMO law has been addressed by WTO Members within the *Committee on Sanitary and Phytosanitary Measures*.[208] However, it is repeatedly stated that the SPS Agreement is not suited to deal adequately with biotechnology and biotechnological applications.[209] Since the Cartagena Protocol is said to address biotechnological risks more adequately,[210] it is suggested to align both agreements with regard to the definitions and procedures employed.[211] Furthermore, it is suggested to carry out the risk assessment on the international level conducted by an international body.[212] The risk management shall be conducted on the national level.[213] The proposal is accompanied by a clear separation of risk management and risk assessment.[214] Another proposal that was raised in the past, is to establish a working group on biotechnology within the WTO framework.[215]

---

[204] For an overview of regulatory approaches worldwide see Menz et al. (2020); Dederer and Hamburger (2019); Turnbull et al. (2021).

[205] *Cf.* Biber-Klemm et al. (2011), p. 302.

[206] *Agreement on the Application of Sanitary and Phytosanitary Measures*, Annex 1 to the *Marrakesh Agreement establishing the World Trade Organization* (concluded 15 April 1994, entered into force 1 January 1995) 1867 UNTS 3.

[207] See above Chap. 6, p 165.

[208] See Committee on Sanitary and Phytosanitary Measures (2018); Committee on Sanitary and Phytosanitary Measures (2019), 3.20–3.23; Committee on Sanitary and Phytosanitary Measures (2021).

[209] *Cf.* Biber-Klemm et al. (2011), p. 304; Sheldon and Josling (2002), p. 14; see also above Chap. 5, p 127.

[210] On the relationship between WTO law and Cartagena Protocol, see above Chap. 5, p 131.

[211] Biber-Klemm et al. (2011), p. 305.

[212] See Biber-Klemm et al. (2011), pp. 305–306.

[213] Biber-Klemm et al. (2011), pp. 306–307.

[214] Biber-Klemm et al. (2011), p. 305.

[215] See General Council (1999a); General Council (1999b); see also Robertson (2001), p. 223; see also above Chap. 5, p 115.

7.4.6.2 Organisation for Economic Cooperation and Development

International exchange on the regulation of new breeding techniques also takes place under the auspices of the *Organisation for Economic Cooperation and Development* ('OECD').[216] Furthermore, the European Commission in a meeting of the *Standing Committee on Plants, Animals, Food and Feed* ('SCoPAFF') in January 2022 presented a project proposal from Japan to the OECD "to collect and share among OECD members publicly available information on regulatory provisions in place and products of New Breeding Techniques".[217]

However, the OECD activities primarily aim at regulatory harmonisation by exchange of information and do not involve proposals on an international framework regulating new breeding techniques.

7.4.6.3 Human Rights Implications

One argument that is also constantly mentioned with regard to the regulation of new breeding techniques is the need of their application to fight worldwide hunger and malnutrition.[218] Accordingly, the question arises whether the right to food as laid down in Article 11 of the *International Covenant on Economic, Social and Cultural Rights*[219] ('ICESCR') requires less strict regulation of genome edited plants in the EU.

The right to food is violated when a state fails to provide within its jurisdiction the minimum level that is necessary to be free from hunger.[220] Under the ICESCR, states are under an obligation to "proactively engage in activities intended to strengthen people's access to and utilization of resources and means to ensure their livelihood, including food security."[221] This obligation could be violated where genome edited plants are compulsory to guarantee a stable agricultural production in light of changing climatic conditions or where these plants would have a major impact to boost crop output.

But probably an agricultural production adapted to changing climatic conditions and the growing need for food will not only depend on the use of genome edited plants but also on adapted agricultural practices.[222] In this respect, it is noted that the use of GMOs could also negatively impact food security by contributing to the loss

---

[216] For an overview of the OECD activities relating to new breeding techniques, see Kearns (2019).

[217] See Standing Committee on Plants, Animals, Food and Feed (2022), para M.02.

[218] See Committee on Sanitary and Phytosanitary Measures (2019), 3.20; see also above, p 262.

[219] *International Covenant on Economic, Social and Cultural Rights* ('ICESCR') (adopted 16 December 1966, entered into force 3 January 1976) 993 UNTS 3.

[220] Committee on Economic, Social and Cultural Rights (1999), para 17.

[221] Committee on Economic, Social and Cultural Rights (1999), para 15; see also the obligation laid down in Article 11 in conjunction with Article 2(1) ICESCR.

[222] *Cf.* also Juma et al. (2014), p. 488.

of traditional crops and to forgetting about traditional agricultural practices which are also necessary to adapt to changing climatic conditions.[223]

Furthermore, there are no genome edited plants adapted to climatic conditions such as drought on the market so far.[224] Also, there are no signs of acute hunger that is caused by changing climatic conditions in the EU.

Therefore, the requirements for a violation of the right to food are not met presently, but this could change in the future.

7.5 Analysis of the EU Commission's Proposal and Other Proposals in Light of Chapter 6

The amendments required by WTO law and its analysis in Chap. 6 comprise amendments to the authorisation procedure and especially to the incorporated comitology procedure. Furthermore, there are cases where the elimination of the authorisation procedure and labelling requirements should be considered. This is the case where genome edited plants are considered as *like products* to conventionally bred plants which is especially the case for the application of targeted mutagenesis techniques. Additionally, the opt-out mechanism should be reconsidered in light of WTO law requirements. This part first deals with the EU Commission's proposal, but then also considers possible effects of other reform proposals.

7.5.1 Exemption of Category 1 NGT Plants from Regulatory Oversight

The EU Commission's proposal to exempt category 1 NGT plants from the scope of Directive 2001/18/EC and Regulation 1829/2003 would help to tackle the inconsistencies that currently arise for the EU regulation of those plants under WTO law since authorisation and labelling requirements would no longer apply to this type of plants. Also, the possibility for Member States to opt out from the cultivation of these plants would no longer be given.

Accordingly, these EU regulations could no longer interfere with WTO law obligations.

223 Hahn (2008), pp. 195–196.

224 See above Chap. 2, p 13.

7.5.2 *Differentiation Between Category 1 and Category 2 NGT Plants*

As laid down in the Commission's proposed regulation, the differentiation between category 1 and category 2 NGT plants is based on the assumption that category 1 NGT plants are equivalent to conventionally bred plants and that their risks are comparable to conventionally bred plants.[225] The criteria to assess equivalence of NGT plants with conventionally bred plants as laid down in Annex I have been developed on the basis of a literature analysis of 90 scientific, peer-reviewed original studies and reviews.[226] Based on this analysis the assumption was made that NGT plants fulfilling the equivalence criteria in Annex I do not carry more risks that conventionally bred plants.[227] Accordingly, the differentiation between category 1 and category 2 plants and the regulatory differences coming along with this differentiation (such as authorisation procedures and labelling requirements) seem to be backed by scientific reasons. Nevertheless, the EU under Article 5.7 SPS Agreement has to show that scientific evidence with regard to the risks of category 2 NGT plants is inconclusive, insufficient or totally lacking to uphold the authorisation requirement for these plants. In light of rapid changes in the field of green biotechnology, the EU constantly has to check whether its differentiation is still compatible with these requirements.

7.5.3 *Can a Product-Based Approach Do Magic?*

A product-based regulation is repeatedly presented as a panacea for solving the problems that arise under the EU GMO law.[228] While such a product-based regulation may not necessarily tackle problems arising out of the comitology procedure, it could be a better approach in light of the national treatment principle as laid down in Article III:4 GATT and Article 2.1 TBT. At least, there would no longer be a differentiation between genome edited plants and identical plants bred by conventional methods carrying the same risks. And this is the most problematic issue in the national treatment analysis.[229] However, such a product-based approach alone is not sufficient, but amendments to the risk management procedure are also necessary. Accordingly, the mere amendment of the GMO definition would not suffice.

---

[225] European Commission (2023b), recital 15.

[226] European Commission (2023a), p. 1.

[227] *Cf.* European Commission (2023a), p. 2.

[228] See above for proposals to incorporate a product-based approach, p 275.

[229] For the analysis under GATT, see above Chap. 6, p 213; for the analysis under the TBT Agreement, see above Chap. 6, pp 231.

7.5.4 Proposals to Regulate Biotechnology on the International Plane

The regulation of GM plants on the international plane would answer the call for an internationally harmonised approach to the regulation of GM plants. This call is not necessarily answered by an amendment of EU GMO law since it can either follow the approach of other States or not.

Such an internationally harmonised approach could also be reached by a universal recognition of the Cartagena Protocol which is not the case so far. Accordingly, the EU could also put effort into convincing North and South American States to join the Cartagena Protocol.

7.5.5 Limited Additional Impact by CETA

As can be seen from the analysis in Chap. 6, the impact of CETA as such is limited since it mostly incorporates the relevant WTO obligations. Also, the Dialogue between Canada and the EU on Biotech Market Access Issues has not had a major impact on EU GMO regulations so far. It remains to be seen whether and how Canada tries to influence a new regulation for genome edited plants in the EU by means of the Dialogue on Biotech Market Access Issues. Such influence can also be exercised by the mean of regulatory cooperation provided for by CETA. While regulatory cooperation and harmonisation of regulations take place on a voluntary basis, it is likely that the European Commission will have to justify future regulatory approaches that differ from the Canadian approach towards the regulation of genome edited plants.[230]

7.5.6 Conclusions

While the EU Commission's proposal on a regulation of plants obtained by new genomic techniques already includes elements that help to overcome the inconsistencies of the current legislative framework with WTO law, there is still room for improvement. While at the moment the EU seems to be able to provide sufficient scientific evidence to justify the different regulation of category 1 and category 2 NGT plants, such evidence can change in the near future making an amendment of the equivalence criteria in Annex I necessary. Accordingly, a product-based approach comprising all GMOs might be more in line with WTO law than the proposed

[230] For further details on the provision on regulatory cooperation and biotechnology in CETA, see above Chap. 5, p. 143.

approach, but this also depends on the concrete design of the product-based approach.

Also, the EU Commission's proposal does not put an end to the comitology procedure with the problematic voting behaviour of Member States. Rather, proposals to amend the authorisation procedure aim at an adaption of the risk assessment to the particularities of genome edited plants. Also not mentioned by the reform proposals is the opt-out mechanism.

While an international regulation of genome edited plants outside the WTO framework would be desirable, it is difficult to create as can be seen from the Cartagena Protocol. The interests and regulatory strategies in the field of plant biotechnology are too different to reach a worldwide agreement.

7.6 Outlook and Recommendations on a Future Regulation of Genome Edited Plants in the EU

7.6.1 The Next Steps at EU-Level

Currently, the EU Commission's proposal is debated in the Council of the EU.[231] While the European Parliament has already taken a decision on amendments to the Commission's proposal and adopted a legislative resolution accordingly in the first quarter of 2024, the Council of the EU is still trying to find a common position on the proposal. As long as such a common position cannot be found, the trilogue procedure on the proposal does not begin. Accordingly, it is not yet clear when a legislative decision on this proposal will be taken.

7.6.2 Concerns Raised by Member States

The German *Bundesrat* has welcomed the EU Commission's proposal and has endorsed it with the exception of a few points.[232] In order to guarantee coexistence between conventional and organic as well as gm-free agriculture, it sees the need for rules on fixed distances and information obligations when cultivating NGT plants.[233] Also, it would be necessary to protect organic farmers from disadvantages and costs that could arise out of unintentional contamination.[234] The *Bundesrat* also addresses

---

[231] See https://eur-lex.europa.eu/legal-content/EN/HIS/?uri=celex:52023PC0411#2024-04-24_ADP_R1_POS_byEP.

[232] See Bundesrat (2023).

[233] See Bundesrat (2023), para 3.

[234] See Bundesrat (2023), para 4.

patent law issues and emphasises the importance of the so-called "breeders privilege" and calls on the Commission to ensure its continued existence.[235]

Other governments have also criticised that the EU Commission's proposal does no longer adequately ensure the consumers' freedom of choice.[236] And, that is does no longer provide for the opportunity of Member States to restrict or prohibit the cultivation on their territory with regard to NGT plants.[237] Also, concerns have been expressed that the current patent regulations could hinder the EU's aim of simplifying the utilisation of genome edited plants for SMEs.[238]

These concerns will probably have to be addressed during the trilogue procedures in order to create a draft that reaches the qualified majority of Member States in the Council of the European Union.

7.6.3 Recommendations for a Future Regulation of Genome Edited Plants in the EU

The proposals brought up for an amendment of the EU GMO law are hardly concerned with WTO law and also the EU Commission's proposal does not discuss the proposal's compatibility with international trade law. Therefore, the present part builds upon the foregoing analyses and tries to give recommendations on a future regulatory framework for GMOs in the EU that are in line with the EU's obligations under WTO law and CETA. It does not constitute a comprehensive proposal, but presents ideas and impulses that should be taken into account when developing a new regulatory framework for genome edited plants in the EU.

7.6.3.1 Improving the comitology procedure

7.6.3.1.1 Change Member States' Voting Pattern Within the Comitology Procedure

As the voting pattern of Member States within the comitology procedure leads to a violation of Article 5.7 SPS by unreasonably prolonging the review time allowed, solutions could be searched to ensure that the Member States take a vote in the SCoPAFF. This could end the existing voting pattern during the comitology procedure since a final decision could already be taken by the SCoPAFF and the decision

[235] See Bundesrat (2023), paras 5–6.

[236] Council of the European Union (2023b), para 2; Council of the European Union (2023d).

[237] See Council of the European Union (2023a), p. 3; see also Council of the European Union (2023b), para 1.

[238] Council of the European Union (2023b), para 4; Council of the European Union (2023c), p. 2; Council of the European Union (2023d).

must not be forwarded to the Appeal Committee in every case but only where this is absolutely necessary. Reasons given by the Member States for their abstention or negative vote concern the lack of a national position or a negative public opinion, different aspects of the risk assessment as well as ethical concerns and an unclear social utility of GMOs.[239] The incompatibility of the comitology procedure with WTO law is only addressed with regard to category 1 NGT plants by the EU Commission's proposal which are exempt from regulatory oversight. However, with regard to other NGT plants, the comitology procedure still applies. Therefore it needs to be assessed whether the comitology procedure could be improved by the Member States taking a definitive opinion on genome edited plants (a.), by amendments to the risk assessment (b.), or by addressing ethical and social concerns raised by the Member States (c.).

7.6.3.1.1.1 Member States Taking a Stance on Genome Edited Plants

In general, the EU Member States should finally formulate an opinion on GMOs and should underpin their opinion with reliable scientific evidence from recognised sources. Such opinion should take account of national public perceptions of GMOs and genome edited plants. A broad public debate about GMOs and genome edited plants is absolutely necessary. Also, Member States should be encouraged to finalise national risk assessment procedures before the risk management process at the EU level starts. So far, some Member States still mention the missing opinion of its national scientific committee or the non-finalisation of the national risk assessment as grounds for their abstention to vote in the SCoPAFF and Appeal Committee.[240]

7.6.3.1.1.2 Adapt Risk Assessment to Member States' Concerns?

With regard to the risk assessment, Member States mention the lack of the 90-day toxicity study and the long-term feeding study. They assert that the risk assessment is not sufficient due to the insufficient assessment of interactions between single events or other uncertainties. These concerns that specific studies or aspects are missing or have not been adequately assessed in the risk assessment could be addressed by an amendment of the risk assessment procedure.

In contrast, it seems rather difficult to address more general concerns mentioned by Member States which are related to the lack of comprehensive data on the long-term potential impact of GMOs, safety concerns for the environment and that potential interactions of GMOs with other plants cannot be excluded. While the risk assessment can try to give an adequate prospect of safety concerns and interactions with the environment, a minimum risk always remains. Furthermore, it is inherent in an authorisation that comprehensive long-term experience is missing. Therefore,

[239] See above Chap. 4, p. 70.

[240] See above, Chap. 4, p. 70.

these concerns cannot only be addressed by amendments to the risk assessment but also require a decision of Member States whether they want to take these risks or not.

7.6.3.1.1.3 Address Ethical and Societal Concerns

Concerns with regard to ethical aspects or social utility could be addressed by including them in the risk management procedure as has already been proposed by scholarship.[241] Such a utility analysis, also including sustainability aspects, might also help to strengthen public acceptance of GM or genome edited plants that have been assessed as useful. However, this requires an amendment to the current legislative framework. Furthermore, when including such aspects in the risk management procedure, it must at the same time be ensured that the final decision is based on scientific evidence in order to comply with WTO law.

7.6.3.1.2 Taking a European Position on GMOs and Genome Edited Plants

Another possibility to tackle problems arising out of the comitology procedure is the formulation of a common European position on GM and genome edited plants. Then, the comitology procedure would no longer be necessary, but the Commission could take a decision in line with the Member States' position. However, it is rather unlikely that all Member States can agree on a common position.

7.6.3.2 Maintain Labelling Requirements for Genome Edited Plants Used as or in Food (Products)

The differentiation between genome edited plants that are identical to conventionally bred plants is less problematic with regard to labelling requirements since these requirements are primarily scrutinised under the TBT Agreement and GATT. Both agreements allow for a differentiation where consumer behaviour differentiates between products. Accordingly, a differentiation between genome edited plants and conventionally bred plants in the food sector is legitimate due to different public perceptions in the EU with regard to GM plants. As long as GM food is not publicly accepted, labelling requirements should be maintained to guarantee that consumers can make informed choices. The continued existence of labelling requirements for genome edited plants could even increase acceptance for a possible exemption of genome edited plants from the current GMO rules.

The differentiation is more problematic in the feed sector. However, labelling in this sector is not as decisive as in the food sector. Products from animals fed with GM feed must not be labelled accordingly. And consumers do not pay attention to whether the meat they eat has been produced from animals fed with GM feed.

---

[241] See above for the proposals to establish a new framework for genome edited plants, p 282.

Labelling is only decisive for organic farmers since they must not use GM feed. In this regard, it is essential that the EU Commission improves its proposal to ensure that organic farmers do not become the victims of a new regulation.

7.6.3.3 Encourage a Public Dialogue on the Use of Genome Edited Plants

The European Commission wants to make use of genome edited plants to tackle problems arising in agriculture and for food security due to climate change. To avoid its plans being thwarted by a lack of public acceptance, it should encourage a broad public dialogue on the use of genome edited plants. The European society should decide whether it sees an advantage in the use of these plants or not. The need for such a broad societal debate about the advantages and potential risks of the use of genome editing techniques is also emphasised by several scholars.[242] It should include social, ethical and sustainability-related aspects as their full consideration is crucial for societal acceptance of new breeding techniques. And the European Union should ensure that there is sufficient information provided by independent scientists. Otherwise, there is the risk that the dialogue will be dominated by the biotech industry and a so-called "anti-GMO coalition".

Another aspect that could help to strengthen public acceptance is more transparency during risk assessment and risk management of GM and genome edited plants. This could include a scientific opinion by EFSA which is not only addressed to the scientific community but more easily understandable for normal citizens. And also, the discussions in the SCoPAFF and Appeals Committee could be published in more detail to make the Member States' and Commission's decisions more understandable.

7.6.3.4 Include a Sustainability/Utility Analysis

An aspect that could help to strengthen public acceptance is the inclusion of a sustainability or social utility analysis as has been proposed by some organisations and has also been asked for by the Member States during the comitology procedure.[243] While such a mechanism would surely improve public acceptance of genome edited plants it is questionable whether it would be compatible with the SPS Agreement requiring that SPS measures are based on a risk assessment and not on sustainability or utility concerns. In order to ensure that the potential benefits of genome edited plants can be deployed, the EU should work towards sustainability criteria being accepted under WTO law and CETA. Otherwise, it risks losing public acceptance for genome edited plants and thus also for their use as envisaged by the EU Green

[242] See *inter alia* Agapito-Tenfen et al. (2018), p. 12; Ammann (2019), p. 4; Araki and Ishii (2015), p. 149; Bogner and Torgersen (2018), pp. 6–7.

[243] See above for new regulatory approaches to genome edited plants, p 282 and Chap. 4, p. 70.

Deal and "farm to fork" strategy.[244] Whether the final legislative act on new genomic techniques will provide for a WTO-conform "sustainability mechanism" remains to be seen.

7.7 Conclusion

The publication of the EU Commission's proposal marks the final stage of a long-running debate. While it was unclear for a long time whether plants obtained by genome editing techniques would fall within the current EU GMO regulation, this question has finally been decided by the CJEU in 2018. However, this judgement was not satisfactory for many stakeholders in the plant breeding sector. They called for a more lenient, in their view scientifically sound regulation of genome editing techniques and emphasised the advantages of these techniques, especially with regard to combatting climate change and building up a sustainable agriculture. This demand was finally heeded by the EU Commission which has set itself the goal of climate neutrality by 2050 and is taking far-reaching steps to achieve this aim. Five years after the CJEU's judgement, the Commission has proposed a regulation that should simplify the use of certain genome editing techniques in plants. How this regulation on new genomic techniques will look like in the end remains to be seen. Member States have already raised concerns regarding the interaction with patent law, the consumers freedom of choice and possible disadvantages for organic agriculture which would run counter to the EU's goal of a sustainable agriculture.

To comply with the EU's obligations under WTO law, the proposal should—in addition to the envisaged changes—also address and amend the currently applicable risk management carried out in accordance with the provisions of the comitology procedure. Also, the planned differentiation between category 1 and category 2 NGT plants should be based on a scientific basis which can also result from serious minority opinions.

The most important point and probably also the largest adjusting screw however is the public opinion in the EU towards genome edited plants. To reach a legislative proposal that has the support of society and Member States, the EU should hold a broad societal debate on the possible use of genome edited plants and involve the society in its decision-making process.

---

[244] *Cf.* also Gordon et al. (2021).

References

Literature

Agapito-Tenfen SZ, Okoli AS, Bernstein MJ, Wikmark O-G, Myhr AI (2018) Revisiting risk governance of GM plants: the need to consider new and emerging gene-editing techniques. Front Plant Sci 9:1–16. https://doi.org/10.3389/fpls.2018.01874

Agra Europe (2020) Häusling erneuert Ruf nach strenger Regulierung der Genscheren: Die Grünen versuchen weiterhin das Verfahren CRISPR/CAS dauerhaft als Gentechnik einzustufen. top agrar ONLINE

Ammann K (2019) Selected innovative solutions for the regulation of GM crops in times of gene editing. In: Khurana SMP, Gaur RK (eds) Plant biotechnology: progress in genomic era. Springer Singapore, Singapore, pp 3–41. https://doi.org/10.1007/978-981-13-8499-8_1

Andersen E, Schreiber K (2020) "Genome Editing" vor dem EuGH und seine Folgen. Natur und Recht 42:99–106. https://doi.org/10.1007/s10357-020-3641-1

Antonsen T, Dassler T (2021) How to do what is right, not what is easy: requirements for assessment of genome-edited and genetically modified organisms under ethical guidelines. Food Ethics 6:1–9. https://doi.org/10.1007/s41055-021-00091-y

Araki M, Ishii T (2015) Towards social acceptance of plant breeding by genome editing. Trends Plant Sci 20:145–149

Association Francaise des Biotechnologies Végétales, Wissenschaftlerkreis Grüne Gentechnik e.V. (2020) Open Letter to EU Commission - Revision of Directive 2001/18/EC: Draft Amendment for regulation of new breeding techniques - Genome Editing, https://www.biotech-gm-food.com/wissenschaft/new-breeding-techniques-regulation-afbv-wgg-open-letter-to-commission

Bauer-Panskus A, Miyazaki J, Kawall K, Then C (2020) Risk assessment of genetically engineered plants that can persist and propagate in the environment. Environ Sci Eur 32. https://doi.org/10.1186/s12302-020-00301-0

Bechtold S (2018) Beyond risk considerations: where and how can a debate about non-safety related issues of genome editing in agriculture take place? Front Plant Sci 9:1–5. https://doi.org/10.3389/fpls.2018.01724

Biber-Klemm S, Burkard M, Cottier T, Jusoh S, Temmerman M (2011) Challenges of biotechnology in international trade regulation. In: Cottier T, Delimatsis P (eds) The prospects of international trade regulation. Cambridge University Press, Cambridge, pp 284–320. https://doi.org/10.1017/CBO9780511792496.009

Bioökonomierat (2019) Genome Editing: Europa benötigt ein neues Gentechnikrecht. BÖRMEMO 07. https://www.biooekonomierat.de/media/pdf/archiv/boermemo-gentechnikrecht-07.pdf?m=1637834225&

Bogner A, Torgersen H (2018) Precaution, responsible innovation and beyond - in search of a sustainable agricultural biotechnology policy. Front Plant Sci 9:1–10. https://doi.org/10.3389/fpls.2018.01884

Bøhn T, Then C, Bauer-Panskus A, Miyazaki J, Defarge N, Lebrecht T, Hilbeck A (2020), Serious shortcoming in the European risk assessment of herbicide tolerant GE plants for human health. RAGES subreport

Brockmann K (2021), Koexistenz: Die Notwendigkeit, neue Gentechnik zu regulieren. In: Arbeitsgemeinschaft bäuerliche Landwirtschaft e.V. (ed) CRISPR & CO: Neue Gentechnik Regulierung oder Freifahrtschein? Texte zur aktuellen Diskussion, pp 44–47

Bundesrat (2023) Vorschlag für eine Verordnung des Europäischen Parlaments und des Rates über mit bestimmten neuen genomischen Techniken gewonnene Pflanzen und die aus ihnen gewonnenen Lebens- und Futtermittel sowie zur Änderung der Verordnung (EU) 2017/625: Beschluss des Bundesrats. *Drs 328/23*

Commissie Genetische Modificatie COGEM (2019) No rose without thorns: Implications of a product-based regulatory system for GM crops in the European Union. COGEM Policy Report

CGM/191010-01, https://cogem.net/app/uploads/2019/12/191010-01-No-Rose-Without-Thorns_ENG_DEF.pdf
Committee on Economic, Social and Cultural Rights (1999) General Comment 12 (Twentieth session, 1999): The right to adequate food (art. 11). E/C.12/1999/5
Committee on Sanitary and Phytosanitary Measures (2018) International Statement on agricultural applications of precision biotechnology: Communication from Argentina, Australia, Brazil, Canada, The Dominican Republic, Guatemale, Honduras, Paraguay, The United States of America and Uruguay. *G*/SPS/GEN/1658/Rev.3
Committee on Sanitary and Phytosanitary Measures (2019) Summary of the Meeting of 1-2 November 2018: Note by the Secretariat. G/SPS/R/93
Committee on Sanitary and Phytosanitary Measures (2021) The European Commission Study on the Status of New Genomic Techniques in the European Union: Communication from the European Union. G/SPS/GEN/1931
Council of the European Union (2023a) Proposal for a Regulation of the European Parliament and of the Council on plants obtained by certain new genomic techniques and their food and feed, and amending Regulation (EU) 2017/625 [11592/23 + ADD 1 - COM(2023) 411 final] - Reasoned opinion on the application of the Principles of Subsidiarity and Proportionality: Cover Note from the Hungarian National Assembly to the President of the Council of the European Union. 14851/23, https://eur-lex.europa.eu/legal-content/EN/TXT/PDF/?uri=CONSIL:ST_14851_2023_INIT
Council of the European Union (2023b) Regulation on plants obtained by certain new genomic techniques and their food and feed products - Information from the Croatian delegation: Note from the General Secretariat of the Council to the Council. 15472/23, https://eur-lex.europa.eu/legal-content/EN/TXT/PDF/?uri=CONSIL:ST_15472_2023_INIT
Council of the European Union (2023c) Proposal for a Regulation of the European Parliament and of the Council on plants obtained by certain new genomic techniques and their food and feed, and amending Regulation (EU) 2017/625 [11592/23 + ADD 1 - COM(2023) 411 final] - Opinion on the application of the Principles of Subsidiarity and Proportionality: Cover Note from the Danish Folketing to the General Secretariat of the Council. 15895/23, https://eur-lex.europa.eu/legal-content/EN/TXT/PDF/?uri=CONSIL:ST_15895_2023_INIT
Council of the European Union (2023d) Proposal for a Regulation of the European Parliament and of the Council on plants obtained by certain new genomic techniques and their food and feed, and amending Regulation (EU) 2017/625 [11592/23 + ADD 1 - COM(2023) 411 final] - Opinion on the application of the Principles of Subsidiarity and Proportionality: Cover note from the Senate of Romania to the President of the Council of the European Union. 15898/23, https://eur-lex.europa.eu/legal-content/EN/TXT/PDF/?uri=CONSIL:ST_15898_2023_INIT
Dederer H-G (2019a) Genomeditierung ist Gentechnik. Europäische Zeitschrift für Umwelt- und Planungsrecht:236–245
Dederer H-G (2019b) Options for the regulation of genome edited plants - framing the issues. In: Dürnberger C, Pfeilmeier S, Schleissing S (eds) Genome editing in agriculture: between precaution and responsibility. Nomos, Baden-Baden, pp 77–122
Dederer H-G, Hamburger D (eds) (2019) Regulation of genome editing in plant biotechnology: a comparative analysis of regulatory frameworks of selected countries and the EU. Springer, Cham, Switzerland
Deutsche Industrievereinigung Biotechnologie, Verband der Chemischen Industrie e.V. (2020) Wie kann Gene-Editing in der EU nutzbar gemacht werden?, Frankfurt
Duensing N, Sprink T, Parrott WA, Fedorova M, Lema MA, Wolt JD, Bartsch D (2018) Novel features and considerations for ERA and regulation of crops produced by genome editing. Front Bioeng Biotechnol 6:1–16. https://doi.org/10.3389/fbioe.2018.00079
Eckerstorfer MF, Dolezel M, Greiter A, Miklau M, Heissenberger A, Steinbrecher RA (2020) Risk Assessment of Plants developed by new Genetic Modification Techniques (nGMs): Biosafety Considerations for Plants developed by Genome Editing and other new Genetic Modification Techniques (nGMs) and Considerations for their Regulation. BfN-Skripten 592

Eckerstorfer MF, Grabowski M, Lener M, Engelhard M, Simon S, Dolezel M, Heissenberger A, Lüthi C (2021) Biosafety of genome editing applications in plant breeding: considerations for a focused case-specific risk assessment in the EU. BioTech 10:1–14. https://doi.org/10.3390/biotech10030010

Engelhard M, Hagen K, Hein A-C, Hendrischke O, Klein M, Reichenbecher W, Simon S, Stracke K, Waßmann F (2021) New developments and regulatory issues in plant genetic engineering. BfN Viewpoint, https://www.bfn.de/sites/default/files/2021-10/Viewpoint-plant-genetic-engeneering_1.pdf

EPSO Agricultural Technology Working Group (2019) On the ECJ Ruling regarding mutagenesis and the Genetically Modified Organisms Directive: Statement, Brussels, https://epsoweb.org/download/epso-statement-on-ecj-ruling-regarding-mutagenesis-and-gmo/

Eriksson D (2019) The evolving EU regulatory framework for precision breeding. Theor Appl Genet 132:569–573. https://doi.org/10.1007/s00122-018-3200-9

Eriksson D, Custers R, Edvardsson Björnberg K, Hansson SO, Purnhagen K, Qaim M, Romeis J, Schiemann J, Schleissing S, Tosun J, Visser RG (2020a) Options to reform the European Union legislation on GMOs: post-authorization and beyond. Trends Biotechnol 38:465–467. https://doi.org/10.1016/j.tibtech.2019.12.015

Eriksson D, Custers R, Edvardsson Björnberg K, Hansson SO, Purnhagen K, Qaim M, Romeis J, Schiemann J, Schleissing S, Tosun J, Visser RG (2020b) Options to reform the European Union legislation on GMOs: risk governance. Trends Biotechnol 38:349–351. https://doi.org/10.1016/j.tibtech.2019.12.016

Eriksson D, Custers R, Edvardsson Björnberg K, Hansson SO, Purnhagen K, Qaim M, Romeis J, Schiemann J, Schleissing S, Tosun J, Visser RGF (2020c) Options to reform the European Union legislation on GMOs: scope and definitions. Trends Biotechnol 38:231–234. https://doi.org/10.1016/j.tibtech.2019.12.002

European Commission (2019) Communication from the Commission to the European Parliament, the European Council, the Council, the European Economic and Social Committee and the Committee of the Regions: The European Green Deal. *COM(2019) 640 final*, https://eur-lex.europa.eu/resource.html?uri=cellar:b828d165-1c22-11ea-8c1f-01aa75ed71a1.0002.02/DOC_1&format=PDF

European Commission (2020) Communication from the Commission to the European Parliament, the Council, the European Economic and Social Committee and the Committee of the Regions: A Farm to Fork Strategy for a fair, healthy and environmentally-friendly food system. COM(2020) 381 final, https://eur-lex.europa.eu/resource.html?uri=cellar:ea0f9f73-9ab2-11ea-9d2d-01aa75ed71a1.0001.02/DOC_1&format=PDF

European Commission (2021a) Study on the status of new genomic techniques under Union law and in light of the Court of Justice ruling in Case C-528/16: Commission Staff Working Document. SWD(2021) 92 final, Brussels

European Commission (2021b) Inception Impact Assessment: Legislation for plants produced by certain new genomic techniques. Ref. Ares(2021)5835503, https://ec.europa.eu/info/law/better-regulation/have-your-say/initiatives/13119-Legislation-for-plants-produced-by-certain-new-genomic-techniques_en

European Commission (2023a) Rationale for the equivalence criteria in Annex I to the proposal for a Regulation on plants obtained by certain new genomic techniques: Technical Paper by the Commission services. https://doi.org/10.2903/j.efsa.2012.2943

European Commission (2023b) Proposal for a Regulation of the European Parliament and of the Council on plants obtained by certain new genomic techniques and their food and feed, and amending Regulation (EU) 2017/625. COM(2023) 411 final, Brussels

European Commission, European Group on Ethics in Science and New Technologies. Main website, https://ec.europa.eu/info/research-and-innovation/strategy/support-policy-making/scientific-support-eu-policies/ege_en

European Commission, European Union Reference Laboratory for Genetically Modified Food and Feed (EURL GMFF). Main website, https://gmo-crl.jrc.ec.europa.eu/

European Commission, Group of Chief Scientific Advisors. Main website, https://research-and-innovation.ec.europa.eu/strategy/support-policy-making/scientific-support-eu-policies/group-chief-scientific-advisors_en

European Commission, Impact assessments. Overview, https://ec.europa.eu/info/law/law-making-process/planning-and-proposing-law/impact-assessments_en

European Commission, Joint Research Centre. Main website, https://joint-research-centre.ec.europa.eu/index_en

European Commission, Legislation for plants produced by certain new genomic techniques. Overview legislative initiative, https://ec.europa.eu/info/law/better-regulation/have-your-say/initiatives/13119-Legislation-for-plants-produced-by-certain-new-genomic-techniques_en

European Economic and Social Committee (2023) Opinion: Plants produced by new genomic techniques. NAT/908, https://webapi2016.eesc.europa.eu/v1/documents/EESC-2023-03330-00-02-AC-TRA-EN.docx/content

European Group on Ethics in Science and New Technologies (2021) Opinion on Ethics of Genome Editing: Opinion no. 32, Brussels. https://doi.org/10.1136/jme.24.4.247

Federal Agency for Nature Conservation (Germany). Official website, https://www.bfn.de/en

Food Standards Australia New Zealand (2019) Final report: Review of food derived using new breeding techniques, https://www.foodstandards.gov.au/consumer/gmfood/Pages/Review-of-new-breeding-technologies-.aspx

Gelinsky E (2021) Warten auf die Superpflanzen: CRISPR & Co wecken übertriebene Erwartungen. In: Arbeitsgemeinschaft bäuerliche Landwirtschaft e.V. (ed) CRISPR & CO: Neue Gentechnik Regulierung oder Freifahrtschein? Texte zur aktuellen Diskussion, pp 10–13

Gelinsky E, Hilbeck A (2018) European Court of Justice ruling regarding new genetic engineering methods scientifically justified: a commentary on the biased reporting about the recent ruling. Environ Sci Eur 30:52–60. https://doi.org/10.1186/s12302-018-0182-9

General Council (1999a) Proposal for the Establishment of a Working Party on Biotechnology in WTO (Communication from Canada): Preparations for the 1999 Ministerial Conference. WT/GC/W/359

General Council (1999b) Proposal of Japan on Genetically Modified Organisms (GMOs) (Communication from Japan): Preparations for the 1999 Ministerial Conference. WT/GC/W365

Gordon D, Jaffee G, Doane M, Glaser A, Gremillion TM, Ho MD (2021) Responsible governance of gene editing in agriculture and the environment. Nat Biotechnol 39:1055–1057

Group of Chief Scientific Advisors (2018) A scientific perspective on the regulatory status of products derived from gene editing and the implications for the GMO Directive

Habets M, van Hove L, van Est R (2019), Genome editing in plants and crops: towards a modern biotechnology policy focused on differences in risks and broader considerations, The Hague

Hahn M (2008) Food security and agricultural production with genetically modified organisms: a comment. In: Wüger D, Cottier T (eds) Genetic engineering and the World Trade System. Cambridge University Press, pp 193–202

Hamburger DJS (2018) Normative criteria and their inclusion in a regulatory framework for new plant varieties derived from genome editing. Front Bioeng Biotechnol 6. https://doi.org/10.3389/fbioe.2018.00176

High Level Group of Scientific Advisors (2017) New techniques in Agricultural Biotechnology. Explanatory Note 02/2017, Brussels

Hissting A (2021) Neue Gentechnik-Produkte sind nachweisbar: Illegale Importe stoppen. In: Arbeitsgemeinschaft bäuerliche Landwirtschaft e.V. (ed) CRISPR & CO: Neue Gentechnik Regulierung oder Freifahrtschein? Texte zur aktuellen Diskussion, pp 64–68

Hjort C, Cole J, Frébort I (2021) European genome editing regulations: threats to the European bioeconomy and unfit for purpose. EFB Bioecon J 1:1–6. https://doi.org/10.1016/j.bioeco.2021.100001

Huang S, Weigel D, Beachy RN, Li J (2016) A proposed regulatory framework for genome-edited crops. Nat Genet 48:109–111

Hüdig M, Laibach N, Hein A-C (2022) Genome editing in crop plant research - alignment of expectations and current developments. Plants:1–27

Jones HD (2019) Future-proofing regulation for rapidly changing biotechnologies. Transgenic Res 28:107–110. https://doi.org/10.1007/s11248-019-00143-4
Jorasch P (2019) The global need for plant breeding innovation. Transgenic Res 28:81–86. https://doi.org/10.1007/s11248-019-00138-1
Jorasch P (2020) Will the EU stay out of step with science and the rest of the world on plant breeding innovation? Plant Cell Rep 39:163–167. https://doi.org/10.1007/s00299-019-02482-2
Juma C, Conceição P, Levine S (2014) Biotechnology and food security. In: Smyth SJ, Phillips PWB, Castle D (eds) Handbook on agriculture, biotechnology and development. Edward Elgar, Cheltenham, pp 488–504
Kawall K, Miyazaki J, Bauer-Panskus A, Then C (2020) Overview of genome editing applications using SDN-1 and SDN-2 in regard to EU regulatory issues, 2020: New methods of genetic engineering (genome editing) and their potential impact on nature protection and the environment
Kearns P (2019) An overview of OECD activities related to modern techniques of biotechnology and genome editing: OECD conference on genome editing, June 2018. Transgenic Res 28:41–44
Kok EJ, Glandorf DC, Prins TW, Visser RG (2019) Food and environmental safety assessment of new plant varieties after the European Court decision: process-triggered or product-based? Trends Food Sci Technol 88:24–32. https://doi.org/10.1016/j.tifs.2019.03.007
Ladeur K-H (2018) Die Entscheidung des EuGH zur Anwendung des geltenden Gentechnikrechts auf CRISPR/Cas9-Verfahren v. 25.7.2018 – eine Entscheidung gegen technologische Innovation! Zeitschrift zum Innovations- und Technikrecht:198-201
Lassoued R, Macall DM, Smyth SJ, Phillips PWB, Hesseln H (2020) How should we regulate products of new breeding techniques? Opinion of surveyed experts in plant biotechnology. Biotechnol Rep 26:1–10. https://doi.org/10.1016/j.btre.2020.e00460
Levidow L (2007) The transatlantic agbiotech conflict as a problem and opportunity for EU regulatory policies. In: Falkner R (ed) The international politics of genetically modified food: diplomacy, trade, and law. Palgrave Macmillan, Basingstoke England, New York, pp 118–137
Menz J, Modrzejewski D, Hartung F, Wilhelm R, Sprink T (2020) Genome edited crops touch the market: a view on the global development and regulatory environment. Front Plant Sci 11:1–17. https://doi.org/10.3389/fpls.2020.586027
Ministerie van Infrastructuur en Waterstaat (2017) Proposal for discussion on actions to improve the exemption mechanism for genetically modified plants under Directive 2001/18/EC
Myskja BK, Myhr AI (2020) Non-safety assessments of genome-edited organisms: should they be included in regulation? Sci Eng Ethics. https://doi.org/10.1007/s11948-020-00222-4
Nationale Akademie der Wissenschaften Leopoldina, Union der Deutschen Akademien der Wissenschaften, Deutsche Forschungsgemeinschaft (2019) Towards a scientifically justified, differentiated regulation of genome edited plants in the EU. Statement, Halle (Saale), Bonn, Mainz, https://www.leopoldina.org/uploads/tx_leopublication/2019_Stellungnahme_Genomeditierte_Pflanzen_web.pdf
Oehen B (2020) Züchten für eine nachhaltige Landwirtschaft. In: Federal Agency for Nature Conservation (ed) Natur und Landschaft: Zeitschrift für Naturschutz und Landschaftspflege. W. Kohlhammer, pp 215–219
Office P (2019) Council Decision (EU) 2019/1904 of 8 November 2019 requesting the Commission to submit a study in light of the Court of Justice's judgement in Case C-528/16 regarding the status of novel genomic techniques under Union law, and a proposal, if appropriate in view of the outcomes of the study
Purnhagen KP, Wesseler JH (2019) Maximum vs minimum harmonization: what to expect from the institutional and legal battles in the EU on gene editing technologies. Pest Manag Sci 75:2310–2315. https://doi.org/10.1002/ps.5367
Rathenau Instituut (Netherlands). Official website, https://www.rathenau.nl/en
Ricroch AE, Ammann K, Kuntz M (2016) Editing EU legislation to fit plant genome editing: the use of genome editing technologies in plant breeding requires a novel regulatory approach for new plant varieties that involves farmers. EMBO Rep 17:1365–1369. https://doi.org/10.15252/embr.201643099

Robertson D (2001) GM foods and global trade. In: Robertson D, Kellow A (eds) . Edward Elgar Publishing, Globalization and the environment: risk assessment and the WTO, pp 206–226
Šefčovič M (2021) Letter to the Portuguese Presidency accompanying the Commission study on new genomic techniques, https://food.ec.europa.eu/system/files/2021-04/gmo_mod-bio_ngt_letter.pdf
Seitz C (2018) Modifiziert oder nicht? - Regulatorische Rechtsfragen zur Genoptimierung durch neue biotechnologische Verfahren. Europäische Zeitschrift für Wirtschaftsrecht:757–764
Sheldon I, Josling T (2002) Biotechnology Regulations and the WTO: Working Paper 02-2
Sowa S, Twardowski T, Woźniak E, Zimny T (2021) Legal and practical challenges to authorization of gene edited plants in the EU. New Biotechnol 60:183–188. https://doi.org/10.1016/j.nbt.2020.10.008
Standing Committee on Plants, Animals, Food and Feed (2022) Summary Report of the Meeting of 20 January 2022, https://food.ec.europa.eu/system/files/2022-02/sc_modif-genet_20220120_sum.pdf
The Norwegian Biotechnology Advisory Board (2018a) A forward-looking regulatory framework for GMO
The Norwegian Biotechnology Advisory Board (2018b) Proposal for relaxation of Norwegian regulations for deliberate release of genetically modified organisms (GMO), with applicability also for EU legislation, http://www.bioteknologiradet.no/filarkiv/2019/03/2019-04-16-Genteknologiloven-komplett-ENGELSK.pdf
Turnbull C, Lillemo M, Hvoslef-Eide TAK (2021) Global regulation of genetically modified crops amid the gene edited crop boom - a review. Front Plant Sci 12:1–19. https://doi.org/10.3389/fpls.2021.630396
van der Meer P, Angenon G, Bergmans, Hans, Buhk HJ, Callebaut S, Chamon M, Eriksson D, Gheysen G, Harwood WA, Hundleby PAC, Kearns P, McLoughlin T, Zimny T (2021) The status under EU law of organisms developed through novel genomic techniques. Eur J Risk Regul, 1–20. https://doi.org/10.1017/err.2020.105
Vollenweider C (2021) *Züchterische Unabhängigkeit bewahren*: Eine Bewertung der neuen Gentechnik aus der Perspektive eines ökologischen Züchters. In: Arbeitsgemeinschaft bäuerliche Landwirtschaft e.V. (ed) CRISPR & CO: Neue Gentechnik Regulierung oder Freifahrtschein? Texte zur aktuellen Diskussion, pp 16–19
Voß U (2006) Die Novelle der Freisetzungsrichtlinie - Richtlinie 2001/18/EG. Schriftenreihe Recht, Ethik und Ökonomie der Biotechnologie, vol 16. Nomos, Baden-Baden
Wasmer M (2019) Roads forward for European GMO policy-uncertainties in wake of ECJ judgment have to be mitigated by regulatory reform. Front Bioeng Biotechnol 7. https://doi.org/10.3389/fbioe.2019.00132
Wember Q (2021) Dürre Argumente der Gentechniklobby: Nur evolutive Züchtungsansätze können Klima-Anpassung erreichen. In: Arbeitsgemeinschaft bäuerliche Landwirtschaft e.V. (ed) CRISPR & CO: Neue Gentechnik Regulierung oder Freifahrtschein? Texte zur aktuellen Diskussion, pp 22–25
Winter G (2021) Regulierungsfragen angesichts Neuer Gentechniken: Wie weiter nach dem Urteil des Europäischen Gerichtshofes? In: Arbeitsgemeinschaft bäuerliche Landwirtschaft e.V. (ed) CRISPR & CO: Neue Gentechnik Regulierung oder Freifahrtschein? Texte zur aktuellen Diskussion, pp 38–42

Jurisprudence – Court of Justice of the European Union (former European Court of Justice)

CJEU (2018) Case C-528/16 - Confédération paysanne et al.

Chapter 8
Concluding Remarks

The analysis of the European Union ('EU') law on genetically modified organisms ('GMOs') and its applicability to genome edited plants under the law of the *World Trade Organization* ('WTO') and the *Comprehensive Economic and Trade Agreement* ('CETA') between Canada and the EU has shown the complexity of multi-level governance of genome edited plants. It is characterised by the tense relationship of different protection goals. While the EU GMO law aims at food safety, environmental and health protection, WTO law and CETA are characterised by the aim of trade liberalisation. They only allow for environmental and health protection in specific narrowly defined cases. Therefore, the Cartagena Protocol is considered a more adequate international treaty to deal with the transboundary movement of GMOs. Also, the Cartagena Protocol is said to be more favourable towards the EU's precautionary approach, one of the key principles of EU GMO law. But in the WTO forum, WTO law takes precedence over the Cartagena Protocol since not all WTO Members are state parties to the Protocol. Whether the precautionary principle is reflected in WTO law and CETA is frequently questioned by scholars and States. In this regard, the present analysis could find that the precautionary principle as applied in EU law is reflected in WTO law. It seems as if the EU has adapted its precautionary action to the requirements laid down in the WTO agreement as can be seen from the EU Commission's communication on the precautionary principle.

Nevertheless, the present analysis also shows the difficulties that arise for the regulation of genome edited plants. The difficulties mainly arise for two points: first, that genetic engineering techniques are subject to constant change and further development. And second, that the release and application of genetically modified plants can potentially have drastic and irreversible effects which cannot be predicted with absolute certainty. The difficulty of capturing these factors in regulatory terms was also clearly demonstrated in the CJEU's judgment in the case *Confédération paysanne* and WTO Panel's report in the case *EC – Biotech*.

E. A. L. Andersen, *Regulation of Biotechnological Risks in a Multi-Level System*, European Yearbook of International Economic Law 46,
https://doi.org/10.1007/978-3-032-02409-1_8

Additionally, a regulation of genome edited plants only makes sense at the European and international level since these plants can easily cross state borders and constitute a popular trading good. But, such a multilateral regulation is much more difficult to achieve in light of the different, sometimes even contrasting views that national governments and societies have on the use and application of genome edited plants. The North (and South) American states, for example, already use genetic engineering in many areas and are therefore much more open to the use of genetic engineering than the European states. These different views on GM plants also reflect the above-mentioned conflict between a more trade- and science-based regulation on the one hand and a precaution-based regulation on the other hand.

The difficulties of reconciling these two regulatory approaches are also evident in the analysis presented here. This analysis has shown that the applicability of the EU GMO regulations on plants modified by targeted mutagenesis is not fully in line with WTO law. This is primarily the case when plants modified by targeted mutagenesis are considered to carry the same or even less risks than conventionally bred plants. The European Commission in its study on new genomic techniques has adopted this view. Accordingly, it is difficult to justify the authorisation procedures for plants modified by targeted mutagenesis techniques. However, it is still possible to label these plants when they are used as or in food. For feed products, these labelling requirements are more difficult to justify. The analysis of the EU regulations under CETA does not substantially add to the analysis under WTO law since CETA mainly incorporates the relevant WTO law provisions. However, CETA may have substantial influence on new rules for targeted mutagenesis techniques in the EU through the Dialogue on Biotech Market Access Issues. The further developments here remain to be seen.

In general, the development of a new regulation for plants modified by targeted mutagenesis techniques as envisaged by the European Commission is likely to be a balancing act. While the European Commission aims at less strict rules for these plants, it must be careful not to lose public acceptance for its reform efforts. Public acceptance could be ensured by the proposed preferences for plants with sustainable traits. Such a "sustainability preference" could also contribute to the EU Commission's aim of applying genome edited plants for the transformation towards a more resilient, climate-adapted agriculture. However, the EU Commission should not forget about other alternatives on its way to a carbon-free Union. Genome edited plants with traits generating for example drought resistance or tolerance to certain diseases can only be one mean out of many for a more sustainable agricultural. It is also important to change agricultural practices or reduce livestock farming. Genome edited plants are not the panacea they are often portrayed as, especially by the plant breeding sector.

Lastly, the European Commission should try to find a position on genome edited plants for society as a whole. Member States have once again emphasised the need to guarantee the consumer's freedom of choice. Accordingly, Member States will only approve a new legislative act that is supported by its population. And, such common standpoint is also necessary for a new regulation to pass the legislative process. A qualified majority is only given when the country votes represent together at least 65% of the EU population.

Chapter 9
Summary of Results

Abstract This chapter includes a summary of the book in 39 short statements.

1. Genome editing techniques and especially the CRISPR-Cas system have great potential to substantially change and improve worldwide agriculture. While many scientists do not associate genetic engineering techniques with specific risks, the long-term effects of genome editing techniques could not have been conclusively researched yet.
2. The Commission of the European Union ('EU') has adopted the assessment by the European Food Safety Authority ('EFSA') that plants modified by targeted mutagenesis, cisgenesis and intragenesis techniques do not carry more risks than plants obtained by conventional breeding methods. It has based its proposal on the regulation of plants modified by new genomic techniques ('NGTs') on this assessment.
3. In its decision in the case C-528/16, the Court of Justice of the European Union ('CJEU'), in a first step, classified all organisms modified by mutagenesis techniques, in particular by targeted mutagenesis techniques, as genetically modified organisms ('GMOs') in the sense of Article 2(2) of Directive 2001/18/EC. The Court implicitly followed a primarily process-based interpretation of the GMO definition laid down in Article 2(2) of Directive 2001/18/EC. In a second step, the CJEU found that targeted mutagenesis techniques do not fall within the *mutagenesis exception* listed in Annex I B of Directive 2001/18/EC.
4. In general, the CJEU stated that all techniques of genetic modification that have been developed since 2001 are comprised by the scope of the Deliberate Release Directive. Accordingly, they also fall within the scope of Regulation 1829/2003 and Regulation 1830/2003 regulating the placing on the market of genetically modified feed and food.
5. The CJEU's decision that organisms modified by targeted mutagenesis techniques are comprised by the EU GMO law brought legal clarity, but it did not end the debate on the adequacy of the EU GMO law and its applicability to genome edited organisms.

E. A. L. Andersen, *Regulation of Biotechnological Risks in a Multi-Level System*, European Yearbook of International Economic Law 46,
https://doi.org/10.1007/978-3-032-02409-1_9

6. The Court's reasoning is reasonable from a legal point of view, but it displays a rather conservative and careful approach. This is consistent and worthy of support in view of the Court's lack of factual and legal powers to conclusively assess the scientific questions at issue in this case. By deciding this way, the Court passes on the question of an adequate regulation of genome edited organisms to the Union legislator which is responsible for these issues.
7. In general, the EU GMO law aims at a high protection of human and animal health and the environment.
8. The EU GMO law is characterised by the precautionary principle which is a central principle of EU environmental law. Not only is it laid down explicitly in Directive 2001/18/EC, but also different elements of the EU GMO legislation, such as the "step by step" approach, the approval reservation before releasing GMOs into the environment and the case-by-case assessment of application can be considered an expression of the precautionary principle.
9. Due to extensive regulations for GMO in the EU it is decisive for the marketing of a plant and its (economic) value whether it qualifies as GMO or not. A GM plant must recoup the high costs incurred for its authorisation and marketing. This is only likely to be worthwhile if the plant has a high economic benefit. Social benefits, on the other hand, are less likely to play a role in this calculation.
10. While no WTO agreement was dedicated explicitly to biotechnology, the WTO Panel in its *EC-Biotech* report has assumed a very broad scope of application of the SPS Agreement with regard to GMO regulation. A finding that cannot be fully endorsed. Since the SPS Agreement does not adequately address biodiversity and environmental protection, GMO regulation to the extent it serves these purposes cannot be qualified as SPS measures.
11. Also, the WTO Panel's findings on the formal precedence of WTO law in relation to the Cartagena Protocol needs to be criticised since it significantly diminishes the role of the Cartagena Protocol in the field of international plant biotechnology regulation. Since the EU is a party to the Cartagena protocol and the CBD it is not only bound by WTO law, but also by these two agreements. Therefore, the regulations of both international regimes have to be aligned.
12. Otherwise, the findings of the WTO Panel in *EC – Biotech* are rather unspectacular. Expectations that the Panel report would clarify crucial questions in the context of biotechnology regulation under WTO law could not be fulfilled. In particular, the legitimacy of the EU's pre-market authorisation procedures has not been analysed since it was not called into question by the claimant States.
13. Both, the WTO regime and CETA, are characterised by their objective to support free trade and remove trade barriers. To this objective, the agreements restrict the States' sovereignty to adopt internal and external measures that fall within the agreements' scopes. With its multilateral agreements, the WTO system is far-reaching and regulates a wide variety of areas, especially in our globalised world where almost every regulatory measure is in some way trade-related. The same applies to CETA with its thirty chapters and numerous attachments.

14. While it is generally assumed that the WTO regime and CETA with their regulatory approach stand in stark contrast to the EU's regulatory approach and especially to the EU's application of the precautionary principle, such stark contrast of opposing regulatory approaches could not be identified.
15. The analysis of the EU GMO law and its applicability to genome edited plants under WTO law and CETA has shown the complexity of multi-level governance of genome edited plants. It is characterised by the tense relationship of different protection goals. While the EU GMO law aims at food safety, environmental and health protection, WTO law and CETA are characterised by the aim of trade liberalisation.
16. The difficulties to qualify EU GMO regulations as falling within or outside of the Agreement's scope show that the SPS Agreement is not adequately designed to cover the risks associated with GMOs. This displays the general difficulty to design comprehensive regulations for scenarios that are characterised by uncertainty. Also, it shows the complexity of comprehensively regulating GMOs with its multi-facetted risk profile, with possible effects on people, animals and the environment in all its dimensions.
17. Regardless of these difficulties, the SPS Agreement is applicable to the authorisation procedures laid down in the Directive 2001/18/EC and the Regulation 1829/2003 to the extent that they are applied for the protection of human and animal life and health. To the extent that these authorisation procedures are applied for the protection of biodiversity and the environment in a way not comprised by the alternatives of Annex A(1) of the SPS Agreement, as well as for the protection of consumer interests, they do not fall within the SPS Agreement's scope.
18. The EU authorisation procedures do not conform to international standards, guidelines or recommendations in the sense of Article 3.2 SPS. Accordingly, conformity of the procedures with the SPS Agreement cannot automatically be presumed.
19. The general requirement for an authorisation procedure for genetically modified plants, accompanied by a temporary marketing-ban, is not based on a risk assessment as required by Article 5.1 of the SPS Agreement.
20. The general requirement for an authorisation procedure for plants modified by targeted mutagenesis or cisgenesis techniques can neither be based on Article 5.7 of the SPS Agreement since there is no lack or inconclusiveness of scientific evidence. The EU Commission has explicitly stated that there are no specific hazards linked to targeted mutagenesis or cisgenesis with regard to risks for human and animal health and the environment. This results in a violation of the science-based obligations Articles 5.1 and 2.2 of the SPS Agreement.
21. But even for GM plants where a lack of scientific evidence, insufficient or inconclusive scientific evidence could be assumed, the general authorisation requirement cannot be based on Article 5.7 SPS at the moment. The review time taken for the approval decision is unreasonably extended by the current EU Member States' voting behaviour in the comitology procedure.

22. For the compliance of the general design of the authorisation procedure with the SPS Agreement, it needs to be differentiated between risk assessment and risk management. The risk assessment carried out in accordance with provisions of the Deliberate Release Directive, the GM Food and Feed Regulation and the guidance issued by EFSA complies with the requirements laid down in Article 5.1 of the SPS Agreement. However, the provisions regulating the risk management provide for the possibility to reject an application although the risk assessment has been overly positive. Such a decision could not be considered to be *based on* the respective risk assessment, thereby violating Article 5.1 SPS. Accordingly, the provisions on risk management harbour the risk of a violation of the SPS Agreement.
23. The fact that plants modified by targeted mutagenesis need to be authorised although they carry the same risks as conventionally bred plants which do not need a comparable authorisation constitutes a discrimination in the sense of Article 5.5 SPS. This also implies a violation of Article 2.3 SPS.
24. In light of EFSA's statement that plants modified by targeted mutagenesis carry the same risks or even fewer risks than conventionally bred plants which has been adopted by the EU Commission, Article 5.6 SPS requires to exempt such plants from the EU GMO law. The envisaged level of protection can also be achieved without an authorisation procedure. Such an exemption substantially improves market access for these genetically modified plants and therefore can be considered a least trade restrictive measure in the sense of Article 5.6 SPS.
25. Whether the EU GMO authorisation procedures violate Article III:4 GATT cannot be determined in general term. An actual violation depends heavily on the circumstances of the individual case. Two criteria are likely to be decisive: first, whether a de facto differentiation between imported and domestic products can be assumed. This is only likely to be the case if imports consist of almost 100 % GM products and domestic products consist of almost 100% non-GM products. The second criterion being, how consumers behave with regard to the specific GM product in comparison to the non-GM product.
26. The justification of a possible violation of the GATT by Article XX GATT is also dependent on the circumstances of the specific case. It is rather unlikely that the EU GMO authorisation procedures would be qualified as relating to the conservation of exhaustible resources in accordance with Article XX lit. g GATT since such a measure must be *reasonably related* to the conservation of a specific endangered plant or animal. This is not the case for the EU GMO authorisation procedures.
27. The EU labelling requirements related to food safety fall within the SPS Agreement's scope and comply with the SPS Agreement's science-based obligations.
28. The labelling requirements laid down in Directive 2001/18/EC and Regulations 1829/2003 and 1830/2003 to the extent that they serve consumer interests and information fall within the TBT Agreement's scope. This is also the case for the application of labelling requirements to plants modified by targeted mutagenesis since these labelling requirements can be qualified as product-related PPMs.

29. There are certain circumstances where the EU labelling requirements could violate Article 2.1 TBT. This could be the case where the majority of imported products is genetically modified while the like domestic products are not genetically modified. Furthermore, the detrimental effect must not be justified by a legitimate regulatory purpose. This could be the case where the genetic modification does not carry any risks and where the GM plant is perfectly comparable to the non-GM plant, as can be the case for plants modified by targeted mutagenesis in comparison to conventionally bred plants.
30. The EU labelling requirements serving the purpose of consumer information fulfil a legitimate objective in the sense of Article 2.2 TBT. However, with regard to plants modified by targeted mutagenesis, it is questionable whether labelling requirements stand up to a cost-benefit analysis. Since these plants are not considered riskier than plants conventionally bred which do not require to be labelled, it is questionable whether the aim of consumer information can still outweigh the high costs that are caused by labelling requirements. Due to these reasons, labelling requirements for plants modified by targeted mutagenesis could also be considered as more trade-restrictive than necessary thereby violating Article 2.2 TBT.
31. The opt-out procedure under Article 26(b) Directive 2001/18/EC, including a cultivation ban for the whole or part of a Member State's territory, would constitute a less favourable treatment in the sense of Article III:4 GATT. However, Article III:4 GATT is only violated when GM and non-GM products are considered *like products*. Whether a cultivation ban for GMOs is justified in accordance with Article XX GATT cannot be assessed properly since the opt-out mechanism laid down in Article 26(b) Directive 2001/18/EC has not yet been applied by the EU Member States.
32. The considerations regarding the compatibility of the EU provisions with the SPS Agreement cannot simply be taken over in the context of CETA, since the SPS Agreement's provisions are not incorporated into CETA. Furthermore, a possible violation of Chapter 5 of CETA could fail because of Article 5.6 CETA. This Article obliges the state parties to accept the exporting party's SPS measure as equivalent if the measure achieves the importing party's appropriate level of SPS protection. However, the principles and guidelines for the determination, recognition and maintenance of equivalence have not yet been adopted. Therefore, no detailed analysis of this obligation is possible.
33. The circumstances leading to a violation of Article III:4 GATT and Articles 2.1 and 2.2 TBT would also lead to a violation of CETA.
34. The Dialogue on Biotech Market Access Issues established by Article 25.2 CETA has an informational character. But it also becomes clear that Canada has very specific interests when it comes to the regulation of biotechnology in the EU. It does not hesitate to name these interests again and again to put (slight) pressure on the EU. However, the EU Commission stands up to this pressure and clearly sets out the EU's regulatory requirements to which it adheres.

35. The analysed violations of WTO leave the EU legislator with no choice but to adapt the EU regulations for targeted mutagenesis techniques to the requirements of the WTO regime and CETA.
36. The EU Commission's proposal on a regulation of plants obtained by new genomic techniques takes up some of the suggestions made in the literature and by industry stakeholders, but also opts for other regulatory approaches in some cases. In general, the Commission is lowering the regulatory requirements for NGT plants. However, the EU Commission does not opt for a product-based approach which would have also comprised the regulation of traditional GMOs, but restricts its proposal to plants modified by targeted mutagenesis and cisgenesis. This does not fulfil the demand for a technology-neutral regulatory approach. Also, societal and ethical aspects which play a major role in GMO regulation are not included in the proposal, but the EU Commission is meeting the demand for a regulation that includes sustainability aspects.
37. While the EU Commission's proposal on a regulation of plants obtained by new genomic techniques already includes elements that help to overcome the inconsistencies of the current legislative framework with WTO law, there is still room for improvement.
38. To also comply with the EU's obligations under WTO law, the proposal should also address and amend the currently applicable risk management carried out in accordance with the provisions of the comitology procedure. In addition, the planned differentiation between category 1 and category 2 NGT plants should be based on a scientific basis, although this can also result from serious minority opinions.
39. Lastly, the EU Commission should encourage a broad public dialogue on the use of genome edited plants to avoid its plans being thwarted by a lack of public acceptance. The EU should try to find a common position on the use of biotech in the plant (breeding) sector.

MIX
Papier aus verantwortungsvollen Quellen
Paper from responsible sources
FSC® C105338

If you have any concerns about our products,
you can contact us on
ProductSafety@springernature.com

In case Publisher is established outside the EU,
the EU authorized representative is:
Springer Nature Customer Service Center GmbH
Europaplatz 3, 69115 Heidelberg, Germany

Printed by Libri Plureos GmbH
in Hamburg, Germany